Anxiety
Theory, Research and Intervention in Clinical and Health Psychology

THE WILEY SERIES IN CLINICAL PSYCHOLOGY

Series Editors

Fraser N. Watts
MRC Applied Psychology Unit
Cambridge

J. Mark G. Williams
Department of Psychology
University College of North Wales, Bangor

Severe Learning Disability and Psychological Handicap
John Clements

Cognitive Psychology and Emotional Disorders
J. Mark G. Williams, Fraser N. Watts,
Colin MacLeod and Andrew Mathews

Community Care in Practice
Services for the Continuing Care Client
Edited by Anthony Lavender and Frank Holloway

Attribution Theory in Clinical Psychology
Friedrich Försterling

Panic Disorder
Theory, Research and Therapy
Edited by Roger Baker

Measuring Human Problems
A Practical Guide
Edited by David Peck and C. M. Shapiro

Clinical Child Psychology
Social Learning, Development and Behaviour
Martin Herbert

The Psychological Treatment of Insomnia
Colin A. Espie

The Challenge of Severe Mental Handicap
A Behaviour Analytic Approach
Bob Remington

Microcomputers and Clinical Psychology
Issues, Applications and Future Developments
Edited by Alastair Ager

Anxiety
Theory, Research and Intervention
in Clinical and Health Psychology
Robert J. Edelmann

Further titles in preparation

Anxiety
Theory, Research and Intervention in Clinical and Health Psychology

Robert J. Edelmann
University of Surrey, UK

JOHN WILEY & SONS
Chichester · New York · Brisbane · Toronto · Singapore

Copyright © 1992 by John Wiley & Sons Ltd,
Baffins Lane, Chichester,
West Sussex PO19 1UD, England

Other Wiley Editorial Offices

John Wiley & Sons, Inc., 605 Third Avenue,
New York, NY 10158–0012, USA

Jacaranda Wiley Ltd, G.P.O. Box 859, Brisbane,
Queensland 4001, Australia

John Wiley & Sons (Canada) Ltd, 22 Worcester Road,
Rexdale, Ontario M9W 1L1, Canada

John Wiley & Sons (SEA) Pte Ltd, 37 Jalan Pemimpin #05–04,
Block B, Union Industrial Building, Singapore 2057

Library of Congress Cataloging-in-Publication Data:

Edelmann, Robert J.
    Anxiety : theory, research, and intervention in clinical and
health psychology / Robert J. Edelmann.
        p.   cm. — (The Wiley series in clinical psychology)
    Includes bibliographical references and index.
    ISBN 0-471-92389-3
    1. Anxiety.   I. Title.   II. Series.
    [DNLM: 1. Anxiety Disorders.   WM 172 E21a]
    RC531.E34   1992
    616.85'223—dc20
    DNLM/DLC
    for Library of Congress   91–30056
                                                                CIP

British Library Cataloguing in Publication Data:

A catalogue record for this book is
available from the British Library.

ISBN 0-471-92389-3   ISBN 0-471-95581-7 (pbk)

Typeset in 10/12pt Palatino by Mathematical Composition Setters Ltd, Salisbury
Printed and bound in Great Britain by Biddles Ltd, Guildford and King's Lynn

To
Mary Bernadette
Thank you for everything

Contents

Series Preface   xi

Preface   xiii

1   Conceptual Issues   1
    Introduction   1
    Three-systems analysis of anxiety   3
    Anxiety as an emotion   6
    The relationship between cognition and emotion   12
    Emotions and anxiety: summary comments   16
    Anxiety—personality trait or situationally determined
    characteristic   16

2   Theoretical Considerations   19
    Classical conditioning   20
    Two-factor theory   28
    Neuropsychological aspects of anxiety   29
    Cognitive conceptions of anxiety   31
    Summary   42

3   Social Anxiety and Social Phobia   45
    Definition and prevalence   45
    The distinctiveness of social phobia   47
    Theoretical perspectives   51
    Assessment   59
    Treatment   63
    Summary   74

4   Panic   76
    Definition and prevalence   76

Theoretical perspectives   83
Assessment   97
Treatment   99
Summary   107

5 Agoraphobia   109
Definition and prevalence   109
Predisposing factors   111
Precipitating factors   116
Theoretical issues   117
Assessment   121
Treatment   126
Summary   137

6 Generalised Anxiety   139
Definition and prevalence   139
Co-morbidity with other anxiety disorders   141
The nature of worry   145
Theoretical perspectives   148
Assessment   150
Treatment   153
Summary   157

7 Obsessions and Compulsions   159
Definition and description   159
Co-morbidity of OCD with other conditions   163
Information processing   167
Theoretical perspectives   169
Assessment   171
Treatment   176
Summary   184

8 Anxiety and Psychosexual Dysfunction   186
Introduction   186
Definitions   188
Prevalence   189
Assessment   190
Anxiety and psychosexual dysfunction   191
Treatment   200
Summary   205

9 Preoperative Anxiety and Preparation for Surgery   207
Introduction   207

Theoretical assumptions 208
Anxiety reduction 210
Summary 228

10 Health Anxiety and Medical Avoidance 230
Introduction 230
Illness phobia, health anxiety and hypochondriasis 231
Blood–injury fear and medical avoidance 242

11 Anxiety and Disease 253
Introduction 253
Asthma 255
Gastrointestinal disorders 259
Coronary heart disease 268
Summary 276

References 278

Index 345

Series Preface

The Wiley Series in Clinical Psychology aims to include authoritative surveys of core fields of clinical psychology. Over the last 30 years or so, work on anxiety has been a central focus for the activity and interests of clinical psychologists. There are few other topics on which such a rich body of theory, clinical practice and research has been developed.

This volume, by Robert Edelmann, presents an up-to-date survey of psychological work with anxiety. After the first two chapters, which present general conceptual and theoretical issues about anxiety, the bulk of the volume is concerned with the various forms in which anxiety presents to the clinician. Some are traditionally regarded as anxiety *disorders* (social anxiety, panic, agoraphobia, generalised anxiety disorder, obsessive–compulsive disorder); others are contexts in which anxiety presents to a greater or lesser extent in most members of the population (psychosexual functioning, preparation for surgery, health and disease). It is one of the unusual strengths of this book that it covers both sets of anxiety problems with equal thoroughness.

Edelmann adopts a systematic approach to provide clinicians with the information they need about anxiety conditions in an easy-to-access format. For each anxiety condition that is considered, information is presented about definition and prevalence, theoretical perspectives, assessment and treatment. Clinicians will find here the clear and reliable account of the scientific background necessary to good practice with anxiety disorders.

I hope the book will be widely used—not only by clinical psychologists, but also by other professions such as psychiatrists and nurses who work with the clinical manifestations of anxiety. It should also be particularly useful to postgraduate students in clinical psychology and psychiatry, and as an advanced undergraduate text.

FRASER WATTS
Series Editor

Preface

This book developed from initial suggestions made early in 1988 by Michael Coombs and Wendy Hudlass of John Wiley. Their assistance and patience in seeing the idea develop from its embryo form through the outline planning stage to final fruition are appreciated. While filled with some initial anxiety of my own at the prospect of drawing together an extensive and disparate literature I was also excited at the idea of writing a book encompassing anxiety in both physical and mental health. This allowed me to draw together my lectures, research and thinking in both clinical and health psychology.

Anxiety is a complex and elusive phenomenon which has occupied the thinking and research endeavours of numerous writers over many years. Ever since Freud's extensive writings a number of theoretical models of anxiety have been proposed. These have emphasised either conditioning experiences or patterns of thinking as fundamental to the genesis and/or maintenance of anxiety, with recent research suggesting that biased cognitive processing may play an important role. It has, however, been increasingly recognised that any comprehensive model of anxiety will, of necessity, be multidimensional in nature incorporating neurophysiological, behavioural and cognitive components which are organised in a hierarchical processing system. This conceptualisation is kept in mind throughout the book.

Given the long history of research relating to anxiety it is perhaps not surprising that there is an extensive literature pertaining to the topic. This literature has increased even more dramatically in recent years with the publication of specialist journals such as *The Journal of Anxiety Disorders* and *Anxiety Research*. A number of handbooks and research monographs, dealing both with specific anxiety disorders and anxiety disorders in general, have also been published recently. I hope that this volume achieves the aim of adding a number of new dimensions to existing work.

The first aim of this book is to go beyond anxiety disorders, which frequently form the focus of research and writing in clinical texts, to explore anxiety as a factor influencing psychosexual dysfunctions, physical symptom presentation, the onset and course of disease and the process of postoperative recovery. The second aim is to provide as up-to-date a review as possible. Approximately one-quarter of all the references cited have been published since the beginning of 1988 and I owe a debt to all those involved in anxiety research in clinical and health psychology in the UK and other European countries, USA and Australia who were kind enough to update me on their work. I hope I have not misquoted or misrepresented anyone. The third aim was to provide a text which would be accessible to undergraduate, postgraduate, professional, academic and research psychologists as well as other health-care professionals. I hope I have succeeded in that aim. The final aim was to provide a consistent framework to the book in order to facilitate accessibility of information. Each chapter is thus organised to reflect theory, assessment and therapy outcome.

The book itself is organised into four broad parts. The first two chapters provide an overview of conceptual and theoretical issues. The following five chapters overview prevalence, co-morbidity, theory, assessment and therapy outcome research in relation to social phobia, panic, agoraphobia, generalised anxiety and obsessive–compulsive disorder. The third part draws away from the anxiety disorders to consider anxiety in another clinical context, that relating to psychosexual dysfunction. The complex relationship between cognitive and physiological parameters of sexual arousal with cognitive and physiological parameters of anxiety has been explored in experimental studies as well as clinical evaluations and therapy. Yet the precise part played by anxiety in the aetiology of sexual dysfunction has still to be fully elucidated. The final part of the book is directed towards anxiety and physical health concerns. There have been numerous evaluations of psychological interventions for noxious surgical procedures within the past 30 years which suggest a positive effect for such procedures in terms of anxiety reduction. Far less attention has been directed towards anxiety related to perceived physical symptoms or anxiety related to expected treatments or investigations. The former may prompt excessive use of, the latter excessive avoidance of, health care facilities. Given the increasing emphasis on preventative medicine it is important to identify those whose anxiety prompts them to avoid treatment. Yet little is known about the extent of such avoidance. As with the need to investigate the links between anxiety and disease this provides an exciting area for future research. I hope that some of the ideas contained in this book act as an impetus for such future endeavours.

Any venture of this kind inevitably involves many solitary hours at the word processor. I would like to thank my wife Mary Bernadette for making the solitude tolerable and the time when I was not working so pleasurable.

ROBERT J. EDELMANN
Department of Psychology
University of Surrey
July, 1991

Chapter 1

Conceptual Issues

INTRODUCTION

Anxiety is a widely used concept within the psychological literature yet is often used uncritically and to reflect diverse meanings. Terms such as fear, phobia, neurosis and anxiety are often used interchangeably, with definitional problems further complicated by the overlap in use of the terms anxiety and stress. Historically, fear and anxiety were differentiated on the basis of the presence or absence of cues, although the terms are frequently equated in the more recent psychological literature. Anxiety is not only presumed to underlie 'anxiety disorders' such as agoraphobia, panic disorder, phobic disorder, obsessive–compulsive disorder and post-traumatic stress disorder, but is also considered to be an important contributor to sexual dysfunction, as a factor influencing symptom presentation, the onset and course of disease and the process of postoperative recovery. The term anxiety thus has many meanings as reflected in both psychological definitions and lay descriptions; it is possible to say that 'I am an anxious person', that 'I am anxious when at the dentist', that 'I feel anxious' or that 'I avoided the party because I was anxious about meeting people'. The first description assumes a relatively enduring characteristic of anxiety which shows little variation across situations; this contrasts with the clearly situationally specific characteristic denoted by the second description. The third description implies a particular affective quality while the final description uses the label as a particular explanation for some behaviour. These different meanings tend to be reflected in the many different definitions of anxiety which appear in the literature:

> Anxiety is a personality characteristic of responding to certain situations with a stress syndrome of responses. Anxiety states are then a function of the situations that evoke them and the individual personality that is prone to stress (Simpson, 1980).

> Apprehension, tension, or uneasiness which stems from the anticipation of danger, the source of which is largely unknown or unrecognised (American Psychiatric Association, 1975).

> An unpleasurable state of tension which indicates the presence of some danger to the organism (Weiss & English, 1957).

> An unpleasant emotional state or condition which is characterised by subjective feelings of tension, apprehension, and worry, and by activation or arousal of the autonomic nervous system (Spielberger, 1972).

This variation in use of the term anxiety is, to some extent, reflected by psychiatric classification systems such as DSM-III (American Psychiatric Association, 1980) and DSM-III-R (American Psychiatric Association, 1987). For example, descriptions of generalised anxiety disorder as a relatively persistent, chronic condition of tension imply an enduring and trans-situational trait of the individual. Other categories such as social phobia or post-traumatic stress disorder are classifications in which anxiety is a relatively transient and/or situationally specific response.

Within the behaviour therapy literature the term anxiety has also been used uncritically and in too many ways (Delprato & McGlynn, 1984). Anxiety can thus be characterised as an inferential construct used to explain behaviours (i.e. he avoided crowds because of his anxiety) or as a categorical concept denoting the occurrence of designated behaviours in specific situations (i.e. the occurrence of trembling, sweating, etc. in a dog phobic confronted by a dog indicate the existence of anxiety).

The distinction between anxiety as an emotional state and a relatively stable personality trait is also emphasised by many writers. Both require careful consideration. In relation to the former supposition Strongman (1987), Gray (1982) and Izard (1972) offer the following observations:

> Anxiety has probably had more written about it than any other emotion (Strongman, 1987, p. 202).

> Whatever else anxiety is, it is undoubtedly an emotion; sometimes, reading the work of psychologists, one is tempted to think that it is the only emotion (Gray, 1982, p. 5).

> I shall present a formulation of anxiety as a variable combination of interacting fundamental emotions.... In particular I propose that anxiety involves fear and two or more of the fundamental emotions of distress, shame (including shyness and guilt), anger, and the positive emotion of interest–excitement (Izard, 1972, pp. 52, 55).

On the basis of a variety of classificatory studies reviewed by Ekman, Friesen & Ellsworth (1982) one may infer that there are five basic emotions of which one is anxiety (or fear), the others being happiness, sadness, anger and disgust. There are many different emotion theories spanning more than a century of psychological writing, with different theories taking different starting points. Yet it has long been clear that emotions are complex phenomena encompassing at a minimum an expression and an emotional experience (James, 1884) or, as recent theorists suggest, that they are: 'complex behavioural reactions that reflect the constructive activity of a multi-component, hierarchical processing system, all of whose levels and components are involved in virtually all emotional experiences and reactions' (Leventhal & Scherer, 1987, p. 8). Yet, perhaps surprisingly, many theorists when discussing anxiety have tended, until relatively recently, to regard anxiety as a unitary phenomenon. Within the past two decades, however, the general thesis has been to regard anxiety as a state expressed via at least three different systems, although this conceptualisation of anxiety has also not been without its critics. The three-systems analysis does, however, have elements in common with theoretical analyses of the expression and experience of emotion. Presenting anxiety as a multidimensional emotion conceptualised in much the same way as other emotional states helps to place anxiety within a clearer conceptual framework.

THREE-SYSTEMS ANALYSIS OF ANXIETY

Lang (1968, 1971) and Lang, Rice & Sternbach (1972) have proposed that human emotion in general, and anxiety in particular, involves responses in 'three main behavioral systems' (Lang, 1968, p. 90) consisting of largely independent components of (i) motor behaviour; (ii) linguistic expressions and (iii) physiological states. This view, which can be contrasted with earlier accounts in which anxiety was treated as a global construct or 'lump' (Lang, 1970), has become known as the three-systems model of fear and anxiety.

The most usual type of motor response in relation to anxiety-eliciting stimuli involves avoidance behaviour, although other aspects of behaviour such as increased or decreased gesturing, changes in posture, trembling, etc., are also involved. While identifying behaviours associated with anxiety may be relatively straightforward, determining the most appropriate target behaviour to be monitored requires careful evaluation.

The linguistic expression component (originally labelled as the verbal–cognitive system by Lang, 1968, 1971) has been largely used to refer to 'cognitive events' or at least to the verbal reporting of such events. In the broadest sense this might include all aspects of the individual's perception and evaluation of the stimuli concerned. These might include past memories or specific thoughts and images. Lang (1985) states that the 'verbal report category includes reports of anxiety, fear, dread, panic, and associated complaints of worry, obsessions, inability to concentrate, insecurity, and the like' (p. 133). Identifying the exact nature of the verbal, linguistic or cognitive component to be assessed is no easy matter. For example, should such verbal reports include the subjects' perceptions of their physiological arousal, their degree of anxiety or their self-critical thoughts? Alternatively, should such a report refer to specific aspects of information processing bias which would be much more in line with current use of the term 'cognitive'?

The physiological component of anxiety is generally assumed to be associated with increased sympathetic nervous system activity with resultant increases in heart rate, respiration, sweat gland activity, muscle tone, etc. As with the behavioural response mode, defining the physiological response is less problematic than defining the verbal/linguistic/cognitive mode, although assessing physiological parameters is also not without its difficulties. For example, major problems arise in the selection of measures (i.e. which individual parameter or multiple set of parameters should be assessed), the reliability of equipment, intrusiveness of the techniques and interpretation of the data (e.g. Ney & Gale, 1988).

When all three response systems are assessed, a number of studies have found low, statistically non-significant correlations between them (e.g. Borkovec, Weerts & Bernstein, 1977). This low correlation between response systems at a particular point in time has been referred to as discordance (Hodgson & Rachman, 1974). It has also been noted that the three systems can covary over time in relation to anxiety reduction procedures, a phenomenon termed desynchrony (Hodgson & Rachman, 1974).

While this is taken to imply that the three systems are partially or functionally independent, with assessment of each system reflecting anxiety, the response system conceptualisation has not been without its critics (e.g. Cone, 1979; Hugdahl, 1981). In view of the inherent difficulties in assessing cognitive and physiological parameters, one possible interpretation of discordance between systems is that it is attributable, at least in part, to measurement error. This possibility is highlighted by the fact that variations have been found among measurements of different aspects within the same system. A particular problem exists in the case of 'cognitive' assessments which usually take the form of verbal reports encompassing a range of self-related thoughts, and often including subjective evaluations of motor behaviour and physiological responses. Thus subjects are in effect making global assessments of all three response systems although the resultant score is taken to reflect cognitive anxiety. As Williams (1987) comments:

The systems are vague and poorly differentiated from one another because they do not clearly specify the range of phenomena they include and exclude. Each system itself is disjointed because it can be readily subdivided into numerous components that show highly mixed degrees of intercorrelation with one another and with the phenomena subsumed under other systems (p. 168).

A further problem noted by Cone (1979) is that evaluations of inter-relationships invariably vary both measurement methods (e.g. self-reports, direct observation) and response modes (cognitive, physiological, and motor behaviour) thus confounding the two. Low interrelationships may therefore be an artefact of using different measurement strategies rather than a reflection of the actual relationship between response systems. Conversely, positive relationships between, say, self-reports of perception of autonomic arousal and self-reports of anxiety may either reflect a real relationship between different parameters of an emotion or may simply reflect the common methodology used.

An issue inherent in the three-systems theory is the problem of identifying the causal agent in relation to 'anxiety'. If one assumes that the three-systems model refers to response modes then, unless feedback loops are incorporated into such a model, the reaction cannot also be the cause. Many would argue, for example, that 'human behaviour, including phobic behaviour, is largely regulated by thoughts . . . people avoid largely because of what they think' (Williams, 1987, p. 174). However, others (e.g. Marks, 1987a) question what they see as the 'fallacy of cognitive supremacy', assuming that thoughts are not necessarily the cause of anxiety but may be a sign of it. The question of cognitions as a cause or consequence of anxiety has frequently been the centre of debate within the literature in the past decade, and is also central to the notion of feeling states (emotions) in general (i.e. does a thought or behaviour precede a feeling or vice versa?). Indeed, the issue of the 'primacy of affect' has not only a long, but a controversial, history, the key elements of which are discussed later.

Although the tripartite response system is not without its difficulties it is now widely accepted within the psychological literature. One important use of such theorising is to match treatments to the person's particular response. Thus individuals with extreme motor responses, or extreme physiological responses, or extreme cognitive responses, who receive a treatment which matches their particular response pattern should show greater improvement than individuals treated with a technique that does not match their response pattern. This notion has been tested in a series of studies by Öst and his colleagues (Öst, Jerremalm & Johansson, 1981; Öst, Johansson & Jerremalm, 1982; Öst, Jerremalm & Jansson, 1984a; Jerremalm, Jansson & Öst, 1986a,b), with varying degrees of success. The benefit of treatment–response system matching was found with social phobic and claustrophobic patients (Öst *et al.*, 1981, 1982) but not with agoraphobic, social phobics using different coping techniques or dental phobics (Öst *et al.*, 1984a; Jansson *et al.*, 1986a,b). Given the inherent difficulties in the assessment of different response systems, such mixed findings are perhaps not surprising.

Further, there is often a dearth of empirical evidence explaining the precise manner in which specific treatments operate. It is often assumed that cognitive restructuring selectively affects cognitive responding, and that direct exposure techniques primarily alter motor behaviour (Hugdahl, 1981), although this may in fact not be the case. A study by Odom, Nelson & Wien (1978), for example, found that cognitive restructuring reduced heart rate more effectively than systematic desensitisation, and that guided participation was more effective than cognitive restructuring in changing self-reported anxiety. Guided mastery was, however, more effective for reducing avoidance behaviour.

The notion of three components of anxiety: affective experience, expressive behaviour and peripheral physiological responding, adopted within the past 20 years shares common ground with views adopted regarding emotions in general. Within the emotion literature the inter-relationships between systems and the question of causality and primacy have been debated in varying ways since the turn of this century. Because of this commonality it is pertinent to examine briefly some of the major theories of emotions and the controversies associated with them which relate to controversies about the nature of the relationship between the three components of emotion/anxiety. It is perhaps inevitable that recent theories stress the complex interrelationship between components of emotion rather than thinking in terms of a simple tripartite response output.

ANXIETY AS AN EMOTION

Emotion probably suffers from as many diverse definitions as anxiety; as Gray (1982) comments: 'it is a moot point whether "anxiety" or "emotion" is the more opaque concept' (p. 5). Kleinginna & Kleinginna (1981) have categorised the many hundreds of definitions of emotion in order to create the following summary definition:

> Emotion is a complex set of interactions among subjective and objective factors, mediated by neural hormonal systems, which can (a) give rise to affective experiences such as feelings of arousal, pleasure/displeasure; (b)

generate cognitive processes such as emotionally relevant perceptual effects, appraisals, labelling processes; (c) activate widespread physiological adjustments to the arousing conditions; and (d) lead to behavior that is often, but not always, expressive, goal directed, and adaptive.

The tripartite distinction inherent in this definition matches that emphasised within the anxiety literature. In addition, however, Kleinginna & Kleinginna's (1981) definition emphasises the fact that the feeling state as well as the tripartite response system is the result of activation of the neural hormonal system presumably in response to a definable stimulus. This assumption is not by any means universally reflected by emotion theories which tend to emphasise either the physiological/peripheral, cognitive or behavioural aspects of functioning in the generation of both emotion in general and anxiety in particular. The ongoing nature of this debate in relation to the cognitive or behavioural generation of anxiety is reflected in the comments referred to previously.

A comprehensive review of emotion theories is beyond the scope of this book, and the reader is referred to relevant texts such as those by Buck (1988) and Strongman (1987). Leventhal & Mosbach (1983) and Leventhal & Tomarken (1986) suggest a useful organisation for emotion theories which they divide into four broad classes: (i) body reaction theories; (ii) central neural theories; (iii) cognition–arousal theories and (iv) Darwinian-evolutionary theories. Other authors have adapted and extended combinations of these broad approaches, regarding emotions as a complex multidimensional process. Each has clear implications for any consideration of anxiety.

Body reaction theories: the James–Lange theory

The central notion of this theory, put forward independently by James (1884) and Lange (1885), is that an 'emotion-evoking' stimulus produces both autonomic activity (heart rate increase, sweating, etc.) and changes in skeletal muscles (running, facial expressions, etc.). The theory holds that the subjective experience, or feeling, of emotion is then a direct result of these changes. No cognitive appraisal relating to emotion precedes the bodily response; rather it is the bodily response which is the emotion. We do not therefore stammer and tremble because we are anxious, but are anxious because we stammer and tremble. In James's terms:

the bodily changes follow directly the PERCEPTION of the existing fact, and that our feeling of the same changes as they occur IS the emotion (1884, p. 189; capitals in the original).

So, for example, if a person feels anxious at the dentist and their stomach churns, they tremble and sweat, in James's terms it is this reaction which results in the feeling of anxiety. The most basic problem with James' theory, however, is in its failure to specify the mechanism by which bodily changes are initiated by the 'perception of the exciting fact'. Other problems have been raised by Cannon (1927).

Central neural theories: Cannon's theory

In 1927 Cannon published a review and critique of the James–Lange theory and proposed an alternative viewpoint. Cannon argued in his critique that bodily sensation is too slow, diffuse and insensitive to account for the speed and wide range of human emotional experience. If feedback from bodily sensations creates an emotional feeling, as the James–Lange theory proposes, then one might also expect that patients who do not receive such feedback, such as those who have suffered injuries to their spinal cord, will report decreased emotional experience. Although some reports suggest that this might indeed be the case (Hohmann, 1966) more recent studies have found no reports of lessened emotional experience from spinal-cord-injury patients (Lowe & Carroll, 1985). The earlier results may be a reflection of the longer hospitalisation which was typical for such patients in the 1950s and hence, as Lowe & Carroll note, a discouraging outlook rather than a disrupted nervous system.

In order to account for the problems he saw with the James–Lange theory, Cannon proposed a theory in which he viewed the generation of emotion as under more central than peripheral nervous system control. His neurophysiological theory proposed that stimuli reach the cortex via subcortical systems. If these stimuli are emotional in nature the subcortical systems not only inform the cortex, thus causing the emotional experience, but also inform relevant peripheral bodily systems causing bodily responses. The subcortical structure assumed to be particularly important in emotion was the thalamus. Although this has subsequently been shown to be incorrect, with the neurophysiological picture being much more complicated than Cannon originally assumed, it provided the groundwork for much later theorising and research. There have also been attempts to answer Cannon's criticisms of the James–Lange theory such as those offered by Schachter & Singer's (1962) self-attribution theory of emotion.

Cognitive–arousal theories

Schachter argued that both cognitive and physiological aspects of emotion are important and that when either component is missing the emotion experienced is incomplete. In their original study, Schachter & Singer (1962) investigated the effects of different cognitions on the subjects' reaction to an injection of epinephrine. Some subjects were told the actual effects of the drug (i.e. your hand will start to shake, your heart will start to pound, and your face may get warm and flushed), while other subjects were misinformed about the effects (i.e. they were told they would experience numbness, itching and a slight headache) while a third group were told nothing about any side-effects. All subjects were thus in a state of epinephrine-induced arousal but differed in the physiological reactions they expected.

Schachter & Singer then manipulated the kind of explanation subjects had for their arousal by manipulating the behaviour of a confederate waiting with the subject following the injection. For half the subjects the confederate behaved in a happy, playful manner, throwing paper aeroplanes, etc., while for the other subjects the confederate was angry and aggressive. On the basis of observed behaviour and self-reports, the uninformed subjects became more angry or happy depending upon the condition in comparison to the informed subjects.

On the basis of this study Schachter & Singer hypothesised that if we are in a state of unexplained physiological arousal we will search the immediate environment for an appropriate explanation. This presupposes that physiological arousal is comparable across emotions with cognitive appraisal providing the differentiating emotion label. The notion that unexplained arousal can be experienced as different emotions depending upon cognitive appraisal of environmental events has generated a great deal of controversy (see Reisenzein, 1983). Further attempts to replicate Schachter & Singer's results have not been successful (Marshall & Zimbardo, 1979; Maslach, 1979), leading Manstead & Wagner (1981) to conclude that this notion has received only limited support. While Schachter & Singer may well have oversimplified and underestimated the importance of physiological systems, while overestimating the importance of cognitions, it nevertheless seems clear that cognitive appraisal does interact with physiological factors in the generation of emotional states.

Darwinian evolutionary tradition

The fourth group of theories can perhaps best be characterised as within the evolutionary tradition, and are identified with the writings of Charles Darwin (1873). He suggested a basic continuity of emotional expressions from lower animals to humans. Emotions thus increase the animals' chances of survival by being appropriate reactions to emergency events in the environment and by acting as signals for future intentions or actions.

A number of theorists can be broadly categorised within this heading (Izard, 1971, 1977, 1990; Plutchic, 1980, 1984; Tomkins, 1962, 1980). Although there are a number of points of departure between the views held by these theorists there are also central points of overlap. For example, both Izard (1971) and Tomkins (1962) emphasise the central role of the face in creating emotional experience. The notion that feedback from one's facial expressive behaviours gives rise to the experience of emotion has a long and chequered history, and has been evaluated in a number of empirical studies.

Two procedures have been used to test the feedback hypothesis directly: (i) direct manipulations of facial expressions and (ii) instructions to hide or reveal expressive reactions. The assumption behind these studies is that expressive changes mediate subjective feeling so that manipulating expressions in the absence of eliciting stimuli nevertheless results in the person reporting feeling that emotion, while hiding an emotion should produce the opposite effect. The results of numerous empirical studies and reviews give rise to contradictory conclusions. Buck (1980) suggests that there does not appear to be convincing evidence in support of the hypothesis; Laird (1984) argues that experimental evidence provides over-whelming support for a facial feedback theory, although both Matsumoto (1987) and Winton (1986) take issue with Laird's conclusion, and Manstead (1988) suggests that the evidence warrants a more cautious con-clusion. Thus while facial expression may not create emotions it seems plausible to assume that expressive changes can alter subjective states, as suggested by other emotion theorists such as Leventhal (1979, 1980, 1984). Feedback may also be more general than purely from facial expression, and may include feedback from other bodily and physiological reactions. It also seems reasonable to assume that such feedback involves an evaluative component and hence the creation of a feeling from a reaction is likely to involve more complex processes than suggested by facial feedback theories.

Multicomponent process models of emotion

Given the possible part played by peripheral, central and cognitive elements in creating emotions some authors have attempted to incorporate these elements into multicomponent process models of emotion. For exam-ple, Leventhal's information-processing model of emotion (Leventhal, 1979, 1980, 1984; Leventhal & Mosbach, 1983; Leventhal & Tomarken, 1986) consists of four integrated systems: (i) an interpretation mechanism which responds to emotional reactions; (ii) an expressive system, feedback from which helps to define the subjective emotional state; (iii) an action system maintained by (iv) the bodily reaction. In an attempt to integrate these systems Leventhal proposes two phases to the model: a perceptual/motor phase and an action phase. The former involves an appraisal phase in which a decision is made about the positive/negative nature of incoming stimuli which are subsequently categorised in emotion terms on the basis of feedback from facial expression and autonomic systems. Taking subsequent action can serve to enhance or detract from subjective experience of the emotion. More recently Leventhal has emphasised three levels of processing involved in emotional experience: an expressive motor mechanism which involves an innate set of expressive reactions; schematic or perceptual memory that codes previous emotional situations, experiences and reactions; and a conceptual or abstract memory which contains rules about emotional experiences and behaviour. Within this framework autonomic activity, expressive behaviour and cognitive appraisal operate interactively with each other in creating emotional experience.

A similar theoretical position in which emotion is regarded as a syndrome of different components has been adopted by Scherer (1982, 1984). He suggests five components for any emotion: (i) precognitive and cognitive evaluation; (ii) physiological reactions; (iii) motivational components and components of preparation for action; (iv) motor expression and (v) subjective emotional state. Scherer's starting point is to describe a series of stimulus evaluation checks (SECs) which he regards as minimally necessary for evaluating or appraising the emotion-producing stimuli. These are concerned with: (i) novelty and unexpectedness; (ii) an evaluation of the inherent pleasantness or unpleasantness of the stimuli; (iii) an evaluation of goal-relevance of the stimulus; (iv) an evaluation of the extent to which the organism is capable of coping with the stimulus; (v) a comparison of stimuli with social norms and self-concept. Each SEC which is experienced helps to further differentiate emotional states, so that within Scherer's framework cognition plays a central part in determining emotional experience.

The importance of cognitive factors in determining emotional state is similarly stressed by Lazarus (1966, 1968) and by Lazarus, Kanner & Folkman (1980), who propose a series of cognitive appraisals which mediate responses to environmental events. Primary appraisal results in the event being evaluated in terms of its relevance to well-being, as benign–positive, or as stressful. He further distinguishes three classes of stressful evaluation: harm–loss (related to injury/loss which has already occurred), threat (related to the anticipation of injury or harm) and challenge (related to chances of obtaining a positive outcome in the situation). Secondary appraisal involves an evaluation of the resources, both personal and environmental, which are available to deal with the situation.

Constant reappraisal of the success of coping efforts and the continuing impact of the event allows the organism to appropriately modify primary and secondary appraisal. If available coping resources are perceived as inadequate, or an event is appraised as threatening or potentially harmful, then negative emotions may result. As with the position adopted by Scherer, and to a lesser extent by Leventhal, for Lazarus it is our cognitive appraisal of stimuli which produces the emotional response.

THE RELATIONSHIP BETWEEN COGNITION AND EMOTION

From the foregoing, albeit brief, presentation of key aspects of theories of emotion it is evident that the weight placed on cognitive aspects of emotion varies considerably between theories. The issue of the role of cognition in emotion emerges from the controversy between the James–Lange theory of emotion and that of Cannon. It could be argued, for example, that the James–Lange theory places an emphasis on cognition, in emphasising that it is the *perception* of a stimulus which causes bodily changes which are subsequently experienced as emotion. In contrast, Cannon's theory, in emphasising that the stimulus acts upon subcortical structures which then provoke cortical and bodily reactions, tends to de-emphasise cognition as a necessary part of emotion. In contrast, Schachter's work suggests that how we label emotional states may be a largely cognitive matter, although as noted this view is not without its critics. Leventhal raises important issues concerning the way in which arousal and cognition combine in emotion. The role of past experience with similar situations and facial or more general bodily feedback may be important here. Scherer, too, assumes that cognitive factors play a central role in emotional experience.

The important role of cognition in emotion is emphasised even more strongly in the work of Lazarus and his colleagues. The notion of cognitive appraisal introduced by Lazarus emphasises the fact that cognitive processes are central to emotion. Lazarus (1984) has argued that:

> cognitive activity is a necessary precondition of emotion because to experience an emotion, people must comprehend . . . that their well-being is implicated in a transaction, for better or worse (p. 124).

He further suggests that appraisal can be a conscious, rational, symbolic process but that it can also be a 'primitive evaluative perception'. In his more recent writings Lazarus has differentiated between appraisal and knowledge as different kinds of cognition.

Knowledge consists of what a person believes about the way the world works in general and in a specific context ... appraisal, on the other hand, is an evaluation of the significance of knowledge about what is happening for our personal well-being (Lazarus, 1991, p. 354).

He further argues that appraisal is a necessary as well as a sufficient cause of emotion while knowledge is necessary but not sufficient (Lazarus & Smith, 1988; Lazarus, 1991).

The notion that cognition influences or determines emotion is, however, not without its critics. The question of what comes first, cognition or affect, has formed a central plank in a debate between Zajonc (1980, 1984) and Lazarus (1982, 1984), which has potentially important clinical implications (Greenberg & Safran, 1984a; Rachman, 1981, 1984a; Watts, 1983).

The 'primacy' of emotion or cognition

Zajonc has argued that affect and cognition can function independently, and that affect can precede cognition (Zajonc, 1980, 1984). This supposition was based upon a series of studies in which subjects were found to respond preferentially to stimuli to which they had been exposed previously, although they were unable to say that they had seen the stimuli previously. This may be because the affective aspects of stimuli are processed independently of their physical attributes. Thus we form positive or negative impressions separately from, and as rapidly as, we perform more cognitively based tasks of classifying and recognising stimuli.

Zajonc's argument has drawn strong criticism from those who argue that emotion cannot occur in the absence of cognitive appraisal (Lazarus, 1982, 1984). Part of the problem within this debate arises over the differential use of central terms 'emotion' and 'cognition'. As previously noted, Lazarus suggests that cognitive activity involved in emotion activation may be a 'highly differentiated process' or some form of 'primitive evaluative perception'. Zajonc (1984) regards cognitive activity as involving some kind of 'mental work' and not the 'most primitive forms of sensory excitation' suggested by Lazarus. It seems plausible, however, that although emotion may involve *'conscious* recognition and affective judgements this does not rule out the possibility ... that affect depends on some degree of *preconscious* cognitive processing' (Brewin, 1988, p. 56; italics in original). The evidence for preconscious processing is now overwhelming (Dixon, 1981) and there is evidence that preconscious or pre-attentive bias in processing information related to personal threat is associated with enhanced reactions of anxiety.

One conclusion from the cognitive/affective debate might be that both Lazarus and Zajonc see some form of cognitive activity as being involved in emotional experience, but that they disagree about the nature of the cognitive activity involved. It is also clear, however, that emotional changes can subsequently influence a person's cognitive processes. Rather than considering whether emotion and cognition can be independent from one another it might be more useful to examine how cognition is involved in different aspects of emotion. The problems inherent in the emotion/cognition debate are to a large extent circumvented by component-process theories of emotion. As Leventhal & Scherer (1987) suggest, the complexity of stimulus appraisal processes may vary at different stages of emotional experience. Plutchik (1985) also concludes that 'the controversy disappears if emotions are conceptualized as complex chains of inferred events with feedback loops that usually begin with an external stimulus and an evaluation of that stimulus' (p. 199). As well as assuming a complex interplay between cognitive, behavioural, physiological and affective components Plutchik's comment also seems to raise the possibility that, although it may be more usual for cognitive/evaluative responses to precede the affective component of emotion, the reverse may also occur.

The emotion/cognition debate is important to research on anxiety for a number of reasons. First, Rachman (1981, 1984a) has related Zajonc's ideas to the observation that clinical patients often show strong emotional reactions to stimuli even though they 'know' them to be objectively harmless. Second, if cognition does not precede emotion then cognitively based therapies might be mistaken in their assumption that affective responses can be modified by altering a person's cognitions. Third, if emotion is a multicomponent phenomenon involving appraisal and reappraisal processes, then presumably anxiety should be discussed within a similar framework.

The 'primacy issue' and clinical psychology

Just as the 1960s witnessed a behavioural revolution in clinical psychology so the 1970s heralded a cognitive revolution. The historical development of theories of the aetiology of anxiety from behavioural models emphasising the role of classical and instrumental conditioning in shaping people's behaviour to cognitive models emphasising the mental processes involved is discussed in Chapter 2. The dichotomy between a concern with behaviours on the one hand and cognitions on the other leads to the assumption within cognitively based theories such as Beck's (e.g. Beck & Emery, 1979; Beck, Emery & Greenberg, 1985) that a person's private meanings determine his or her emotional responses.

Thus, according to Mahoney (1974), cognitive approaches all share the following assumptions:

1. The human organism responds primarily to cognitive representations of its environments rather than to those environments *per se*.
2. These cognitive representations are functionally related to the processes and parameters of learning.
3. Most human learning is cognitively mediated.
4. Thoughts, feeling, and behaviors are causally interactive (pp. 7–8).

This could be taken to imply that affect is a postcognitive phenomenon and that affect and cognition operate within the same system. These notions underlying cognitive theories have been criticised by both Wilson (1984) and Rachman (1981). Rachman has drawn on the views advanced by Zajonc (1980) and elaborated them in relation to the three-systems analysis of anxiety. In addition to the subjective, behavioural and physiological systems Rachman suggests that if affect is precognitive, as Zajonc suggests, a new type of discordance is produced—discordance between affective and cognitive systems. Problems can then be located in behavioural, physiological, cognitive or affective systems. If affect is precognitive then changing cognitions will not necessarily result in affective change, hence challenging a basic assumption of cognitive theories. Further, if affect and cognition operate within separate systems there is no reason to believe that changing one will result in changes in the other. Wilson has drawn on Rachman's conclusions to further question the assumption that cognitions have a large influence upon emotional systems or that one can identify automatic (anxiety-producing) thoughts prior to emotional arousal.

It seems clear, however, as Watts (1983) points out, that Rachman's suggestions go beyond the propositions made by Zajonc. As he notes: 'If some cognitive processes are preconscious, then an absence of awareness of cognitive processes associated with affective reactions cannot be used as evidence for the absence of *any* involvement of cognition in affective reaction' (p. 89). Greenberg & Safran (1984b) in a similar vein note that the experience of emotion is likely to be the result of information-processing activities in which cognition and affect are seen to operate in a combined manner, with one influencing the other, rather than independently. In their model they draw heavily on the work of Leventhal to propose a model in which emotions are viewed as being linked to expressive-motor reactions, autonomic reactions, memories, images and ideas so that activation of any one component can lead to activation within other components.

EMOTIONS AND ANXIETY: SUMMARY COMMENTS

The literature alluded to raises several key points in relation to anxiety. First, confusion about definitions of anxiety reflects the extent to which different definitions emphasise different aspects of the same phenomenon (i.e. a feeling, a behaviour or an explanation for a behaviour). Second, the tripartite model of anxiety, while useful, implies three relatively independently functioning systems, and it seems unlikely that such components operate independently one from the other. Third, the emotion literature illustrates the long history of the debate about which component of emotion plays the dominant role in creating the feeling state. Fourth, it is possible to extend the tripartite model to include an affective component which, unlike the cognitive component, does not involve evaluative perception of external stimuli. Fifth, the evidence seems to suggest that cognitive aspects of anxiety can involve both preconscious evaluation and ongoing evaluative appraisal of a stimulus.

Rather than conceptualising anxiety as either a 'lump' or simple multi-component reaction it seems more useful to regard it as a hierarchical multicomponent construct which can be conceptualised in similar terms to recent information-processing models of emotion. It is thus an ongoing rather than static reaction which can not only change in form over time, but can also change in the extent to which one 'system' predominates over time. Also of importance are appraisal and reappraisal processes not only of the eliciting stimulus but also reactions to that stimulus, including subsequent coping attempts (see Edelmann, 1987, for a recent example of such a model in relation to embarrassment). Given the multicomponent nature of anxiety it seems reasonable to assume that any explanation or therapy for anxiety will have to reflect this complexity. Theories have, however, tended to focus upon one aspect of anxiety and have thus, not surprisingly, been found wanting as explanations for the totality of a complex phenomenon. These issues are discussed in the following chapter. Before moving on to such explanations one further aspect of anxiety requires comment. It is clear that different people show different reactions to the same phenomenon. Whether such differences are due to some inherent variations in bodily sensitivity, appraisal processes, or behavioural reactivity is clearly a central issue in anxiety research.

ANXIETY—PERSONALITY TRAIT OR SITUATIONALLY DETERMINED CHARACTERISTIC

An adequate theory of anxiety must distinguish conceptually and operationally between anxiety as a transitory state and as a relatively stable personality trait (Spielberger, 1972, p. 38).

The impetus for considering a distinction between anxiety as a transient state and as a relatively stable personality disposition came from Cattell & Scheier (1961) and Spielberger (1966). Trait anxiety has been defined as 'relatively stable individual differences in anxiety proneness', while state anxiety is 'characterised by subjective, consciously perceived feelings of tension and apprehension, and heightened autonomic nervous system activity' (Spielberger, Gorsuch & Lushene, 1970, p. 3).

Trait anxiety correlates between 0.6 and 0.8 with neuroticism. Eysenck's (1967, 1981) theory of personality posits neuroticism–stability and extraversion–introversion as two major axes. The endpoints of the latter axis are determined by relatively low and high levels of cortical arousal, respectively. Thus extraverts have to seek out higher levels of cortical arousal while introverts find that lower levels of arousal provide sufficient stimulation. Biological determinants of neuroticism–stability are autonomic nervous system reactivity, with neurotics characterised by intense autonomic nervous system activity and very slow rates of habituation to stimuli.

In relation to Eysenck's theory, Gray (1982, 1985) emphasises an axis of impulsivity–anxiety, the endpoints of which fall between the extraversion/stability dimensions and the introversion/neuroticism dimensions, respectively. Individuals with high trait anxiety thus possess characteristics which reflect a combination of introversion and neuroticism. Anxiety is related to a highly active behavioural inhibition system, composed of the septohippocampal system, its monoaminergic afferents from the brain stem, and its neocortical projections in the frontal lobe.

In relation to trait theories in general, it has been argued that personality characteristics are determined, at least in part, by hereditary factors. Studies assessing the hereditability of neuroticism seem to suggest that this might indeed be the case. Shields (1962) found inter-pair correlations of 0.53 for monozygotic twins reared apart, 0.38 for monozygotic twins reared together and 0.11 for dizygotic twins reared together. Although the correlation for monozygotic twins reared together is, surprisingly, less than that for those reared apart, and the correlation for dizygotic twins is rather low, the overall pattern is suggestive of some hereditary determination of personality. A further large-scale study of 12 898 twin pairs (Floderus-Myrhed, Pedersen & Rasmussen, 1980) reported estimated hereditability for neuroticism of 0.50 for males and 0.58 for females. Shields (1973), reviewing evidence from available twin studies, concluded that many studies show evidence of a significant hereditary component of neuroticism or anxiety. As a result of findings such as this, Eysenck & Eysenck (1985) have concluded that 'no serious worker in this field denies that genetic factors account for at least something like half the variance' (p. 96).

A complicating factor is that trait and state anxiety tend to correlate quite highly with each other. There is also some evidence from twin studies of a possible genetic basis for anxiety disorders (Slater & Shields, 1969). One possibility is that the inherited aspect of fears and phobias is the 'vulnerability' to develop such difficulties—trait anxious individuals may be more likely to exhibit state anxiety given the required conditions. Thus, Spielberger, Pollans & Worden (1984) state that:

> Persons who are high in Trait-Anxiety are more vulnerable to stress and respond to a wider range of situations as dangerous or threatening. Since individuals who are high in Trait-Anxiety are more disposed to see the world as dangerous or threatening, they experience State-Anxiety reactions more frequently, and often with greater intensity than do people lower in Trait-Anxiety (p. 276).

State anxiety, then, is an emotional state identified in conceptions of anxiety as a multicomponent process; trait anxiety merely reflects individual differences in anxiety proneness.

The notion that people have stable, highly consistent personality traits that influence behaviour across a range of situations has, however, not been without its critics. Mischel (e.g. 1973), for example, while not denying the existence of some consistency across situations emphasises the importance of complex person–environment interactions in producing behaviour. Rather than global traits, the central focus is the individual's cognitive processing and behavioural actions in relation to specific situations. Variables identified by Mischel as important determinants of behaviour include competencies, expectancies, subjective values and the categorization of events. Derived from this, specific vulnerability factors for anxiety include the tendency to selectively attend to threat stimuli with those who believe that they have little control over events being particularly vulnerable (see Chapter 2).

In summary, while not denying some element of genetic transmission, perhaps via an underlying biological 'vulnerability', specific reactions will be influenced to a not-insignificant degree by environmental factors. The 'vulnerability' factor may relate to Eysenck's (1967, 1982) notion of an overly responsive nervous system, or Gray's (1971, 1985) notion of a highly reactive behavioural inhibition system. It seems reasonable to assume, however, that any conceptualisation of anxiety must take into account individual differences in proneness, perhaps in the form of 'vulnerability' to anxiety. These differences will clearly impinge upon the individual's appraisal of their bodily reactions and information-processing activities, and hence influence their interpretation of external environmental events.

Chapter 2

Theoretical Considerations

Anxiety (or dread) itself needs no description; everyone has personally experienced this sensation, or to speak more correctly this affective condition, at some time or other. But in my opinion not enough serious consideration has been given to the question why nervous persons in particular suffer from anxiety so much more intensely, and so much more altogether than others ... one thing is certain, that the problem of anxiety is a nodal point, linking up all kinds of most important questions: a riddle of which the solution must cast a flood of light upon our whole mental life (Freud, 1969, p. 341).

Ever since Freud's pioneering work (Freud, 1926/1959) a number of theoretical models of anxiety have been proposed, each with their own derivative set of treatment techniques. Freud's own views on the role of anxiety in the so-called neuroses underwent many revisions, leading to his publication of 'Inhibitions, symptoms and anxiety' (Freud, 1959), in which he differentiated between 'primary anxiety' which could be traced to somatic sources, often the birth process, and later 'subsequent anxiety' resulting from separation from either mother of other significant object, castration fears, or other crises in psychosexual development.

Within Freud's familiar tripartite model, anxiety could be separated into realistic, moral and neurotic forms. Realistic anxiety was a direct response to real external threat and on its own could not cause psychological difficulties. Moral anxiety, associated with shame and guilt, resulted from conflict between ego and superego. Neurotic anxiety was composed of three elements: (i) focused symptoms such as phobic anxiety; (ii) free-floating feelings of displeasure caused by many and varied stimuli; and (iii) fully developed sensations of panic.

Freud's psychoanalytic view of anxiety has undergone many subsequent additions and revisions, and has given detailed insights into the phenomenology of anxiety; unfortunately, however, the complexity of some of the theoretical constructs has posed practical problems both in terms of definition and for empirical scrutiny. This has led some writers to claim that 'Freudian theories are untestable because they cannot be falsified by any conceivable experimental or clinical event' (Eysenck, 1976, p. 252). Indeed, there is an unfortunate lack of empirical studies within the psychoanalytical literature. While others have been less vociferous in their criticism of Freudian theories subsequent historical developments of theoretical perspectives concerning anxiety have trodden a path heavily rooted in experimental psychology and the individual's learning history. As Wolpe & Rachman (1960) comment in their critique of Freud's psychoanalytical propositions:

> Phobias are regarded as conditioned anxiety (fear) reactions. Any 'neutral' stimulus, simple or complex, that happens to impact on an individual at about the time that a fear reaction is evoked acquires the ability to evoke fear subsequently (Wolpe & Rachman, 1960, p. 145).

Since the 1950s, however, as it became clear that the basic learning theory paradigm could not explain all cases of anxiety reaction, it too has undergone many revisions. Over the past decade there has been increasing emphasis upon cognitively based theories. Initially these emphasised the importance of mental events as intervening variables between an environmental event and the reaction of the individual to this event. While there is a continuing debate about whether mental events can be seen as causal or moderating variables or, indeed, whether they are merely one component of an anxiety response, much recent theorising has emphasised the importance of particular patterns of thinking as causally implicated in the generation of anxiety. In describing and discussing theoretical contributions to anxiety this historical trend will form the basis for organising the presentation of material.

CLASSICAL CONDITIONING

The traditional classical conditioning paradigm focuses on the acquisition of specific phobic reactions. According to the model initially proposed by Watson & Morgan (1917) an initially neutral, non-anxiety-provoking event, when paired with an aversive experience (the unconditioned stimulus or UCS), which results in experienced anxiety (the unconditioned response or UCR), becomes associated with the aversive experience (becomes a conditioned stimulus or CS) and hence is able to elicit a similar anxiety reaction (the conditioned response or CR). Stimulus generalisation is invoked to explain anxiety reactions to stimuli similar to, but never actually paired with, a UCS. Watson & Rayner (1920) illustrated the basic principles in their widely cited study with 11-month-old Albert:

> Just as the right hand touched the rat (CS) the bar was again struck (UCS—loud sound). Again the infant jumped violently, fell forward and began to whimper (UCR) (p. 4; sections in italics not in original).

Within a week of the second CS–UCS pairing, Albert not only showed avoidance and cried when the rat was presented alone, but showed such reactions when presented with similar stimuli (rabbit, dog, fur coat, cotton) which had not previously resulted in such reactions. A number of subsequent laboratory and clinical studies have shown supportive evidence for the classical conditioning theory (for reviews see Bandura, 1969; Beecroft, 1966), although many theorists have raised doubts about the adequacy of the theory (e.g. Bandura, 1977a; Mahoney, 1974). Even strong proponents of the classical conditioning model have substantially modified their earlier positions (e.g. Eysenck, 1976; Rachman, 1978).

It has also been suggested that subsequent attempts to replicate Watson & Rayner's study have failed to demonstrate successful conditioning of young children (Bregman, 1934; English, 1929). Both these studies used evolutionary 'neutral' stimuli (toy duck, wooden blocks) rather than stimuli which we might be predisposed to fear. The lack of conditioning evidenced in these studies would suggest that conditioned fear occurs only with objects having an inherent biological significance. Having become an influential notion this issue is discussed later, but careful examination of the English and Bregman studies suggest that they neither present an adequate refutation of Watson & Rayner's study nor provide evidence of conditioning of stimuli of biological significance. In pairing a loud noise with exposure to a toy duck English comments that the loud noise failed to evoke fear at any time. Rather than the nature of the pre-aversive stimuli (the toy duck) the lack of an aversive stimulus may have been responsible for failure to produce conditioned fear (for a full discussion of these studies see Delprato, 1980).

Conditioning theory has nevertheless generated much support. Rachman (1979) has summarised six factors which he suggests were used as evidence that anxiety is acquired through the process of conditioning. Firstly, the large number of experiments on the induction of fear in animals; secondly, the development of anxiety states in combat soldiers; thirdly, experiments on the induction of fear in small children; fourthly, clinical observations of anxiety in cases such as dental phobia; fifthly, incidental findings from the use of aversion therapy and sixthly a few experiments of the effects of traumatic stimulation. In contrast, many reservations have been expressed about the theory over the intervening years which have been discussed by Rachman (e.g. 1977, 1978, 1984b, 1990, 1991), Eysenck (e.g. 1967, 1976) and others. As a result of such reservations these authors have salvaged the theory with many subsequent revisions. Rachman and Eysenck raise six major concerns in relation to a conditioning theory of anxiety.

First, Rachman (1977, 1990) discusses instances of individuals exposed to air-raids who did not develop anxiety reactions in spite of repeated exposure to theoretically fear-evoking situations. On the basis of conditioning theory one might expect that people exposed to the trauma of an air-raid would not only show acute emotional reactions immediately after such exposure, but that fear reactions would endure and be subsequently strengthened by further exposure to air-raids. Although short-lived fear reactions are common in such circumstances, enduring anxiety responses seem to be rare (Janis, 1951).

Second, clients frequently present with severe anxiety in the absence of any clearly identifiable aversive experience. It has been suggested that between 40% and 80% of individuals with fears or phobias cannot recall any traumatic experience associated with onset (Brewin, 1988), although studies examining the recall of aversive experiences in relation to phobias have produced mixed results. Thus, Öst & Hugdahl (1981) report that 47.5% of their animal-phobic subjects attributed their fears to conditioning experiences, while in comparable samples, McNally & Steketee (1985), Rimm et al. (1977), and Hekmat (1987) report figures of less than 25%, 35% and 26% respectively (the latter two studies used analogue animal phobias). In a further study of the origins of snake fear in college students, Murray & Foote (1979) found that few subjects reported experiences that could be construed as conditioning events, while Kleinknecht (1982) reports that none of his spider-phobic subjects recalled direct traumatic events. In fact findings suggest that evidence for direct conditioning is less striking in relation to animal phobias than other categories of human fears. Öst & Hugdahl (1981) found that across patient groups 58% of patients ascribed their phobias to conditioning experiences, while Öst (1985, 1987) reports a figure of 64%.

Öst & Hugdahl (1983) and Öst (1985, 1987) further report that the majority of their agoraphobic patients ascribed the onset of their phobia to conditioning experiences (87%, 88.8% and 81%, respectively). This finding is perhaps particularly surprising as others have found that the onset of agoraphobia is rarely preceded by a conditioning event (Goldstein & Chambless, 1978 refer to only 12% of such cases) and Mathews, Gelder & Johnston (1981) have concluded that classical conditioning is largely irrelevant to the aetiology of agoraphobia.

The inevitable reliance on the retrospective self-reports in such studies is no doubt one reason for the variable nature of these findings; an additional problem, however, lies with the definition of what precisely qualifies as a conditioning event. The possibility that many self-reported conditioning experiences are really 'false alarms' (i.e. a panic attack in a context which prevents escape rather than an aversive experience with an object *per se*) has recently been raised by Barlow (1988) and assessed in a further retrospective study of phobias by Merckelbach *et al.* (1989). In this latter study it was found that only 29% of phobic patients referred only to past conditioning experiences, but that 78% referred to conditioning experiences in conjunction with vicarious informational learning experiences. Further, the majority of conditioning experiences could be classified as the 'false alarm' variety.

In addition to the absence of identifiable aversive experiences in relation to phobias, DiNardo, Guzy & Bak (1988a) found that about two-thirds of both dog-fearful and non-dog-fearful college students had experienced a conditioning event in which a dog featured. It seems that conditioning experiences do not necessarily give rise to fear, that they are at best only one of a number of pathways to fear acquisition and that conditioning stimuli are more complex than simple painful events. One possibility is that the interpretation placed upon the event differentiates between those who become frightened and those who do not. As DiNardo *et al.* (1988b) comment, 'dog fearful Ss showed a marked expectation of harm upon encountering a dog, as compared to non-fearful Ss' (p. 243).

A third problem raised by Rachman is that a simple conditioning theory of anxiety acquisition assumes that any stimulus can be transformed into a fear signal, and that given comparable exposure all stimuli would have an approximately equal chance of being transformed into fear stimuli. The studies of English (1929) and Bregman (1934), although of questionable validity, had raised the possibility that this may not in fact be the case. Subsequent conditioning studies both with animals (see Milgram, Kames & Alloway, 1977) and humans (see Ohman, Dimburg & Öst, 1985) suggest that not all stimuli are likely to evoke fear when they signal a given aversive event. The notion of equipotentiality (Seligman & Hager, 1972) has been criticised by Seligman (1971), who suggested that we are biologically prepared to fear certain stimuli which facilitate species survival.

A fourth problem is that, following from the notion of equipotentiality, anxiety should be distributed in a way which would be predicted from expected ratios for traumatic interactions with objects or situations. Yet clinical phobias are restricted to a relatively well-defined range of objects and situations with fears often not associated with likely exposure to the feared object. For example, a number of surveys suggest that fears of snakes and spiders are considerably more prevalent than dental or injection fears (e.g. Agras, Sylvester & Oliveau, 1969) when on the basis of sheer exposure the reverse might be expected. Further, fears of insects, snakes and spiders are common while fear of other potentially dangerous stimuli, such as electric sockets and gas fires, are not. This is in spite of the fact that unpleasant experiences may have been experienced with the latter but not the former.

Fifthly, conditioning theory requires direct exposure to both the CS and the UCS, yet there is evidence from studies both with humans (Venn & Short, 1973) and animals (Mineka, 1987) that observers can develop fear reactions by watching others display fear in the presence of those stimuli.

Finally, although there is substantial experimental evidence that CS presentations in the absence of contingent UCS presentations result in progressive diminution of the CR, anxiety states are remarkably persistent over time and are liable to increase. Indeed, in clinical phobias anxiety is likely to increase in the absence of subsequent exposure to the object or situation.

In line with these limitations Rachman and Eysenck have both sug-gested that conditioning theory requires additional components in order to provide a complete account of fear acquisition, and each has suggested modifications. Rachman (1977, 1978) has suggested additional routes to fear acquisition, and emphasised the multidimensional concept of, and innate aspect to, anxiety responses. Eysenck (1968, 1976, 1979, 1982, 1985, 1987) has discussed variations of potential UCSs and contiguity of CS–UCS pairings, and introduced the notion of incubation to account for enhancement of fear following repeated CS-only presentations.

Suggested revisions to classical conditioning theory

Rachman (1977, 1978) has suggested that in addition to conditioning there are two further pathways for the acquisition of human fear reactions: modelling and transmission of information. There is evidence from experimental studies that modelling is implicated in the development of anxiety reactions. For example, Mineka and her colleagues (Cook *et al.*, 1985; Mineka, 1987; Mineka *et al.*, 1984) have shown that laboratory-reared monkeys, not initially afraid of snakes, develop fearful reactions when exposed to the sight of wild monkeys behaving fearfully with snakes and non-fearfully with other objects. Further, the degree of disturbance exhi-bited by the observer monkeys was related to the degree of disturbance shown by the fearful model. There is also evidence that the converse applies, so that exposing phobic patients to non-fearful models reduces levels of fear (Bandura, 1971). Particularly striking evidence of this comes from the use of videotaped displays of a coping model used to reduce anxiety in hospitalised patients, particularly children (e.g. Melamed & Siegel, 1975; Pinto & Hollandsworth, 1989) (see Chapter 9). Observational learning may also explain why children often experience the same kind and number of fears as their mothers. Solyom *et al.* (1974) noted that 30% of mothers of phobic patients were also phobic, while Bandura & Menlove (1968) report that 35% of dog-phobic children had parents who were also fearful.

A second revision, already discussed in Chapter 1, was to view fear not as 'some hard phenomenal lump that lives inside people, that we may palpate more or less successfully' (Lang, 1968) but as a set of three loosely coupled systems—behavioural, physiological and verbal. According to Lang the three systems are partially independent. A number of studies have been derived from this hypothesis, and it has been proposed that concordance among the three components of fear is likely to be high during strong emotional arousal and that high levels of demand will produce discordance among components (Rachman & Hodgson, 1974).

The third revision centres on the notion that not all stimuli are likely to become cues for fear, but that evolution has predisposed organisms to learn easily those associations that facilitate species survival. Thorndike (1935), explaining Watson & Rayner's findings, suggested that humans have an inherited attachment between rats and fear. Seligman (1970, 1971) has elaborated this view, holding that phobias are best understood as instances of biologically prepared learning because they commonly involve objects and situations that have threatened the human species throughout its evolutionary history. Preparedness theory has been tested in a number of experimental studies with both humans and animals (see reviews by Delprato, 1980; Ohman, 1979; Ohman, Dimburg & Öst, 1985; McNally, 1987). Cook & Mineka (1989) report two experiments in which laboratory-reared rhesus monkeys watched wild-reared monkeys display intense fear to fear-relevant compared with fear-irrelevant stimuli. In both experiments, videotapes were spliced so that the model monkeys appeared to be reacting fearfully to both fear-relevant (toy snakes or toy crocodiles) and fear-irrelevant stimuli (flowers or toy rabbits). Results indicated that observers acquired a fear of fear-relevant but not fear-irrelevant stimuli.

Laboratory conditioning experiments conducted by Ohman and his colleagues to evaluate preparedness have typically involved comparisons between autonomic responses conditioned to slides of fear-relevant and fear-irrelevant stimuli. Fear-relevant stimuli (e.g. snakes, spiders) are associated with common phobias, were dangerous for prehistoric people, and are held to be prepared for fear conditioning. Fear-irrelevant stimuli (e.g. pictures of flowers and geometric figures) are rarely associated with phobias, presented minimal danger for prehistoric people, and are considered unprepared for fear conditioning. Preparedness theory suggests that Pavlovian conditioned responses established to fear-relevant stimuli should mimic characteristics associated with phobias, such as ease of acquisition, irrationality, a relationship between fear and likely prehistoric threat and finally resistance to extinction.

Although some have concluded that the 'observations and arguments of the preparedness view of phobias are impressive' (Sturgis & Scott, 1984, p. 99), McNally in his review of experimental studies of preparedness concludes that:

> laboratory studies have provided mixed support for the preparedness theory of phobias. Hypotheses regarding ease of acquisition have rarely been substantiated, and those concerning irrationality have been corroborated in some experiments but disconfirmed in others. That SCRs established to fear-relevant stimuli are slow to extinguish has been the most consistent positive finding (McNally, 1987, p. 295).

Further, in contrast to evidence from experimental studies with college or analogue populations, the limited clinical data provide little evidence to support preparedness theory. De Silva, Rachman & Seligman (1977) developed a procedure for rating fears and obsessions on the degree to which these responses should have had survival value for pretechnological people. They found that the vast majority of the fears and obsessions of 82 obsessive–compulsive and 69 phobic patients were evolutionarily significant. However, contrary to expectation, preparedness was not related to suddenness of onset, severity, lifestyle impairment, or therapeutic outcome. Similar results are reported by Zafiropoulou & McPherson (1986) with a sample of 49 phobic subjects.

As a fourth revision, in order to explain the fact that fear responses sometimes fail to extinguish with repeated CS-only presentations, Eysenck (e.g. 1968, 1976, 1979, 1982, 1985, 1987) has attached considerable importance to the phenomenon of incubation in which the expected process of fear extinction does not occur. That is, although it is likely that the CS (e.g. a dog) will be encountered in the absence of further pairings of the UCS (e.g. biting/attack) the CR (e.g. fear of dogs) continues to grow in strength. Eysenck argues that a CS signalling an unpleasant UCS may be experienced by the person as having an effect equivalent to the original UCS. Thus the person's reaction to the CS (e.g. fear of dogs) is virtually identical to their reaction to the UCS (e.g. fear of being bitten/attacked). Because it then becomes impossible to expose the person to the CS in the absence of the UCS, their reaction being similar in both instances, repeated exposure to the CS still tends to be aversive. Eysenck suggests that there is a critical point in the relationship between CS exposure and the strength of the CR. If the CS exposure is brief, but there is a strong CR, then incubation or strengthening of the conditioned response of anxiety will occur. With a longer CS exposure but a weaker CR, the conditioned response will tend to extinguish. Although Eysenck (1987, p. 18) suggests there is a large body of research supporting the incubation phenomenon, others argue that there is a need for more empirical support (see commentaries accompanying Eysenck, 1979), while Bersh (1980) has concluded that empirical evidence for incubation is weak and that 'its potential for contribution ... must remain in doubt' (p. 16). However, in one of the few empirical studies directly evaluating predictions from the incubation model with human subjects, Sandin & Chorot (1989) report evidence consistent with the theory. In a laboratory demonstration of heart rate conditioning, responses were sustained when the UCS was high noise (compared to low noise) and the CS presentation (slides of snakes and spiders) was brief rather than long.

A fifth revision is based upon Eysenck's (1968, 1976) observation that while the majority of laboratory-based conditioning studies have typically used pain as the UCS, fear generated under other circumstances may result from alternative UCSs. He thus argues that 'Frustrative non-reward' can be shown to have physiological and behavioural consequences which are identical with those of pain' (Eysenck, 1976, p. 254). Such frustration-arousing circumstances may include withdrawal of positive reinforcement or situations involving conflict. In the context of clinical fears, extending the type of UCSs which may be implicated in fear generation seems reasonable, although it does then make it more difficult both to verify the theory and to define exactly which stimuli might be regarded as UCSs within that context.

The sixth revision is based upon Eysenck's (1975) suggestion that while CS onset preceding UCS by a short period of time is considered the basic procedure within classical conditioning, there are numerous examples within the experimental literature of backward conditioning (i.e. UCS–CS presentations). Evidence for backward conditioning is also reviewed by Spetch, Wilkie & Pinel (1981). Eysenck further argues that such backward conditioning can play an important part in the acquisition and extinction of anxiety. As with the extension of UCSs implicated in the generation of anxiety, the notion of backward conditioning seems inherently reasonable in the context of clinical anxiety. Verifying such propositions in non-laboratory contexts, does, however, present considerable difficulties.

Clearly in moving away from a laboratory context to a real-life setting, respondent interactions become more complex and defining terms more difficult. In attempting to modify classical conditioning theory to explain the complexities of human fear responses some would argue that the theory becomes untenable. Nevertheless Rachman (1991) has recently commented that 'there appears to be strong evidence to support the idea that fears can be acquired by a conditioning process' (p. 161) and that 'the weaknesses of the classical theory are serious but not necessarily fatal'

(p. 165). Even with revisions, however, it is still not clear how one might account for the fact that different people manifest anxiety in quite different ways, such as through rituals or panics. Such difficulties are also encountered by extensions of the classical conditioning paradigm which include accounts of subsequent avoidance behaviour.

TWO-FACTOR THEORY

One extension of the conditioning theory of fear, in what has become known as the Miller–Mowrer or two-factor theory, was to additionally provide an explanation of avoidance behaviour (Dollard & Miller, 1950; Miller, 1951; Mowrer, 1939, 1960; Mowrer & Lamoreaux, 1946). The seeds for the theory were lain by Mowrer (1939) who comments:

> Anxiety (fear) is the conditioned form of the pain reaction, which has the highly useful function of motivating and reinforcing behavior that tends to avoid or prevent the recurrence of the pain-producing (unconditioned) stimulus (p. 555).

Thus, individuals will either attempt to avoid anxiety by avoiding exposure to classically conditioned stimuli or, when exposed to such stimuli, will try to reduce anxiety by taking direct actions that have been associated with reduction of anxiety in the past. Avoidance behaviour is then maintained because fear reduction acts as a powerful secondary reinforcer. Several theorists (e.g. Eysenck & Rachman, 1965) have argued that two-factor theory can account for certain aspects of a wide range of clinical problems including phobic avoidance and obsessional behaviour.

Over the past two decades there has been extensive criticism of the two-factor theory (e.g. Gray, 1971; Rachman, 1976a). One of the difficulties with the model lies with the prediction that a fear reaction that is no longer paired with the UCS will eventually extinguish, resulting in diminution of avoidance behaviour. However, in both laboratory and clinical observations avoidance behaviour tends to persist, irrespective of the intensity of the fear associated with it. This is especially marked in the case of compulsive rituals. Rather than diminishing, compulsions tend to become more complex, increasingly difficult to perform and often with their own aversive qualities. Yet in spite of their aversive nature compulsive behaviours do not seem to diminish.

In his 1960 account, however, Mowrer had shifted away from fear as the primary motivating factor in learning, drawing a distinction between danger signals and safety signals: 'Hope is no less essential than fear to a genuinely adequate behavior theory' (Mowrer, 1960, p. 61). The central feature of Mowrer's revised position was the postulation of two types of secondary reinforcement. In Type 1 secondary reinforcement, fear is initiated by the onset of some danger signal and is reduced with the termination of the signal. In Type 2 secondary reinforcement, fear is generated by some unconditioned aversive stimulation and is reduced by the onset of a stimulus that signals the termination of the aversive stimulation. Because of its pairing with the termination of the aversive event, the safety signal functions as a secondary reinforcer. Variations of Mowrer's safety signal analysis have also developed in relation to human avoidance behaviour, particularly in relation to agoraphobia (Gray, 1971; Himadi, 1987; Rachman, 1984b).

It is clear, given the clinical complexity of anxiety, that many alternative explanations may be required to account for their development. Thus, respondent conditioning, modelling, vicarious learning, information transmission and operant or instrumental factors may all be involved. At one level it could be argued that the various theoretical revisions which have taken place have done so without abandoning the basic conditioning framework. On the other hand it could be argued that anxiety is such a complex phenomenon that in order to provide an adequate account of the phenomena the way in which information is perceived and appraised needs to be taken into account. As a bridge between those theories which emphasise the conditioning framework and those which take a more cognitive approach lie theories which focus on the neurophysiological substrates of normal emotional behaviour (Eysenck, 1967; Gray, 1982).

NEUROPSYCHOLOGICAL ASPECTS OF ANXIETY

In a series of papers and monographs Gray (e.g. 1975, 1982) has set out an extensive analysis of the role of the reward and punishment systems in the brain in relation to anxiety. According to him, anxiety consists of activity in the behavioural inhibition system (BIS), which comprises the septohippocampal system, its monoaminergic afferents from the brain stem, and its neocortical projections in the frontal lobe. The BIS does not store information but has access to it (transmitted from the prefrontal cortex) and may modify information stored elsewhere. The system inhibits behaviour in response to cues associated with punishment (e.g. passive avoidance in relation to fear-relevant stimuli) and frustrative non-reward (e.g. expectations of safety which do not occur) or novel stimuli. Phobic anxiety states are handled within this model by the suggestion that certain classes of stimuli may have the innate capacity to trigger the BIS. These stimuli are comparable with the 'prepared' stimuli discussed by Seligman (1971), but as well as stimuli of danger to specific species they include stimuli that arise during within-species interaction such as threatening looks or calls (Gray, 1982).

The system acts to compare actual with expected stimulus input. If actual stimuli match expected stimuli then the system remains in a 'checking mode' and behavioural control is not exerted by the BIS. If an actual stimulus does not match what is expected, either because an unpredicted environmental event occurs, or because a predicted event fails to occur, or because the predicted event is aversive, then the BIS operates in 'control mode', taking over direct control of behaviour. When this occurs there is an immediate inhibition of any ongoing behaviour. An additional outcome is that any future execution of this same behaviour will be conducted with a certain degree of restraint. In addition, the BIS initiates exploratory behaviour allowing the organism to identify the nature of the stimuli associated with punishment or non-reward. The responses mediated by this system are illustrated in Figure 2.1. The evaluative aspect of the BIS may well be comparable with the evaluative systems referred to in cognitive models of anxiety discussed below.

Within Gray's model the major function of the BIS is to monitor ongoing behaviour, checking continuously that it coincides with expectations. If, in the course of checking, threatening or unexpected events occur, the signs of anxiety (raised autonomic activity, avoidant behaviour and subjective experience) are an inevitable consequence as the BIS halts behaviour to evaluate the nature of the threat. Should the system become overactive, this excessive checking of the BIS is manifest as obsessive–compulsive

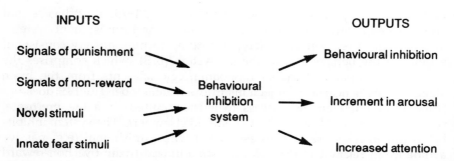

Figure 2.1 The behavioural inhibition system. This responds to any of its adequate inputs with all of its outputs. (Adapted from Gray, 1982, p. 12)

symptoms. The final assumption behind Gray's model is that individuals who are especially susceptible to anxiety have highly reactive BISs. It is not altogether clear, however, how such variations in sensitivity might arise, or why different individuals develop anxiety in relation to differing events and circumstances. One possible explanation has to do with individual variations in the processing of information which, together with conditioning, need to be incorporated within neuropsychological models. As Mathews & Eysenck (1987) suggest, there are likely to be several complex systems operating at different levels in parallel, and influencing each other at various points.

COGNITIVE CONCEPTIONS OF ANXIETY

Cognitive approaches to anxiety are varied both in terms of the range of explanations offered and the background to their development; hence the way in which different theories are formulated is highly divergent. They range from theories which emphasise the existence of mental events between the recognition of an aversive event and the subsequent response (e.g. Reiss, 1980), through those which provide detailed cognitive accounts of the development and maintenance of avoidance behaviour (e.g. Bandura, 1977a; Seligman & Johnston, 1973) to those which emphasise that faulty thinking causes anxiety (e.g. Beck & Emery, 1979; Beck et al., 1985; Ellis, 1962, 1979; Meichenbaum, 1977) and subsequent theories addressing the question of faulty information processing in relation to anxiety (Williams et al., 1988).

Cognitive expectancy theories

The model maintains that what is learned in Pavlovian conditioning is an expectation regarding the occurrence, or nonoccurrence, of a US onset or a change in US magnitude or duration. Expectations are considered to be mediating responses with covert stimulus properties that can become elicitors of a number of anticipatory responses (Reiss, 1980, p. 387).

Although primarily based upon learning principles, the central assumption behind cognitive expectancy theories is that some 'cognitive mediating process' occurs between the occurrence of an initial stimulus and the resultant response. The presence of initiating (danger) expectancies and anxiety expectancies is used to explain the development of fears. Thus expectancies initiating anxiety include anticipation of social or physical danger. These expectations arise, not only from respondent conditioning but also from observations of models and transmission of information, or from any combination of these factors (Carr, 1979; Riess, 1980). Anxiety expectancies result from what the person thinks will occur when a particular stimulus is encountered. Reiss (1980) additionally links this to the 'fear of fear' concept proposed by Goldstein & Chambless (1978) to explain the development and maintenance of agoraphobia reformulated as anxiety sensitivity (Reiss & McNally, 1985). In a recent summary and review of his expectancy model, Reiss (1991) holds that there are six fundamental factors underlying fears: danger expectancy, injury sensitivity, anxiety expectancy, anxiety sensitivity, social evaluation expectancy and social evaluation sensitivity. Within this framework not only are we likely to anticipate becoming anxious if we know a feared stimulus will be encountered but, because anxiety is feared, the anticipation of anxiety can of itself be anxiety-provoking.

The notion that associative learning or acquisition of knowledge takes place during respondent conditioning is not a new one. Tolman had offered a cognitive account of learning almost half a century before (1932), and both animal learning studies and laboratory-based conditioning studies with humans have shown that conditioning is as dependent upon outcome expectancies as upon the simple pairing of two events. The shift towards the Tolman-like view of conditioning with its emphasis on association formation or stimulus–stimulus (S–S) explanation means that theories of conditioning more closely resemble 'cognitive' explanations (see for example Davey, 1987). As Rescorla & Wagner (1972) point out in their description of S–S conditioning, 'certain expectations are built up about the events following a stimulus complex; expectations initiated by that complex and its component stimuli are then only modified, when consequent events disagree with the composite expectation' (p. 75). As Rescorla (1988) notes, stimuli provide information. The anticipation of an expected negative outcome is thus likely to influence the development of anxiety in some instances, and may also be responsible for the development of some kinds of avoidance behaviour. The question of avoidance from a cognitive perspective is, however, dealt with in differing degrees of complexity by different theorists. Carr (1979), for example, gives only a very brief discussion of avoidance behaviour, and Reiss (1980) advocates a version of the two-process theory of avoidance learning, suggesting that 'avoidance is at least sometimes reinforced by anxiety reduction' (p. 390). Other cognitive expectancy theorists (e.g. Bandura, 1977a,b; Seligman & Johnston, 1973) provide a more comprehensive account of avoidance. For Bandura the critical factor appears to be a judgement regarding one's ability to cope with potentially threatening events, or perceived self-efficacy.

Efficacy expectations

In terms of self-efficacy theory (Bandura, 1977b) those who adjudge themselves to be capable of managing difficulties have little reason to fear or avoid them, whereas those who doubt their ability will quickly give up attempts to cope, feeling vulnerable and fearful. Bandura distinguishes two major determinants of behaviour: (i) people's self-efficacy judgements, i.e. their perception of their ability to perform specific actions successfully; and (ii) response–outcome expectancies, i.e. their expectations regarding the likely consequences of performing an action. The extent to which self-efficacy and outcome expectancies determine behaviour will vary according to the situation. High perceived self-efficacy or maximum confidence in relation to a task is likely to mean that outcome expectancies will determine variations in performance. With strong incentives to perform a particular task (e.g. giving a public speech to achieve promotion) then perceived self-efficacy will influence whether the task is attempted and how successful these attempts are. Bandura (1978) suggests that fearful behaviour is more likely to be determined by self-efficacy judgements than by outcome expectancies.

Bandura (1977b) further suggests that efficacy expectations develop from four main sources: the individual's successful performance history (i.e. personal mastery experiences); vicarious experiences (i.e. seeing others perform successfully); verbal persuasion and from awareness of one's own emotional arousal. In relation to exposure-based therapies, Bandura holds that performance success serves to strengthen perceived self-efficacy, and that it is the cognitive rather than the behavioural change which is the important therapeutic ingredient. Similarly, treatments involving modelling are successful because self-efficacy can be altered by observing others cope with a particular situation, while verbal persuasion can also help to influence self-efficacy. Finally, awareness of one's emotional state (such as trembling, shaking and sweating when in a social setting) can provide information about self-efficacy.

A number of studies have investigated the relationship between self-efficacy, behavioural functioning and anxiety (Bandura, 1977b; Bandura, Adams & Beyer, 1977; Bandura et al., 1980; Williams, Dooseman & Kleifield, 1984; Williams, Kinney & Falbo, 1989; Williams, Turner & Peer, 1985; Williams & Watson, 1985). The basic principle of these studies is for subjects to complete a pre-treatment behavioural assessment in order to evaluate the extent to which they can progress in a hierarchy of tasks of increasing difficulty. Thus Williams *et al*. (1984) assessed height phobics by testing the maximum storey they could reach in order to stand on a semi-open balcony in a 12-storey building. Similarly, driving phobics were asked to complete routes of increasing difficulty (in terms of traffic density and length of route) until unable to complete one. Following this assessment subjects are assigned to one of a number of treatment conditions such as guided mastery, modelling, exposure-based treatments or no treatment. Subsequent to treatment subjects again perform the behavioural assessment. Ratings indicating the tasks they think can perform, and the degree of certainty with which they can perform them, are completed by subjects prior to and after the initial behavioural assessment and again following treatment. These studies report that performance-based treatments, particularly those involving attempts to enhance the subject's coping attempts, are most likely to enhance self-efficacy. They also report that self-efficacy ratings are a better predictor of treatment effects than anticipated outcome or performance-related anxiety.

While there is therefore some evidence that self-efficacy theory might provide a mechanism for therapeutic change, and hence could be used to direct treatment procedures, the theory is not without its critics (e.g. Kirsch, 1985a; Smedslund, 1978; Wolpe, 1978a). There are also studies using subjects other than height, driving or snake phobics, in which the predictive power of self-efficacy is not as good as in those studies cited above (e.g. Lane & Borkovec, 1984; Meier, McCarthy & Schmeck, 1984). Lane & Borkovec (1984), for example, using speech-anxious subjects, found that although efficacy judgements of aspects of performance such as voice quality, posture, dysfluencies and eye contact were related to self-report measures of outcome such as anxiety ratings, they were not related to measures of behaviour or physiological reactivity. One major difference between the simple phobias and the more complex interpersonal performance-based anxieties relates to the degree of certainty about the performances required. In Bandura's and Williams's studies the hierarchy of behaviours is well mapped out, with obvious points at which subjects can decide whether or not to continue. In contrast, while speech-anxious subjects may make a decision about giving a public talk, exerting control over voice quality or eye contact is much more difficult to achieve. Feedback about success is also less precise than in the case of the hierarchical progression associated with simple phobias. The subject may succeed in speaking in public, but may not ascertain from feedback the standard with which this performance has been achieved.

Other critics have raised issues which are as much related to cognitively based theories in general as to self-efficacy theory in particular. These relate to issues of whether thoughts which accompany anxiety are causing anxiety or are a sign of anxiety, and whether we should expect people to know how they come to have their cognitions. It is possible tha judgements, rather than providing access to internal determiiiants or behaviour, merely reflect knowledge of behavioural characteristics. Correspondence between verbal reports and behaviour does not necessarily mean that the individual's expectations cause subsequent actions. As Brewin (1988) points out, however, Bandura's theory is not so much a theory of fear acquisition and reduction but an attempt to explain the maintenance of anxiety. Other cognitively based theories such as those of Ellis (1962) and Beck (1967) emphasise the fact that emotions such as anxiety arise directly from perceptions and evaluations of events.

Cognitions as a cause of anxiety

The most comprehensive view of anxiety from a cognitive perspective is contained in Beck & Emery (1979) and Beck et al. (1985). They offer the proposition that cognitive schemas and automatic thoughts that are typical of anxiety states play a crucial role in the development and maintenance of anxiety disorders. The cognitive features of anxiety include cognitive propositions or content, cognitive operations, cognitive products and cognitive structures (Goldfried & Robbins, 1983; Ingram & Kendall, 1986, 1987). Thus Ingram & Kendall (1987) state that:

> Cognitive propositions (content) refer to the information that is actually represented and considered. Cognitive structure (schemata) can be viewed as the organised manner in which information is internally arranged and represented in memory. Cognitive operations are the processes and procedures by which the cognitive system operates. Cognitive products are the result of the interaction of content, by operations, and within structures (p. 524).

The key relationship with anxiety revolves around schema content and functioning which reflect themes of danger or harm to the individual. As Beck (1985) noted:

> When a threat is perceived the relevant cognitive schemas are activated; these are used to evaluate and assign meaning to the event . . . there occur a series of adjustments to 'fit' appropriate schemas to a specific threat. One's final interpretation is the result of interaction between the event and the schemas (p. 56).

Perceived threats related to specific phobias would be fear of possible negative evaluation by others in relation to social anxiety, fear of negative sensations in relation to panic, fear of being attacked in relation to specific animal fears and so on. Such fear relates to the self-schema of the individual and the perceived danger to oneself. Ingram & Kendall (1986) suggest that while anxious people have general schemata consisting of propositions relevant to the self, a shift occurs away from these while actually in situations perceived as threatening or dangerous, towards schemata designed to facilitate the processing of danger cues either externally in the environment or internally within oneself. This proposition relates to the distinction between state and trait anxiety.

A further proposition of Beck & Emery's model of anxiety is that anxious individuals selectively process information relevant to personal danger as a result of the activation of associated schemata (i.e. schemata being the way in which information is arranged and represented in memory). Schemata are thought to be further organised into constellations or subsystems ('modes') corresponding to broad motivational concerns such as fear and danger. Accordingly one would predict a bias towards material which holds a particular concern for a specific individual.

Bower (1981, 1987) has similarly proposed that emotions are associated with unique, special-purpose units (or 'nodes') embedded in each person's associative network which encodes concepts, actions and events. The network theory of emotion leads to a number of hypotheses—one of which, 'mood-congruity' closely matches the selective processing hypothesis of Beck & Emery. The notion of 'mood-congruity' implies that stimuli whose affective significance matches the person's emotional state will provoke greater attention, faster perception, and more elaborate processing, with the result that these stimuli will be better learned than neutral or mood-incongruent materials. It is as if people have an attentional bias for material which matches their emotional state.

Models such as those proposed by Beck & Emery (1979, 1985) and Bower (1981, 1987) have generated a number of empirical investigations of cognitions associated with anxiety.

Attentional bias and anxiety

A number of studies using dichotics listening tasks or modified Stroop tests have found positive effects when assessing processing bias in relation to anxiety. Burgess et al. (1981) had six agoraphobic and social phobic patients, six control subjects and 12 highly fearful non-patients shadow prose passages presented to each ear, and to detect occasional presentations of a target word in the attended (shadowed) or unattended (non-shadowed) ear. The target word was either a neutral word or a threat word relevant to the person's phobia (e.g. seminar, shopping alone). They found that patients and fearful non-patients were better at detecting the fear words—they were able to perceive and respond to fear-relevant stimuli without any loss of performance on responding to targets in the shadowed message. However, as both Mathews & Eysenck (1987) and Williams et al. (1988) note, the effect found in this study may be attributable to the greater frequency of usage made of phobic-related words by these subjects, hence facilitating their detection.

In an attempt to overcome this problem Foa & McNally (1986) repeated Burgess et al.'s design with 11 obsessional–compulsive patients undergoing a three-week exposure and response prevention treatment, testing them both before and after treatment. They argued that treatment would make the stimuli more familiar but less feared; if responding was influenced by familiarity then there would be an enhanced difference in responding to salient stimuli following treatment, whereas if responding was influenced by fear, treatment would lead to less difference. Patients did in fact show greater sensitivity to salient stimuli than neutral stimuli before treatment, whereas following treatment the difference did not reach significance.

Evidence for an attentional bias also comes from a study by Parkinson & Rachman (1981), who found that mothers of children about to have an operation showed increased detection rates for words embedded in a background noise when the words related to surgery and were hence concern-related (e.g. bleeding, operation) in comparison with auditorily confusable neutral words (breeding, operatic) and dissimilar words (e.g. newspaper, uniform). Unfortunately, because subjects were asked to verbally report any word they heard it is possible that they were prompted to guess at words relating to their current concern; hence a response bias explanation for the results is as plausible as an attentional bias explanation.

An ingenious study by MacLeod, Mathews & Tata (1986) does, however, substantiate the claims for an attentional bias towards threat words. They tested generally anxious patients and non-anxious controls on their speed of detecting a visual dot (probe) which sometimes appeared as they were reading the top word of a pair of words presented on a visual display unit. The probe could appear in either the upper (attended) or lower (unattended) location, with some of the words being threat words (e.g. inept, foolish) and others neutral. Anxious and control subjects showed different patterns of responding dependent upon the location of the threat word and probe. Regardless of upper (attended) or lower (unattended) location, anxious subjects responded more rapidly to probes that replaced threat rather than non-threat words. The opposite pattern of shifting away from threat words was found for non-anxious controls. It is as though anxious subjects shift attention to information relating to threat rather than diverting attention away from it, while the non-anxious are able to avoid emotionally threatening information. The possibility that anxiety is associated with the capture of attention by threat cues has also been illustrated by Mathews *et al.* (1990a). They required subjects to ignore distractors while searching for a target word. Threat distractors led to slower detection of the target for anxious patients relative to controls. In a further study (Mathews, Richards & Eysenck, 1989b) anxiety was associated with a tendency to interpret ambiguous cues as threatening.

A further important finding (Mathews & MacLeod, 1986) relates to evidence that selective processing of threat cues can occur outside conscious awareness. Using a dichotic listening experiment, anxious patients and controls were exposed to threat and non-threat words on the unattended channel while shadowing neutral stories on the attended channel. Although subjects were not consciously aware of any of the words presented in the unattended message, threat-related words in the unattended message disrupted shadowing of the attended message more than neutral words for the anxious patients, but not for normal controls. The same pattern of results was obtained with a simultaneous reaction time task. This suggests the presence of an automatic selective processing bias in anxious patients diverting processing resources towards information related to threat.

In a replication of the MacLeod *et al.* (1986) study in a non-clinical sample, Broadbent & Broadbent (1988) examined the relationship between response time with trait and state anxiety. They report that the most reliable results were obtained using trait rather than state anxiety, with a curvilinear relationship such that anxiety makes little difference to responding at low levels but becomes increasingly important at high levels. Attentional bias to threat may thus only become severe in relation to extreme anxiety. In a study referred to by Eysenck, MacLeod & Mathews (1987), replicating the MacLeod *et al.* (1986) study but utilising the auditory modality with a non-clinical sample, a similar correlation was obtained between anxiety and a tendency to react faster to a probe following a threatening word. Thus, independently of subject groups studied, stimulus modalities used and procedural details, it seems that subjects differing in anxiety levels differ in their allocation of processing resources to threatening and non-threatening words.

An alternative paradigm used to assess attentional bias in relation to anxiety has involved adaptations of the Stroop colour-naming test (Stroop, 1935). The basic prediction of these studies is that whereas attentional bias would facilitate performance in the shadowing and dot-probe tasks, it would impede performance in the Stroop-type tasks where attention is allocated to some other, more salient stimuli. In one of the first studies of this type Ray (1979) found that students in a pre-examination period showed longer colour-naming latencies for words related to examination anxiety (e.g. exam, failure) than for neutral words, and that this effect was strongest for subjects who were most anxious about their examinations. Similar results were found by Mathews & MacLeod (1985) using anxious patients. They tested two groups of patients, one group with worries about social relationships and another with worries about physical health, on four sets of Stroop cards related to physical threat (disease, cancer), social threat (failure, pathetic) or two sets of matched positive words. While all anxious subjects took longer to name the social threat words in comparison to a control sample, only the subjects reporting predominantly physically related concerns showed slower responding in relation to the physical threat words. While in line with an attentional bias explanation, extra processing resources may well have been allocated by the anxious subjects to the threatening stimuli, as the authors themselves note, it may have been the emotional arousal arising from the perception of relevant words that indirectly interfered with colour-naming.

In a replication of this study (Mogg, Mathews & Weinman, 1989), clearer evidence was obtained of specific attentional bias, with slower responding to social or physical threat words matching the predominant worry, social or physical, reported by the anxious subject. However, evidence for a relationship between reactions to specific types of threat words and reported domain of worry was not obtained in another recent study with panic patients (Ehlers et al., 1988). These authors did nevertheless find evidence for an attentional bias towards threat cues in general with both clinically defined and non-clinical panickers.

In a further study Watts et al. (1986) found that spider phobics were slower in colour-naming words related to their phobia (e.g. hairy, crawl) when compared to control subjects. Furthermore, the interference in naming the ink colour of the phobia-related words was significantly reduced by desensitisation treatment. These results need to be qualified to some extent, however, by the fact that a non-treatment control group also showed a reduced interference effect when tested a second time (the average spider interference scores went from 18.9 to 2.9 for the treated patients and from 20.4 to 7.9 for the untreated patient controls).

Further evidence for selective processing of threat cues has been obtained in modified Stroop tasks with panic patients (Hope et al., 1990; McNally, Rieman & Kim, 1990), socially phobic patients (Hope et al., 1990), patients with post-traumatic stress disorder (McNally et al., 1990) and in one report with high trait anxiety non-patient subjects (Richards & Millwood, 1989) but not in two other recent reports (Mogg & Marden, 1990; Martin, Williams & Clark, 1991). Indeed, in one study Martin et al. (1991) found that anxiety disorder patients were significantly slower at colour-naming threat words than equally anxious non-patients. In summarising the results of four studies these authors suggest that 'anxiety disorders may be characterised and maintained by a more specific kind of selective attention to threat, namely attention to stimuli that are perceived as threatening because they reflect idiosyncratic beliefs' (p. 159).

Overall, the series of experiments referred to seem to offer good evidence for the possibility that threatening stimuli capture the attention of anxious patients. There is less evidence, however, that threatening stimuli are preferentially encoded into, or retrieved from, memory. In their Stroop study, Mathews & MacLeod (1985) tested incidental recognition memory for stimulus words but failed to find a memory bias for threat words in anxious subjects, a finding replicated by Mogg, Mathews & Weinman (1989). Mogg & Mathews (1990) also failed to find a recall bias for self-referent mood-congruent information in generally anxious patients, a finding consistent with Foa, McNally & Murdoch's (1989) failure to demonstrate similar memory effects in anxious non-clinical subjects. In contrast, studies with panic patients (McNally, Foa & Donnell, 1989) and non-clinical panickers (Norton et al., 1988) have found enhanced recall of anxiety information in such groups in contrast to normal controls. One study suggesting memory bias in agoraphobic patients has also been reported by Nunn, Stevenson & Whalan (1984). They found that agoraphobic patients were more likely than controls to remember prose passages with a potentially phobic content and to recall more phobic words (e.g. crowd, street). However, Pickles & van den Broek (1988) failed to replicate Nunn et al.'s findings. Whether the effect obtained by Nunn et al. was due to a recall bias for selectively processed information, or a response bias favouring all negative information, is difficult to interpret; clearly the words and passages would have implied very different things to the agoraphobic and control groups.

In an attempt to overcome these problems Mogg, Mathews & Weinman (1987) required clinically anxious subjects and normal controls to judge whether positive (e.g. amused, secure), negative, threatening words (e.g. humiliated, trapped) or negative non-threatening words (e.g. bored, gloomy) applied to themselves or to a well-known television personality. Not only was there no recall effect favouring negative or threatening words, but a signal detection analysis of subsequent recognition revealed a trend suggesting poorer discrimination of negative words by anxious subjects.

Taking all the data together it seems that the dichotic and Stroop studies favour an attentional bias towards threat-related information in anxiety. However, with a few exceptions, recall and recognition studies suggest that the attentional bias present is not associated with superior memory for threat-related information in anxiety (see Dalgleish & Watts, 1990, for a recent review). One explanation for these findings, suggested by Mogg et al. (1987) is that biases may operate in opposite directions at different stages of processing in anxious individuals: they show attentional vigilance but inferior immediate memory for threat, establishing a vigilance–avoidance pattern of cognitive processing. Vigilance to threat cues will facilitate detection of danger, while cognitive avoidance inhibits subsequent processing of information. Such a cognitive avoidance response may be an involuntary reaction to excessive anxiety, but may also be a deliberate distraction strategy responsible for short-term but not long-term anxiety reduction and hence partly responsible for maintaining anxiety (Foa & Kozak, 1986; Watts, 1989).

That the issue is even more complicated is illustrated by a further recent study (Mathews et al., 1989a), where anxious, recovered anxious and normal control subjects were tested on implicit (word completion) and explicit (cued recall) memory tasks. Implicit memory is implied when stored information affects subsequent responses, although the information is not necessarily available for recall, while explicit memory is reserved for processes that lead to the ability to recall information on demand. The explicit measure was correlated with trait anxiety scores, but did not reliably distinguish between subjects with clinical anxiety states and normal control subjects (i.e. in line with previous studies, clinically anxious subjects when compared with non-anxious subjects do not show a memory bias for threatening words). On the implicit memory measure, however, clinically anxious subjects produced more threat word completions, but only from a set to which they had recently been exposed (i.e. priming activated internal stronger representations of non-threatening than threatening words for the non-anxious subjects while the reverse (though non-significant) pattern emerged for anxious subjects). The authors conclude that: 'in normal subjects, non-threatening representations are better integrated, whereas in anxious subjects, threatening representations are (relatively speaking) better integrated' (p. 240).

Taken as a whole, the evidence points to anxious individuals being more vigilant to threat-related cues, although they fail to show subsequent superior recall or recognition. The differential effects can be explained by the use of cognitive avoidance strategies by anxious individuals (Foa & Kozac, 1986; Watts, 1989) which prevents the elaboration of threatening material. Thus although anxious individuals may initially perceive threat more readily they then show subsequently poorer recall of such events. Although such information processing bias exists in relation to anxiety this does not infer that such biases cause anxiety. As Mathews & Eysenck (1987) conclude:

> None of the research discussed so far conclusively demonstrates that biased cognitive processing either causes or contributes to the maintenance of pathological anxiety. It remains possible that clinical anxiety states arise in

quite different ways, and the cognitive effects documented here are secondary consequences of emotional disorder rather than being one of its causes (p. 228).

SUMMARY

As indicated in Chapter 1 it is clear that anxiety is a multifaceted phenomenon and thus any comprehensive account of the genesis and maintenance of anxiety will also, of necessity, be complex. In spite of this, theories of anxiety have tended to concentrate on one aspect of the phenomena and, perhaps not surprisingly, have thus left gaps which remain to be explained. Even in the case of phobias where the presumed external stimulus can be specified, conditioning theories are not able to explain a number of factors associated with such states, such as the failure of fears to extinguish and their non-random distribution. The original theory has thus undergone many revisions. Some of these revisions have proved more acceptable than others. For example, some have suggested that there is considerable evidence supporting the notion of incubation (Eysenck, e.g. 1987), while others have argued that there is little unambiguous evidence for such a notion (e.g. Bersh, 1980). Other revisions, such as the evidence that fears are acquired not only by conditioning but also via modelling and information transmission, have received more general support. In spite of such revisions, however, it is clear that 'as models of psychopathology they still have many shortcomings ... and need to be supplemented in various ways if they are to provide an adequate account of the clinical phenomena' (Brewin, 1988, p. 47).

Such supplementation has taken many forms, some retaining conditioning as the central component while emphasising the multilevel nature of anxiety, others emphasising the central part played by patterns of thinking. In relation to the former, for example, Eifert (1990) and Staats & Eifert (1990) in their theory of anxiety suggest that: (a) a central emotional response is at the core of anxiety problems and that (b) this emotional response can be acquired directly through aversive classical conditioning or indirectly through language experiences. Again, however, such explanations tend to be restricted to phobias rather than anxiety in general.

Other more recent models have drawn on the patterns of thinking associated with anxiety offering explanations for both phobias and general anxiety. These have ranged from those emphasising the part played by expectations regarding the potential outcomes of behaviour, such as Bandura's self-efficacy theory (1977), to those emphasising the part played by cognitive processes characteristic of anxiety (Williams *et al.*, 1988). In relation to the former, empirical evidence suggests that perceived self-efficacy is a better predictor of phobic behaviour than self-rated anxiety (e.g. Williams *et al.*, 1984), although this relationship is less evident when subjects other than those with simple fears are assessed. Others have suggested that efficacy judgements may merely reflect knowledge of behavioural characteristics rather providing access to internal determinants of behaviour. Bandura's theory is much more a theory of general motivation, and it is thus questionable whether he ever intended self-efficacy theory to be a theory of fear acquisition in particular. Further, while there is considerable empirical evidence from laboratory-based studies that anxiety is associated with a cognitive bias for threat-related information, it is not possible at present to ascertain whether this bias is a consequence of anxiety rather than a causal factor.

The central issue, then, is whether one adopts a linear model of anxiety in which learning processes lead to cognitively based reactions and behaviour change or whether anxiety is viewed as a complex multifaceted phenomenon in which different components are interactive. Thus, in line with theories of emotion outlined in Chapter 1, the neurophysiological, behavioural and cognitive processing components are likely to be organised in a hierarchical processing system with input from components varying from time to time. Within this framework each model outlined in this chapter would be seen as providing additive rather than competing information. In view of this a number of writers have formulated multi-level theories of anxiety. Barlow (1988), for example, comments that

> In my view, anxiety is a diffuse cognitive–affective structure consisting of a negative feedback cycle characterized to varying degrees by components of high negative affect; a sense of both internal and external events proceeding in an unpredictable, uncontrollable fashion; and maladaptive shifts in attention . . . each individual component contributes to the cycle in a manner that in turn affects other components of the structure (p. 72).

The multidimensional nature of anxiety will be evident throughout this book, in which anxiety in both clinical and medical contexts will be examined. In relation to the former, the aetiology, assessment and treatment of social phobia, panic disorder, agoraphobia, generalised anxiety disorder, obsessive–compulsive disorder and psychosexual dysfunction will be discussed. Anxiety also pervades everyday life in relation to medical procedures and illness. Although these are often central concerns within the health psychology literature they are often overlooked in general discussions of anxiety. In both clinical and health psychology dispositional anxiety, whether anxiety sensitivity, trait anxiety or neuroticism can serve as a vulnerability factor which determines the individual's reaction to external events or internal reactions. In some instances this may take the form of pathological anxiety where the individual chronically focuses upon anxiety cues. In other instances dispositional anxiety may act as a vulnerability factor in the development of disease. Reactions to disease may mimic reactions to clinical anxiety—attention to symptoms leading to anxious apprehension which leads to further anxiety and so on in a vicious cycle. One possible reason for the lack of integration between research and practice relating to anxiety in clinical and health psychology is that anxiety has been considered 'pathological' or 'normal', rather than as a continuum. One aim of this book is to consider the broad continuum of anxiety in diverse medical and clinical settings.

Chapter 3

Social Anxiety and Social Phobia

DEFINITION AND PREVALENCE

European researchers have long recognised the fact that for some people social encounters may be anxiety-provoking. Marks (1970) refers to 8% of his clients treated at a general psychiatric hospital as socially phobic; defined as clients with excessive anxiety and a tendency to avoid certain interpersonal situations. Similar prevalence rates for social anxiety have been found in the USA, Curran *et al.* (1980a) estimating that 7% of a psychiatric population struggled with such difficulties. In a general population survey in the UK Bryant & Trower (1974) found that 10% of 223 students had difficulties in, or avoided, social situations. Milder forms of social anxiety may indeed be widely experienced. Zimbardo (1977) refers to the fact that 42% of a sample of American college students described themselves as shy; Arkowitz *et al.* (1978) report that nearly one-third of college men and women report anxiety about dating; while Pilkonis & Zimbardo (1979) report prevalence rates between 31% and 60% for shyness in different cultural groups, although not all shy people are socially phobic (Turner, Beidel & Townsley, 1990).

It is only within the past decade that extreme social fear or social phobia has been included as a diagnostic entity within the *Diagnostic and Statistical Manual of Mental Disorders* (DSM-III; American Psychiatric Association, 1980). Indeed, as recently as 1985 Liebowitz *et al.* referred to social phobia as a 'neglected anxiety disorder'. The DSM-III defines social phobia as:

> Persistent, irrational fear of and compelling desire to avoid a situation in which the individual may be exposed to possible scrutiny by others. There is also fear that the individual may behave in a manner that will be humiliating and embarrassing (American Psychiatric Association, 1980, p. 227).

Using DSM-III-based diagnostic criteria DiNardo *et al.* (1983) report a figure of 13.3% as representing the proportion of patients presenting at a phobia clinic whose main problem was social phobia. Further general population-based data are available from the Epidemiological Catchment Area (ECA) programme, conducted in five different US locations with over 3000 subjects from the general population in each site. Data have been published regularly from this programme since its initiation in 1981 (e.g. Myers *et al.*, 1984) although the first comprehensive presentation of data about phobias has only appeared recently (Boyd *et al.*, 1990). Using a diagnostic interview schedule to classify social phobia according to DSM-III criteria, data from the five sites provide one-month prevalence rates of 1.8% in Baltimore, 1% in St Louis, 2.3% in Durham, 0.8% in Los Angeles but too few cases for statistical analysis in New Haven. Based upon these figures the estimated prevalence of social phobia in the US is 1.3%.

The possibility that these latter figures underestimate the extent of the problem is suggested by Pollard & Henderson (1988), who interviewed a random population of 250 male and 250 female community residents. Of these, 22.6% were diagnosed as having a social phobia, defined as becoming very nervous as a result of fear of criticism or embarrassment in one or more specified social situations, avoiding the situation if at all possible. Of the initial sample, 2% met the DSM-III criterion of creating 'significant distress because of the disturbance and recognition by the individual that his or her fear is excessive or unreasonable'. The authors suggest that lower prevalence figures may under-represent the extent of social interaction difficulties as some situations (e.g. public speaking) can be avoided without necessarily disrupting life—the person is disabled by such a situation but, because the situation need never be confronted, distress is prevented. Further, individuals who are socially anxious may avoid seeking help as the idea of talking about themselves and their difficulties may itself be anxiety-provoking and distressing (Heimberg & Barlow, 1988).

It seems likely that interaction difficulties may be a widespread concern within the general population while chronically disabling social phobia is far less prevalent. Social anxiety in its myriad forms—such as shyness, stage fright, heterosocial anxiety, dating anxiety, embarrassment, audience anxiety, reticence and communication apprehension—is likely to occur along a continuum of severity with social phobia as the extreme endpoint, marked by significant distress associated with a compelling desire to avoid social situations. Heimberg, Dodge & Becker (1987) suggest that many features of social phobia are likely to be commonly experienced within the general population, while Turner & Beidel (1989) note that 'degree of impairment may be an important distinction between shyness and social phobia' (p. 8).

With the recent revision of the DSM-III (DSM-III-R, 1987) there have been only minor changes to the DSM-III definition of social phobia. The new criteria specify, however, that social phobia may be either a generalised social apprehension or may be restricted to specific situations in which the person may be observed by others. These include fear of public speaking, eating in public, drinking in public, using a public lavatory or writing while under the scrutiny of others.

These variations in social fears may well account for some of the variations in prevalence rates obtained between studies. Fear of public speaking is frequently found to be the most commonly avoided social situation, reported by over 70% of socially phobic samples (Pollard & Henderson, 1988; Turner et al., 1986c) followed by eating in public and writing in public. There is also evidence that generalised social phobics may differ in degree from public speaking phobics, although they appear similar on the key dimension, fear of evaluation and scrutiny by others (Heimberg et al., 1990c). Generalised social phobics appear to have suffered more anxiety and disruption of function, and to have done so at an earlier point in their lives.

THE DISTINCTIVENESS OF SOCIAL PHOBIA

A further issue concerns the extent to which social fears are distinct from simple fears, agoraphobia and panic attacks (see DiNardo & Barlow, 1990 and Mannuzza et al., 1990, for recent reviews) and from avoidant personality disorder, the latter being characterised by hypersensitivity to criticism or rejection and social withdrawal in spite of the desire for social interaction.

Relationship to other anxiety disorders

With regard to simple fears and agoraphobia, Marks (1970) has suggested that social phobia occupies a position intermediate between simple fears and other anxiety problems on a continuum of severity. This corresponds with Ohman's (1986) functional–evolutionary classification of fears in which he distinguishes between fear of inanimate objects, fear of animals and fear of people, with agoraphobia having a unique evolutionary origin related to separation anxiety. Studies comparing features of anxiety disorders have, however, shown a degree of overlap between categories.

Rapee, Sanderson & Barlow (1988b) compared the extent to which patients with social phobia, agoraphobia, panic disorder, generalised anxiety and simple phobia reported features assumed to be characteristic of social phobia (e.g. fear and avoidance of parties, meetings, dating, etc.). Fear and avoidance behaviour reported by social phobics was also commonly experienced by other patients, although the extent of disruption to functioning in the specified situations was greater for the social phobics. Solyom, Ledwidge & Solyom (1986) have noted that among their socially phobic sample 35% were also agoraphobic, while among their agoraphobic sample 55% were also socially phobic. Figures presented by Boyd *et al.* (1990) from the ECA programme suggest that more than half those identified as socially phobic are also agoraphobic. Cerny, Himadi & Barlow (1984) and DiNardo & Barlow (1990) have also suggested that socially phobic behaviour can be seen in a number of clinical syndromes. DiNardo & Barlow (1990) report that 27% of their socially phobic patients received an additional anxiety disorder diagnosis, while of 271 anxiety disorder patients with a primary diagnosis other than social phobia 10% received an additional diagnosis of social phobia. Further, Turner *et al.* (1991) have recently reported that of 71 socially phobic patients, 24 (33%) also presented with generalised anxiety and eight (11%) with simple fears such as fear of flying, heights, spiders and snakes. Others have noted, however, that social fears are distinctive from other fears both in terms of the demographic characteristics of the patients concerned as well as in observed behaviours and patient cognitions.

A number of reports have found that, unlike other phobias where females predominate, social fears are present in males and females in about equal numbers (Amies, Gelder & Shaw, 1983; Marks, 1970; Solyom *et al.*, 1986) although Turner *et al.* (1986c) and Pollard & Henderson (1988) report socially phobic samples with a higher percentage of women (81% and 64.6% respectively). The high female percentage in the former sample may, however, be due to the exclusion of a number of males identified by the authors as patients with avoidant personality disorder (see below). Other findings are that social phobics are less likely to be married, and that age of onset is earlier in life for social phobics in comparison to agoraphobics (Amies *et al.*, 1983; Marks, 1970; Solyom *et al.*, 1986). Age of onset for social phobia is typically between 15 and 20 years (Liebowitz *et al.*, 1985; Turner *et al.*, 1986c). There is also some evidence that social phobics differ in certain aspects of parental rearing in comparison to agoraphobics. Arrindell *et al.* (1989) found that, in comparison to controls, agoraphobics rated both their parents as being less emotionally warm but only their mothers as being rejective, while social phobics rated both their parents as being rejective, as having lacked emotional warmth, and as having been overprotective. Stravynski, Elle & Franche (1989) also found evidence that patients with avoidant personality disorder (see below) in comparison to controls regarded their parents as more rejecting and less affectionate but only marginally overprotective. Others have noted that social phobics tend to be of higher social class and educational status than other phobics (Persson & Nordlund, 1985; Solyom et al., 1986).

Liebowitz et al. (1985) note that agoraphobics respond to anxiety by seeking out others, while social phobics tend to avoid interactions with others. This divergent reaction characterises attempts made by the two groups to reduce anxiety, a point also made by Gorman & Gorman (1987). The latter authors note specific autonomic symptoms of palpitations, trembling, sweating and blushing associated with social phobia. Amies et al. (1983) also found that blushing and muscle twitching were more common in social phobics while the primary somatic complaints reported by agoraphobics were dizziness, difficulty breathing, weakness in limbs, fainting episodes, and buzzing or ringing in the ears; a similar distinction is made by Solyom et al. (1986). Blushing as a characteristic of social fears has been discussed in other recent reports (Edelmann, 1990a, 1991). Cognitions of agoraphobics and social phobics are also quite different, with agoraphobic thoughts characterised by fear of losing bodily control or experiencing a physically catastrophic event (Chambless et al., 1984) while the cognitions of social phobia are characterised by fear of negative evaluation or fear of blushing (Edelmann, 1990a,b). Although there may be similarities in the manner that interactions between cognitions, bodily sensations and behaviour give rise to the subjective state of anxiety, the ingredients of each constituent part are likely to differ between anxiety types.

Relationship to avoidant personality disorder

A further conceptual difficulty relates to the distinction drawn in the DSM-III-R between social phobia and avoidant personality disorder. Barlow (1988), Marks (1985) and Turner & Biedel (1989) note the similarity between shyness as a trait and the DSM-III-R diagnosis of avoidant personality disorder. Barlow, for example, comments that 'it would certainly seem that the trait of shyness is on a continuum. Avoidant personality would represent one extreme of that continuum' (p. 537). Heimberg, Dodge & Becker (1987) suggest that while social phobics make efforts to confront their fears or actually enter feared situations, those with avoidant personalities have little desire to enter or confront the phobic event, and have adopted avoidance as a safe but unsatisfying lifestyle. Recent reports have also suggested that some socially phobic patients may also be avoidant personalities (Klass, DiNardo & Barlow, 1989), Turner et al. (1990) reporting that 15 (21%) of their sample of 71 socially phobic patients were also categorised as avoidant personality disorder.

In one study investigating the distinctiveness of social phobia and avoidant personality disorder, Turner *et al.* (1986a) compared 10 socially phobic and eight avoidant personality patients on a range of self-report inventories, a series of behavioural ratings taken during structured interactions and physiological parameters. Although no differences were found on psychophysiological or cognitive variables there were considerable differences between the two groups on both self-report inventory scores and behavioural skill factors as judged by raters blind to the diagnostic groupings when viewing the role-played interactions. The avoidant personality group were consistently rated as less skilful both on global ratings and specific parameters (e.g. gaze) and obtained higher scores on measures of social avoidance and distress. The distinction between pure social phobics who have normal social skills and patients with avoidant personality disorder who lack social skills has also been emphasised by Marks (1985). The latter are 'social isolates. Perhaps half also have anxiety, depression, withdrawal, and work inhibition' (Marks, 1985, p. 615). Stravynski & Greenberg (1989) also refer to social phobia as more anxiety- than skill-related, and avoidant personality disorder as marked by a lack of ability to act skilfully with associated anxiety. Certainly a number of studies, reviewed below, clearly illustrate that many socially phobic patients and analogue populations with social anxiety do not lack social skills in spite of feeling anxious and believing that others perceive them as anxious. As discussed later, both a comprehensive assessment of presenting difficulties and the appropriate tailoring of interventions to patients' needs seem essential.

Useful conceptualisations of the myriad forms of social anxiety have also been suggested by a number of authors within the social psychology literature. Within this framework there is a linking of shyness and audience anxiety on the one hand and embarrassment and shame on the other (e.g. Buss, 1980; Edelmann, 1987; Schlenker & Leary, 1982), the former being associated with anticipatory concerns, the latter with actual social predicaments or transgressions. Audience anxiety is differentiated from shyness because the former is guided primarily by internal plans, while in the latter case behaviours are contingent on the responses of others. Embarrassment involves interpersonal exposure while shame is much more a private feeling. However, the relationship of these constructs to social phobia remains unclear. As Turner *et al.* (1990) comment in their review, the relationship of social phobia and shyness remains elusive, and the link between embarrassment and social fears has only recently been explored (Edelmann, 1990a, 1991).

A further point emphasised by the social psychology literature is that while people may become anxious in a variety of situations, for social anxiety the central precipitating factor is the part played by the prospect or presence of interpersonal evaluation (Leary, 1982, 1983a; Leary & Schlenker, 1981; Schlenker & Leary, 1982). This issue forms a central thread in relation to theoretical explanations of social anxiety. As with the historical development of theories concerning the aetiology of anxiety in general there has been a recent extension of cognitively based explanations with regard to social anxiety in particular, emphasising the interaction of environmental and self concerns with learning experiences.

THEORETICAL PERSPECTIVES

Classical conditioning

In line with the classical conditioning perspective outlined in Chapter 2 an assumption with regard to social anxiety is that difficulties occur because stimuli in those settings have been associated with aversive experiences in the past. Two assumptions underlie this explanation: first, it is necessary to assume that all people referred to as socially anxious have experienced an aversive social encounter which has served to condition the person to become anxious in similar settings in the future. The second assumption is that we are able to explain the individual's aversive experiences in social encounters without recourse to his/her own behaviours in the situation or thoughts about it (Edelmann, 1987). Alternative assumptions might be: (i) that the person is unsure how to behave or does not possess the necessary repertoire of behaviours, or (ii) that he/she perceives the situation inappropriately or in an unnecessarily negative light, while possessing the necessary behavioural skills.

Skills deficit model

A number of authors have referred to the fact that anxiety in social situations is a result of an inability to handle the demands of a particular encounter (Bellack & Hersen, 1979; Curran, 1977). This may be because: (a) the person has not had the opportunity to learn and/or practise the necessary repertoire of behaviours; (b) although the behaviours are learned the person concerned is unable to put them into practice; (c) the person has learned the behaviours but puts them into practice inappropriately.

If the skills deficit model is correct then one would expect discernible differences between low and high socially anxious individuals on measures of social skills. Results are, however, rather mixed, although there are a number of possible explanations for this. First, the method-ology used differs between studies, with some assessing actual behaviours and others reporting observer judgements of those behaviours. Second, the subject groups studied differ between studies, some being clinically defined while others involve analogue populations. Third, a deficit in socially skilled behaviour may not be a prerequisite for an individual to experience social anxiety.

Studies using observers' ratings of analogue populations identified as socially anxious by questionnaire scores or behavioural assessment suggest that socially anxious individuals are less socially skilled than those who are low in social anxiety (e.g. Arkowitz et al., 1975; Farrell et al., 1979; Twentyman & McFall, 1975; Halford & Foddy, 1982). The finding that judges rate socially anxious people as less skilled than their non-socially anxious counterparts has been replicated using a number of different raters (trained raters, confederates, other naive subjects) and in a number of contexts (role-played tasks and real-life interactions). It seems that socially anxious people are *perceived* as being less skilled than those who are not socially anxious.

In contrast, studies which have directly assessed the amount/content of behaviours have frequently found no differences between socially and non-socially anxious groups or differences on only a few measures. Thus Daly (1978) found that although high-anxious in comparison to low-anxious subjects talked less while listening, and held gaze for less total time and in bouts of shorter duration while they were talking, there were no differences between subject groups for number of arm movements, self-touching behaviours or eye contact while listening.

In a further study Newton, Kindness & McFadyen (1983) found marked overlap between clinically identified socially anxious patients and non-socially anxious subjects on the percentage of time spent speaking, number of questions asked and number of smiles during a semi-structured encounter with a confederate. Some patients' social performance was as adequate as the non-clinical group, with some patients scoring well within the range of the more skilful members of the non-clinical group. Interest-ingly, when observers' ratings of the two groups were compared the patient group were perceived as less skilled than the non-clinical group, in line with findings from previous rating studies.

A similar finding is reported by Biedel, Turner & Dancu (1985), who again found little difference between socially anxious and non-socially anxious subjects on actual behaviours, although observers rated the non-socially anxious subjects as more skilful. Some people presenting with interaction difficulties seem to have adequate social performance but nevertheless have high social anxiety. In addition, it would seem that even when there are no real differences between socially anxious and non-socially anxious individuals in terms of behaviours displayed, the latter are nevertheless judged by others to have behavioural deficits, possibly having some deficit in general style of behaviour.

There are a number of ways of interpreting these results. Firstly, there might indeed be two groups of socially anxious patients, those with and those without a skills deficit. This would match to some extent the distinction made by Marks (1985) and others between social phobia with normal social skills and avoidant personality disorder with a social skills deficit. However, this would not explain why some socially anxious subjects with apparently normal skills are nevertheless rated as less skilled and more socially anxious than their low socially anxious counterparts. A second possibility arises from the fact that socially skilled behaviour is not just composed of discrete motor responses but is made up of a series of steps (skills) leading to those responses (McFall, 1982). It thus seems likely that no single skill in and of itself will be associated with a deficit in general social competence. Further, investigators have inevitably restricted themselves to assessing certain component behaviours so that, given the complexity of human behaviour, crucial parameters may have been omitted. There is, for example, evidence that socially anxious students are less accurate in their perception of relevant cues from others (Cowan, Conger & Conger, 1989) which may lead to a stilted performance (e.g. gaze at inappropriate times), although there may be no alteration in gross measures of quantity of behaviour (e.g. amount of gaze).

If one assumes that there is a real behavioural deficit associated with social anxiety a remaining issue concerns the cause of such difficulties. This might lie either in deficient or aversive learning experiences or alternatively with inappropriate or excessive performance concerns (although clearly the latter may also be generated by the former). Given that a particular behavioural style, rather than behavioural deficits *per se*, may be the central feature of social anxiety it seems quite likely that particular patterns of self-perception or cognitive style will give rise to a stilted or distorted performance. As outlined in Chapter 2 it seems inevitable that a hierarchical multicomponent model provides the most comprehensive account of anxiety. Thus variations in individual vulnerability will influence both perception and reaction to learning experiences in an interactive fashion. The way in which events are perceived will thus play a central role in influencing style of performance.

Cognitive factors

A number of different patterns of faulty thinking or cognitive styles have been implicated in the generation and maintenance of social anxiety.

These include negative self-evaluations of social performance (Edelmann, 1985a; Glasgow & Arkowitz, 1975; Clark & Arkowitz, 1975; Curran, Wallander & Fischetti, 1980b); negative self-statements before and during social encounters (Biedel *et al.*, 1985; Glass *et al.*, 1982; Cacioppo, Glass & Merluzzi, 1979; Dodge *et al.*, 1988; Glass & Furlong, 1990; Halford & Foddy, 1982; Heimberg *et al.*, 1990a); irrational beliefs (Glass *et al.*, 1982; Sutton-Simon & Goldfried, 1979); selective memory for negative versus positive information about one's social performance (O'Banion & Arkowitz, 1977); attentional bias to social threat cues (Hope *et al.*, 1990) and lower expectations about ability and performance (Maddux, Norton & Leary, 1988).

Negative self-evaluations

The central thesis of this supposition is that socially anxious subjects experience social anxiety as a result of negatively evaluating their own performance. Thus Clark & Arkowitz (1975) found that an analogue population of high socially anxious male subjects underestimated positive aspects of their performance (i.e. their social skill) and overestimated negative aspects of their performance (i.e. their degree of social anxiety) following a conversation with a female confederate. Similarly, Edelmann (1985a) found that although a socially anxious patient group did not differ from a non-socially anxious group in their knowledge about how to cope with embarrassing events, they reported being less clear about how to react, and felt that they would not have dealt as effectively with the situation. In a further study Curran *et al.* (1980c) divided subjects into high-anxious/high-skill, high-anxious/low-skill and low-anxious/high-skill groups. Following a simulated interaction with an opposite sex confederate high-anxious/high-skill subjects underestimated (in comparison to judge's ratings) their own skill, while high-anxious/low-skill subjects accurately assessed their poor performance. Doubts about one's ability to perform effectively may then influence both behavioural style and feelings of anxiety.

Negative self-statements

A number of studies have assessed the role of negative self-statements in relation to social anxiety. This follows Meichenbaum's (1977) suggestion that thoughts that contain negative feedback and poor self-evaluation, or are task-irrelevant, interfere with adaptive functioning and result in anxiety. Thus, Cacioppo *et al.* (1979) found that the anticipation of a discussion with an unfamiliar woman led to the spontaneous generation of more negative self-statements and a more negative self-evaluation by an analogue population of high in comparison to low socially anxious men. Similarly Glass *et al.* (1982) found that high socially anxious female subjects scored significantly higher on negative self-statements and significantly lower on positive self-statements than low socially anxious female subjects using the Social Interaction Self-Statement Test (SISST, described below). Similar findings using this scale are reported by Biedel *et al.* (1985). In a further study with clinically defined social anxious patients (Dodge *et al.*, 1988) negative self-statements were much more likely than a lack of positive self-statements to be related to anxiety. The authors also report that those seeking treatment for social interaction difficulties showed evidence of more negative self-statements than those seeking treatment for anxiety about speaking in public. This finding no doubt reflects the more general anxiety experienced by the former group. More negative than positive self-statements on the SISST have also been reported in two further studies with socially phobic subjects who participated in a role-played interaction. Heimberg *et al.* (1990a) report a mean score on the negative self-statement subscale of the SISST of 52.67 and a mean score on the positive self-statement subscale of 35.07; corresponding figures reported in another recent study (Glass & Furlong, 1990) were 50.27 and 38.85 respectively.

Using a different self-statement checklist Halford & Foddy (1982) also found that socially anxious subjects made more negative statements but not less positive statements than a non-socially anxious control group. These latter findings tie in with suggestions that negative self-statements may play a more important role in psychopathology than positive self-statements (Kendall & Hollon, 1981; Heimberg, Keller & Peca-Baker, 1986). Others have pointed to the importance of balancing negative and positive cognitions. In their States of Mind (SOM) model Schwartz & Garamoni (1986, 1989) argue that optimal adjustment is represented in a balance of positive and negative cognition such that the ratio of positive thoughts to the sum of positive and negative thoughts approaches 0.618. Mild, moderate and severe pathology have values averaging 0.5 (internal dialogue of conflict), 0.38 (negative dialogue) and 0.32 (negative monologue) respectively. Heimberg *et al.* (1990a) report an evaluation of the SOM model with 51 socially phobic subjects who participated in a role-played interaction. A mean SOM ratio of 0.40 was obtained from the negative and positive subscales of the SISST completed prior to the interaction, placing the average subject in the negative dialogue range. A similar figure of 0.436 is reported by Glass & Furlong (1990) from the SISST filled out after the interaction, for their sample of socially anxious volunteers. These two studies also used a similar thought listing procedure, Heimberg *et al.* asking subjects to list their thoughts after the interaction while Glass &

Furlong asked subjects to list their thoughts about the impending inter-action. SOM ratios from these two methods were 0.25 and 0.39 respect-ively, suggesting that thought listing may reflect a rather more negative balance generated by the role-played interaction. A central feature of social anxiety relates to concern about performing inadequately, saying the wrong thing and receiving a negative evaluation; such thoughts may well predominate subsequent to an interaction.

Irrational beliefs

A further cognitive variable which has been investigated in relation to social anxiety is the existence of irrational beliefs. That is, a tendency to maintain absolutist beliefs and imperative assumptions about oneself and the world, even in the face of contradictory evidence (Ellis, 1962; Ellis & Harper, 1975). In one study of relevance Sutton-Simon & Goldfried (1979) assessed 25 male and 33 female adults requesting therapy at a community clinic on the Irrational Beliefs Test, which consists of 100 statements of rational and irrational content, and the Situations Questionnaire which taps negative self-statements. Degree of social anxiety (as measured by the Social Avoidance and Distress Scale (Watson & Friend, 1969) was corre-lated with irrational beliefs and also with negative self-statements, although the latter figure was not significant. A relationship between irra-tional beliefs, social anxiety and negative self-statements on the SISST is also reported by Glass & Furlong (1990).

Selective memory

As discussed in Chapter 2, there is evidence that anxious individuals are more vigilant to threat-related cues, although they do not show sub-sequent superior recall or recognition. There is some evidence that social anxiety may operate in a slightly different manner with studies showing both increased recall of negative information about themselves by socially anxious individuals and increased preoccupation with the evaluation of others. In a study by O'Banion & Arkowitz (1977) high and low socially anxious women interacted with a male confederate trained to respond positively to half the subjects and negatively to the other half. Subsequent to the interaction subjects were given identical feedback, consisting of positive and negative adjectives and supposedly indicating the confeder-ate's impression of them. They were then asked to perform a recall task. Consistent with predictions, highly socially anxious women recalled more negative adjectives than low socially anxious women.

In a further study, Smith, Ingram & Brehm (1983) investigated recall of self-relevant information by socially anxious subjects. Subjects expecting to perform a speech in public took part in a depth-of-processing task. After listening to 48 adjectives they had to either identify whether the word was read by a male or female (structural processing); whether it meant the same as/opposite to other presented words (semantic processing); whether the word described themselves (private self-referent processing); or whether someone who knew them or had just met them would use the word to describe them (public self-referent processing). Subjects then performed a recall task.

Results indicated that socially anxious subjects showed increased recall of words processed on the public self-referent task but no difference in recall for words processed on the other three tasks in relation to non-socially anxious controls. One explanation for this effect is the fact that socially anxious individuals spend excessive time ruminating about what others might think of them, and thus perceive threat much more readily. Smith *et al.*'s processing task seems more likely to reflect vigilance to threat cues pertinent to social anxiety rather than recall of specific events *per se*, and thus more likely to match the suggestions outlined in Chapter 2 in relation to information processing and anxiety. Hypervigilance to social threat cues is in fact suggested by a more recent report. Using the revised Stroop colour-naming task Hope *et al.* (1990) found that social phobics had longer latencies for social threat words than for physical threat or neutral words.

A multicomponent process framework

Interactive models of varying complexity incorporating psychobiological, behavioural, physiological and cognitive parameters have been suggested as explanations for social anxiety by a number of authors (e.g. Barlow, 1988; Trower & Turland, 1984; Trower & Gilbert, 1989). The starting point for these conceptions is to posit a psychobiological basis to social anxiety. Drawing on the work of Ohman (1986) and others, social fears are viewed as originating in a dominance/submission system, the function of which is to establish social order. It has been reasoned that, biologically, humans are predisposed to react to threatening social cues, particularly those conveyed via facial signals. In a series of papers Dimburg and Ohman have argued that facial cues play a decisive role in social fears (Dimburg, 1987; Ohman, 1986; Ohman & Dimburg, 1984; Ohman, Dimburg & Öst, 1985). This is based on the finding that fear conditioned to angry faces is more resistant to extinction than responses to happy or neutral expressions, and that this effect is obtained only when the stimulus person directs his or her anger towards the subject. If conditioning to facial stimuli plays a particularly important role in the generation of social anxiety then social phobics should be particularly sensitive to facial cues. However, in one study investigating this supposition Merckelbach *et al.* (1989a) found that, although angry faces elicited greater skin conductance responses and fewer eyeblinks than happy face stimuli or neutral face stimuli, no difference in reaction was found between social phobics and control subjects. Thus although facial stimuli may be salient cues, social phobics do not seem to be particularly sensitive to them.

It may be the case, however, that socially anxious individuals have either an innate capacity to recognise more general social threat, selectively perceiving and interpreting cues in terms of dominance–submission hierarchies (Trower & Gilbert, 1989) or be biologically and psychologically vulnerable to anxious apprehension (Barlow, 1988), being particularly prone to focus on bodily sensations and the evaluative opinions of others.

This supposition can be related to social psychological theorising which has interpreted social anxiety in terms of self-awareness theory (Duval & Wicklund, 1972; Wicklund, 1975). This proposes that attention can be focused either outward towards the environment or inward towards the self. This focusing of attention can be influenced by both situational and dispositional factors (e.g. Buss, 1980; Fenigstein, Scheier & Buss, 1975; Schlenker & Leary, 1982). The former has been referred to as self-awareness; the latter as self-consciousness. Both these parameters have a public component, referring to an awareness of one's observable thoughts and feelings, and a private component, referring to an unobservable awareness of one's thoughts and feelings. Public self-consciousness but not private self-consciousness as measured by the Self-Consciousness Scale (Fenigstein *et al.*, 1975) is positively related to measures of shyness (Cheek & Buss, 1981), interaction anxiousness and audience anxiety (Leary, 1983b) and with general measures of social anxiety (Buss, 1980; Fenigstein, 1979; Fenigstein *et al.*, 1975) in non-clinical samples. This has led Fenigstein (1979) to suggest that public self-consciousness may be a necessary, but not sufficient, precondition of social anxiety.

In a sample of socially phobic patients Hope & Heimberg (1988) found that public self-consciousness was similarly related to most measures of social anxiety. Public and private self-consciousness were, however, highly related and the latter was related to self-reported cognitive and somatic symptoms. This raises the possibility that both types of self-consciousness may relate to social anxiety (Hope, Gansler & Heimberg, 1989), private self-consciousness via attention to bodily sensations and public self-consciousness via overperception of oneself as the focus of others' observations.

Experimental studies have shown that awareness of physiological processes (e.g. heart beat) increases self-awareness (e.g. Fenigstein & Carver, 1978). It has also been found that phobic individuals are attuned to their

own heart rate changes, with social phobics particularly accurate in estimating their heart rate changes in phobic situations (Johannson & Öst,
1982). In addition, socially anxious individuals with elevated somatic
symptoms report that they display significantly more signs of anxiety than
are noticed by their peers (McEwan & Devins, 1983). Highly socially
anxious people may rely on internal cues to estimate the salience of their
anxiety while excluding other salient cues. Sensitivity to bodily changes
may thus play a particularly important role in social anxiety by acting as
fear-producing cues in a fear-of-fear cycle. In the same way that panic and
agoraphobia seem to be related (see Chapters 4 and 5) fear of specific bodily
cues such as blushing may play an important part in relation to social
anxiety. Edelmann (1990a,b) has argued that fear of blushing generates an
emotional state (embarrassment or social anxiety) which in turns generates
a specific negative pattern of thinking. This matches suggestions by
Trower & Gilbert (1989) that subjective experience consists of (a) characteristic physical sensations which arise from physiological arousal contributing to (b) an emotional state in turn linked to (c) a perceived threat to the
desired self-schema. Allied to this is the fact that the socially anxious
person is sensitive to external evaluation being more likely to predict,
perceive and recall negative appraisal from others (i.e. negative self-
evaluation).

In summary, socially anxious individuals may, by nature, be particularly
sensitive to specific bodily sensations and the evaluations of others (i.e.
publicly and privately self-conscious). This may lead to a set of anticipatory expectations about the potentially negative outcome of social encounters with a possible subsequent detrimental effect upon performance.
Trower & Gilbert (1989) and Trower & Turland (1984) conceptualise this
in terms of an appraisal system in which negative stimulus expectancies
elicit anxiety experiences and a subsequent behavioural response system
in which the individual attempts to cope; lack of appropriate skills at this
stage would, they argue, lead to escape or avoidance. Like anxiety in
general, social anxiety and social phobia are multifaceted phenomena with
cognitive appraisal in general, and fear of negative self-evaluation in
particular, playing seemingly central roles.

ASSESSMENT

As indicated in the preceding section, a number of cognitive and
behavioural elements have been addressed in relation to social anxiety.
Some of these relate to constructs such as irrational beliefs assumed to be
causally implicated in anxiety in general (assessed with the Irrational

Beliefs Test, Jones, 1969), while others such as negative self-statements are directed towards social anxiety in particular (assessed with the Social Interaction Self-Statement Test, Glass et al., 1982). Both categories of assessment have been addressed in relation to social anxiety in recent reviews (Arnkoff & Glass, 1989; Glass & Arnkoff, 1989). The aim of the present section will be to comment upon the most widely used assessment strategies cited in both theoretical and treatment studies.

Behavioural assessment

Given the assumption that socially anxious patients may lack social skills it is perhaps not surprising that an evaluation of social behaviour and social skills should form an essential part of any adequate assessment. Naturalistic observation would inevitably provide the most valid method of behavioural assessment; however, it is not always practical to implement such assessments, and role-play methods are often used as an alternative. These can take the form of either a structured or unstructured role-play. In the former, subjects are presented with a description of a social situation and a confederate who may provide prompts; subjects are inevitably aware that they are in an 'experimental' situation and are being observed (e.g. Higgins, Frisch & Smith, 1983). In unstructured role-plays subjects are instructed to interact with a confederate for a brief period of time (e.g. five minutes) behaving as they typically do in social situations (e.g. Curran, 1975).

It is inevitable that ratings of behaviour obtained under such different conditions may be highly variable. Indeed, Bellack, Hersen & Lamparski (1979) found little relationship between behavioural measures derived from a structured role-play and those derived from a naturalistic interaction. More recently, however, Merluzzi & Biever (1987), using global ratings of social skill rather than assessments of specific behaviours, found no differences between judges', confederates' and subjects' ratings across structured and unstructured role-plays and naturalistic interactions.

A further issue concerns the number of situations in which a subject needs to be observed in order to gain a realistic assessment of their level of functioning. Curran and his colleagues (Curran, 1982; Curran et al., 1980b; Farrell et al., 1983) have developed the Simulated Social Interaction Test for use with inpatients. This consists of eight brief social interactions each initiated by a series of two confederate prompts delivered in face-to-face interactions. The situations used are representative of a good range of social encounters with judges' ratings from the role-plays relating to nurses' ratings of the patients' everyday interactions.

Others have used extended interactions with confederates of the opposite or same sex, with the general instructions to initiate and maintain a conversation with the other person for some specified time period. Trower, Bryant & Argyle (1978a) have used such an interaction (the Social Interaction Test) lasting 12 minutes with patients subsequently rated for 29 items (e.g. voice tone, pitch, volume and clarity; posture; gestures; gaze) on a five-point scale (0–4) to indicate acceptability of behaviours.

Self-report inventories

There are a range of self-report inventories which either assess fears and phobias in general, and include questions pertaining to social anxiety in particular (e.g. the Fear Survey Schedule, Wolpe & Lange, 1964; Fear Questionnaire, Marks & Mathews, 1979), or which measure constructs related to social anxiety (e.g. Shyness Scale, Cheek & Buss, 1981; Social Reticence Scale, Jones & Russell, 1982; Embarrassibility Scale, Modigliani, 1968; Edelmann, 1985b; Edelmann & McCusker, 1986). There are also a range of measures which assess discomfort in social situations (e.g. Situation Questionnaire, Rehm & Marston, 1968; Social Anxiety Questionnaire, Arkowitz et al., 1975; Interaction Anxiousness Scale, Leary, 1983b) or which assess the perceived likelihood of performing a range of behaviours in social situations (e.g. Social Situations Questionnaire, Bryant & Trower, 1974; Social Performance Survey Schedule, Lowe & Cautela, 1978).

Perhaps the most frequently used scale in studies of social anxiety and social phobia is the Social Avoidance and Distress Scale (SADS) and to a lesser extent the Fear of Negative Evaluation Scale (FNE) developed by Watson & Friend (1969). These consist of 28 and 30 true–false items which were standardised on a population of undergraduates. The SADS in particular has since been used in numerous clinical studies, often as the sole criterion for distinguishing between socially and non-socially anxious subjects and as an important outcome variable for treatment programmes. The scale has not, however, been without its critics. Turner, McCanna & Beidel (1987) have suggested that the SADS and FNE are better suited as measures of general emotional distress than social anxiety. They administered the two inventories in addition to measures of anxiety, depression and general emotional distress to 206 outpatients with agoraphobia with panic attacks, agoraphobia without panic attacks, social phobia, simple phobia, panic disorder, generalised anxiety disorder or obsessive–compulsive disorder. On the SAD and FNE social phobics did not differ significantly from the other anxiety conditions with the exception of simple phobics; the SADS and FNE were significantly correlated with measures of anxiety and depression.

In commenting upon these findings Heimberg *et al.* (1988) suggest that social anxiety may to a greater or lesser degree be present in all the anxiety conditions. This is consistent with Barlow *et al.*'s (1986b) finding that social anxiety may be common across anxiety conditions (i.e. 35% of panic patients, 33% of generalised anxiety patients, 17% of agoraphobic patients and 29% of simple phobic patients also being identified as socially phobic). It is clear, however, that reasons for social distress may differ between groups (e.g. the panic patient may feel embarrassed by panicking in public, the socially phobic patient may feel embarrassed at the prospect of exposure to public scrutiny), the SADS and FNE may not satisfactorily discriminate between them and hence may not reflect the specific features of social phobia (Turner & Beidel, 1988a). This has led Turner and his colleagues to develop a new empirically derived self-report inventory, the Social Phobia and Anxiety Inventory, as a more specific measure of social phobia (Beidel *et al.*, 1989; Turner *et al.*, 1989a,b).

The 45-item scale comprising two subscales (social phobia and agoraphobia) was developed according to Goldfried & D'Zurilla's (1969) behavioural-analytic method so that items were derived from the population of interest (Beidel *et al.*, 1989). The authors report that the scale has high test–retest reliability (Turner *et al.*, 1989a) and adequate concurrent and external validity (Beidel *et al.*, 1989) reliably distinguishing between social phobics and agoraphobics (Turner *et al.*, 1989b). It remains to be seen whether this scale replaces the SADS as the instrument of choice in clinical studies.

A further widely used measure with socially anxious subjects is the Social Interaction Self-Statement Test (SISST; Glass *et al.*, 1982). This is a 30-item questionnaire that assesses the frequency of positive and negative self-statements in heterosexual social situations. Subjects use a five-point scale to rate how frequently they experience each thought during an immediately preceding role-played interaction. It has become one of the most frequently used self-statement measures in social anxiety research. Glass *et al.* report that the scale reliably distinguishes between high and low socially anxious individuals. Merluzzi, Burgio & Glass (1984) also report correlations between both positive and negative subscales of the SISST and shyness ratings obtained from clinicians and clients, and with the social introversion subscale of the MMPI. There is also evidence that the measure shows situational specificity (Turner, Beidel & Larkin, 1986a).

In this latter study three groups of subjects (non-clinically socially anxious, clinically socially anxious and non-socially anxious) took part in an unstructured interaction with a same-sex and opposite-sex confederate and gave an impromptu speech. Non-socially anxious subjects reported more positive cognitions and less negative cognitions than either of the two socially anxious groups. All subjects reported more positive thoughts during the same-sex interaction than during the opposite-sex interaction or the speech condition. The clinically socially anxious group had more negative thoughts in the impromptu speech than the same-sex task and actually had fewer negative cognitions during the opposite-sex task than the non-clinically socially anxious subjects.

In a further study with DSM-III diagnosed socially phobic subjects Dodge *et al.* (1988) found that negative but not positive thoughts on the SISST correlated in the expected direction with self-report measures of social anxiety and depression. Subjects' reports of negative thoughts obtained via a thought-listing procedure were also related to the SISST negative self-statement score; the scale also discriminated between those whose primary concern involved social interactions and those whose primary concern was confined to public speaking situations. However, in a further report Glass & Furlong (1990) found a lack of relationship between thoughts generated by a thought-listing procedure and thoughts on the SISST for a sample of socially anxious volunteers although thoughts (low positive, high negative) on the SISST were related to irrational beliefs, fear of negative evaluation and social anxiety.

TREATMENT

While there are numerous studies evaluating treatment approaches to social anxiety, a great many of these are directed towards subclinical populations among college students and community volunteers. In a recent review Heimberg (1989) identified only 19 treatment studies using socially phobic subject populations defined in terms of DSM-III (1980) or DSM-III-R (1987) criteria. Treatments can be broadly grouped into those which are based upon a conditioning model using relaxation procedures and associated techniques such as systematic desensitisation and exposure-based methods, social skills training based upon the assumption that social phobics lack the necessary interpersonal skills to function effectively in social situations, and cognitive techniques based upon the assumption of faulty thinking patterns.

Exposure-based methods

The assumption that exposure to the feared stimuli is essential for fear reduction has a long history (Emmelkamp, 1982; Marks, 1972, 1973, 1978). The effectiveness of exposure-based treatments, in particular for obsessive–compulsive difficulties and agoraphobia, has been evaluated in relation to a variety of parameters. Although results are mixed, optimal treatment seems to involve graduated, repeated and prolonged exposure with practice tasks which are clearly specified. Social phobia, however, differs in a number of ways from other phobias. As Butler (1985) notes, social situations are often time-limited (e.g. saying good morning); social phobics often seem to avoid relatively few situations, yet this repeated exposure is not apparently beneficial; and thirdly thoughts and attitudes, particularly a fear of negative evaluation, seem to play a central role in social phobia. This latter suggestion has led some to comment that, in contrast to other phobias, cognitive change is more likely to play a therapeutic role in social phobia (Biran, Augusto & Wilson, 1981; Emmelkamp, 1982; Marks, 1987b). Despite this, there is some evidence that exposure-based treatments have some degree of efficacy. In a recent report Fava, Grandi & Canestrari (1989) found significant reductions in both observer-rated and self-rated assessments of social phobia and observer-rated anxiety for seven out of 10 socially phobic patients who completed a programme of behavioural exposure homework without therapist-aided exposure. Treatment gains were maintained at one-year follow-up. However, the absence of a control group or groups receiving other treatments means that it is not possible to deduce whether treatment gains were due to exposure *per se* or whether exposure is the most beneficial treatment. Other studies have compared exposure-based treatments to no-treatment controls or to other treatments.

In one recent report Renneberg *et al.* (1991) compared patients with avoidant personality disorder, the majority of whom were also diagnosed with social phobia, treated with a comprehensive group treatment package (group systematic desensitisation, behavioural rehearsal and self-image work) involving an element of exposure, to a waiting list control group. Treatment resulted in significant improvement on measures of fear of negative evaluation, assertion, depression and self-image. The authors themselves refer to the study as a pilot report, and note that assignment to treatment and control groups was not entirely random. In addition, although the authors note anecdotal therapist and patient reports of decreased behavioural avoidance this was not assessed directly; it is also not possible to ascertain whether there is a specific effective ingredient of the treatment package used.

Alstrom *et al.* (1984) compared 42 socially phobic patients randomly assigned to one of four treatment conditions: all groups received a 'basal therapy' consisting of information, encouragement and anxiolytic medication. In addition the second group received therapist-aided *in vivo* exposure, the third group dynamically oriented supportive therapy and the fourth group relaxation training. Improvement on measures of phobic severity and global functioning was greatest in the group which had additional therapist-aided exposure. Interpreting the results should, however, be treated with some degree of caution as subject groups differed in terms of medication received, degree of psychological difficulty and gender distribution.

Butler *et al.* (1984), Mattick & Peters (1988) and Mattick, Peters & Clarke (1989), in studies discussed in further detail in relation to cognitive therapies, used exposure for one of their two treatment groups. Butler *et al.* report that their exposure group improved more than a waiting list control with improvement maintained at follow-up, while Mattick *et al.* found an improvement in anxiety and avoidance with exposure-based treatment but not on attitudinal measures (fear of negative evaluation, irrational beliefs and locus of control).

In a further study Emmelkamp *et al.* (1985) compared exposure *in vivo* with self-instructional training and rational emotive therapy. Each of the three therapeutic procedures resulted in significant reductions in anxiety which were either maintained or improved upon at follow-up. Exposure treatment was superior to other treatments on pulse rate reduction but only cognitive treatments produced significant changes in cognitions.

In a more recent study Wlazlo *et al.* (1990) compared exposure *in vivo* received either in groups or in individual sessions with social skills training for patients with 'social inhibition' (subsequently diagnosed as primary social phobia or primary skills deficit). All three treatments led to clinically and statistically significant improvements for both groups of patients at the end of treatment in social anxiety and skills deficits and in associated complaints. These treatment gains were either maintained or improved upon at 3 months and $2\frac{1}{2}$ years follow-up assessments. There was a tendency for the socially phobic subgroup to show slightly superior gains at long-term follow-up and for the skills deficit group to show superior outcome with group exposure.

There seems, then, to be some evidence that exposure-based treatments are effective for reducing anxiety and avoidance in social phobics although cognitive parameters are less affected by such treatment. In discussing the reasons for the possible effectiveness of exposure for social phobia, Butler (1985) notes that cognitive and behavioural factors might be responsible for patient change. She thus suggests that implicit cognitive factors such as reinterpreting the situation and problem-solving, as well as non-cognitive factors such as identifying specific skills, may form an integral part of therapy during exposure treatment. This suggests that treatments directed towards cognitive factors may be more effective than exposure-based treatments alone. It is also possible that skills training (as in the Wlazlo *et al.* (1990) study referred to above) is effective because it, of necessity, involves an element of exposure to the feared situation during behavioural practice.

Social skills training

The basic assumption of the skills deficit approach is that the source of anxiety in social situations is due to an inadequate or inappropriate behavioural repertoire, although as noted this is not necessarily the case. Nevertheless, an objective of therapy is for the patient to acquire the specific verbal and non-verbal skills required to achieve a specific social target or goal. A number of training manuals have been developed with this aim in mind (e.g. Goldstein, Sprafkin & Gershaw, 1976; Liberman et al., 1975; Trower, Bryant & Argyle, 1978a). Initially a list is drawn up of the social difficulties experienced in particular social situations, and techniques for dealing with those situations are specified. Then specific skills are taught through instruction, modelling, role-play and feedback from videotaped recordings and social reinforcement. The various skills identified by Trower et al. include observational skills (e.g. recognising emotions), listening skills (e.g. appropriate use of head-nods), speaking skills, meshing skills (e.g. regulating a conversation through turn-taking) and finally non-verbal deficits (e.g. inappropriate actions or mannerisms).

Although there are a plethora of studies evaluating social skills training the majority of these have been directed towards heterosexual–social anxiety and dating anxiety in college students (Curran (1977) reviews 12 such studies) or towards patients presenting with skills deficits rather than phobic reactions per se (e.g. Brady, 1984a,b; Falloon et al., 1977; Hall & Goldberg, 1977). There are few studies directed towards clinically defined socially phobic groups. In the Falloon et al. study, for example, 51 outpatients with skills deficits, of whom 18 were identified as socially phobic, were treated with either group discussion sessions or social skills training alone or together with homework assignments. There were no treatment differences between the groups. In the first study directed specifically towards socially anxious patients, Marzillier, Lambert & Kellett (1976) compared social skills training to systematic desensitisation and a waiting list control group. Both treatments led to significant within-group improvements with the social skills patients maintaining improvement at six-month follow-up. However, the treatment gains were not significantly greater than those achieved by the waiting list control group.

Trower et al. (1978b) also compared social skills training with systematic desensitisation for patients characterised as either socially phobic (anxious in social settings) or socially inadequate (lacking in social skills). Socially phobic patients showed reduced anxiety with both treatments but little change in social behaviour; socially inadequate patients showed greatest improvement in terms of both anxiety reduction and behaviour change with skills training. In an extension of this study comparing a group treated with imaginal flooding to the other two treatments, Shaw (1979) found all three treatments to be equally effective.

A similar lack of differential effectiveness of treatments for socially dysfunctional patients has been reported in two further studies. Stravynski, Marks & Yule (1982) compared social skills training with social skills training plus additional cognitive therapy. Both treatment groups improved, reporting increased social interaction and decreased anxiety with no additional benefit provided by the cognitive therapy. Falloon, Lloyd & Harpin (1981) compared social skills training with a pharmacologically based treatment. Post-treatment measures of specific fears, generalised social anxiety, self-image and global tension and anxiety showed significant improvements for both groups.

In a further study Öst, Jerremalm & Johannson (1981) divided patients presenting with anxiety in a wide range of social situations into either 'behavioural reactors' or 'physiological reactors', based on standardised scores obtained from two sets of measures. The behavioural measures consisted of 17 items concerned with voice, posture, gesture, proximity, orientation, speaking, and turn-taking derived from video recordings of a brief interaction between the subject and one male and one female confederate. The physiological measures consisted of a continuous record of the patient's heart rate taken during the interaction with the confederates.

The 'physiological reactors' were 16 patients with high heart rate reactions but small overt behavioural reactions, while the 16 'behavioural reactors' had large behavioural reactions but low heart rate reactions. The two groups of 16 subjects were then randomly assigned to two treatments which either matched the patient's response pattern or did not accord with it (i.e. relaxation matching the 'physiological reactors' response pattern and skills training matching 'behavioural reactors' response pattern). While both treatments yielded significant improvements, social skills training was significantly more effective for the 'behavioural reactors' while applied relaxation was significantly more effective for the 'physiological reactors'.

In a similar vein, Mersch et al. (1989) divided 74 socially phobic patients into behavioural and cognitive reactors on the basis of their scores on a behavioural test (Simulated Social Interaction Test) and a cognitive measure (the Rational Behaviour Inventory). Half the patients within each response pattern received a behaviourally focused treatment (social skills training) while the other half received a cognitively oriented treatment (rational emotive therapy). While all treatment groups showed considerable improvement, there was no evidence for any greater effectiveness of the treatment matched to patient's response pattern. Other studies matching treatment to reaction pattern with agoraphobics (Öst, Jerremalm & Jansson, 1984) and dental phobics (Jansson, Jerremalm & Öst, 1986) have also not met with differential success. As discussed below, however, these results do not necessarily mean that patient characteristics are not related to effects of treatment for social phobia.

Over the past two decades social skills training has had a mixed history, being considered a panacea for the social difficulties of many psychiatric patient groups and for heterosexual–social anxiety in analogue populations in the 1970s but having engendered a rather more cautious approach in the 1980s. Certainly for extreme social anxiety there is little evidence either for the efficacy of social skills training or for a firm theoretical rationale for the treatment. On the whole the few comparative treatment outcome studies show little difference between social skills training and other treatments, and the only study using a waiting list control (Marzillier et al., 1976) found no superior effect for the treatment group. Social skills training is clearly most appropriate when patients actually have inadequate skills, which is not the case for all socially anxious patients. Certainly in both the Trower et al. (1978b) and Öst et al. (1981) reports, treatment outcome was a function of the patients' specific difficulties (although, as mentioned, similar results have not been obtained in other studies).

If, however, one assumes that social skills training is effective, a question remains concerning the precise mechanism of change. Clearly in any skills training programme patients may role-play activities which engender anxiety and receive feedback on performance as well as having the opportunity to practise in real-life settings between sessions. As Stravynski & Greenberg (1989) comment: 'social skills training also affords exposure in vivo to the feared situations: first in a simulated fashion during the practice in the clinic and second in vivo during the performance of social tasks assigned as homework' (p. 216). This has led a number of authors to suggest that the essential ingredient of social skills training is anxiety reduction as a result of exposure to phobic cues. Thus Stravynski, Grey & Elie (1987), re-analysing data from Stravynski et al. (1982), suggest that anxiety reduction acts as a mediator of behaviour change rather than a skills acquisition process per se. In a test of the therapeutic mechanism of skills training Stravynski et al. (1989) randomly assigned 28 patients with avoidant personality disorder to either social skills training plus homework or group discussion plus homework in a crossover design. No significant differences between treatment groups or treatment modalities were found, questioning the centrality of skills acquisition as the effective therapeutic process in social skills training. Indeed the homework practice (and hence exposure) may have been a potentially important therapeutic ingredient.

As Barlow (1988) comments: 'most clinicians have recognised that the exposure elements of social skills training may be the important ingredient for those patients suffering primarily from social phobia' (pp. 555–556). Edelmann (1987) has also argued that 'social skills training may thus alleviate behavioural difficulties in social situations, as well as anxiety occasioned by those situations, through exposure to the problem situation as in desensitization' (p. 179). Heimberg, Dodge & Becker (1987) have also suggested that the effect of social skills training may result from the exposure to phobic cues inherent in social skills training procedures and homework assignments. In contrast, others have argued that cognitive change is inherent in social skills training, even if this is at the level of patients re-evaluating themselves in the light of successful (i.e. skilled) performance in the therapeutic environment. Thus Trower (1981) comments that when cognitive biases exist they appear to inhibit socially appropriate behaviour regardless of available skill, and that social skills training (SST):

> cannot well succeed while the cognitive processes of agency are dysfunctional, and while SST may facilitate the growth of agency by chance and nonspecific factors, therapy had best be applied purposefully and systematically to resolving cognitive blocks, lest training becomes another of the client's failed experiences, and leaves him worse off than before (Trower, 1984, p. 83).

Cognitive techniques

The main cognitive component in social phobia is the fear of being negatively evaluated, criticised or rejected (Beck, Emery & Greenberg, 1985; Butler, 1985) suggesting that cognitive strategies may be helpful therapeutically. There have been many developments in relation to cognitive therapies over the past two decades and numerous applications of these methods to social anxiety, performance anxiety or public speaking anxiety. Some have emphasised Ellis's rational emotive therapy (RET) (Ellis, 1962) and the need to alter clients' irrational cognitive responses (e.g. Kanter & Goldfried, 1979; Lent, Russell & Zamostny, 1981; Shahar & Merbaum, 1981), others have followed Meichenbaum's emphasis of self-verbalisation or self-instructional training (SIT) (Meichenbaum, Gilmore & Fedoraviciua, 1971) (e.g. Hayes & Marshall, 1984; Jerremalm, Jansson & Öst, 1986a) or Suinn & Richardson's (1971) anxiety management training (e.g. Butler et al., 1984) or combinations of RET with rational restructuring (Goldfried & Goldfried, 1980) (e.g. Mattick & Peters, 1988; Mattick et al., 1989; McCann, Woolfolk & Lehrer, 1987).

Kanter & Goldfried (1979) compared the efficacy of rational restructuring and self-control desensitisation as interventions for 68 socially anxious community residents. The former intervention involved training clients to recognise unrealistic and self-defeating thoughts related to their anxiety and then substituting more realistic ones. The latter intervention involved a modification of systematic desensitisation using relaxation and imagery after suggestions by Goldfried (1971). Subjects were randomly assigned to either systematic rational restructuring, self-control desensitisation, a combination of the two treatments or a waiting list control. Each of the three therapeutic groups showed significant decrements in anxiety post-treatment which were either maintained or improved upon at follow-up. Between-group comparisons showed that rational restructuring was more effective than desensitisation in reducing state anxiety, trait anxiety and irrational beliefs. Finally when compared to waiting list controls, rational restructuring was significantly more effective on a greater number of variables than desensitisation.

Butler et al. (1984) compared exposure to exposure plus anxiety management training with a waiting list control group. Anxiety management consisted of relaxation, distraction and rational self-talk techniques. Both treatment groups improved more than the waiting list group, and this improvement was maintained at six-month follow-up. At the end of treatment and at six-month follow-up the exposure plus anxiety management group had lower scores than the exposure group on both the Social Avoidance and Distress Scale and Fear of Negative Evaluation Scale (Watson & Friend, 1969). No patient in the exposure and anxiety management group requested further treatment within a year, whereas 40% of the exposure group did so.

Although Butler et al.'s results suggest that anxiety management facilitates exposure it is difficult to ascertain the precise component involved, although anecdotal data collected informally by the therapist before and after treatment, and reported by the authors, serves to shed some light on this issue. About half the patients in each group were using a recognisable anxiety management technique before treatment began; after treatment, use of distraction and relaxation techniques had doubled, but use of rational self-talk had increased more than five times, suggesting that this may be the effective ingredient of anxiety management training. As the authors comment, 'attention to cognitive factors may be important in the treatment of social phobia because negative evaluation of social behaviour is an important part of this disorder' (p. 649).

Others have attempted to match cognitively based treatments to patient characteristics. Thus studies by Fremouw & Zitter (1978), Shahar & Merbaum (1981) and McCann et al. (1987) with interpersonally anxious, speech anxious and socially anxious subjects respectively show some support for the notion that matching enhances treatment effectiveness. The former two studies suggest that people with strong physiological reactions do better with a treatment technique based upon relaxation, while rational restructuring is better suited for altering strong physiological perceptions and cognitive components. The latter study found that subjects who received rational restructuring showed improvement on self-report measures, while subjects who received behavioural rehearsal had the greatest treatment gains on behavioural measures.

In a further study Jerremalm *et al.* (1986a) classified subjects as physiological or cognitive reactors on the basis of heart rate measures taken during a social interaction test and cognitive reactions assessed immediately after the test. Within each category subjects were randomly assigned to a physiologically focused method (applied relaxation), a cognitively focused method (SIT) or a waiting list control group. For both treatments there were significant improvements on most measures. For the physiological reactors the two treatment groups did equally well on most measures (i.e. SIT was as effective as applied relaxation in reducing heart rate during the behavioural test). Among cognitive reactors the SIT group improved more than the relaxation group on four of the 11 measures. The authors suggest that the division of social phobics into cognitive and physiological reactors does not predict differential outcome with a physiologically and cognitively focused method. This corresponds with Mersch *et al.*'s failure to find increased treatment effectiveness when cognitive and behavioural treatments were applied to cognitive and behavioural reactors.

These negative results do not necessarily mean that patient characteristics are unrelated to the effects of treatment. The failure might be due in part to the difficulty of deciding on the appropriate cognitive measure with which to assess subjects. The measure used by Jerremalm *et al.* (1986a) was specifically devised by the authors, and psychometric data for the scale not presented. The question of what cognitions to measure, and when and how to assess them, is a general difficulty referred to in Chapter 1. The question of comparing such a self-report measure to direct physiological assessments was also discussed at that time. The authors may thus simply not have assessed the relevant cognitive parameters; as Mersch *et al.* note: 'Perhaps it is better to simply abandon the term "cognitive reactor" until further research has delineated specific cognitive types' (p. 432).

In this context it is interesting to note that Turner & Beidel (1985) suggest the existence of subtypes of non-clinically socially anxious individuals characterised by specific patterns of cognitions (as assessed by the Social Interaction Self-Statement Test) and physiological reactivity (systolic blood pressure). Both groups, however, were characterised by negative cognitions, with one group having a high level and the other a low level of physiological reactivity. Given that the vast majority of socially anxious subjects or socially phobic patients might be characterised by negative thoughts, the strategy of using a median split to divide patients into response categories (used by Jerremalm *et al.*, 1986a and by Mersch *et al.*,

1989) might understate the magnitude of negative cognitions for the 'low' scoring group.

In addition to difficulties associated with cognitive assessment, the assessment of social skills is not without its difficulties adding to the inherent problems of matching treatments to patients' specific deficits. An alternative to attempting to match treatments to individuals is to use treatments in combination.

Two studies reported by Mattick & Peters (1988) and Mattick *et al.* (1989) assessed the efficacy of cognitive restructuring (described by the authors as a combination of systematic rational restructuring, after Goldfried & Goldfried, 1975) and elements of RET, after Ellis (1962). In the first study 51 socially phobic patients were randomly assigned to one of two treatment conditions: either therapist-guided exposure or a combined treatment of therapist-guided exposure and rational restructuring. While there was significant improvement in both treatment conditions patients receiving the combined treatment showed greater improvement on actual behaviour and self-rated avoidance of the target phobic situation. At follow-up 24% of the combined group stated that they felt the need for additional treatment, whereas 47% of the exposure-only group asked for further treatment.

In the second study (Mattick *et al.*, 1989) 43 socially phobic subjects were randomly allocated to either a waiting list control group or one of three treatment conditions comprising exposure, cognitive restructuring without exposure or a combined exposure/cognitive restructuring group. In comparison to the exposure treatment the combined exposure and cognitive restructuring groups improved significantly on fear of negative evaluation and irrational beliefs immediately post-treatment, although this difference was less evident at three-month follow-up. On the behavioural avoidance test the exposure alone and exposure plus cognitive restructuring groups showed most post-treatment gains with only modest change shown by the cognitive restructuring group. At follow-up, however, the exposure-alone group had deteriorated while the cognitive-alone group had improved, with both groups now at a similar level but below that of the combined treatment group who had also shown modest gains since the end of treatment.

Interestingly both studies found that changes in fear of negative self-evaluation was most predictive of long-term improvement, supporting Butler's (1985) assertion that excessive concern over the opinion of others plays a major role in social phobia. Exposure-based treatments would clearly not address such attitudinal concerns, supporting the view that they might not be the most effective intervention for social fears. The view that socially phobic patients overestimate the probability of negative social outcomes is also supported by findings from a further small-scale treatment outcome study.

Lucock & Salkovskis (1988) treated eight socially phobic patients referred for social skills training with cognitive therapy techniques such as 'thought monitoring, reality testing (behavioural experiments), activity scheduling, challenging and looking for alternatives to negative automatic thoughts' (p. 299). Following treatment, which involved eight weekly group sessions, the treated group in comparison to four waiting list control subjects showed specific changes in appraisal with decreased social avoidance and distress scores and ratings, indicating that they believed the probability of negative social outcomes to be less likely.

The most effective treatment may thus involve a multicomponent cognitive–behavioural treatment package similar to that described by Heimberg and his colleagues (Heimberg *et al.*, 1985, 1987). The six components described by Heimberg *et al.* (1987) involve: (a) providing patients with a cognitive–behavioural explanation of social phobia and a rationale for treatment effectiveness; (b) through the use of structured exercises patients are taught to identify, analyse and question problematic cognitions; (c) during treatment groups patients are exposed to simulations of anxiety-provoking situations; (d) using cognitive restructuring procedures patients are taught to control their maladaptive thinking before, during and after simulated exposures; (e) patients are given homework assignments for *in vivo* exposure to situations confronted during the exposure situations; (f) patients are taught a self-administered cognitive restructuring routine for use before and after completion of exposure assignments.

In one study using an earlier version of this treatment package with seven socially phobic patients, Heimberg *et al.* (1985) report a significant reduction on all anxiety self-report measures, as well as demonstrating significant improvement in behavioural performance and quality of performance during behavioural simulations. Several patients also showed a decrease in heart rate during the behavioural simulation. Gains were maintained at six-month follow-up for six of the seven patients.

Heimberg *et al.* (1990b) have presented a more recent evaluation of a similar cognitive–behavioural treatment consisting of exposure to simulated phobic events, cognitive restructuring of maladaptive thoughts and homework for self-directed exposure and cognitive restructuring between sessions. Forty-nine socially phobic patients were assigned to either the cognitive–behavioural treatment or a credible control consisting of lecture–discussion and group support. Although both groups improved on a number of measures in no case did the scores for the control group show significantly greater improvement than those of the cognitive–

behavioural group; the cognitive–behavioural group were also more likely to have maintained treatment gains at six-month follow-up.)

Cognitively based techniques do seem to be related to positive outcomes, although multicomponent treatments do not allow for identification of the effectiveness of particular ingredients, and the precise mechanisms by which cognitive interventions might operate are not clear. Whether cognitive strategies reduce anxiety directly or whether they facilitate exposure which subsequently facilitates anxiety reduction remains to be seen. Many cognitively based interventions have involved an element of exposure, meaning that it is not possible to attribute change to the cognitive component *per se*. Examining the contribution of cognitive interventions in comparison to other treatments, and the relative contribution of the cognitive component of multicomponent treatments, are clearly questions for future research.

SUMMARY

Social anxiety, as trepidation and concern about social encounters, is a very common and distressing condition reported by as many as 40% of the general population. In its more extreme form social phobia, or almost total avoidance of social situations, is less common, with prevalence rates of about 2% of the general population. Theoretical perspectives have suggested that social anxiety may result from aversive learning experiences, a lack of social skills or a particular pattern of thinking relating to over-concern with negative evaluation. In line with theoretical proposals relating to anxiety in general it seems more appropriate to adopt a multi-component hierarchical conceptualisation of social anxiety and social phobia. This necessitates taking account of: (i) biological vulnerability which might include individual differences in self-consciousness and hence a tendency to be over-aware of bodily sensations and the evaluations of one's performance by others (i.e. a tendency to selectively perceive and interpret cues as threatening to one's sense of self); (ii) the fact that this is reflected in a particular set of behavioural, cognitive and physiological expectancies about the outcome of social encounters; and (iii) the fact that this in turn relates to a particular pattern of responding in relation to social events. The latter two elements are interactive and not sequential in nature.

While socially phobic and socially anxious individuals can be recognised by others as more anxious and less skilful than their non-socially anxious counterparts there appears to be little evidence that they are necessarily deficient in social skills. There may well be subgroups of socially phobic and socially anxious individuals some of whom lack social skills and some of whom do not. The former may correspond to those categorised as avoidant personality disorder within DSM-III-R while the latter are socially phobic. This may reflect the dispositional–situational dimensions suggested by social psychologists in relation to notions of dispositional constructs such as shyness and situational constructs such as audience anxiety. While such constructs are clearly related, the extreme severity endpoint of shyness may relate to avoidant personality disorder while the extreme endpoint of audience anxiety may relate to the specific forms of social phobia referred to in DSM-III-R. Some interactive element may reflect the generalised social phobia category.

There seems to be clearer evidence that social anxiety is characterised by a particular pattern of thinking relating to fear of negative self-evaluation. Socially anxious individuals are more likely to generate negative cognitions in stressful encounters, underestimate their own level of social skill in social situations and are more likely to recall negative encounters, suggesting that cognitive interventions may prove to be effective therapeutically. There does seem to be evidence from intervention studies that this is indeed the case, although there is also some evidence for the efficacy of both exposure- and skills-based interventions. One possibility is that the latter two interventions are effective because they have an exposure-based element in common, although all three interventions may involve some element of cognitive change which is incidental to the main treatment component in the case of exposure- and skills-based interventions.

Chapter 4

Panic

DEFINITION AND PREVALENCE

Discussion of anxiety attacks and panic has a lengthy history (see Baker, 1989, for a review). Freud's (1894) description of anxiety attacks closely parallels the current description of panic. He refers to anxiousness that can break through into consciousness, thus provoking an anxiety attack (i.e. anxiety neurosis precedes anxiety attacks). Further landmark research by Klein (e.g. 1964) reversed this notion, proposing that panic attacks appear spontaneously and that after a series of such unpleasant experiences secondary anticipatory anxiety develops between panic attacks. Klein further proposed that avoidance of situations where an attack is likely to occur results from anticipation of panic attacks, i.e. agoraphobic avoidance develops as a consequence of panic attacks. Panic disorder only emerged as a distinct psychiatric entity with the publication of DSM-III (1980). The characteristic features are described as discrete periods of intense fear or discomfort and at least four of the following symptoms which appear during each panic attack: dyspnoea (shortness of breath); palpitations or accelerated heart rate; chest pain or discomfort; choking or smothering sensations; dizziness, unsteady feelings or faintness; trembling or shaking; paraesthesias (tingling sensations); sweating and hot-and-cold flushes; fear of dying, going crazy or doing something uncontrollable. Recognition was also given to the fact that avoidance behaviour is frequently associated with panic attacks; if this avoidance is extreme then the term agoraphobia with panic attacks was used.

With the publication of DSM-III-R (1987) three specific categories of agoraphobia and panic disorder were recognised: panic disorder with agoraphobia, panic disorder without agoraphobia and agoraphobia without a history of panic disorder. DSM-III-R also states that the panic attack: (a) must be unexpected, that is not occurring immediately before or on exposure to a situation that almost always causes anxiety, and (b) must not be triggered by situations in which the person is the focus of others' attention.)As a result of these revisions in classification there has inevitably been a surge of interest in panic attacks with the publication of a number of recent monographs (Baker, 1989; Rachman & Maser, 1988), treatment manuals (Barlow & Cerny, 1988; Clark & Salkovskis, 1991), theoretical reviews (McNally, 1990) and reviews of treatment outcome (Mattick *et al.*, 1990; Michelson & Marchione, 1991).

Epidemiological studies investigating the prevalence of panic disorder have also recently appeared. The Epidemiological Catchment Area Survey (Karno *et al.*, 1987) using DSM-III criteria obtained from the Diagnostic Interview Schedule reported a 1.5% lifetime prevalence rate for panic disorder across four sites in the USA (Los Angeles, Baltimore, New Haven and St Louis). As DSM-III criteria were employed, panic and agoraphobia were classified separately; combining the rates for panic and agoraphobia the prevalence increases to 5.4%. A summary of the five-site ECA sample provided a rate of 0.8% for six-month prevalence (Weissman *et al.*, 1986) and 1.6% for a lifetime diagnosis of panic disorder (Regier, Burke & Burke, 1990). A telephone survey of 410 residents of the greater Houston metropolitan area found a 0.8% one-year prevalence for panic disorder using DSM-III criteria (Salge, Beck & Logan, 1988); 14.1% were classified as having infrequent (at least one) panic attack. Similar rates (12% and 9.3% respectively) for at least one panic attack within their lifetime are reported for a population sample in Munich (Wittchen, 1986) and from a survey of over 2000 US college students (Telch, Lucas & Nelson, 1989b); in the latter study 2.6% of the sample met DSM-III-R criteria for panic disorder. Other studies have also found that 2–3% of general populations report a sufficient frequency of panic to meet DSM-III criteria for panic disorder (Norton, Dorward & Cox, 1986; Norton *et al.*, 1985).

There is also some evidence that life events are associated with panic attack onset. Pollard, Pollard & Corn (1989) found that the prevalence of life events in the year preceding panic onset was greater for panic patients than for matched controls over a similar time period. In a further survey 72% of 162 panic patients with and without agoraphobic avoidance reported that their initial panic attacks were associated with a recognised stressor (Craske *et al.*, 1990a). Pollard *et al.* report that 62% of the life events reported by their sample involved loss, separation or conflict, while the comparable figure reported by Craske *et al.* was 38.8%. However, this difference may be due to the different questioning procedures and methods for categorising stressors used in the two studies. In contrast to the above findings Rapee, Litwin & Barlow (1990) report no differences in the number of reported life events for a panic with an agoraphobic group compared with an anxiety disorder group or non-anxious controls. However, in comparison to non-anxious subjects both panic and anxiety groups rated their life events as having a significantly greater negative impact. The frequency of life events may therefore not be peculiar to panic or anxiety, and the negative perception of such events may be a general feature of psychopathology.

Non-clinical panic

Evidence suggests that panic attacks are not limited to those presenting for treatment, but are occasionally experienced by a high percentage of adults. Prevalence figures range from a low of 3% of a sample of community residents who had experienced at least one panic attack in the last six months (von Korff, Eaton & Keyl, 1985) to a high of 59% of a sample of 136 undergraduate students who had experienced a panic attack within the past year (Margraf & Ehlers, 1988). An even higher figure of 63.3%, who had experienced at least one panic attack in the past year, has been obtained from a sample of 660 adolescents (aged 13–18 years). However, for only 5.4% of the total sample were the panic attacks described as severe; for 75% of those reporting panic attacks, severity was only moderate, with the attack described as mildly distressing (Macaulay & Kleinknecht, 1989). Figures intermediate to the high and low estimates are those most consistently reported in the literature. Norton *et al.* (1985), for example, found that 35% of people attending evening university courses had experienced one or more panic attacks in the past year, a figure closely replicated in studies by Norton, Dorward & Cox (1986a) and Brown & Cash (1989).

In a review of 23 separate studies of 18 627 subjects surveyed, Norton, Cox & Malan (1990) report that the average proportion of subjects reporting one or more panic attacks was 27.6%. As they point out, the variable frequencies obtained appear to be a function of three factors: the type of survey method used (questionnaires or structured interviews); the definition of panic attacks (based upon number of symptoms or screening questions) and the population sampled (university students or general population samples).

The way panic definition can influence prevalence rates is illustrated in the study by Brown & Cash (1989). When subjects were given a more detailed description of panic attacks the prevalence rate was reduced from 37.1% to 25.7%, a finding replicated in a further study by the same authors (Brown & Cash, 1990). The higher figures obtained from questionnaire studies may thus overestimate the extent of the problem, although even the more modest figures suggest that panic attacks are commonly experienced within the general population.

Studies of non-clinical panickers suggest several similarities with those identified as panic disorder patients. Many similar symptoms are reported, although clinical populations inevitably report more symptoms and greater severity of symptoms. However, symptoms such as dizziness, dyspnoea, fear of going crazy and fear of losing control, commonly reported by clinical populations (Barlow *et al.*, 1985), are reported with relative infrequency by non-clinical panickers (Norton *et al.*, 1985). Fear of panic attack reoccurrence, common in clinical populations, is also far less common in non-clinical populations (reported by 91% and 22% respectively in a study by Telch *et al.*, 1989b). In a further study of non-panickers, non-clinical panickers, and clinical panickers, Rapee, Ancis & Barlow (1988a) found that although physiological sensations characteristic of panic attacks were commonly experienced by non-clinical subjects the main distinguishing feature for panic disorder patients was that they were likely to respond with anxiety to the sensations. In a similar comparison of clinical and non-clinical panickers on a variety of measures Cox, Endler & Swinson (1991) conclude that 'in general, the results of the present study support the existence of a continuum' (p. 32).

As Norton *et al.* (1990) note, the difference between clinical and non-clinical panickers is possibly due to the difference in meaning or importance that the attacks have for people in the different groups, with non-panickers, non-clinical panickers and panickers lying along a continuum of catastrophising about bodily sensations experienced. This supposition would be in line with cognitive theories of panic which suggest that the evaluation of somatic symptoms experienced during a panic attack is central in the development of the disorder.

The notion of a continuum in relation to panic is also supported by findings that non-clinical panickers typically score midway between non-panickers and clinical panickers on general measures of anxiety, depression and anxiety sensitivity (Norton *et al.*, 1990). The latter construct refers to a belief that anxiety has undesirable consequences apart from its immediate unpleasantness (Reiss & McNally, 1985). It is assessed with the Anxiety Sensitivity Index (Reiss *et al.*, 1986) a 16-item measure developed to assess a person's beliefs about the social and somatic consequences of anxiety symptoms. The scale is factorially independent of other anxiety measures (Peterson & Heilbronner, 1987) with evidence for the validity of the scale as a measure of fear and anxiety (Maller & Reiss, 1987). Several studies (e.g. McNally & Lorenz, 1987) have shown that panic disorder patients obtain high scores on the scale and that non-clinical panickers obtain higher scores than non-panickers (e.g. Brown & Cash, 1989; Telch *et al.*, 1989b).

The continuity hypothesis

The evidence for a panic continuum extending to normals raises issues concerning the relationship of panic to general anxiety. Some have argued for an anxiety–panic continuum with panic merely representing an extreme form of anxiety (i.e. quantitatively distinct); others suggest that panic is in some way qualitatively distinct from general anxiety. In this latter instance a normal–clinical panic continuum would be distinct from a normal–clinical generalised anxiety continuum.

The assumption that panic is a qualitatively different state from generalised, chronic or anticipatory anxiety has formed the central tenet of biologically based models of panic which assume some disordered physiological mechanism requiring appropriate pharmacological correction (Lesser & Rubin, 1986). Klein (1964) was a forerunner of such a notion based upon his observation that the drug imipramine reduced or eliminated panic attacks but had little effect on chronic levels of anticipatory anxiety. However, a number of different pharmacological agents have since been used in treating panic.

The possibility that panic might be qualitatively different from extreme anxiety also comes from evidence that panic disorder and generalised anxiety disorder show different patterns of childhood and family characteristics (Torgersen, 1986) and that the two disorders follow a different course (Breier, Charney & Heninger, 1985). Such evidence could, however, be consistent with a quantitative distinction between conditions, and as Hallam (1989) notes, 'care must be taken to ensure that differences between PD and GAD are not simply an elaboration and consequence of the criteria to select the groups' (p. 98). (The distinction between panic and generalised anxiety is discussed further in Chapter 6.)

It is also possible that a panic continuum extends to all anxiety disorders, studies having found that panic attacks are frequently reported by all anxiety disorder patients. Barlow et al. (1985) evaluated the nature and extent of panic in 108 patients diagnosed variously as agoraphobia with panic, social phobia, simple phobia, panic disorder, generalised anxiety disorder, obsessive–compulsive disorder and depression. At least 83% within each category admitted to having had a panic attack, and almost all these panic attacks were associated with four of the 12 DSM-III panic criteria. Also, few differences emerged between groups in panic symptomatology (patients in the simple phobia, social phobia and generalised anxiety groups had less frequent attacks; in relation to diagnostic symptoms, patients in the social phobia, simple phobia and depression groups reported less severe dizziness than panic patients).

Evidence suggesting that panic might be an extreme form of generalised anxiety is obtained from physiological data. Taylor et al. (1986) found that heart rate averaged 108.2 beats per minute during panic but 89.2 during anticipatory anxiety for these episodes monitored during day-to-day activities. A similar pattern of results is reported by Freedman et al. (1985), who compared heart rate recorded during panic attacks and during states of anxiety that were matched in terms of intensity but were not labelled as panic.

The possibility that panic is an extreme manifestation of certain anxiety characteristics is suggested by a study of experimentally induced panic (Holt & Andrews, 1989a). These authors report higher somatic ratings for panic patients followed by socially phobic, then generalised anxiety patients and finally normal controls. This finding is consistent with data from questionnaire studies suggesting that while there are few differences between generalised anxiety and panic patients on measures of cognitive anxiety, general anxiety or personality, panic patients score significantly higher on measures of somatic anxiety (Anderson, Noyes & Crowe, 1984; Barlow et al., 1984; Borden & Turner, 1989; Hoen-Saric, 1982). Findings such as these have led Barlow and Turner and their colleagues (e.g. Barlow, 1988; Barlow & Cerny, 1988; Barlow & Craske, 1989; Borden & Turner, 1989) to conclude that panic is distinguishable from other anxiety disorders while noting that the qualitative/quantitative issue is not resolved. Thus Barlow (1988) states that 'panic is a unique event distinguishable from generalized anxiety on the basis of presenting characteristics' while maintaining that 'it is not possible to infer a fundamental qualitative difference' (p. 96). Clearly the qualitative/quantitative distinction is a topic which will occupy the endeavours of much future research, remaining an unresolved issue at present.

Spontaneous panic

A defining feature of panic attacks according to DSM-III-R is that they are unexpected, i.e. do not occur immediately before or on exposure to a situation that almost always causes anxiety. In contrast, panics associated with specific anxiety disorders are assumed to be directly triggered by the cues associated with that fear (i.e. exposure to social settings for social phobics, etc.). As mentioned, there appear to be only minor differences between the two types of panic (e.g. Barlow et al., 1985). In fact, it seems appropriate to recognise that both external and internal cues can act as panic triggers. Thus, perception of changes in somatic sensations may act as an internal cue for panic patients while other anxiety disorders have clearly definable external cues. As Street, Craske & Barlow (1989) comment: 'a "cued" panic is one perceived by the individual as being clearly associated with an *internal* or *external* stimulus' (p. 189; italics in original).

Implicit in such an assumption is that interoceptive or bodily sensation fears are specific to panic attacks and do not occur in non-anxious controls or other anxiety disorders. In a questionnaire study assessing how fearful they were of 14 bodily sensations van den Hout *et al.* (1987) found that panic patients were significantly more fearful than a non-anxious control group and a mixed group of non-anxious neurotic controls. Chambless & Gracely (1989) have also found that fear of somatic sensations, as measured by the Body Sensation Questionnaire (Chambless *et al.*, 1984) was greater among agoraphobic patients than among other anxious or depressed patients. However, fear of bodily sensations is not necessarily specific to panic (cf. fear of blushing and social anxiety, Edelmann, 1990a,b, 1991). Future research could be usefully directed towards further evaluation of the nature and specificity of fear of bodily sensations in relation to anxiety disorders.

A further dimension, suggested by Rachman & Levitt (1985), is the extent to which fear is expected or predicted on exposure to a given situation. In a study of student claustrophobics, of 67 episodes of panic experienced upon exposure to a small, dark room, 50 were correctly predicted and 17 were unexpected. Those who experienced unexpectedly high levels of fear tended to overpredict their level of fear/panic experienced upon re-exposure to the same situation. These results were subsequently replicated with 20 panic patients (Rachman, Lopatka & Levitt, 1988b). It is thus possible to distinguish between cued–uncued and expected–unexpected panics as orthogonal dimensions.

These dimensions were investigated in a recent study by Street, Craske & Barlow (1989). Forty-four panic patients (18 of whom were also moderately to severely agoraphobic) rated their expectancy of panic and presence of external panic cues. Of these panics, 70% were rated as cued–expected and only one panic as uncued–expected. The cued–unexpected and uncued–unexpected comprised approximately 15% of all panic attacks each. It seems, then, that patients perceive their panics as predictable and as more likely to be triggered by external stimuli than might have been assumed. Further, there were few reported differences between the panic groups in terms of somatic sensations or cognitions. However, consistent with the findings of Rachman and his colleagues a far greater number of subjects experienced an increase in the probability of experiencing future panic following unexpected panic in comparison to those experiencing expected panic (64% vs 14%). Although subjects changed their expectations of experiencing a panic, those with unexpected panic remained less sure that they would experience another panic than those who had experienced an expected panic; i.e. expected panic was associated with a higher expectation of future panic in similar circumstances. In order to address factors influencing the likely development of future panic attacks research could usefully be directed towards monitoring change in expectancy of panic, anxiety and perception of panic cues.

THEORETICAL PERSPECTIVES

For many years panic was considered mainly from a biological perspective, largely as a result of research by Klein and his colleagues starting in the 1960s (see for example Klein, 1964, 1980, 1981). This was initially based upon the finding that the tricyclic antidepressant drug imipramine suppressed the anxiety attacks of agoraphobic patients but did not act directly on anticipatory anxiety or avoidance behaviour. Benzodiazepines and other minor tranquillisers, however, were effective in reducing anticipatory anxiety but not panic attacks.

The fact that a wide range of biochemical agents induce panic has also been used as supportive evidence for a biological explanation of panic. Biochemical agents which have been used include sodium lactate infusion (see reviews by Ehlers, Margraf & Roth, 1986; Margraf, Ehlers & Roth, 1986a; Margraf & Ehlers, 1989 and Ley, 1988a), carbon dioxide inhalation (e.g. van den Hout & Griez, 1984), caffeine (e.g. Charney, Heninger & Jatlow, 1985) and oral or intravenous yohimbine (e.g. Charney, Heninger & Breier, 1984). The assumption is that panic patients, because of some biological, genetically determined dysfunction, will respond to such physiological challenges with panic attacks while controls rarely or never do. Margraf & Ehlers (1989) provide an extensive critique of studies investigating the experimental induction of panic, suggesting that the results from such research do not provide evidence for biologically based models. They conclude that:

> Although the response to lactate infusion and similar challenges has reasonable validity as a model for panic attacks, the anxiety observed in these models on the average is only moderately intense. No psychophysiological or biochemical variable studied so far is a necessary or sufficient condition for panic. Control subjects show responses that are qualitatively similar to those of panic patients (p. 164).

While the involvement of some biological events and processes is inevitable (e.g. individual differences in autonomic reactivity such that panic patients are physiologically more vulnerable to panic attacks), emerging psychological explanations offer a challenge to purely biological conceptualisations. As Clark (1986) points out, the wide range of biological panic-provoking agents used have little in common other than their propensity to produce bodily sensations. The effects of provocation experiments may well be mediated .by psychological factors, a possibility suggested by a number of studies. For example, van der Molen et al. (1986) administered lactate to two groups of non-clinical subjects provided with differing information. One group was told that the lactate would produce unpleasant sensations similar to those experienced when anxious; the other group were told that lactate would produce feelings of pleasant tension, such as those experienced during sports. The former group reported considerable anxiety while the latter reported little or no change in anxiety ratings during the lactate administration.

The fact that instructions can influence degree of anxiety and panic experienced has also been demonstrated in a clinical group by Rapee, Mattick & Murell (1986). They found that a group of panic patients who received explicit information regarding the source of unusual somatic sensations during inhalations of carbon dioxide/carbon gas mixture reported fewer catastrophic cognitions, a reduced degree of panic, and less similarity to natural panic attacks than a control group not receiving such information. Extending this study Sanderson, Rapee & Barlow (1989) provided half a group of 20 panic patients with the illusion that they could control the amount of CO_2-enriched air they were receiving. All subjects were instructed that illumination of a light directly in front of them would signal that they could decrease the amount of CO_2—for half the subjects the light was illuminated the entire time, while for the remainder the light was never illuminated. Unbeknown to the subjects the control dial was ineffective and all subjects experienced full CO_2. In spite of this the subjects who thought they were in control reported less symptoms of less intensity, less subjective anxiety, fewer catastrophic cognitions and were less likely to report a panic attack.

Psychological variables can clearly influence responses to panic-provoking agents in both non-clinical and clinical subjects. Indeed, three recent psychological theories—the hyperventilation interpretation, the cognitive model and the interoceptive conditioning model—have emphasised in varying degree the part played by interpretation of the bodily sensations in the generation of acute panic attacks (e.g. Beck, 1988; Clark, 1986, 1988; Ehlers & Margraf, 1989; Ehlers, Margraf & Roth, 1988b; Ley, 1985a,b, 1987a,b, 1988a,b, 1989; Margraf & Ehlers 1989; Margraf, Ehlers & Roth, 1986a,b; Ottaviani & Beck, 1987; Salkovskis, 1988a; van den Hout, 1988; van den Hout et al., 1987). It is towards such explanations that the present discussion is directed.

Hyperventilation formulations

The hyperventilation model posited by Ley (see also Lum, 1976) suggests that panic results from dysfunctional breathing patterns which cause chronic hyperventilation. The theory maintains that stress-induced arousal produces an increase in the volume of air breathed so that respiration exceeds metabolic demands. As a result body tissue suffers excess loss of CO_2, the direct result of which is an increase in blood pH and a decrease in arterial CO_2 tension. The increased blood pH reduces the amount of oxygen that haemoglobin can release to body tissue (hypoxia) while reduced CO_2 in the blood reduces the calibre of the arteries, thus impeding the flow of blood to body tissue (ischaemia). In order to compensate for the decreased CO_2 and increased pH the heart has to beat with greater rapidity and power. Heart palpitations, shortness of breath and breathing difficulties follow, with intensity of symptoms a direct consequence of the degree of hyperventilation.

As with many chemical agents, therefore, hyperventilation can clearly induce symptoms associated with panic. As Ley (1988a) points out, however, it is important to distinguish 'between the phenomenal panic *attack* and the experience of the *symptoms* . . . the symptoms can occur without reported fear . . . the attack is defined by the reported experience' (p. 8; italics in original). Indeed, the fact that hyperventilation produces symptoms of panic but not a full-blown panic attack has been shown in a number of studies (e.g. Gorman *et al.*, 1984; Beck & Scott, 1988) with some individuals actually finding the experiences enjoyable (Clark & Hemsley, 1982). This necessitates the implication of additional causal factors in determining the nature of panic attacks.

In this respect a number of further assumptions are crucial within Ley's formulation. The first assumption is that it is the misattribution of the sudden, unexpected and unaccountable somatic consequences of hyperventilation which result in the fear experienced in panic attacks. As Clark (1988) suggests, hyperventilation is only likely to produce panic if the bodily sensations which it induces are perceived as unpleasant and interpreted in a catastrophic manner. The importance of symptom interpretation is illustrated in a study by Salkovskis & Clark (1990). Non-clinical subjects were provided with a positive or negative interpretation of the sensations produced by equivalent amounts of voluntary hyperventilation. Subjects in the positive interpretation condition experienced hyperventilation as pleasant, and subjects in the negative interpretation condition experienced hyperventilation as unpleasant, even though both groups experienced similar bodily sensations and did not differ in their prior expectations of the affective consequences of hyperventilation.

Interpretation of sensations is thus likely to differentiate those who just experience the symptoms from those who experience an attack. Other related aspects concern the relative degree of safety and control envisaged by subjects. In one study which illustrates this point, Rapee (1986) recorded physiological changes from panickers under conditions of hyperventilation. Although the symptoms reported were very similar to those reported during naturally occurring panics, none of the subjects reported an actual panic. As Rapee notes: 'a number of subjects reported that although physical symptoms were the same, they did not panic because they knew what was causing the symptoms and felt in a safe environment' (p. 26). It seems that hyperventilation, like pharmacological provoking agents, is not sufficient on its own to produce panic attacks. In line with Ley's (1988a) supposition Rapee suggests that misinterpretation of sensations may mediate panic.

The second assumption is that the fear generated by the misattribution of the somatic consequences of hyperventilation activates the autonomic nervous system in preparation for fight or flight. As ANS responses include increased heart rate and respiration the result will be further sensations of palpitations in addition to further decreases in CO_2 and increases in pH. As a result, symptoms will quickly intensify. As Ley points out, if this process continued unabated death or fainting would occur, yet panic victims do not die and few faint. Termination of a panic attack according to Ley occurs when CO_2 levels drop below the level necessary to stimulate the respiratory reflex centre of the brain, thus slowing involuntary respiration. A recent report suggests that even when CO_2 levels are maintained at a constantly low level during extreme hyperventilation panic symptoms decline (van den Hout et al., 1990). The authors suggest that habituation or local physiological changes may both play a role in the reduction of symptoms.

The assumption that panic attacks result from the misattribution of the sensations produced by hyperventilation is not, however, without its difficulties. A number of studies suggest that panic attacks are not always associated with fearful cognitions (e.g. Rachman, Levitt & Lopatka, 1987; Rachman, Lopatka & Levitt, 1988b) and that fearful cognitions sometimes do not occur until after the fearful event of the panic attack (Wolpe & Rowan, 1988). This has led Ley to revise his original hyperventilation thesis, suggesting that the fear experienced during a hyperventilatory panic attack is caused by severe dyspnoea (difficulty breathing) under circumstances in which the person feels unable to terminate the attack (i.e. lack of control) (Ley, 1989). Although a number of lines of evidence lend some degree of support to both the original and revised hyperventilation hypothesis there is also contrary evidence for the supposition.

Supportive evidence is derived from the fact that hyperventilation symptoms are reported more frequently by patients with agoraphobia or panic than by generalised anxiety patients (e.g. Hoehn-Saric, 1982; Rapee, 1985a). Second, some studies suggest that agoraphobia and panic patients show lower levels of partial pressure of arterial CO_2 while at rest than do generalised anxiety patients (Rapee, 1986) or non-anxious subjects (e.g. Salkovskis et al., 1986b). Thirdly, there is a degree of resemblance between the sensations associated with panic and those produced by voluntary hyperventilation (e.g. Clark & Hemsley, 1982). Fourthly, treatment approaches aimed at breathing retraining in panic patients have met with some degree of success (e.g. Clark, Salkovskis & Chalkely, 1985).

There is also, however, evidence contrary to some of these propositions. For example, Beck & Scott (1988) found that although both frequent and infrequent panickers showed increases in skin conductance and heart rate in response to voluntary hyperventilation, contrary to predictions the infrequent panickers reported greater overall distress. As the authors themselves note, this finding is counterintuitive, particularly in relation to an interpretation of sensations model.

In two further studies Woods *et al*. (1986) failed to find significant differences between agoraphobic patients and normals on measures of resting partial pressure of arterial CO_2, while Holt & Andrews (1989b) failed to find any difference between agoraphobia, panic, generalised anxiety and social phobia patients and normal controls on the same measure. The latter authors also note in a further report of this study (Holt & Andrews, 1989a) that in response to voluntary hyperventilation or inhalation of 5% CO_2 in air all subjects, irrespective of diagnosis, showed heightened ratings of somatic symptoms and degree of worry, fearfulness and nervousness in comparison to normal controls.

Interestingly, however, Holt & Andrews (1989b) report that the panic and agoraphobia patients reported higher ratings of perceived hyperventilatory symptoms than the social phobia/generalised anxiety patients, who in turn reported higher ratings than the normal controls. In addition the degree of perceived symptoms was not related to measures of partial pressure of arterial CO_2 but was highly related to measures of anxiety. Further, Holt & Andrews (1989a) report that during the provocation test fears of impending doom were the only aspect of the panic reaction which separated panic/agoraphobic patients from the social phobic/generalised anxiety groups. From these two sets of findings the authors conclude that 'the greatest differences between groups lay in their *perception* of the effects of the experimental procedures rather than in the degree to which the procedures reduced their pCO_2 levels' (1989b, p. 458) and 'Cognitions appeared to be the only discriminator between panic and non-panic patients' (1989a, p. 259). Taken together, these results suggest that hyperventilation *per se* is insufficient on its own to produce panic attacks. As Holt & Andrews (1989a) conclude, 'the criteria for a panic attack should emphasize three elements: a sudden attack of fear, the perception of distressing somatic anxiety symptoms and, as a separate category, the expectation of catastrophic outcome' (p. 260). In a review of hyperventilation and panic attacks Kenardy, Oei & Evans (1990) similarly conclude that 'in summary, hyperventilation provides a plausible model for the physiological processes that underlie panic attacks but requires the incorporation of a cognitive component to explain panic attacks' (p. 266). Catastrophic misinterpretation of bodily sensations forms a central feature of the cognitive model of panic.

Cognitive theory of panic

Several alternative yet complementary cognitive theories of panic have been developed which share as their central assumption the notion that people who experience such panics have an enduring tendency to interpret bodily sensations in a catastrophic fashion. Thus sensations normally involved in anxiety reactions (e.g. breathlessness, palpitations) are perceived as more threatening than they are in reality (e.g. evidence of impending cessation of breathing or a heart attack). This interpretation results in further, anxiety-induced bodily sensations which fuel the catastrophic interpretation in a vicious cycle resulting in a panic attack.

Margraf, Ehlers and their colleagues (e.g. Ehlers & Margraf, 1989; Ehlers et al., 1988b; Margraf & Ehlers, 1989; Margraf, Ehlers & Roth, 1986a,b) have proposed a psychophysiological model of panic incorporating a complex interaction between perceived control, available coping resources, internal and external panic cues and threat appraisals. This is consistent with multicomponent models of emotion discussed previously. Three central elements of the model involve physiological or cognitive changes consequent upon any one of a number of possible causes (e.g. physical exercise, situational stressors, emotional responses); perception of these changes by the person; and interpretation of these bodily or cognitive changes as threatening. The central theme then involves the interpretation of bodily sensations as frightening or dangerous.

As Clark et al. (1988) note, there are two further consequences which result from catastrophically interpreting bodily sensations. First is the tendency to be hypervigilant to bodily sensations, noticing sensations others may be unaware of. Secondly, patients may engage in subtle (not necessarily agoraphobic) avoidance to maintain negative beliefs (such as avoiding exercise in response to palpitations with the belief that this has prevented a heart attack; Salkovskis, 1988a).

Such cognitively based models can account for both panic attacks subsequent to anxiety and panic attacks which occur 'out of the blue'. In the former case panic may result from catastrophic interpretation of sensations consequent upon anxiety either prompted by specific situations (e.g. supermarket) or general worrying events; in the latter case panic is prompted by misinterpretation of bodily sensations caused by innocuous events (e.g. drinking coffee) or by a different emotional state (e.g. excitement). Although this has clear parallels with the 'fear of fear' model (Goldstein & Chambless, 1978) discussed in the subsequent chapter, one major difference noted by Clark (1988), and also acknowledged by Chambless *et al.* (1990) is that in the fear-of-fear hypothesis panic must always be triggered by an anxiety response while the model developed by Clark and his colleagues also allows for misinterpretation of sensations triggered by innocuous events.

Indeed there is considerable evidence that not everyone is likely to interpret bodily sensations catastrophically. For example, Beitman and his colleagues have documented cases of non-fearful panic attacks (see Kushner & Beitman, 1990, for a recent review). These individuals meet DSM-III or DSM-III-R criteria for panic attacks while current attacks do not include any cognitive panic symptoms. Kushner & Beitman suggest that such cases occur with varying prevalence of between 20% and 40% in medical populations with negative medical findings (primary care, cardiology, neurology) with the possibility that non-fearful panic attacks occur in non-clinical panickers. Such cases appear to manifest somatic and/or behavioural characteristics of panic but not self-report/cognitive characteristics (cf. concordance/discordance of fear responses, Rachman & Hodgson, 1974).

One factor suggested by several studies as a characteristic determining the likelihood that an individual will engage in catastrophic misinterpretation of bodily sensations is anxiety sensitivity (i.e. fears of anxiety symptoms that are based on beliefs that these symptoms have harmful consequences; Reiss *et al.*, 1986). Anxiety sensitivity is strongly associated with panic disorder (Rapee, Ancis & Barlow, 1988a), although this relationship is not unique. Following hyperventilation, anxiety sensitivity has been found to be related to more intense hyperventilation and higher levels of subjective anxiety in college students (Holloway & McNally, 1987) even if they have never experienced a spontaneous panic attack (Donnell & McNally, 1989). In addition, high anxiety sensitivity college students have an excess of first-degree relatives who had experienced panic (Donnell & McNally, 1990). One possibility then is that in response to usual bodily sensations 'preexisting beliefs about the harmfulness of such sensations may predispose individuals to interpret them catastrophically and thereby panic' (McNally 1990, p. 408). Given that some people are more prone than others to interpret bodily sensations catastrophically, a number of further assumptions are incorporated within the cognitive model of panic:

1. Bodily sensations should be identifiable as preceding panic, i.e. it is the perception of the symptoms which produces panic.

2. Panic patients should be more likely to interpret bodily sensations as dangerous. Thus catastrophic misinterpretations of bodily symptoms will predominate particularly during panic attacks.
3. Treatment packages which aim to modify a patient's misinterpretations of bodily sensations should be effective in treating panic attacks. As detailed subsequently, a number of studies based upon this rationale have met with apparent success.

There is now an accumulating body of empirical work evaluating the above propositions, much of which has produced results consistent with the cognitively based model of panic; this has been reviewed by Clark (1988), Clark et al. (1988) and Margraf & Ehlers (1989).

1. The perception of bodily sensations precedes panic onset

A number of studies using structured interviews to elicit subjective information about the phenomenology of panic suggest that patients themselves perceive panic onset as a response to the perception of bodily sensations. Hibbert (1984), after interviewing 24 patients, comments that 'the ideational content in those experiencing panic attacks can be understood as a reaction to the somatic symptoms, a connection insisted upon by all but 2 of the patients' (p. 622). Ottaviani & Beck (1987) interviewed 30 patients with panic disorder and identified ideation centred on themes of physical, mental or behavioural catastrophes: they further report that a misattribution of a physical sensation triggered panic in all their patients. However, Zucker et al. (1989) only partially replicated these results. They found that although more panic patients than controls reported thoughts centred on fears of losing control and shame when anxious, most panic patients reported that feelings of anxiety preceded anxious thoughts. These findings imply that faulty cognitions may not be the initial event in a panic attack. Indeed, the authors suggest that anxious thoughts may exacerbate or maintain, rather than cause, a panic attack. However, results based upon retrospective self-reports do not necessarily provide the most reliable data; indeed this latter study relied on a telephone interview. One of the few studies to directly monitor heart rate changes and associated perceptions of these changes, does, however, provide evidence that bodily sensations precede panic with anxious thoughts subsequently exacerbating the reaction.

Pauli et al. (1991) recorded ambulatory EEG over a 24 hour period in addition to self-reports of cardiac perception and anxiety elicited by these perceptions for 28 panic attack patients and 20 healthy controls. The actual heart rate of the two groups prior to the heart rate perception was a similar acceleration, but subsequent to the perception the heart rate for the patient group accelerated while that for the controls decelerated. This study illustrates that physiological changes after the perception of cardiac reactivity are directly related to the anxiety these changes elicit; i.e. bodily changes precede the panic with anxious thoughts subsequently exacerbating the reaction.

The fact that hyperventilation and pharmacological provoking agents produce physical sensations which result in panic attacks in some subjects, also provides evidence that it is the interpretation of bodily sensations which precede panic attacks which results in a full-blown panic attack (Margraf & Ehlers, 1989). However, contrary evidence is provided by Wolpe & Rowan (1988), who suggest that the cognitions occur after the fearful event of the panic and are 'probably attempts by the subject to rationalize what has happened to him' (p. 446), i.e. they are not causally implicated but are epiphenomena. A recent preliminary report also suggests a possible physiological mechanism responsible for panic attacks in some patients. Lynch et al. (1991) found higher chest EMG activity in a subgroup of highly anxious panic disorder patients in response to CO_2 inhalation. In this instance the physiological component would interact with the subsequent cognitive evaluation to produce the panic attack. On balance, however, the evidence does seem to point to the fact that it is the manner in which sensations are interpreted which provides the key to whether they subsequently do or do not develop into panic attacks.

2. *Panic patients should be more likely to interpret bodily sensations in a catastrophic manner in comparison to non-panic patients and controls*

In one study of relevance to this proposition, Rapee (1985a) found that panic patients were more likely than generalised anxiety patients, who did not have panics, to have thoughts concerned with the anticipation of having a heart attack, fainting, dying or going mad. Findings by Argyle (1988) also suggest that the content of cognitions during a panic attack is much more likely to be of personal catastrophe, mental or physical, than is the case for non-panic anxiety patients. Indeed, a finding by Kenardy et al. (1988b) of a bias towards causal attribution of cognitive factors in panic attacks suggests that patients themselves recognise the importance of the relationship between cognitions and their panic attacks.

In a further recent study Chambless et al. (1990) evaluated the relationship of cognition to fears of internal sensations in 155 agoraphobic patients with panic disorder. As predicted, self-rated fear of specific physical and psychological symptoms was related to the frequency of specifically logically related catastrophic thoughts (e.g. thoughts of a heart attack with fears of heart palpitations or chest pressure).

As well as expecting panic patients to be more likely to interpret bodily sensations in a catastrophic manner, there should also be clear links during panic attacks between catastrophic cognitions of bodily sensations and panic. In one such study Rachman, Levitt & Lopatka (1987) evaluated panic and non-panic episodes which occurred in 20 panic disorder patients when entering a series of feared situations. They report meaningful links between fearful cognitions and bodily symptoms, with particularly clear links between fearful cognitions and combinations of bodily symptoms. Twelve out of 14 patients were able to identify catastrophic thoughts during some or all of their attacks. Street, Craske & Barlow (1989) also report some interesting correlations between cognitions and physical sensations (i.e. feelings of nausea with thoughts of throwing up; feelings of faintness with thoughts of passing out) in relation to naturally occurring panics. This again emphasises the possible role of catastrophic interpretation of bodily sensations in producing panic attacks. Findings reported by Pauli et al. (1991) also support the notion of catastrophic cognitions. They found that, while panic attack subjects reported no more cardiac perceptions during a 24 hour monitoring period than a group of healthy controls, they reported significantly greater anxiety related to cardiac perceptions.

The link between cognitions and panic is further illustrated in a study where heart rate and ambulatory activity, cognitions using frequent cognitive sampling, and subjective anxiety were recorded throughout panic attacks for three subjects with agoraphobia with panic attacks (Kenardy, Evans & Oi, 1988a). The results suggest a preliminary period of heightened anxiety characterized by high, unstable, but not accelerating heart rate, and a negative, catastrophic cognitive bias, with high subjective anxiety.

In contrast to the above findings, however, Rachman, Lopatka & Levitt (1988b) note that 25% of the panics reported by their patients were non-cognitive, in contrast to an absence of non-cognitive panics reported by student claustrophobic subjects (Rachman et al. 1987, 1988a). In interpreting these results in relation to cognitive theories of panic they comment that 'These non-cognitive panics can be regarded as unexplained exceptions to the theory, or as a signal that the theory is insufficient'. On balance the findings by Rachman and his colleagues seem an important exception to the general thesis favouring cognitive explanations of panic.

Other studies have used experimental methods based upon information processing paradigms to evaluate memory bias for anxiety information and attentional bias to threat cues in panic patients. McNally, Foa & Donnell (1989) found that panic patients recalled more anxiety than non-anxiety words while normal controls recalled more non-anxiety than anxiety words, and that this memory bias was enhanced (though non-significantly) in panic patients under conditions of heightened arousal. A similar recall bias for anxiety/danger words is reported by Norton et al. (1988b) for non-clinical panickers, especially after having read a paragraph about a person having a panic. These results contrast with the lack of memory bias in patients with generalised anxiety disorder (Mogg, Mathews & Weinman, 1987).

A number of further studies suggest that panic patients show an attentional bias for processing threat-related information. Ehlers *et al.* (1988a) assessed reaction times of 24 panic patients and 24 controls in a modified Stroop colour-naming task using threat words and matched neutral words. Panic patients showed a larger interference effect (i.e. slower reaction times) when colour-naming physical threat words (e.g. disease, stroke) than normal controls. In a subsequent study a similar result was obtained for non-clinical panickers in relation to controls. In two recent reports Hope *et al.* (1990) found that panic patients had longer latencies for colour-naming physical threat words than did social phobics, while McNally, Reimann & Kim (1991) found that panic patients exhibited longer latencies for colour-naming bodily sensation words, fear words and catastrophe words than did normal controls. Issues relating to these studies have been discussed in Chapter 2. Taken together the results suggest that panic patients have a bias for interpreting ambiguous bodily sensations as threatening and, in contrast to generalised anxiety patients, may be characterised by a memory bias favouring anxiety information.

The misattribution hypothesis as a psychological theory of panic clearly has its strengths and is favoured by the balance of evidence. Contrary evidence is provided by Rachman *et al.* (1988b), who have demonstrated the existence of panics without fearful cognitions, and Wolpe & Rowan (1988), who refer to the cognitively based theory as a 'blind alley', suggesting that it is 'superimposed on the facts and not derived from the reports of patients' (p. 444). Evidence from subjective reports does, however, seem to be consistent with the theory, and evidence from various experimental and questionnaire studies has further pointed towards a misattribution hypothesis as well as suggesting promising treatment avenues. Caution is always advisable but the evidence certainly seems to be promising.

Nocturnal panic attacks

One further difficulty for a cognitive model of panic relates to the occurrence of nocturnal panics. Mellman & Uhde (1989) note that 71% of a panic disorder group reported experiencing at least one nocturnal panic attack. In order for these to be explicable in terms of cognitive theories some form of cognitive event would need to be associated with such night-time panics. The cognitive event could either be the person's interpretation of the reason for awakening, or based upon the content of a dream preceding awakening.

Nocturnal panics have been illustrated in a number of studies which have used continuous monitoring of naturally occurring panic attacks over a 24 hour period (Margraf *et al.* 1987; Taylor *et al.* 1986b). Taylor *et al.* (1986) found that five out of 41 panic attacks occurred between 1.30 and 3.30 a.m., waking subjects from sleep. Roy-Byrne, Mellman & Uhde (1988) report that nocturnal panics occur in non-REM sleep and are preceded by autonomic activation, suggesting that it is difficult to associate them with cognitive factors. It is unlikely that nocturnal panics are explicable on the basis of sleep patterns. In general, the sleep pattern of panic patients does not seem to differ from that of control subjects (Dube *et al.*, 1986), although Hauri *et al.* (1985) and Uhde *et al.* (1984) report increased movement time in panic patients in the sleep laboratory.

In a descriptive study investigating the phenomenology of nocturnal panic, Craske & Barlow (1989) compared 56 panic patients who reported never having experienced a nocturnal panic with 37 who reported having had such an experience within the past month. There was no difference between the two groups on degree of avoidance or distress, although the nocturnal panickers reported more frequent daytime panics and general somatic sensations. About half the nocturnal panics were reported as occurring within the second or third hour after sleep onset. Only six subjects recalled a dream preceding their panic, two-thirds reported that they were first aware of a somatic symptom upon wakening, and one-third reported a cognitive symptom. Ley (1988c) estimates from his hyperventilation theory of panic that about 70% of nocturnal panics will not be associated with dreams. In a further report Craske & Krueger (1990) note the occurrence of uncued nocturnal panic attacks in 5.1% of a sample of 294 college students; the same percentage reporting uncued daytime panics. Of those reporting nocturnal panic half did not report the occurrence of daytime panic. The tendency to experience nocturnal panics was related to the tendency to experience somatic sensations under other circumstances, while anxiety about these sensations was related to their belief that they are potentially harmful.

The small number of studies to date concerning nocturnal panics makes it difficult to construct a comprehensive theory about their occurrence, although suggestions have been made about their relationship to relaxation-induced panic (Cohen, Barlow & Blanchard, 1985), interoceptive cues (Craske & Barlow, 1989), CO_2 hypersensitivity (Mellman & Uhde, 1989) and chronic hyperventilation (Ley, 1988c). Ley (1988c) argues that in normal subjects the drop in blood pH which occurs during non-REM sleep would be accommodated by blood bicarbonate buffers so that pH is maintained within the normal range. For chronic hyperventilators, however, renal compensation for respiratory alkalosis may leave available blood bicarbonate levels so low that the drop in pH resulting from deep sleep would produce a state of acute hypoventilatory acidosis. Because the kidneys could not adjust rapidly enough to balance pH, the lungs, and hence rapid and deep breathing required to blow off CO_2, would be the only available means of raising pH. A marked increase in heart rate would result, the person awakening from deep sleep with rapid heart beats and shortness of breath. As Ley (1988c) notes,

> [if] panic attacks during sleep are a manifestation of severe chronic hyperventilation . . . then the clinical profile of panic patients who experience attacks during sleep should differ on respiratory indices and somatic complaints from those panic patients who do not experience panic attacks during sleep (p. 190).

Similar group differences should exist in response to CO_2 challenge if panic attacks during sleep result from CO_2 hypersensitivity. However, a recent evaluation of both the hyperventilatory and CO_2 hypersensitivity hypotheses (Craske & Barlow, 1990) found no differences in response to hyperventilation or CO_2 inhalation challenges between subjects who experienced nocturnal panic attacks and those who experienced daytime panic attacks only. These authors conclude that 'the results to date suggest that nocturnal panic is not linked specifically with indices of hyperventilation or CO_2 hypersensitivity'.

In contrast Craske & Barlow (1989) propose that nocturnal panickers are characterised by a higher rate of respiration; interoceptive cues, such as breathing rate, become conditioned stimuli that can subsequently elicit a panic attack (see below). This would also be in line with Ley's (1989) revised hyperventilation theory of panic, placing as it does an emphasis on dyspnoea (difficulty breathing). Associated with this is a hypervigilance for certain somatic cues and fear of somatic sensations. As a result Craske & Barlow hypothesise that fluctuations in internal state that occur during the course of sleep may be sufficient to trigger anxiety and panic. The mechanisms underlying nocturnal panic and daytime panic would then be essentially similar.

Allied to this are the parallels drawn between nocturnal panic and relaxation-induced panic (Adler, Craske & Barlow, 1987). Barlow (1988) draws upon the fact that panics mostly occur within the first few hours of sleep onset when slow-wave sleep, which is associated with reduced eye movements, lowered blood pressure and reduced heart rate and respiration, is most prevalent. As he points out, these are the characteristic features associated with relaxation. For some people the triggers of panic can involve sensations which are not only innocuous but also those which many people consider to be pleasant, such as relaxation (Heide & Borkovec, 1983, 1984). Daytime relaxation-induced panic may be associated with fear of somatic sensations and fear of losing control; there is no reason why these should not also be triggers for nocturnal panics, perhaps triggered by cues outside immediate awareness.

Interoceptive conditioning

As an alternative to, or incorporated into, the cognitive model a number of authors have suggested that conditioning to internal sensations accounts for the escalation of panic (Griez & van den Hout, 1986; van den Hout, 1988; van den Hout et al., 1987; Wolpe & Rowan, 1988). Wolpe & Rowan (1988) propose that 'the initial panic is an unconditioned response to a bizarre stimulus complex produced by excessive hyperventilation, and panic disorder is the result of contiguous stimuli, especially endogenous stimuli, being conditioned to the elicited anxiety' (p. 441).

In a similar vein van den Hout (1988) comments that 'panic patients become frightened by the perception of interoceptive sensations that happen to be part of the anxiety response; that is, they suffer from an interoceptive phobia' (p. 247). In this view anxiety is the aversive event; because bodily sensations are in temporal association with this event they may acquire CS characteristics and hence the capacity to elicit anxiety as the CR. As the CS is part of the CR an intensification of reactions would ensue. As van den Hout (1988) notes, however, there are at least two major problems with the model. Firstly, one would expect that everyone exposed to intense anxiety would become interoceptive phobics, and this is clearly not the case. Secondly, panic patients are frequently exposed to feared sensations and yet the conditioned response does not diminish. McNally (1990) also raises a number of concerns about the interoceptive-conditioning hypotheses; for example, as he points out, it is unclear what is the CS and what is the CR—'does a "skipped heartbeat CS" elicit a "dizziness CR" or vice versa?' (p. 406).

A major source of support for the model comes from studies investigating the effect of repeated and prolonged administrations of lactate or CO_2 to panic patients. The interoceptive conditioning model would predict that the prolonged exposure to fear-eliciting bodily sensations which would result from such administrations should lead to the extinction of interoceptively conditioned fear and hence panic. Treatment studies outlined subsequently have indeed found this to be the case.

Van den Hout (1988) suggests that both the cognitive version of the interoceptive fear hypothesis (i.e. based upon the catastrophic misinterpretation of interoceptive cues) and the interoceptive conditioning hypothesis itself share the notion that panic patients become frightened by the perception of bodily sensations. The accounts are thus additive rather than exclusive. A similar position is adopted by Margraf & Ehlers (1989), who suggest that 'in addition to cognitive processes, interoceptive conditioning could account for at least part of the association between internal cues and anxiety responses' (p. 220). While an explanation incorporating both the role of interoceptive fear conditioning and cognitive misinterpretation seems to provide a useful way forward, others feel that 'This explanation suffers from a lack of parsimony in requiring both cognitive and conditioning components in the explanatory account' (Teasdale, 1988, p. 196). Although each theory has led to the development of a specific treatment, the integration of explanatory accounts is perhaps reflected in the fact that initial psychologically based treatment studies used multifaceted treatment programmes. As will be seen, this inevitably makes it difficult to evaluate either the effective ingredient or the robustness of a specific theory.

ASSESSMENT

Self-monitoring

The most detailed information relating to panic attacks is clearly derived from continuous monitoring, either from self-reports or ambulatory monitoring of physiological reactions. Self-monitoring forms typically involve an anxiety rating, sensations experienced, time of onset and offset, whether anyone was present and whether the panic is associated with a stressful event or not (Barlow, 1988). On the basis of this information number and intensity of panic episodes per week can be obtained. Rapee, Craske & Barlow (1990) have recently evaluated the use of a standard self-monitoring form, used by 62 panic patients defined according to DSM-III-R criteria, to monitor panic attacks continuously over a two-week period (one form per panic attack to be completed either during the attack or immediately following its cessation). The authors report that subjects found the forms understandable, descriptive and convenient to use.

Ambulatory monitoring of physiological reactions

The availability of microcomputer technology has made the ambulatory monitoring of panic possible within the past decade, and several reports of the use of such devices have appeared (Freedman et al., 1985; Kenardy et al., 1988a; Shear et al., 1987; Taylor, Telch & Haavik, 1983; Taylor et al., 1986b; White & Baker, 1987). For example, Taylor et al. (1986b) used a

Vitalog solid-state device programmed to record heart rate with a precision of about two beats per minute for 12 patients and 12 control subjects. Freedman et al. (1986) recorded heart rate, finger temperature and ambient temperature continuously over two 12-hour periods using a Medilog cassette recording system. As Freedman (1989) notes in a recent review, ambulatory monitoring offers the obvious advantage of being able to record patients in their natural environment over extended periods of time. This must be balanced against the lack of experimental control possible, and the fact that only relatively technically simple measures can be taken. However, Margraf (1991), in a paper reviewing 10 studies involving ambulatory monitoring, suggests that such studies give a more accurate impression of panic than clinical and case reports which often rely upon retrospective recall. He suggests this as a likely explanation for his review findings that naturally occurring panic attacks are of moderate intensity with respect to heart rate, blood pressure and skin temperature, in contrast with the intense and dramatic nature of panic attacks suggested by clinical reports.

Self-report inventories

Standardised self-report forms typically used to monitor somatic symptoms and cognitions associated with panic include the Chambless Body Sensations Questionnaire and Agoraphobic Cognitions Questionnaire (Chambless et al., 1984) the Cognitive–Somatic Anxiety Questionnaire (Schwartz, Davidson & Goleman, 1978) and the Psychosomatic Rating Scale (Cox, Freundlich & Meyer, 1975).

One specific measurement instrument, the Panic Attack Questionnaire (PAQ), has been used in a number of studies to assess panic attack symptoms in general population samples. Devised by Norton et al. (1986) the scale provides information on frequency and symptom profile of panic as originally defined by DSM-III, information about first-degree relatives who have experienced panic attacks, and the effects of the panic attacks on the person's lifestyle. The PAQ has been shown to have adequate test–retest reliability for all items except those evaluating onset to peak severity and reports of unexpected panic (Margraf & Ehlers, 1988). The questionnaire has been used in its original or revised form (specifically asking about the number of attacks in the past four weeks in order to conform with DSM-III-R criteria) in a number of studies designed to assess panic symptomatology, frequency and severity in non-clinical panickers (Brown & Cash, 1989, 1990; Macaulay & Kleinknecht, 1989; Norton et al., 1985, 1986, 1988).

Clum et al. (1990) have recently reported the development of two self-report instruments designed to assess the symptoms and cognitions associated with panic attacks: the Panic Attack Symptom Questionnaire (PASQ) and the Panic Attack Cognitions Questionnaire (PACQ). The PACQ consists of a shorter version of 12 items generated from the DSM-III description of panic, and a longer version with an additional free-response item and 12 further items derived from specific subject input and the Agoraphobic Cognitions Questionnaire. Each item is rated on a four-point scale, indicating degree of preoccupation with each cognition during a panic attack. The PASQ also consists of a shorter version with 21 items generated from the DSM-III description of panic, and a longer version with an additional free-response item and 15 further items derived from specific subject input and the Body Sensations Questionnaire. The authors report adequate reliability for the scales which successfully differentiated a group of anxiety-disordered individuals with panic attacks from a group of anxiety-disordered individuals without panic attacks. Initial data thus appear promising, although the recent development of the scales means that there are few data available at present and further evaluative studies would be useful.

TREATMENT

Given that, until recently, panic was largely considered from a biological perspective, it is perhaps not surprising that many authors argue that medication is the treatment of choice for alleviating panic attacks (e.g. Rickels, Schweitzer & Lucki, 1987). Benzodiazepines and other minor tranquillisers have been shown to be effective in reducing anticipatory anxiety, but have also been used in the treatment of panic symptoms. Noyes et al. (1984), for example, found that high doses of benzodiazepines resulted in reduced panic attacks in 18 out of 21 patients. In a recent large-scale, multicentre study using alprazolam, Ballenger et al. (1988) randomly assigned over 500 panic patients to alprazolam or placebo; 55% of alprazolam and 32% of placebo subjects were panic-free following eight weeks of treatment or at the time they dropped out. However, of those subjects who completed the alprazolam or placebo treatment 59% of the alprazolam and 50% of the placebo subjects were free of panics, a non-significant difference between the groups. A recent study has also compared treatment for panic by alprazolam with a cognitive–behavioural treatment, a medication placebo and a waiting list control group (Klosko et al. 1990). The proportion of the subjects completing the study who were free of panic attacks following treatment was 87% for the cognitive–behavioural treatment, 50% for alprazolam (although the difference between these figures did not reach significance), 36% for the placebo and 33% for the waiting list group. Further, the cognitive–behavioural treatment was more effective in

reducing intensity of somatic panic attack symptoms generally, and shortness of breath (dyspnoea) in particular.

The development of effective psychologically based treatments is
particularly important given the major concerns raised about the utility of
drug-based treatments by many authors. These include the problems of
withdrawal from the medication and increasing tolerance to the medication over time, with resulting psychological and physical dependence
(e.g. Fyer *et al.*, 1987; Tyrer, Rutherford & Huggett, 1981). In one study,
for example, Fyer *et al.* (1987) found that when alprazolam treatment was
reduced, 15 out of 17 patients suffered a recurrence of panic attacks, with
four patients reporting attacks which exceeded pretreatment attacks in
terms of severity and frequency, and with nine patients reporting new
symptoms (insomnia, dizziness) during withdrawal.

In addition to the use of tranquillisers, antidepressant medication has
long been argued to be particularly effective in the treatment of panic (e.g.
Klein, Zitrin & Woerner, 1977; Sheehan, Ballenger & Jacobsen, 1980; Zitrin
et al., 1983). However, both careful interpretation of the results of these
studies and more recent research studies yield a far from unambiguous
picture of the effects of antidepressants on panic. The studies by Klein,
Zitrin and colleagues (cited above) suggest that antidepressant medication
adds somewhat to the 70% improvement gained by exposure-based
therapy for 'mixed phobics' (those who reported experiencing at least one
spontaneous panic). As Barlow (1988, p. 432) notes, however, the effects
were apparent only for some ratings of panic, and then only reached very
marginal levels of significance. The possibility that medication adds little
to exposure-based treatments is further attested to in other studies. Telch
et al. (1985), for example, found that imipramine administered to
agoraphobics with instructions to the patient not to enter the feared
situation produced no reduction in panic.

Even if one assumes the efficacy of antidepressant medication in the
short term a number of authors have pointed to the fact that there can be
high relapse rates on termination of medication. Sheehan (1986), for
example, found that of 106 patients treated with imipramine, phenelzine,
alprazolam or a combination of imipramine and alprazolam, from 71% to
95% had relapsed within a matter of months of terminating medication.
The problems of relapses and withdrawal, as well as issues relating to
resistance to medication and intolerance of side-effects, have also been
noted by other authors (e.g. Telch, Tearnan & Taylor, 1983).

Given the limitations of drug treatment there is clearly a need for a non-
pharmacological alternative, and psychological interventions for panic
attacks have steadily been emerging over the past decade. These have
largely been based on the assumption that somatic sensations and the
manner in which these are interpreted provide the basis for panic attacks.

Treatments have thus focused on breathing retraining or relaxation in order to control the somatic sensations, and/or cognitive restructuring involving identifying and modifying catastrophic beliefs associated with panic attacks and/or through systematic exposure to somatic sensations (Rapee, 1987; Rapee & Barlow, 1989).

Before discussing these emerging treatments it is worth pausing to reflect upon recently published reviews examining the relative effectiveness of pharmacological treatments and psychological interventions (both the emerging treatments and exposure-based interventions) for panic and agoraphobia with panic attacks (Clum, 1989; Mattick *et al.*, 1990; Michelson & Marchione, 1991). In Clum's analysis, behavioural treatments were found to be at least as effective as pharmacological treatments in reducing panic attacks, and to have a generally lower relapse rate. One of Clum's summary comments is that 'Behavior therapies . . . are the treatment of choice for panic attacks.' It should be kept in mind that this review is based on treatment studies examining both patients with panic attacks and agoraphobia with panic attacks and many of the studies with the latter involved exposure-based treatment, the effectiveness of which has been well documented (see Chapter 5). Nevertheless, seven studies of cognitive–behavioural treatments for just panic attack patients are included in Clum's review, highlighting the promising nature of such treatments. In their review Mattick *et al.* report only limited evidence for the efficacy of low-potency benzodiazepines or monoamine oxidase or behaviour therapy not involving exposure to the symptoms of panic or to the feared situation. Substantial improvement in panic symptoms and frequency was reported by studies examining the efficacy of imipramine, high-potency benzodiazepines such as alprazolam and exposure *in vivo*, particularly if combined with imipramine or anxiety management. The effects on panic produced by exposure were maintained over long follow-up periods. The authors conclude that 'cognitive behaviour therapy involving exposure to symptoms of panic and to the feared situation under guidance of skilled personnel reduces panic and phobia on a permanent basis' (p. 572). Although the studies reviewed again include patients with both panic and agoraphobia with panic attacks it seems from this review that cognitive–behavioural interventions involving an element of exposure effectively reduce panic symptoms as well as avoidance behaviour. Finally, Michelson & Marchione (1991) review the comparative efficacy of cognitive, behavioural and pharmacological treatments for panic with agoraphobia in relation to drop-outs, the achievement of clinically significant improvement, and relapse. They summarise the studies reviewed by examining these issues in relation to a hypothetical *N* of 100. This clearly documents the very high relapse rate from beta-blockers and benzodiazepines (approximately 90%); the lower relapse rates for monoamine oxidase and tricyclic antidepressants (40% and 35% respectively); the modest numbers showing clinically significant improvement with the latter two medications (45% and 60% respectively); the very low relapse rates for exposure-based treatments with or without cognitive therapy (10–15%); the high numbers showing clinically significant improvement with cognitive–behavioural interventions (65–87%). As with the previous two reviews these authors also conclude that 'the treatment of choice for panic disorder with no or mild phobic avoidance is cognitive–behavior therapy aimed at panic cessation'. Some of the studies which have led to these conclusions are discussed below.

Breathing retraining

A number of studies have evaluated the efficacy of breathing retraining in the treatment of panic attacks (Bonn, Readhead & Timmons, 1984; Clark, Salkovskis & Chalkley, 1985; Gitlin et al., 1985; Hibbert & Chan, 1989; Salkovskis, Jones & Clark, 1986a; Rapee, 1985b; de Ruiter et al., 1989b). With the exception of de Ruiter et al. (1989b) these studies seem to suggest beneficial effects for breathing retraining. The results should, however, be treated with some degree of caution. The studies by Clark, Salkovskis & Chalkley (1985) and Salkovskis, Jones & Clark (1986a) evaluated a treatment involving several stages. First, patients were asked to overbreathe and to introspect on the sensations produced; second, they were given an explanation of how hyperventilation produces panic; third, they were trained in slow breathing. Provision of information and training were also incorporated into Rapee's (1985b) single case report.

In a further uncontrolled trial Gitlin et al. (1985) treated 11 patients with panic disorder with a package that included education, abdominal breathing and exposure. Ten of the 11 patients were panic-free at post-treatment and at an average of five months follow-up.

Although all these reports indicate a marked reduction of panic attacks both during treatment and at follow-up it is difficult to assess whether this was due to the educational component inherent in the treatment package or the breathing training involved. Indeed, the efficacy of the treatment might be due to cognitive parameters such as reattribution of panic attacks to hyperventilation. In the Gitlin et al. study subjects specifically indicated that education and reassurance about panic attacks which altered catastrophic cognitions had been the most helpful factor in the treatment package, followed by the abdominal breathing. In addition the lack of control or comparison groups makes it difficult to evaluate the actual effectiveness of the intervention.

In the first of three controlled studies (Bonn et al., 1984) 12 agoraphobic with panic attack patients were randomly allocated to treatment with either respiratory control training plus *in vivo* exposure, or *in vivo* exposure alone. Although there was only a non-significant trend for the respiratory group to experience fewer panic attacks than the exposure-alone group at post-treatment, at six-month follow-up the exposure-alone group had deteriorated and the difference between groups was significant. Also at the follow-up the respiratory group had a significantly lower respiratory rate than in the exposure-alone group, suggesting that breathing control was indeed the effective treatment ingredient.

In a further study Hibbert & Chan (1989) randomly assigned 40 patients who experienced panic attacks to either a respiratory control or a placebo treatment condition. The former group were subdivided into those whose panics most clearly resembled hyperventilation (hyperventilators) and those whose panics did not (non-hyperventilators). After two weeks' treatment there was little difference between groups on measures of anxiety or avoidance. The brief treatment period used, and the mixed subject groups studied (both phobic and non-phobic, social phobic as well as agoraphobic), suggest that the results should be treated with a considerable degree of caution. As the authors suggest, the failure of the respiratory treatment may well be due to the absence of the cognitive component used in the Clark *et al.* (1985) study, although such interpretations are not really warranted given the design issues mentioned.

In a final comparison study de Ruiter *et al.* (1989b) randomly assigned 49 panic disorder with agoraphobia patients to one of three treatment conditions: breathing retraining/cognitive restructuring (a treatment adapted from that used by Clark, Salkovskis & Chalkley (1985) and Salkovskis, Jones & Clark (1986a), graded self-exposure *in vivo* or a combination of breathing retraining/cognitive restructuring plus exposure therapy. Treatments resulted in a reduction in symptomatology on self-report measures and a decrease in respiratory rate, with no differential effect of treatments. Contrary to expectations, however, breathing retraining/cognitive restructuring was generally ineffective in reducing panic frequency. Although the authors suggest that hyperventilation may be less important in panic than previously thought, as they further note, a follow-up assessment may modify the picture. Although Clark *et al.* (1985) and Salkovskis *et al.* (1986a) found a marked decrease in panic frequency during treatment, Bonn *et al.* found a differential effect for respiratory training only at follow-up. The relative effectiveness of respiratory control may become evident only in the longer term, although clearly more controlled comparisons are needed.

Cognitive techniques

Given the assumption behind cognitive models that the misattribution of somatic sensations is central to the generation of panic, therapeutic interventions have been directed towards modifying patients' responses to such cues. The effectiveness of the breathing retraining package used by Clark *et al.* (1985), Rapee (1985b) and Salkovskis *et al.* (1986) could well have been due to the cognitive component involved in the treatment programme.(Rapee *et al.* (1986), as noted previously, found that panic was less likely to be experienced when subjects were provided with an explanation for their sensations; while Gitlin *et al.* found that education and reassurance were the most important components of a behavioural treatment package.)

There are, however, few studies to date which have specifically used cognitive interventions as treatment for panic, although a number have now used cognitive treatments in combination with either breathing retraining, relaxation training or as part of a treatment package. In one such study Öst (1988) compared 14 one-hour sessions of either applied relaxation training or progressive muscular relaxation training in the treatment of 18 panic patients. In the applied relaxation treatment patients were taught to observe the first signs of panic and to use relaxation as a technique for coping rapidly with the sensations. The technique was taught within the framework of alerting the patient to sensations followed by negative thoughts followed by further physiological sensations. The treatment could thus be conceptualised either in terms of identifying negative cognitions, even if not overtly, or from a coping framework. While both treatments yielded significant post-treatment improvements (38% for progressive and 75% for applied), applied relaxation was significantly better than progressive relaxation on six of 11 outcome measures at post-treatment and on 11 measures at follow-up.

Cognitive interventions have been used as one component of a treatment package in a number of outcome studies. Barlow *et al.* (1984) randomly assigned 11 subjects with panic disorder (and nine with generalised anxiety) to a treatment or waiting list control. Treated subjects were given progressive muscular relaxation, frontalis EMG biofeedback and cognitive therapy. The latter component of treatment was divided into three phases: an introduction and education phase, a rehearsal phase and an application and practice phase. Strategies taught included coping self-statements and cognitive restructuring of anxiety-provoking thoughts(Compared to the controls, treated patients improved on clinical ratings, psychophysiological measures, frequency of self-monitored panic and questionnaire measures of anxiety; continued improvement was noted at follow-up.) Similar success rates are reported by Beck (1988) for a cognitive treatment programme of 16 panic patients whose panic frequency was reduced from an average of 4.62 per week to zero at treatment termination, results which were maintained at one-year follow-up. The treatment consisted of explanation, reappraisal of thoughts, relaxation, breathing exercises, distraction

and exposure. A similar multifaceted treatment package reported by Shear
et al. (1988) also resulted in a reduction of panic frequency from 4.8 in the
three weeks prior to treatment to zero at post-treatment for 10 of 11 panic
patients; treatment gains were maintained during the follow-up period of
between three and 12 months. Michelson *et al.* (1990a) have also evaluated
a cognitive–behavioural treatment derived from the work of Clark,
Salkovskis & Chalkley (1985) and Beck (1988). They report statistically significant improvement across all outcome domains for 10 patients treated
for 13 sessions of $2\frac{1}{2}$ hours each over a 12-week period.

A further recently published account of this treatment by Beck and his
colleagues also suggests promising results (Sokol *et al.*, 1989). A consecutive series of 17 patients requesting treatment for panic disorder (nine of
whom were diagnosed as primary panic disorder patients) were treated
with a focused cognitive therapy based upon the treatment used, for
example by Clark, Salkovskis & Chalkley (1985). Patients had weekly sessions (ranging from 10 to 40 sessions) and were trained to control symptoms through breathing exercises, coping self-statements, and refocusing
techniques. They were also encouraged to enter into previously avoided
situations in order to apply these techniques *in vivo*. At the end of treatment panic attacks were reduced to zero, an improvement which was
maintained at one-year follow-up. As the authors themselves note, however, in the absence of a suitable control group the results inevitably need
to be treated with a considerable degree of caution. Also, given the multifaceted nature of the treatment programme it is not possible to ascertain
whether exposure, breathing retraining or the cognitively based coping
self-statements and refocusing techniques was the important component
in the treatment package.

[The exposure to somatic cues/breathing retraining/cognitive reassessment treatment developed by Beck, Barlow, Clark, Salkovskis and their
colleagues, in the studies cited above, has been evaluated in relation to
relaxation, a combined relaxation and exposure/cognitive package and a
waiting list control group in one recently published report (Barlow *et al.*,
1989). All three treatment groups showed superior outcome on a variety
of measures in relation to the waiting list control group. In the two treatment conditions containing exposure to somatic cues and the cognitively
based therapy 85% of patients were panic-free at post-treatment, results
which were maintained at one-year follow-up. In contrast, patients in the
relaxation group showed greater reductions in generalised anxiety associated with the panic attacks, although this group also had a substantial
drop-out rate (33%). A further two-year follow-up assessment found that
81.3% of patients in the exposure/cognitive treatment group were still
panic-free compared with 42.9% in the combined relaxation and exposure/
cognitive treatment and 35.7% in the relaxation-alone group. Treatment

gains were thus maintained in the exposure/cognitive group while relaxation seems to interfere with the effectiveness of this treatment (Barlow, 1990; Craske, Brown & Barlow, 1991).)While it is well established that, in general, relaxation is effective in reducing anxiety, evidence suggests that for some individuals relaxation may instead result in heightened anxiety (Heide & Borkovec, 1983) and even panic (Adler, Craske & Barlow, 1987; Cohen, Barlow & Blanchard, 1985). This suggests that relaxation should not be the treatment of choice for panic attacks.

Overall these studies provide promising results for cognitively based interventions, although further controlled comparisons are necessary to evaluate the relative success of such treatments. Also given that the evaluation studies described all involve a multifaceted treatment programme it is difficult to ascertain whether the cognitive element is the effective treatment component or whether treatment must of necessity also address the need to provide coping resources (breathing retraining) or exposure to the feared sensations in the clinical context. However, in a recent report Salkovskis, Clark & Hackman (1991) provide preliminary evidence that cognitive procedures without any exposure to feared situations or sensations (subjects were specifically requested not to increase or decrease the extent to which they went into situations they would tend to avoid), and without training in breathing control, can reduce panic attack frequency. Seven patients were assigned to differing length baselines followed by two sessions of cognitive treatment within a week, designed to change catastrophic interpretations of bodily sensations. After the treatment a further baseline was instituted. The short-term reduction in panic frequency resulting from this intervention suggests that treatment success is likely to be due to cognitive elements. Although this is encouraging for cognitive theorising, at the end of the second baseline phase patients were offered unrestricted further treatment, including exposure, as appropriate. As the authors themselves note,

> we would not wish to suggest that therapists should rely entirely on cognitive procedures in routine clinical practice . . . the majority of chronic patients with extensive avoidance are likely to need some exposure practice in order to achieve substantial and sustained improvement (p. 166).

In reviewing seven uncontrolled studies and three controlled studies evaluating cognitive–behaviour therapy (CBT) as treatment for panic attacks Michelson & Marchione (1991) conclude that:

> These CBT studies evince consistently positive findings. Therapeutic gains appear to be substantive, with elimination of panic attacks and anticipatory anxiety in the vast majority of clients. Although these results are highly encouraging, long term follow-up studies are needed (p. 105).

The promising two-year follow-up results reported by Barlow (1990) and Craske, Brown & Barlow (1991) represent the first step in this direction.

Exposure-based techniques

Exposure-based treatment has been widely used in the successful treatment of phobias. Exposure is typically to feared external stimuli; in the case of panic attacks, however, the stimuli which are feared are internal sensations. As Rapee (1987) and Rapee & Barlow (1989) note, treatment of panic can be conducted via exposure to interoceptive (somatic) sensations. Such treatment necessitates the invoking of a panic attack in order to expose the client to panic symptoms in the clinical context. One such method which has been used involves the repeated inhalation of a CO_2/ oxygen mixture (Griez & van den Hout, 1983, 1986).

Griez & van den Hout (1986) compared the effects of CO_2 inhalations against propranolol in 14 patients with panic attacks in a crossover design. Treatments were administered for two weeks in counterbalanced order with two weeks break between. CO_2 inhalations produced a significant mean reduction in panic attack frequency while propranolol produced a non-significant reduction, although the difference between the two treatments was not significant. The breathing retraining package outlined previously, by involving a provocation element, contains by its very nature an exposure element. While exposure to interoceptive cues such as the cognitively based treatments and breathing retraining may be effective in treating panic, because each treatment contains elements of the others, it is difficult to isolate which component forms the most effective ingredient, or indeed how the components can be most effectively linked into one package. Future research could usefully address this issue.

SUMMARY

Until the 1970s panic attacks were largely conceptualised from a biological perspective which assumed some disordered physiological mechanism requiring appropriate pharmacological correction. Psychological research over the past two decades suggests that panic attacks are frequently experienced within the general population, and may be more usefully conceptualised as involving an element of anxious apprehension about the occurrence of the next unexpected panic attack. Clinical panickers may be differentiated from non-clinical panickers and non-panickers along a continuum of catastrophising about bodily sensations experienced. Cognitive models of panic have certainly provided the most comprehensive psychological account of panic phenomenology, although this has been complemented by theoretical assumptions emphasising hyperventilation and fear of somatic sensations.

The hyperventilation account suggests that panic results from dysfunctional breathing patterns which cause severe hyperventilation. Although emphasis has been placed on the misattribution of the somatic consequences of hyperventilation, the model has recently been revised by Ley (1989) to decrease the significance of cognitions and emphasise the part played by breathing difficulties as the initial panic trigger. Recent findings that some panics do not have a cognitive component (Rachman, Lopatka & Levitt, 1988b), that cognitions can occur after panic onset (Wolpe & Rowan, 1988), in addition to the existence of nocturnal panics, provide difficulties for a cognitive model of panic. Non-cognitive panics may, however, be an exception to the rule, and the balance of evidence suggests that it is the perception of symptoms which produces panic.

The past decade has also seen the advent of psychological interventions derived from the hyperventilation, cognitive and interoceptive conditioning models; namely: breathing retraining, cognitively based interventions and exposure to somatic sensations. Each of these interventions has seemingly met with success, although the majority of treatment studies to date have rarely used a comparison group, and have tended to use a multifaceted treatment programme involving a combination of breathing retraining, exposure to somatic sensations and cognitive restructuring—thus not allowing determination of the effective therapeutic ingredient. Reviews attesting to the efficacy of cognitive–behavioural interventions suggest that these and not pharmacologically based treatments will be the future treatment of choice for panic attacks.

Both theoretical advances and the treatments derived from them offer important psychological alternatives to purely biological explanations. The problems of relapse on withdrawal of medication, resistance to medication and intolerance to side-effects point to the need for a non-pharmacological alternative. Psychological contributions are beginning to build such an alternative, although a great deal of work remains to be done in fully evaluating psychological interventions and the theoretical models upon which they are based.

Chapter 5

Agoraphobia

DEFINITION AND PREVALENCE

(The term 'agoraphobia' was first used by Westphal (1871) to describe complete avoidance of walking through certain streets or squares, or extreme anxiety when doing so.)It originates from the Greek words 'phobos' or fear and 'agora' or market place/place of assembly, and thus literally means 'fear of public places'. The definition provided by DSM-III (1980) includes a marked fear of being in public places from which escape might be difficult, or help not available in the case of a sudden incapacitation; avoidance of situations involving crowds such as on a busy street or in crowded stores or being in tunnels, on bridges or on public transportation.) DSM-III also includes the statement that the initial phase of the disorder often consists of recurrent panic attacks. The interrelationship of agoraphobia and panic was recognised by identifying diagnostic categories of agoraphobia with panic attacks, agoraphobia without panic attacks and panic disorder. The central role of panic attacks in agoraphobia is made even more prominent in DSM-III-R (1987), where the categories are now panic disorder with agoraphobia, panic disorder without agoraphobia and agoraphobia without a history of panic disorder. In assigning categories the severity of avoidance exhibited by the patient is assessed as mild, moderate or severe. Thus the old DSM-III category of agoraphobia with panic attacks becomes panic disorder with agoraphobia: severe agoraphobic avoidance. This shift in classification appears to be consistent with the behavioural model promulgated by Goldstein & Chambless (1978), who proposed 'fear of fear' (or fear of having a panic attack) as a central component in agoraphobia. It could thus be argued that 'agoraphobic avoidance behaviour is simply one associated feature of severe unexpected panic' (Barlow, 1988, p. 358) and that, clinically, agoraphobia rarely occurs in the absence of panic. This draws into question the very existence of agoraphobia as a distinct anxiety-related condition, which reflects dilemmas with both the use of the tripartite model of anxiety and attempts to treat anxiety-related behaviours as diagnostic categories.

At the most basic level one might argue that panic is the extreme physiological response to anxiety-inducing circumstances, with avoidance the subsequent behavioural response. Cognitive parameters may determine whether bodily sensations or external circumstances are the focus of the individual's attention and hence whether panic, avoidance or both the likely outcome. This can be compared to the association of blushing and social phobia referred to in Chapter 3, where individual patterns of responding (either internal/bodily focus or external focus) can act as the trigger for social phobia. In fact, fear of anxiety has been related theoretically to a wide range of phenomena (Reiss, 1987). Thus both cognitive factors and individual sensitivity to bodily cues, together with other parameters, may determine the association of panic with avoidance.)

Notwithstanding these issues, there is an extensive history of research and hence a vast body of literature pertaining to agoraphobia. In one recent report Watts (1988) comments that 'research and theory on agoraphobia continues unabated (80 entries in a recent *Psychological Abstracts*)' (p. 53). Prior to the publication of DSM-III-R, (agoraphobia was regarded as one of the commonest anxiety disorders, accounting for between 50% and 80% of patients seeking professional help for anxiety-related problems) (Burns & Thorpe, 1977; Chambless, 1982). In epidemiological surveys estimates of prevalence rates range from six out of every 1000 individuals (Agras, Sylvester & Oliveau, 1969) to between 27 and 58 per 1000 (Myers *et al.*, 1984). A comprehensive summary of ECA data from five US sites indicates a one-month prevalence ranging from 2.1% (St Louis) to 4.8% (Baltimore) with an average suggesting that 2.9% of the US population are agoraphobic (Boyd *et al.*, 1990). These figures would suggest that between 1.25 and 12 million people in the USA suffer from agoraphobia, and if the figures are applicable to other countries, between 0.3 and 3 million people in the UK. While the latter figure may, to some extent, reflect an increased awareness and hence greater reporting of the problem, it is no doubt an overestimate of the extent of the prevalence of agoraphobia. Agoraphobia is nevertheless a common clinical difficulty.)This is perhaps reflected by the appearance of many monographs on the topic within the past decade (e.g. Chambless & Goldstein, 1982; Hallam, 1985; Mathews, Gelder & Johnston, 1981; Thorpe & Burns, 1983).

Gender and age of onset

(One consistent finding across studies is the preponderance of women amongst agoraphobics.) Women rarely constitute less than two-thirds of agoraphobic populations (Thorpe & Burns, 1983) with recent reports (Bourdon et al., 1988) confirming earlier suggestions (Marks, 1969) that women represent 75% of all agoraphobics. In general there tend to be few differences on demographic, clinical symptoms and personality variables between male and female agoraphobics (Mavissakalian, 1985; Oei, Wanstall & Evans, 1990). One suggested explanation for the greater preponderance of female compared with male agoraphobics is that sex-role stereotyping of women as helpless and dependent leads them to fear and avoid a wider range of situations (Fodor, 1974). One might thus expect a changing gender distribution in recent years to reflect women's changing roles within society; this does not seem to be the case. Indeed, a recent preliminary report by Gournay (1989) suggests little difference between agoraphobics and non-psychiatric controls on feminine sex type behaviour.

A further consistent finding is that the majority of agoraphobic patients report a mean age of onset in their mid-20s. In a summary of findings from 11 studies of agoraphobic patients (Öst, 1987) the mean age of onset varied from 19.7 to 32 years with an average across the samples of 27.62 years. Öst's own study of 100 agoraphobic patients refers to a mean age of onset of 27.74 years. This age of onset, which is significantly older than for other anxiety states, may relate to increasing requirements for independence and the development of responsibilities within relationships and families which occur during the 20s. The consistent pattern to the age of onset has led to the search for precipitating factors which may interact with personality characteristics to explain the aetiology of agoraphobia.

PREDISPOSING FACTORS

Personality

Specific personality traits have long been assumed to be predisposing factors for the development of agoraphobia. As Tearnan, Telch & Keefe (1984) note: 'the premorbid personality of the agoraphobic has often been characterised as soft, infantile, passive, anxious, dependent, obsessive, introverted, emotionally immature, retiring and highly neurotic' (p. 55). There is, however, surprisingly little empirical evidence that a clear 'agoraphobic personality' exists. Many reports are correlational in nature and do not include comparisons with reference groups. In their review of the evidence Foa, Steketee & Young (1984) concluded that 'the literature provides meagre support for the existence of a consistent "agoraphobic personality"' (p. 18). In two studies conducted since that review mixed results were obtained. Van der Molen, van den Hout & Halfens (1988) found that while their agoraphobic patients had a more external orientation than normal controls on Rotter's I–E locus of control scale they did not differ significantly from a mixed phobic and depressed comparison group. In a further study Arrindell & Emmelkamp (1987) administered a battery of questionnaires to 32 agoraphobic patients, 12 non-phobic psychiatric subjects and 38 normal controls. Compared to both groups of controls agoraphobics were characterised by higher levels of neuroticism, seclusion (low on extraversion and sociability and showing greater tendencies towards isolating themselves from social contacts), situational dependency (higher scores on a restricted style of living), passivity (low activity, little energy and need for rest), and self-directed hostility. The groups did not differ on measures of dependency. Given the large number of measures used, the number of group comparisons made, and the relatively small N, the possible personality differences between agoraphobic and other groups must be treated with considerable caution. Further, as Arrindell & Emmelkamp themselves note, and Tearnan et al. comment, by the time agoraphobics are evaluated they may evidence many 'traits' mistakenly assumed to have existed premorbidly.

A more promising avenue of research relates to anxiety sensitivity (fear of anxiety symptoms—see Chapter 4). It has been found that agoraphobics score highly on this construct in relation to normal controls (McNally & Lorenz, 1987; Wardle, Ahmad & Hayward, 1990) and that scores decrease post-treatment (McNally & Lorenz, 1987). Although anxiety sensitivity relates specifically to cognitive appraisal of anxiety cues it is plausible to assume that agoraphobics also have abnormal vulnerability to the physiological reactions that cue anxiety (Watts, 1988) (i.e. they have more frequent and severe physiological reactions even in the absence of anxiety cues). This issue no doubt relates to panic sensitivity, characteristic of many agoraphobics.

Given that studies of personality characteristics of agoraphobics have met with such mixed results it seems reasonable to conclude that 'there is only meagre support for the existence of a consistent "agoraphobic personality"' (Emmelkamp, 1988).

Family characteristics and relationships

Many reports suggest that agoraphobics perceive their families as overprotective (e.g. Solyom, Silberfeld & Solyom, 1976) although this finding has not been replicated in other studies (e.g. Arrindell et al., 1983). Some reports suggest that agoraphobics, in comparison to other groups, rate their parents as less caring (e.g. Parker, 1979), or lacking in emotional warmth, and their mothers as having been rejective (e.g. Arrindell *et al.*, 1983, 1989). Others have argued that agoraphobics have a history of separation trauma or childhood separation anxiety, although this notion is largely based upon clinical observations or descriptive studies (e.g. Mendel & Klein, 1969). The few controlled studies do not tend to favour the separation hypothesis. Thyer *et al.* (1985a), for example, found no difference between agoraphobics and simple phobics on questions pertaining to childhood separation anxiety experiences; unfortunately a non-phobic comparison group was not included.

Other studies report a high incidence of psychiatric disturbance amongst agoraphobic families. For example, Burns & Thorpe (1977) found that 28% of the mothers and 13% of the fathers of agoraphobics required psychiatric treatment, while in 35% of cases at least one sibling had received such help. Other studies have, however, produced very different results, reporting little difference between the parents of agoraphobics and matched controls in the incidence of psychiatric difficulties (e.g. Buglass *et al.*, 1977). Much of the data relating to family relationships is derived from retrospective studies using a variety of measuring instruments (Mathews, Gelder & Johnston, 1981), while many of those studies purporting to show raised incidence of psychiatric morbidity in families of agoraphobics suffer from the lack of an adequate comparison group. In addition, as Tearnan, Telch & Keefe (1984) point out, there is a lack of specificity and clarity of the definitions of parental rearing practices employed in many studies. These issues no doubt account to some extent for the array of conflicting results. The extent to which early family environment might be considered causal in the genesis of agoraphobia is thus questionable on the basis of available evidence.

The marital context

A number of authors have suggested that the relationship of agoraphobic patients with their marital partner may be of critical importance in the precipitation and maintenance of agoraphobic symptoms. Goldstein & Chambless (1980) concluded that agoraphobics wish to flee the marriage but cannot do so because of their dependency and fears of being alone. Further, it has been noted that improvement in the agoraphobic spouse may not always be welcomed with joy and enthusiasm by the non-phobic partner, who may seemingly impede or reverse the positive effects of treatment (Hafner, 1977a,b). These observations have led to the suggestion that agoraphobic symptoms serve to maintain the marital *status quo*.

The evidence that agoraphobia and relationship difficulties are interlinked is, however, far from convincing. The initial impetus for the development of such views stems from clinical reports. Fry (1962), for example, concluded on the basis of data from an unspecified number of female, mainly agoraphobic, patients, that the patients and spouses resembled one another, and that the spouses had a vested interest in maintaining the phobia in the partner. As Kleiner & Marshall (1985) conclude in their review of this literature, 'it is difficult to sort out observation from interpretation in these studies, so that at best these reports are suggestive' (p. 584).

Controlled studies comparing agoraphobic marriages with marriages of comparison groups are also not without their difficulties. Of those reviewed by Kleiner & Marshall few actually assessed marital conflict, and some relied on case notes and within-group comparisons. The latter studies tended to provide some evidence for marital dissatisfaction and dependency. In one of the few controlled studies examining the quality of agoraphobic marriages Buglass et al. (1977) compared agoraphobic women and their spouses with normal control couples in terms of domestic activities, decision-making in a number of areas and 'manifest interaction' ratings made on the basis of a tape-recording of a conjoint interview. The most striking feature of the comparison of the two groups of couples was their similarity with respect to these measures. This lack of difference was also found in a comparison of 30 agoraphobics with three groups of control couples (non-phobic female psychiatric patients and their husbands, maritally distressed couples and happily married couples) assessed on a battery of measures relating to marital adjustment, intimacy and needs (Arrindell & Emmelkamp, 1986). In fact agoraphobics and their spouses were found to be more comparable to happily married couples than to maritally distressed controls. Fisher & Wilson (1985) also found no difference between agoraphobic and non-agoraphobic controls on a measure of marital adjustment. Kleiner & Marshall, in their review published prior to the publication of the above two papers, conclude that 'although agoraphobic patients do not differ from normals in their overall interpersonal relations, the interaction between their personal characteristics and marital dissatisfaction might nevertheless be important in the development and maintenance of the phobia' (p. 588). Marital difficulties may thus interfere with treatment outcome or may be adversely affected by treatment gains.

The picture is complex, however, as shown by studies investigating the relationship between treatment gains and changes in marital adjustment. Barlow, Mavissakalian & Hay (1981) found two patterns of change in the group treatment of six agoraphobic women treated with their husbands by exposure and cognitive restructuring. For two couples, improvements in phobia were correlated with decreases in marital satisfaction, while for the remaining four subjects as phobia improved marital satisfaction increased.

Hafner (1984) also reports two patterns of change in 32 agoraphobic women treated with exposure-based methods. For half the subjects treatment gains were associated with increased marital conflict. The remaining subjects are described as protected from personal conflict by a mutual adherence to sex-role stereotypes. If conflict over sex-role stereotypes emerged then further treatment gains were dependent on the couples' success in resolving these conflicts. Other findings suggest that a reduction in agoraphobic complaints is accompanied by either stable (e.g. Monteiro, Marks & Ramm, 1985) or improved (e.g. Cobb et al., 1984) marital and sexual adjustment.

A further line of evidence relates to the suggestion that the poorest treatment results are obtained by patients from families with the severest pathology (e.g. Hudson, 1974) or who were maritally dissatisfied (e.g. Milton & Hafner, 1979; Bland & Hallam, 1981). However, a number of authors (e.g. Emmelkamp, 1982; Monteiro, Marks & Ramm, 1985) have pointed to statistical and methodological flaws in some of the earlier studies conducted in this area. Further, other studies (e.g. Arrindell, Emmelkamp & Sanderman, 1986; Emmelkamp, 1980; Himadi et al., 1986) have found no relationship between improvement in agoraphobic complaints and initial marital and sexual adjustment. Reviewing nine studies examining the relationship between marital satisfaction and treatment outcome Jansson, Öst & Jeremalm (1987) found that three studies showed a positive relationship immediately post-treatment and three at follow-up (two of which showed no such relationship at post-treatment). In their own study they report no relationship between marital satisfaction and behavioural, subjective or overall improvement up to 15 months after treatment. In a further meta-analytic review which included six studies assessing marital adjustment and treatment effectiveness, Dewey & Hunsley (1990) conclude that 'higher pretreatment marital functioning is associated with greater reductions in agoraphobic symptomatology at posttreatment and up to one year following completion of treatment' (p. 77), although the effect size was small.

Although results are mixed, a difference seems to lie in change at follow-up. While immediate post-treatment differences between patients with 'good' and 'bad' marriages may be negligible, the latter seem more likely to relapse at follow-up. This may well relate to the finding reported by some studies that involving the spouse as co-therapist in exposure-based treatments for agoraphobia appears to enhance the effectiveness of treatment (e.g. Barlow, O'Brien & Last, 1984; Cerny et al., 1987). However, a meta-analytic review of seven published studies on the use of spouse involvement in exposure-based therapy suggests no significant benefits from spouse compared with no-spouse involvement (Dewey & Hunsley, 1990). Nevertheless, it is possible that treatment changes may reflect spouse involvement either directly through therapy or indirectly through encouragement and support. The latter is no doubt related to degree of marital conflict, and may thus account for the mixed results of treatment gains in relation to marital adjustment. It seems less likely that agoraphobia is characterised by a particular marital pattern.

PRECIPITATING FACTORS

A number of reports suggest that traumatic events often precede the onset of agoraphobic symptoms. Öst & Hugdahl (1983) report that 82% of their sample could identify a precipitating cause, while Sheehan, Sheehan & Minichiello (1981) found that 91% of a large sample of agoraphobics could identify life changes that appeared to be related to the onset of their symptoms. The two most frequent precipitants appear to be loss of a significant other and physical threat (Foa, Steketee & Young, 1984; Liebowitz & Klein, 1979). In studies by Klein and his colleagues (e.g. Liebowitz & Klein, 1979) between 30% and 50% of patients referred to physical threat (assault, car accident) or serious illness as a precipitating factor; similar figures are reported by other studies. In a study of 50 agoraphobic patients asked to record details of stressors and conflicts experienced in the year preceding the development of agoraphobic symptoms (Kleiner & Marshall, 1987), 84% reported experiencing marital or relationship conflicts, 64% family conflicts, 2% divorce, 22% marriage, 22% social isolation, 22% death of a loved one and 18% relocation of residence. Although subjects clearly reported a range of predicted stressors, whether their incidence exceeds that which would be expected for a general population cannot be determined in the absence of comparison data.

In summarising findings relating traumatic events to agoraphobia Foa et al. (1984) suggest that:

> If agoraphobia is brought about primarily by an actual or anticipated death of an important person or by the psychological concomitants of illness, the realization of one's own physical vulnerability, then perhaps agoraphobic symptoms can be construed as manifestations of fear of death (p. 14).

Other studies have, however, failed to find such specific predictors of agoraphobia. Although 88% of Öst & Hugdahl's (1983) sample recalled a precipitating circumstance the authors report that 'one cannot conclude that any specific predictor seems to have been at hand for these patients' (p. 630). Findings such as these led Tearnan, Telch & Keefe (1984) to conclude that 'the range of precipitating factors related to onset is quite extensive and appears to include any stressful experience' (p. 58). As Foa *et al.* (1984) note, 'that symptom onset follows a stressful period is a trite observation' (p. 14). But if this is indeed the case, and general stress factors rather than specific precipitating factors are involved, then this would not provide an explanation for the specific development of agoraphobia.

THEORETICAL ISSUES

Predisposing and precipitating factors are incorporated into most theoretical analyses of agoraphobia. These include the behavioural model set forth by Goldstein & Chambless (1978) who proposed that a 'fear of fear' (i.e. fear of having a panic attack) is a central component in the genesis of agoraphobia and Rachman's (1983a, 1984c,d) revised learning-theory based formulation emphasising the balance of danger and safety signals (see Chapter 2). Both theories are mutually compatible, emphasising to differing degrees the part played by panic (unconditioned emotional stimuli or 'danger' signals) and stimuli which signal safety, as well as the part played by interpersonal factors, separation and loss.

Fear of fear

According to the fear-of-fear model proposed by Goldstein & Chambless (1978) (see also Chambless & Goldstein, 1981) fear of panic forms the central component of agoraphobia. Thus fear develops through the occurrence of panic attacks as unconditioned emotional responses to prolonged chronic conflict and stress. The latter refer to the specific predisposing factors discussed above and include person variables (lack of assertion, low self-sufficiency) and psychological loss or physical trauma as well as a specific cognitive style. Given such circumstances the individual is vulnerable to unpredictable panics and, being hypersensitive to internal sensations such as heart rate or breathing, anxiety is conditioned to these consistent internal cues. Subsequent second-order conditioning of specific to-be-avoided situations also occurs. These are situations where flight would be difficult in the occurrence of panic so that even if panics should cease these situations will continue to evoke anxiety in a secondary manner.

A further component of the model concerns the part played by maladaptive cognitions concerning the potential harm that will befall the agoraphobic because of anxiety (e.g. I'll die or go crazy). Chambless & Goldstein (1981) note that these cognitions are maladaptive in two ways:

firstly because they contribute to the spiralling panic once the anxiety response is triggered, and secondly because they prevent the individual from recognising and resolving the problem.

Reiss & McNally (1985) have expanded on the origins of 'fear of fear' by suggesting a role for such factors as biological constitution, and personality needs to avoid embarrassment, illness, danger and loss of control, in addition to the actual experience of panic. According to this model, anticipation of panic is composed of a combination of anxiety expectancy and anxiety sensitivity (see Chapter 2). A similar model of panic-related avoidance has been outlined by Telch et al. (1989a). They emphasise the interaction between beliefs in one's ability to execute effective coping strategies (cf. self-efficacy), estimation of panic likelihood and appraisal of negative anxiety/panic consequences as determinants of avoidance behaviour.

The shift from the DSM-III to the DSM-III-R diagnostic subcategories is consistent with the fear-of-fear notion. This would assume that panic is primary in most cases of agoraphobia as suggested by a number of authors (Barlow, 1988; Goldstein & Chambless, 1978; Klein, 1981) so that panic–anxiety is viewed as the construct which results in avoidance behaviour (Klein, 1988; Klein & Gorman, 1987; Klerman, 1986). Klein, for example, has argued that agoraphobia is caused by biologically driven panic attacks that are conditioned to increasingly broad circumstances so that the person's life becomes ever more circumscribed (Klein, 1988). Others have argued that agoraphobia has a variety of causes including, but not limited to, panic attacks (e.g. Lelliott & Marks, 1988). Within this view the contention is that, given appropriate predisposing and precipitating factors, it is as likely that panic attacks and avoidance will be acquired simultaneously or avoidance behaviours acquired first, as it is that panic will precede agoraphobia.

There are a number of lines of evidence which provide some support for the view that panic precedes the development of agoraphobia. It seems that patients do report the development of varying degrees of avoidance behaviour after, rather than before, experiencing one or more panic attacks (Garvey & Tuason, 1984; Uhde et al., 1985). Thyer & Himle (1985) found that 79% of a sample of 115 agoraphobics attributed the development of their agoraphobia to their experience of panics. Rapee & Murrell (1988) report that 80% of their 88 agoraphobic subjects reported an age of onset for their agoraphobic concerns as identical to or closely following their first panic attack. Lelliott et al. (1989) found that only 23% of a clinic sample reported onset of agoraphobia-related avoidance preceding the first panic, while for 32% avoidance began within days after the first panic and for an additional 41% avoidance began after more than one panic. In a further study Schneier et al. (1991) report that agoraphobic avoidance preceded the onset of panic disorder in only approximately 17% of cases.

It should be borne in mind, however, that these results all rely on retro-spective reports with the inevitable problems inherent in such information.

A further line of research investigating whether panic precedes the development of avoidance or vice versa concerns the sequence of symptom improvement in relation to treatment. If panic is primary then decrease in avoidance would be unlikely prior to improvement in panic symptoms; conversely if avoidance is primary then a decrease in panic attacks would be unlikely prior to a decrease in avoidance behaviour. However, the results of a large sample of panic patients from several European and North and South American centres failed to find any particular symptom as central in terms of the sequence of improvement (Deltito et al., 1991).

A further suggestion is that agoraphobia without panic attacks is a relatively rare disorder (Garvey & Tuason, 1984; Torgersen, 1983). In one report of a series of 115 patients receiving a diagnosis of agoraphobia, 83% met the criteria for agoraphobia with panic attacks while only 17% were diagnosed as agoraphobia without panic attacks (Thyer et al., 1985a). This has led some to view agoraphobia as merely a more severe form of panic disorder (e.g. Klein, Ross & Cohen, 1987). However, the figures for co-occurrence of agoraphobia and panic may well be an overestimation. As Eaton & Keyl (1990) note, both agoraphobia and panic can lead to the person seeking treatment; if the person experiences both problems he or she is much more likely to seek help than if either problem is experienced in isolation. Clinic-based figures of co-occurrence may thus exceed those taken from population-based studies. Indeed, in one such study Wiessman et al. (1986) found a higher prevalence for agoraphobia without panic attacks than agoraphobia with panic attacks. Recent data from the ECA programme (Eaton & Keyl, 1990) also suggest a higher proportion of agoraphobics who report no history of panic attacks than indicated by clinic-based estimates. Of 260 new cases of agoraphobia, identified by DIS/DSM-III criteria from a community-based sample or over 11 000 people interviewed on two occasions a year apart, over two-thirds reported no history of panic.

The relationship between agoraphobia and panic in clinic-based samples has led some to suppose that panic severity and frequency are directly related to degree of avoidance. However, there is little evidence to support this view. Diary (Mavissakalian, 1988), interview (Craske, Sanderson & Barlow, 1987) and questionnaire data (Rapee & Murrell, 1988) all suggest that severity and frequency of panic is not related to avoidance behaviour. In one recent paper comparing 20 panic with agoraphobia with 20 panic without agoraphobia patients there were no differences between the two groups on measures of severity and frequency of panic (Fleming & Faulk,

1989). Craske & Barlow (1988), reviewing the evidence, comment that 'overall, the data suggest that the relationship between panic severity and avoidance is not direct, but is mediated by other variables' (p. 672). These other variables include access to safety signals (see below), perceived consequences of panicking and anticipation of panicking in a given situation, somatic focus and generalised expectancy of panic. Thus, although 'fear of fear' may be one factor contributing to avoidance there are many other contributory factors.

Although a number of authors have suggested that one or more unexpected panic attacks are essential for the occurrence of agoraphobic avoidance, there is clearly not a one-to-one relationship, and many other factors are likely to be implicated. Given that the research investigating factors predisposing individuals to agoraphobia has produced mixed results this is clearly an area where more detailed investigation is required. Panic and agoraphobic avoidance evidently interlink to some extent, but as Rapee & Murrell (1988) comment, 'to say that there exist no differences between panic disorder and agoraphobia is to risk ignoring a wealth of potentially important information' (p. 204).

Safety signals

The historical antecedents of the safety signal perspective can be traced to Mowrer's two-stage theory of fear and avoidance, with Pavlovian conditioned stimuli giving rise to a 'drive state' which motivates the organism to execute avoidance behaviour (see Chapter 2). Subsequent revisions by Mowrer (1960) postulated two types of reinforcement emphasising danger and safety signals. Drawing on this notion Rachman (1984c) has suggested that avoidance behaviour is motivated both by avoidance of fear and approach to safety. The balance between perceived danger and perceived safety will determine avoidance. Stimuli associated with escape from the feared situation serve as safety signals and hence acquire positive reinforcement properties.

Rachman (1984c) further suggests that reliance upon safety signals is determined in part by psychological loss and a history of overprotection. Given the evidence reviewed above the interpretation of psychological loss and overprotection as predisposing factors in agoraphobia is not without its critics, and thus their actions as determinants of safety signals not proven. Further, panic is viewed as a 'danger' signal which is likely to reduce perceived safety and hence strengthen avoidance. This interlinking should also be treated with caution given the lack of a consistent link between panic frequency/intensity and avoidance. Rachman further postulates that within exposure-based treatments the individual should be encouraged to travel towards safety signals rather than away from them. Barlow (1988), for example, asks clients as part of the assessment interview to detail their reliance upon safety signals. The therapeutic value of the safety signal perspective has, however, also drawn notes of caution (Himadi, 1987; Watts, 1988). The strength of the safety signal perspective lies rather in its integrating theoretical perspective (Watts, 1988).

ASSESSMENT

Self-report instruments

A number of phobia questionnaires contain items pertaining to agoraphobia (e.g. the Fear Survey Schedule (FSS), Wolpe & Lang, 1964; Fear Questionnaire (FQ), Marks & Mathews, 1979). For example, the FQ has a five-item Agoraphobia factor which has good test−retest reliability (Michelson & Mavissakalian, 1983) and has been shown to be sensitive to treatment change. Mavissakalian (1986) has provided further data relating to the validity of the agoraphobia subscale with a sample of agoraphobic patients, further suggesting that a cut-off point of 30 on this subscale may be a useful diagnostic aid.

A self-report scale specifically developed for assessing agoraphobic avoidance behaviour and panic frequency has been developed in part from the Fear Survey Schedule. The Mobility Inventory (MI) for Agoraphobia (Chambless et al., 1985) is a 27-item scale that is rated four times each on a five-point Likert scale. On this instrument 26 situations are rated for avoidance both when the individual is accompanied and when alone. The items are then rated for discomfort elicited, again when alone and when accompanied. A final question refers to panic frequency—a report of the number of panic attacks experienced within the past seven days. The authors report high internal consistency and reliability for the scale, and sensitivity to change with treatment. The scale also discriminates agoraphobics from patients with other anxiety disorders (Craske, Rachman & Tallman, 1986).

The Body Sensations Questionnaire (BSQ) and the Agoraphobia Cognitions Questionnaire (ACQ) (Chambless et al., 1984) are two related self-report inventories designed to assess cognitive and physiological aspects of agoraphobia. The ACQ is a 15-item scale referring to thoughts concerning the negative consequences of anxiety rated on a scale from the thought never occurs (1) to the thought always occurs (5). The BSQ is a 17-item scale referring to such symptoms as dizziness, nausea and sweating rated on a five-point scale rated from not worried or frightened by this sensation

(1) to extremely frightened by this sensation (5). The authors report high internal consistency and good test–retest reliability for both scales, as well as sensitivity to treatment change and ability to distinguish between agoraphobics and normal controls.

A further scale devised by Johnston *et al.* (1984) consists of 25 items designed to assess agoraphobic avoidance. The scale seems to have a variable factor structure, Johnston *et al.* obtaining a two-factor solution ('avoidance of going places' and 'avoidance of situations where the subject may feel trapped or restricted'), while Hamann & Mavissakalian (1988) report a five-factor solution. The scale has, however, been used as a means of assessing agoraphobic status (Watts, 1989) with a score above 70 seeming to indicate extreme avoidance.

Most recently Öst (1990) has described the Agoraphobia Scale (AS) consisting of 20 items depicting agoraphobic situations. Each item is rated twice, once on a five-point scale to indicate degree of anxiety or discomfort and a second time on a three-point scale to indicate degree of avoidance. Öst provides data indicating that the AS is significantly correlated with the agoraphobia factor of the FQ and with the avoidance when alone but not the avoidance when accompanied component of the MI. The AS also correlates moderately but significantly with the ACQ and BSQ but not with more general measures of anxiety or depression. Öst reports further data indicating high internal consistency for the AS which also discriminated between an agoraphobic and normal sample and a sample of simple phobic patients; it was also sensitive to change subsequent to treatment. The scale is clearly promising and could become a useful self-report measure in agoraphobia research.

While self-report instruments give some indication of self-assessed anxiety or thoughts associated with that anxiety, they do not provide a record of the person's thoughts while actually exposed to a threatening situation. A number of studies have attempted to assess thought samples during *in vivo* exposure. Williams & Rappoport (1983) asked subjects to report anything they were thinking about every 90 seconds during behavioural testing. A timed bleeper activated a portable tape-recorder for 20 seconds. Thoughts were subsequently coded as fearful, about bodily states, coping thoughts, diversionary thoughts and thoughts about the actual task. Inter-rater reliability is reported as quite satisfactory for all codes, although only 62% agreement between raters was obtained for coping thoughts.

A further method reported by Michelson (1987) is for subjects to continuously dictate their thoughts into an unobtrusive microphone during a behavioural test. Thoughts are subsequently coded as negative/self-defeating, positive/coping or neutral/task irrelevant. Schwartz & Michelson (1986) and Michelson (1986) report good inter-rater reliability, reasonable test–retest reliability and sensitivity to treatment change for cognitions obtained in this way.

Behavioural assessment

Three general types of behavioural measures are typically referred to within the literature (e.g. Barlow, 1988; Michelson, 1987; O'Brien & Barlow, 1984): standardised walks or behavioural avoidance tests; individual behavioural avoidance tests and self-monitoring or self-directed exposure.

The method of standardised walks has been used in a number of studies spanning the past two decades since first reported by Agras, Leitenberg & Barlow (1968). These typically involve clients walking alone along a course of specific length until they either reach the end of the course or feel too anxious to proceed. The course is usually divided into relatively equal parts. Thus Mavissakalian (1986) describes a standard walk 0.4 miles in length, leading from the front door of the hospital to a crowded urban centre and ending at a crowded bus stop. Patients were asked to walk the course alone until their anxiety reached a degree which could not be tolerated. The course was divided into 20 parts with performance assessed as the number of parts completed.

Some studies have obtained self-reports of anxiety at specific points on the walk (e.g. Barlow, Mavissakalian & Schofield (1980) subjects carried a small tape-recorder to record subjective assessments of anxiety) or have taken continuous physiological recordings (e.g. Mavissakalian (1987) obtained a continuous recording of heart rate).

One obvious advantage of a standardised walk is that it allows both a direct comparison across clients and across treatments, as well as allowing direct monitoring of both subjective reports and physiological responses *in vivo*.

One obvious disadvantage is that only one behavioural parameter is assessed (i.e. walking); thus it does not provide an adequate assessment for clients whose primary difficulty relates to shopping, driving, etc. A further problem relates to the issue of demand characteristics. Experimental demand effects have been shown to influence the behaviour of mildly fearful subjects (Borkovec, Weerts & Bernstein, 1977), although it is not known whether similar effects are evident in agoraphobics. However, in aiming to 'please the therapist' the standardised test may not reveal the true nature of the person's difficulties. As Williams (1985) points out, if standardised behavioural avoidance tests are to minimise demand characteristics and be adequately sensitive to treatment-induced change then they must cover a broad enough range of differentially difficult items.

Given these difficulties an alternative is to tailor the behavioural avoidance test to the specific individual. Mathews and his colleagues (1977, 1981) developed an individualised 15-item hierarchy of feared situations with each client. When the therapist first visited the client's home, the client was asked to attempt the item which they felt was most difficult for them. If successful they proceeded to items of increasing difficulty, if unsuccessful they proceeded to items of decreasing difficulty until they failed an item having completed the one immediately below it or when they refused to attempt a higher item. The number of items successfully completed during assessment provided an overall score. As O'Brien & Barlow (1984) point out, however, the number of items completed is largely influenced by the client's initial choice of item to attempt, and the client's performance provides no index of the absolute level of difficulty of the completed phobic tasks.

\A number of other studies have used variations of individualised tests / (e.g. Greist *et al.*, 1980; Hand, Lamontagne & Marks, 1974; Mavissakalian & Michelson, 1983, 1986).\In the latter study, agoraphobic subjects were asked to attempt five items specifically selected from their own completed phobic anxiety and avoidance scales\ The number of situations subjects could attempt and remain in for five minutes, and their peak self-reported anxiety level at this time, were recorded.)While an individually tailored assessment clearly provides a personally relevant and hence clinically sensitive assessment, its very nature means that comparison with other individuals, groups or studies is inherently limited. Its use is likely to be most appropriate for within-group comparisons and single case investigations or for specific clinical assessments.

, A final method of behavioural assessment used extensively in clinical practice is the daily recording of information relating to the client's fear.) Several studies report the use of behavioural diaries or weekly records to monitor a range of variables such as the destination and reason for the trip, the distance travelled and time spent away from home, whether the person was accompanied or alone, whether the trip was a specified practice session or part of the client's usual routine, as well as overall and peak anxiety levels (e.g. Greist *et al.*, 1980; Jannoun *et al.*, 1980; Mathews *et al.*, 1977; Mavissakalian & Michelson, 1983; Michelson *et al.*, 1986). The question of reliability and validity of self-report diaries is obviously open to question, as with diary methods in general. However, they clearly do provide essential clinical data, especially when used in conjunction with direct behavioural observation.

Physiological assessment

In comparison to the use of self-report and behavioural assessments there are fewer studies reporting the recording of psychophysiological responses in agoraphobia. In studies which have taken such assessments, the most frequently taken measures are heart rate and skin conductance. In one early study Stern & Marks (1973) continuously monitored heart rate during phobic and neutral imagery tasks and during imaginal and *in vivo* exposure. Heart rate increased in the early stages of *in vivo* exposure relative to baseline measures, and subsequently decreased with prolonged exposure. There were then few studies addressing psychophysiological responding in relation to agoraphobia until the 1980s, when the potential importance of triple-response measurement (cognitive, behavioural and physiological) in order to discriminate treatment success was emphasised (see Himadi, Boice & Barlow, 1985, for a review of the perceived need for assessment of agoraphobia across the three response systems).

Within the past decade Barlow, Mavissakalian, Michelson and their colleagues have produced a number of studies examining the relationship of psychophysiological measures to other measures of agoraphobic responsiveness (Barlow, Mavissakalian & Schofield, 1980; Holden & Barlow, 1986; Mavissakalian, 1987; Mavissakalian & Michelson, 1982, 1983; Michelson & Mavissakalian, 1985; Michelson, Mavissakalian & Marchione, 1985; Michelson *et al.*, 1990b; Vermilyea, Boice & Barlow, 1984). Suggestions to emerge from this research are firstly, that significant desynchrony of measures exists with significant treatment improvements often evident from behavioural and cognitive measures while only weak or inconsistent improvements are evident in heart rate; secondly, there is some evidence, although this is inconsistent, that desynchrony is associated with either poorer outcome and/or a greater likelihood of relapse.

The latter suggestion was raised by a preliminary small-scale report of three agoraphobic subjects (Barlow *et al.*, 1980) within which the desynchronous responding of one subject was associated with poor outcome. Subsequent studies have, however, not substantiated this notion. Vermilyea *et al.* (1984) found that desynchronous subjects did as well as synchronous subjects by the end of treatment. At follow-up of a year or more desynchronous subjects were doing as well as synchronous subjects (Craske, Sanderson & Barlow, 1987).

Studies by Michelson, Mavissakalian and their colleagues have also produced mixed results. Thus Michelson & Mavissakalian (1985) and Michelson, Mavissakalian & Marchione, (1985, 1988) report that 'synchrony' was associated with greater improvement at post-treatment and follow-up. Unlike the earlier studies, however, 'synchronisers' were identified on the basis of mean physiological, behavioural and cognitive parameters at post-treatment. As Barlow (1988, p. 399) notes, this assessment at one point in time is really referring to a concordance/discordance dimension rather than a synchronous/desynchronous dimension, and is thus dealing with correlations between measures rather than using synchronous/desynchronous changes over time to predict outcome. In a study comparing post-treatment assignment with assignment according to pre- to post-increases or decreases in behavioural and physiological parameters, Mavissakalian (1987) reports no relationship between synchrony and treatment outcome, thus supporting Vermilyea *et al*. (1984) rather than his previous findings with Michelson. However, in a subsequent study including additional subjects to those included in Michelson *et al*. (1985), Michelson *et al*. (1990b) report that synchronisers exhibited superior end-of-treatment outcome and follow-up compared to desynchronisers on all parameters except physiological measures.

Such mixed results make it difficult to evaluate the usefulness of predicting outcome on the basis of synchronous/desynchronous treatment responses. The contradictory results are no doubt due in part to definitional differences, but may also reflect difficulties with the reliability of physiological measures taken repeatedly over time. Holden & Barlow (1986), for example, found that while heart rate decreased in agoraphobics during treatment, there was a similar decrease in a non-treated control group over sessions. This has led to suggestions that avoidance and subjective anxiety are the most useful outcome measures. Care clearly needs to be exercised both in monitoring physiological parameters, particularly in terms of which parameter or multiple set of parameters to assess, the reliability of equipment and in the interpretation of results (see Chapter 1).

TREATMENT

Exposure-based treatments

Behavioural treatments of agoraphobia during the 1960s involved either systematic desensitisation (e.g. Gelder & Marks, 1966) or imaginal exposure (Marks, Boulougouris & Marset, 1971) and generally met with only limited success. The increasing use of real-life exposure during the 1970s and 1980s has met with far more success. Exposure to phobic stimuli under conditions conducive to habituation or extinction is often assumed to be the active therapeutic ingredient in the reduction of agoraphobic anxiety and avoidance (although a number of cognitive variables have recently been suggested as the crucial variables in fear reduction due to exposure).

In their review of behavioural treatments for agoraphobia published nearly a decade ago, Jannson & Öst (1982) detail 21 studies treating approximately 400 agoraphobic subjects by *in vivo* exposure treatments, 12 outcome studies treating 140 subjects with imaginal exposure either alone or in conjunction with real-life exposure, and five further studies evaluating systematic desensitisation. They conclude that the data show a consistent picture of clinical improvement with real-life exposure, that imaginal exposure is effective in relation to controls although there is conflicting evidence regarding its effectiveness in relation to real-life exposure, while systematic desensitisation is generally not effective. Similar conclusions are presented in a further review by Emmelkamp (1982) published at about the same time, in a more recent review by Michelson (1987) and a meta-analytic review of 19 outcome studies by Trull, Nietzel & Main (1988). The latter review was specifically concerned with 'clinical significance', i.e. changes in a presenting problem that result in the client being within the normal limits of the outcome measure used, in this instance the FQ. The authors summarise their findings by commenting that: 'behaviour therapy produces clinically significant outcomes . . . these outcomes are well-maintained at follow-up . . . treatments involving exposure were associated with greatest improvement' (p. 527).

There are surprisingly few studies reporting long-term follow-up results for exposure-based therapy, although the available results are promising (Marks, 1971; Emmelkamp & Kuipers, 1979; McPherson, Brougham & McLaren, 1980; Cohen, Monteiro & Marks, 1984; Jansson, Jerremalm & Öst, 1986; Hand et al., 1986; Fiegenbaum, 1988). It should be borne in mind, however, that there are limitations with many of these follow-up findings. They are often based upon postal follow-up data (e.g. Emmelkamp & Kuipers, 1979); may only include a relatively small percentage of those initially treated (e.g. McPherson et al., 1980 included at follow-up only those who had improved after treatment, and of those only 69% participated at follow-up); also, follow-up assessments have tended to involve relatively circumscribed patient self-assessments or therapist reports, and it is worth bearing in mind that on average a quarter to a third of patients do not improve. Recent follow-up studies include the report of Cohen, Monteiro & Marks (1984), showing that, two years after treatment, two-thirds of agoraphobic patients remained improved or much improved on self-report and independent assessor ratings; 89% of those initially treated were assessed at follow-up. In a further follow-up study Jansson, Jerremalm & Öst (1986) report that of 32 agoraphobic patients treated with exposure *in vivo* or applied relaxation, the proportion reaching clinically significant improvement was 50% at the end of treatment and 66% at 15-month follow-up. These figures were based upon the average percentage of subjects falling outside the normal agoraphobic range on behavioural, physiological and self-ratings. Hand et al. (1988) report that four years after treatment 70% of 75 agoraphobic patients treated with exposure-based therapy (88% of those initially completing treatment) reported a marked reduction in phobic anxiety, while Fiegenbaum (1988) reports that at five-year follow-up 78% of 104 patients treated with exposure-based therapy were symptom-free.

Given that approximately 30% of clients fail to improve with *in vivo* exposure, a number of authors have attempted to unravel variables predictive of such failure (e.g. Chambless & Gracely, 1988). These include marital dissatisfaction (discussed previously), demographic characteristics and phobic severity. Although some studies suggest that an unsatisfactory marital relationship (e.g. Milton & Hafner, 1979) or initial phobic severity (e.g. Fischer *et al.*, 1988) may be predictive of treatment failure, there are few consistent results within the literature. Others have pointed to a number of procedural variations in exposure therapy, some of which may affect outcome.

Procedural variations in exposure therapy

Procedural variations in the actual practice of *in vivo* exposure include prolonged exposure of varying duration (or flooding), successive approximations (or graded practice/shaping), therapist-directed or client-directed exposure, home-based or clinic-based treatment and individual versus group treatment. Studies suggest that some of these procedural variations make little difference to treatment outcome. Thus Emmelkamp (1974) and Everaerd, Rijken & Emmelkamp (1973) found equal treatment gains for flooding and shaping procedures, while Hafner & Marks (1976) and Emmelkamp & Emmelkamp-Benner (1975) found equal treatment gains for *in vivo* exposure conducted in groups and when conducted individually. Others have found that while a group approach *per se* may not enhance therapeutic gain relative to individual treatment, the involvement of friends or the encouragement of support groups can enhance such gains. Thus Hand, Lamontagne & Marks (1974) found that structured groups designed to facilitate social cohesion showed significant improvements in comparison to unstructured groups at three- and six-month follow-up. Also Sinnott *et al.* (1981) found that agoraphobics selected from the same neighbourhood and treated as a group showed superior outcome on many measures in comparison to a group from a wider geographical area whose opportunities for informal socialising and support were presumably not as easy.

Other procedural variations seem to be more consistently associated with differential treatment effects. Stern & Marks (1973) found that prolonged *in vivo* exposure (two hours of uninterrupted real-life exposure) was superior to brief *in vivo* exposure (four 30-min real-life trials separated by 30-min rest intervals). In a further study comparing time between exposure sessions, Foa *et al.* (1980a) found that massed practice (daily sessions of exposure) was more effective than spaced practice (once-weekly sessions of exposure). In a more recent report, however, Chambless (1991) found no difference between massed and spaced exposure (daily versus weekly) in the treatment of 19 agoraphobic and 17 simple phobic patients.

A further procedural variation involves the use of therapist-directed or client-directed exposure. As Mathews, Gelder & Johnston (1981) suggest, 'Practice as self-exposure is not considered incidental to some other procedures it forms the core of treatment' (p. 110) Self-directed exposure can be established with the aid of a self-help instruction manual and hence minimal or no therapeutic contact, although there are obviously variations in the amount of therapist contact time involved in establishing self-directed exposure programmes. This degree of contact is no doubt one variable affecting the efficacy of such a treatment strategy. Holden *et al.* (1983) examined the efficacy of a client-conducted treatment package for agoraphobics using a self-help manual evaluated in a multiple-baseline design with six severely agoraphobic females. The results suggest little therapeutic gain with just the self-help manual in the absence of direct therapist contact; when therapist contact was subsequently introduced modest improvement was shown by most patients. In a further study evaluating the relative and combined effectiveness of therapist-assisted *in vivo* exposure, self-directed *in vivo* exposure, imipramine and a placebo, subjects assigned to the self-directed treatment showed significantly inferior post-treatment outcome.

The way in which procedural variation affects outcome is clearly complex. At one level one might assume that massed practice, like prolonged exposure, allows time for the patient's anxiety to reduce substantially while in the feared situation; brief and spaced practice may allow the patient to leave the situation while still anxious. It has generally been assumed that escape from the situation while anxiety is increasing (or at least not decreasing) is likely to reinforce escape and avoidance. As Mathews, Gelder & Johnston (1981) note, 'The golden rule is to try never to leave the situation until the fear is going down' (p. 182). Yet empirical evidence now seems to contradict this notion. In two studies (De Silva & Rachman, 1984; Rachman *et al.*, 1986) agoraphobic subjects were exposed to a fear-provoking situation and instructed either not to leave the situation until the anxiety had dropped at least to half of peak anxiety felt (endurance condition) or to leave when subjectively felt anxiety reached about 75% of the maximum anxiety the subject felt she would feel in the target situation (escape condition). Both groups of patients showed significant and equivalent improvement on all measures of agoraphobia which were maintained at three-month follow-up. Interestingly, subjects in the escape condition reported greater pre-session estimates of control which may well be an important cognitive variable in fear-reduction therapies.

Cognitive parameters and exposure therapy

A number of authors have suggested that cognitive parameters are responsible for exposure-based treatment gains. Williams (1991) draws on self-efficacy theory (see Chapter 2), arguing that effectiveness of exposure therapy is not based on extent of approach to phobic stimuli or attention to them, but in people's appraisal of their effectiveness in coping with whatever stimuli are present. The aim of therapy based upon this premise is enhanced personal mastery. The therapist plays an active role in supporting, assisting, and guiding people towards success; factors not inherent in exposure-based treatments. In a comparison of guided mastery and exposure treatment as therapy for 20 agoraphobics, Williams & Zane (1989) found the former to be significantly more effective in reducing anxiety both at the end of treatment and follow-up; at follow-up the effectiveness differential between treatments actually increased. Williams and his colleagues (Williams, Dooseman & Kleifield, 1984; Williams, Kinney & Falbo, 1969; Williams, Turner & Peer, 1985; Williams & Watson, 1985) have also found that self-efficacy is a better predictor of treatment effects than anticipated outcome- or performance-related anxiety.

A further related cognitive variable that may be an important mediator of the effects of *in vivo* exposure is the role of clients' anxiety expectations (Kirsch, 1985b). In an interesting study Southworth & Kirsch (1988) treated 20 agoraphobic subjects for 10 sessions over two weeks with *in vivo* exposure therapy. For each session all subjects were instructed to walk away from their homes until they became anxious and then to return; half the subjects were told the procedure was part of therapy (high-expectancy group) while the other half were told it was an assessment procedure (low-expectancy group). Subjects provided with therapeutic expectancies showed substantially greater behavioural improvement and improved more rapidly than subjects who were led to believe that exposure was for the purpose of assessment. Although both groups reported equal improvement in the experience of fear, subjects in the high-expectancy group were able to travel twice as far from home before reaching that reduced fear level (i.e. fear reduction was greater among subjects given therapeutic instructions).

A further paradigm positing cognitive mechanisms for change is the State-of-Mind model (Schwartz & Garamoni, 1986). Although primarily considered a model for studying cognitive change across therapy, the model posits five distinct states-of-mind: negative monologue, negative dialogue, internal dialogue of conflict, positive dialogue, and positive monologue (see Chapter 3). In one specific study, Schwartz & Michelson (1987) found that at pretreatment, agoraphobic subjects were characterised by negative dialogue; at post-treatment a number of subjects were characterised by positive dialogue and effectiveness of treatment was related to extent of positive dialogue. Interestingly both cognitively and exposure-based treatments produced significant changes in subjects' internal dialogues, again suggesting that exposure-based procedures may not operate via Pavlovian extinction procedures (i.e. promoting prolonged exposure to fear-evoking stimuli until anxiety declines) but via cognitive parameters.

Exposure therapy improvement rates

As noted, overall improvement rates of 60–75% have been reported for exposure-based strategies for agoraphobia, although these figures are closer to 50% when treatment drop-outs are included in the analysis (Barlow & Wolfe, 1981). Studies involving *in vivo* exposure treatments have reported drop-out rates that range from 8% to 40% with a median of 22% (Mavissakalian & Barlow, 1981). These drop-out rates are considerably higher for intensive *in vivo* exposure administered over a short period of time (e.g. Emmelkamp & Ultee, 1974; Emmelkamp & Wessels, 1975) and lower for a more gradual, self-initiated programme introduced over a longer time period (e.g. Mathews *et al.*, 1977). A recent reanalysis of 11 previously published studies involving clinical trials of exposure-based treatment for agoraphobia suggests that while improvement figures of 58% are achieved (excluding drop-outs) actual recovery rates are only 33% (Jacobson, Wilson & Tupper, 1988). Many patients who show treatment gains may be far from symptom-free. McPherson, Brougham & McLaren (1980) report that among clients who showed some improvement following behavioural treatment, only 18% rated themselves as being completely free of symptoms. Further, Munby & Johnston (1980) found relapse occurring in as many as 50% of clients who had benefited clinically. Nevertheless, follow-up research over two to seven years suggests that therapeutic gains induced by behavioural, exposure-based treatments can be maintained (e.g. Mavissakalian & Michelson, 1986; Munby & Johnston, 1980).

Although real-life exposure for agoraphobia has been considered the treatment of choice, and results from such treatments have certainly been promising, the reporting of very high treatment gains may be overly optimistic and exposure-based treatment alone may not be the total solution to the problem. Jacobson *et al.* (1988) note that certain treatment innovations seem to enhance the efficacy of exposure-based treatments. These include the home-based, spouse-involved treatment developed by Mathews and his colleagues (Gelder *et al.*, 1973; Jannoun *et al.*, 1980; Mathews *et al.*, 1976, 1977) and the spouse-involved treatment reported by

Barlow and his colleagues (Barlow, O'Brien & Last, 1984; Cerny *et al.*, 1987).

Spouse involvement in exposure treatment

In one report Munby & Johnston (1980) observed that the treatment in which spouses were involved produced continuing improvement and results that at four- to nine-year follow-up were superior to those in which treatment was more intensive but spouses were not involved. In a further study (Barlow *et al.*, 1983, 1984) 28 agoraphobic women were treated in small groups in a self-paced exposure-based programme. Although the husbands of all the women agreed to accompany their wives to all the 12 weekly sessions if necessary, only the husbands of 14 of the women were invited to do so. When the results of the 14 agoraphobic women accompanied with their husbands were compared to the results of the 14 women treated without the presence of their husbands a substantial advantage was found for the spouse group on measures of agoraphobic avoidance. The spouse group also showed more rapid improvement in social, work and family functioning, although this comparative advantage had disappeared at post-test. Agoraphobics treated with their spouse maintained an improving trend over a two-year follow-up period (Cerny *et al.*, 1987) in comparison to the non-spouse group who did not show continued improvement at one-year follow-up and even deteriorated slightly, although their improvement trend resumed at two-year follow-up.

In contrast a study by Cobb *et al.* (1984) failed to reveal any positive effect of including the spouse compared to a non-spouse group at post-test or six-month follow-up. As Barlow (1988) notes, this study took place in the patient's home and included the spouse in the initial assessment and subsequent measurement sessions for both the spouse and non-spouse groups. In the study by Barlow and his colleagues therapy took place at the clinic, with the therapist never meeting the spouse. It is therefore plausible to assume that in the Cobb *et al.* study all spouses had, to some extent, an active input to treatment.

The possible importance of the spouse in enhancing therapeutic gain is highlighted in a further study by Arnow *et al.* (1985) in which agoraphobics and their spouses were exposed to phobic situations in a standard manner for four weeks, after which they were divided into two matched groups. One group then received communication training aimed at dealing with agoraphobic situations while the other group received couples-based relaxation training. Although both groups showed some improvement in outcome results (unaccompanied excursions; self-report scores) at both post-test and eight-month follow-up, the group receiving communication training maintained their post-test improvement to a greater extent than the relaxation group.

The balance of evidence then seems to suggest that spouse involvement enhances therapeutic gains. There are a number of possible reasons for this. An involved spouse may facilitate between-sessions practice, although this does not seem to have occurred in the Barlow et al. (1984) study. Other studies have, however, found a direct relationship between the frequency and duration of practice during treatment and increased post-treatment functioning (e.g. Michelson et al., 1986). Increased practice as one mechanism facilitating therapeutic improvement in the spouse group cannot be ruled out. There are, however, alternative explanations, as Barlow et al. (1984) point out; these include the possibility that a spouse may facilitate more efficient and effective practice rather than more practice per se; also a newly cooperative and supportive spouse may reduce general levels of tension and anxiety. This latter supposition may be associated with the finding reported by Arnow et al. (1985) that improved spouse communication and problem-solving skills in particular were associated with therapeutic gains. It is also worth noting that Hafner and his colleagues (Hafner, 1977b; Hafner & Ross, 1983; Milton & Hafner, 1979) have found that marital conflict has a negative impact on therapy, usually after exposure has produced therapeutic gains. Commonly, maritally dissatisfied clients improve during treatment but show partial relapse at follow-up, while clients who are satisfied with their marriage continue to improve. Mathews et al. (1977) have also found that poor marital adjustment was related to treatment failure.

As Kleiner, Marshall & Spevack (1987) point out, however, not all agoraphobics are married; nor do they necessarily have cooperative spouses. Training agoraphobics to identify interpersonal conflicts and ways of coping with them more appropriately and assertively may be the important ingredient in promoting therapeutic success rather than the spouse per se. Kleiner et al. (1987) thus compared an in vivo exposure and coping skills training package to in vivo exposure plus coping skills training plus a 'problem-solving skills training' programme. The problem-solving skills programme focused on increasing the client's awareness of ongoing interpersonal problems and training in basic skills to deal with them. All patients improved significantly after 12 treatment sessions while at three- and six-month follow-ups the problem-solving group continued to improve on all measures whereas the exposure plus cognitive skills training group showed a slight relapse. Improved ability to cope with interpersonal distress may thus enhance behavioural treatment gains.

Cognitive strategies

A number of studies have appeared within little more than a decade evaluating the efficacy of cognitive treatments for agoraphobia. In one of the first such studies Emmelkamp, Kuipers & Eggeraat (1978) compared cognitive restructuring with prolonged exposure *in vivo* in a crossover design. Exposure *in vivo* was found to be more effective than cognitive restructuring on both behavioural measures and self-report inventories. Treatment was, however, very brief (one week), which as Emmelkamp (1982) himself acknowledges is unlikely to be sufficient time to promote cognitive change. In a subsequent study Emmelkamp & Mersch (1982) compared cognitive restructuring to prolonged *in vivo* exposure and a combination of self-instructional training and prolonged exposure *in vivo*. At the post-test, prolonged exposure *in vivo* and the combined procedure were clearly superior to cognitive restructuring, although the differences between treatments disappeared at one month follow-up due to continuing improvement of the cognitive group and a slight relapse for the exposure group.

In a further study Williams & Rappoport (1983) compared exposure *in vivo* with exposure *in vivo* plus self-instructional training in the treatment of 20 agoraphobic females. Results of the study were mixed, with the cognitive group performing as well as the exposure group on some measures, better on one and worse on others. Mavissakalian *et al.* (1983) investigated the impact of two different cognitive strategies (self-instructional training and paradoxical intention) combined with *in vivo* exposure. At post-treatment, paradoxical intention plus exposure showed greater treatment gains than self-instructional training plus exposure. Subsequently the self-instructional group continued to improve with resultant follow-up showing equivalent effectiveness of treatments. In the absence of an exposure group alone, however, it is not possible to comment on the effectiveness of cognitive interventions *per se*.

In a further report Emmelkamp (1986) randomly assigned 43 agoraphobic subjects to either exposure *in vivo*, rational emotive therapy or self-instructional training. Treatment in each case involved six $2\frac{1}{2}$-hour sessions conducted over a period of three weeks. At post-test all groups showed significant improvement on behavioural measures and self-report scales with superior treatment gains for exposure on all measures except the Irrational Beliefs Test, where the cognitive intervention produced greater improvement. After the post-test, subjects received no further treatment for a month followed by six $2\frac{1}{2}$-hour sessions of *in vivo* exposure. Between treatments the exposure group continued to evidence improvements while the subsequent additional exposure sessions led to further improvement in all groups with the exposure–exposure group showing greatest treatment gains. The authors conclude that exposure was more effective than the cognitive treatment in reducing agoraphobics' anxiety and avoidance. It could still be argued, however, that the three-week duration of cognitive interventions was insufficient time for the cognitive intervention to be fully effective. Further, the between-treatment exposure gains could be explained by continuing practice on the part of these subjects, for whom the importance of practising between sessions had been emphasised.

In a further report Michelson, Mavissakalian & Marchione (1985) randomly assigned 39 agoraphobics to one of three treatment conditions: paradoxical intention, therapist-guided *in vivo* exposure or relaxation training. In addition, all subjects received an extensive rationale emphasising the importance of self-directed, graduated, prolonged *in vivo* exposure practice. Although all three groups improved, there were a number of differences across treatments. Paradoxical intention was less effective on a number of measures at post-test; further, while both the exposure and relaxation groups showed significant improvements on physiological measures, the paradoxical group actually showed an increase in physiological reactivity during treatment with equivalent physiological functioning not achieved until three-month follow-up. One explanation for different treatment effects lies in the different pattern of self-directed exposure evidenced by the three treatment groups (Michelson *et al.*, 1986). Both the relaxation and exposure treatments were effective and rapid in fostering self-directed exposure practice, with marked increases during treatment and only a modest decrement at follow-up. Paradoxical intention showed more variation in practice sessions during treatment and decreases between post- and follow-up phases with regard to exposure practice. Further, self-directed exposure was significantly associated with high endstate functioning at post-treatment. In a further report on this study with an additional 49 subjects Michelson, Mavissakalian & Marchione (1988) report statistically significant improvement across all domains and treatments, and few between-group differences. In a subsequent extensive analysis of the physiological data Michelson *et al.* (1990b) report significant and beneficial effects on heart rate of relaxation and exposure, but no improvement on heart rate measures for paradoxical intention.

In a further study comparing cognitive therapy plus exposure with relaxation training plus exposure with exposure alone Marchione *et al.* (1987) report statistically significant and clinically meaningful improvements on behavioural, physiological and cognitive assessments across all conditions. However, both the combined treatments were more effective than exposure alone.

Taken together, these studies yield mixed results for cognitively based interventions for agoraphobia. As Michelson (1987) notes, however, 'Part of the existing difficulty in appraising the potential value of cognitive treatments for agoraphobia so far may stem from differences and variations in procedures employed' (p. 261). Treatments have often been of only brief duration, paradoxical techniques may not be the treatment of choice for many cognitively oriented theorists and cognitive interventions often integrate behavioural components into treatment. The study by Kleiner et al. (1987) refers to a treatment involving in vivo exposure plus a cognitive modification and relaxation training package as 'a standard behavioural treatment'. The coping skills training programme consisted of relaxation training and cognitive modification training which focused upon increasing awareness of negative thoughts, insight into irrational beliefs and self-instructional training. Given the broad-ranging nature of such programmes it becomes very difficult to unravel the effective contributing ingredients. Given also that cognitive parameters might be the effective ingredient in exposure-based therapeutic gains, the issue of which treatment is effective, and why, clearly warrants detailed and careful investigation.

Treatment consonance and response profiles

Two studies have examined the role of individual differences and treatment consonance for agoraphobia. Öst et al. (1984a) assessed heart rate and self-rating of experienced anxiety during a behavioural test for 40 agoraphobic subjects. On the basis of their reactions during the test the subjects were divided into two groups—behavioural reactors (those who had completed five situations in the behavioural test and had a low heart rate increase) and physiological reactors (those who had completed less than five situations and had a high heart rate increase). Within each group, subjects were randomly assigned to a behaviourally focused method (exposure in vivo) and a physiologically focused method (applied relaxation). Both treatments yielded significant improvements on most measures while the between-group comparisons showed that both treatments did equally well for both groups. In terms of the percentage of clinically improved patients, however, the figures were 80% for the matched method and 50% for non-matched patients, suggesting possible clinical if not statistically significant effects. At seven- and 15-month follow-up, exposure-treated subjects maintained treatment gains in all three response systems; for the relaxation group there was a relapse on heart rate at seven months for the physiological reactors although earlier improvement was regained at 15 months (Jansson, Jerremalm & Öst, 1986).

In a further report Michelson (1986) presents a reanalysis of data obtained in the Michelson et al. (1985, 1986) reports in which 39 agoraphobics were randomly assigned to one of three treatment groups: paradoxical intention, relaxation training and *in vivo* exposure. Subjects were subsequently classified as behavioural, physiological and cognitive response types according to a procedure developed by Michelson (1984). Subjects were rank-ordered on the three domains with subjects who exhibited the highest one-third rank ordering on the separate distributions of each measure classified according to the most clinically pronounced domain. Comparisons were then made according to whether subjects had received treatments which were consonant or non-consonant with their particular response profile. Consonantly treated subjects showed enhanced levels of functioning and short-term maintenance.

There are clearly difficulties in assigning subjects to particular response groupings in either of the ways outlined above. It is obviously difficult to obtain 'pure' groups, and deciding which treatment matches the group's responding is no easy matter given the difficulty of ascertaining the precise mechanism responsible for therapeutic change. It might thus be more appropriate to direct attention towards the question of which therapy works and why, rather than towards the difficult task of assigning subjects to 'pure' reaction categories.

SUMMARY

Agoraphobia, or fear and avoidance of public places, is frequently associated with a history of panic attacks. This has been recognised in the DSM-III-R classification by placing panic disorder as the prominent defining criterion. Although there is evidence that one or more panic attacks often precede agoraphobic avoidance it is clear that there is not a one-to-one relationship between panic severity/frequency and avoidance. Cognitive parameters are likely to play an important part in determining the extent of internal/bodily focus or external focus and hence the panic/avoidance relationship.

Research prior to the DSM-III-R integration of panic and agoraphobic avoidance suggests that agoraphobia is one of the commonest anxiety disorders accounting for between 50% and 80% of patients seeking professional help. Epidemiological surveys suggest prevalence rates of approximately six per 1000 individuals, although some studies report higher figures. Studies have consistently found a predominance of females (approximately 70% of all agoraphobics) and a mean age of onset of 27 years, which is later than for other phobias. Explanations for these factors centre around dependence/independence conflicts associated with sex role stereotyping and the development of responsibilities, although there is little supportive evidence for such suggestions. Others have sought to investigate the existence of specific vulnerability factors (such as personality characteristics and the marital context) and precipitating events. A number of studies suggest that traumatic events, especially those associated with interpersonal issues, precede the onset of agoraphobia, although the search for specific precipitating events has been inconclusive. Predisposing and precipitating factors have, however, been incorporated into both the 'fear-of-fear' model (Goldstein & Chambless, 1978) and Rachman's (1984c) safety signal perspective. Both theoretical models also emphasise to differing degrees the part played by panic (unconditional emotional stimuli or 'danger signals') and stimuli which signal safety.

Although there seem to be some differences between agoraphobics and comparison groups on certain measures of personality there is little evidence for the existence of an 'agoraphobic personality'. Also, in spite of some clinical observations, there is little evidence that agoraphobia is characterised by a particular marriage pattern. Agoraphobics within 'good' relationships do, however, seem to sustain treatment gains, and spouse involvement in therapy seems to enhance treatment gains.

The treatment of choice for agoraphobia has been exposure therapy targeted specifically towards avoidance behaviour. Although outcome of such treatment is generally favourable, individuals differ markedly in the extent to which they benefit from such treatment. This has led recent investigators to question the mechanisms of change inherent in exposure therapy with suggestions that cognitive parameters are the important ingredient. Given the changing face of agoraphobia inherent in DSM-III-R, and the acknowledged part played by cognitions in panic attacks, the future may well see an increasing trend towards investigations of the part played by cognitions in the aetiology and treatment of agoraphobic avoidance both with and without associated panic attacks.

Chapter 6

Generalised Anxiety

DEFINITION AND PREVALENCE

Generalised anxiety disorder (GAD) was referred to for the first time in DSM-III (1980), its defining characteristics being: (1) symptoms from three of the following four areas—motor tension, autonomic hyperactivity, apprehensive expectations and hypervigilance and scanning; (2) presence of anxiety for at least one month; and (3) anxiety that is not part of another disorder or a reaction to recent life stress. Generalised anxiety was diagnosed only in the absence of 'specific symptoms that characterise Phobic Disorders, Panic Disorder or Obsessive–Compulsive Disorder (obsessions or compulsions)' (DSM-III, p. 232). By its very nature the DSM-III definition of GAD presents difficulties; anxiety, whether specific or general, is associated with the defining symptoms of GAD. This has led some to doubt the validity of GAD as an independent problem (e.g. Breslau & Davis, 1985). Indeed, the overlap between GAD and other problems is illustrated in a study by Barlow *et al.* (1986a). These authors report that almost all their sample of 108 anxiety patients comprising agoraphobic, social phobic, panic disorder, GAD and obsessive–compulsive disorder patients presented with the symptoms defining GAD. The exception was simple phobia, where only 40% met criteria for GAD. The authors conclude that the feature which distinguishes GAD from other anxiety disorders is the nature of the person's anxious apprehension. In panic or social fears the person may worry about panicking or social encounters. GAD, on the other hand, is characterised by 'chronic worry' about a multitude of life circumstances.

This issue has been addressed directly with the advent of DSM-III-R (1987). GAD is defined as unrealistic or excessive anxiety and worry (apprehensive expectation) about two or more life circumstances, such as worry about possible misfortune to one's child (who is in no danger) or worry about finances (for no good reason) for a period of six months or more. There should be more days when the person is bothered by these concerns than worry-free days.) In one recent study Sanderson & Barlow (1991) found that the most frequently reported focus of anxiety for GAD patients was related to family issues (reported by 11 out of 14 patients) followed by excessive or unrealistic concerns about finances (seven out of 14), about work (six out of 14) and personal illness (two out of 14). Twenty out of a sample of 22 GAD subjects reported that they worried excessively about minor things.

Given the recent inclusion of GAD as a specific diagnostic category within the anxiety disorders, and the poorly defined criteria proposed in DSM-III, the prevalence of GAD is difficult to establish.) Weissman (1985) reports a one-year prevalence rate of 2.3/100 to 6.4/100 making it the most frequent anxiety disorder, occurring two to five times more frequently than panic disorder. The lower figure is similar to an estimate of 2.6% identified as the prevalence of 'definite generalised anxiety disorder' by Anderson, Noyes & Crowe (1984). In a further report of 437 women who were attending their family doctor, and who had moderately high scores on a self-report scale of depression, 7.6% reported mild general anxiety and 1% intense general anxiety on the basis of ratings obtained according to Present State Examination criteria (actual responses indicating free-floating autonomic anxiety) (Costello, Devins & Ward, 1988). A prevalence rate of 4.6%, intermediate to the above figures, has been reported by Von Korff et al. (1987) using, for the purpose of their study, a general anxiety section added to the Diagnostic Interview Schedule (DIS).

An even higher prevalence rate of 8.12% was obtained from the Epidemiologic Catchment Area (ECA) programme (George, Hughes & Blazer, 1986) from a survey of 3643 adult community residents in North Carolina. Classification was determined by the DIS, which at the outset of the study did not include GAD. GAD was therefore not included as a category in the first interview of respondents but only at the second follow-up interview a year later. Prevalence rates for other anxiety disorders reported in this paper (obsessive–compulsive disorder, 2.00%; agoraphobia, 6.37%; social phobia, 3.11%; simple phobia, 12.51% and panic disorder, 1.02%) are similar to those reported for other ECA sites (Myers et al., 1984). As with other anxiety disorders (except social phobia) the prevalence rate for GAD was higher for women (9.51%) than for men (6.22%).

As more figures emerge it is likely that generalised anxiety will prove to be common amongst the general population. Currently available data suggest that it is at least as prevalent as simple phobias and three to four times more prevalent than panic. As Barlow (1985, 1988) notes, however, this contrasts with figures for patients presenting at clinics where approximately 10% will be diagnosed as general anxiety disorder, while as many as 50% are diagnosed as panic disorder. There are a number of possible reasons for this discrepancy. Clinic and survey data are based upon differential diagnostic criteria; specific symptoms are not detailed with the same degree of precision in surveys compared to clinics, where general symptoms may be easier to report. Secondly, the nature of the two populations is very different; as Barlow (1988) notes, many generalised anxiety patients may be 'chronic worriers' who seek treatment only as a last resort and who are managed in the community by their doctor. In contrast, because the symptoms of panic are more distressing and disabling, they may be more likely to be referred for, or present for, psychological treatment. Generalised anxiety, epitomised by unrealistic and excessive worrying, is thus likely to be very common in community samples with many people managing their difficulties by self-help or GP-prescribed medication. Those referred to specialist psychological services may represent the tip of the iceberg.

CO-MORBIDITY WITH OTHER ANXIETY DISORDERS

The overlap between anxiety disorders and the high probability of finding one or more additional diagnoses in individuals who meet DSM-III-R criteria for anxiety disorders has been discussed by a number of authors (e.g. Barlow, 1988; Barlow et al., 1986b; Boyd et al., 1984; DiNardo & Barlow, 1990; Last, Strauss & Francis, 1987). Research suggests that patients with GAD report a high degree of social anxiety (Rapee, 1985a; Rapee, Sanderson & Barlow, 1988b, Sanderson et al., 1990) simple phobia (de Ruiter et al., 1989c) and panic attacks (Barlow et al., 1984; Sanderson & Barlow, 1991).

Rapee, Sanderson & Barlow (1988b) report that 41.7% of their 36 subjects with a diagnosis of GAD also received a diagnosis of social phobia. Three-quarters of their GAD subjects also expressed fears about being observed, and concerns about public humiliation, which are identifying features of social phobia. In further studies Barlow et al. (1986a) report that four of their 12 GAD subjects also received a diagnosis of social phobia, while Sanderson et al. (1990) report a figure of 59% (13 of their 22 GAD subjects). Further, Turner et al. (1991) note that for a sample of 71 socially phobic subjects 24 (33%) had a concomitant diagnosis of GAD, making it the most common secondary diagnosis for their socially phobic sample. Turner et al. (1986b) present Social Avoidance and Distress scores for GAD subjects elevated relative to Social Phobics and Fear of Negative Evaluation scores which are not dissimilar for the two groups. Clearly apprehension and overconcern are common to both social phobia and GAD: in the former these concerns will, by definition, be audience-related; although GAD is characterised by more general life concerns, for a far from insubstantial subgroup it may be concomitantly associated with more focused concerns.

Panic attacks are also frequently reported by GAD patients. Barlow *et al.* (1984) note that 83% of a sample of GAD patients reported having at least one panic attack, although this figure was exceeded by patients from other anxiety disorder groups. Sanderson & Barlow (1991) and Sanderson *et al.* (1990) found that 73% of their sample of 22 GAD patients reported experiencing at least one panic attack as defined by DSM-III-R with 27% (six of the subjects) meeting DSM-III-R criteria for panic disorder.

As discussed in Chapter 4, a number of authors have conceptualised panic as the extreme endpoint of a continuum of general anxiety with symptom interpretation playing a central part in the development of panic. Others have argued that panic and GAD are qualitatively distinct. The latter argument is largely founded on the basis of differential responsiveness to drug treatment; hence the hypothesis that the two disorders have a distinct biological basis (Klein, 1964). This supposition receives some support from the findings of family studies of panic. Crowe *et al.* (1983) found an increase in panic disorder among the first-degree relatives of probands with panic disorder but no increase in generalised anxiety disorder or other psychiatric conditions. The morbidity risk for panic disorder among the relatives of probands with panic disorder was 24.7% compared with 2.3% among the relatives of control probands. The risk for GAD among the relatives of panic disorder probands was 4.8% compared with 3.6% among the relatives of control probands. As these categories were based upon DSM-III criteria a diagnosis of GAD was not made if panic was identified (i.e. co-morbidity of GAD and panic was not allowed for); the incidence of GAD may thus be underrepresented. However, data from twin studies also tend to suggest a genetic predisposition to panic disorder, with no clear evidence for such a predisposition to generalised anxiety disorder (Torgersen, 1986).

A number of further avenues of research, such as comparison of physiological responses, age and type of onset, symptom pattern, course and outcome, as well as personality characteristics, have been pursued in attempting to distinguish between panic and generalised anxiety disorder (see reviews of these issues by Aronson, 1987 and Barlow & Cerny, 1988).

Evidence from ambulatory monitoring indicates that heart rate is lower for panic patients during periods of anticipatory or non-panic anxiety than during panic attacks (Freedman *et al.*, 1985; Taylor *et al.*, 1986b). These differences emerge in spite of the fact that ratings of intensity and anxiety are similar for both panic and non-panic anxiety. Barlow *et al.* (1984) also report significantly higher frontalis EMG and higher heart rate (though non-significantly) for panic patients compared to GAD patients assessed under laboratory conditions. There is also some evidence that GAD patients are characterised by inhibition of some sympathetic systems (Hoehn-Saric & McLeod, 1988). Findings such as these have been regarded as support for the distinctiveness of panic and general anxiety (Barlow, 1988). However, other studies suggest no difference between GAD and panic patients on physiological measures (de Ruiter et al., 1989a).

Data regarding the onset and course of GAD and panic also suggest a number of differences. Rapee (1985a), in a comparison of 38 panic disorder and 48 generalised anxiety disorder subjects, found that while panic disorder was characterised by sudden onset (reported by 81.6% of the sample) around the mid- to late 20s, generalised anxiety was characterised as having a slow, gradual onset (reported by 76.6% of the sample). Gradual onset for generalised anxiety has also been reported by Anderson et al. (1984). Thyer et al. (1985c) report a mean age of onset of 26.6 years for panic and 22.8 for generalised anxiety, and a gender distribution biased towards females in panic disorder (57% females; 43% males) and towards males in generalised anxiety (44% females; 56% males). Others have suggested that panic attacks follow a prolonged period of generalised anxiety. Cloninger et al. (1981), for example, report that symptoms of generalised anxiety preceded the onset of panic disorder in all their patients. In a further study Aronson & Logue (1987) report that 12 out of 46 (21.6%) consecutive referrals with panic disorder reported that GAD symptoms predated the onset of their panic disorder. However, a further 20 (43.5%) described current daily, chronic GAD so that 70% of the total sample presented with both GAD and panic (this markedly exceeds the figure of 27% co-morbidity referred to above, Sanderson & Barlow, 1991; Sanderson et al., 1990).

Comparisons of generalised anxiety and panic patients on questionnaire measures, while suggesting some differences, also indicate a great deal of overlap between the two conditions. Cameron et al. (1986) found no difference between panic and GAD patients on self-reported symptoms of panic, somatic and psychic anxiety. Gross & Eifert (1990a) found that anxiety sensitivity contributed significantly to severity of generalised anxiety as well as panic frequency in a sample of college students. In a further report Borden & Turner (1989) note that although panic patients and GAD patients reported the same panic symptoms, the panic disorder patients reported greater distress from trembling, heart pounding, trouble getting breath, and spells of terror/panic than the GAD patients.

Further differences between panic and GAD have been noted by Rapee (1985a). In his sample, panic was characterised by blurred vision, tingling sensations and chest pain as the prominent somatic symptoms with fear of dying, fainting or having a heart attack as typical accompanying thoughts. In contrast, generalised anxiety subjects were more likely to realise that their symptoms were due to their own anxiety, and hence harmless. Hibbert (1984) has also referred to the fact that panic subjects report experiencing cognitions associated with disastrous consequences while generalised anxiety subjects report less dramatic cognitions. Gross & Eifert (1990a) in a comparison of high-anxious and high-panic college students found that the former were characterised by worry about minor events while the latter were characterised by worry about major events. In a further study Anderson et al. (1984) note that frequent reporting of somatic symptoms, especially those related to the cardiovascular system, was common in panic patients but not generalised anxiety patients. Similarly, although Hoehn-Saric (1982) found that subjects with GAD and panic had very similar symptom self-report profiles, they differed slightly on severity of somatic symptoms, especially those related to hyperventilation and cardiovascular change.

The relationship between somatic concerns and panic but not GAD has also been noted in other studies. Barlow et al. (1984) report that panic patients obtained significantly higher somatic scores on the Cognitive–Somatic Anxiety Questionnaire (Schwartz, Davidson & Goleman, 1978) than GAD patients, while scores on the cognitive scale did not differ between the two groups. In a further report Chambless & Gracely (1989) found that while anxious thoughts were common across the anxiety disorders there was a tendency for panic patients, in comparison to GAD patients, to report more cognitions related to physical concerns. Gross & Eifert (1990b) also report that panic is characterised primarily by hyperventiliation while generalised anxiety is characterised primarily by worry. In a further study Gross, Oei & Evans (1989) compared GAD, panic, social phobic and agoraphobic patients on items from the Hamilton Anxiety Scale (Hamilton, 1959). GAD was characterised by anxious mood, while agoraphobia and panic were characterised by fear symptoms and social phobia by autonomic arousal. The authors interpret anxious mood as representative of worry.

It is interesting to note that on measures of trait anxiety panic patients are often found to obtain similar or even lower scores than GAD patients (e.g. Borden & Turner, 1989). This would not be expected if panic was simply an intense version of GAD. In Rapee's (1985a) study panic patients obtained lower manifest anxiety scores than his generalised anxiety subjects. Anderson et al. (1984) report little difference between the two groups on trait anxiety as measured by the State–Trait Anxiety Inventory, or neuroticism as measured by the Eysenck Personality Inventory.

Clearly, then, panic and GAD can co-occur in the same way that social phobia and GAD co-occur. The difference seems to lie both in the nature of concomitant concerns (far less focused in the case of GAD) and the interpretation of bodily symptoms (panic symptoms are less likely to be interpreted as catastrophic by GAD patients). This would be consistent with the notion that GAD patients are chronic worriers about broadly based life circumstances. It seems plausible to assume that, in some instances, somatic reactions generated by this diffuse worry and associated focused concerns would not be uncommon (hence the overlap of GAD with panic and social phobia).

THE NATURE OF WORRY

The notion that worry is a component of anxiety separate from somatic aspects has a long history within the test anxiety literature. For example, worry is a better predictor than somatic anxiety of the performance decrements of test-anxious students (Deffenbacher, 1980). Worry is also a common feature of everyday life, with the content of worry varying according to life circumstances. The most frequent concern for children is their family (Simon & Ward, 1982), academic worries are rated as most frequent for college students (Borkovec et al., 1983) whilst health concerns are most highly rated amongst the elderly (Wisocki, 1988).

As noted, Sanderson & Barlow (1991) report that the most frequent worries of GAD patients are related to family issues, finances, work and personal illness. In their study the worries of GAD subjects were judged to be excessive or unrealistic in 30 out of 35 cases. In a further report Craske et al. (1989) found that the worries of non-anxious controls were more likely than GAD subjects to be related to financial issues, while the worries of the latter were more likely to be related to injury, illness and health issues. Borkovec, Shaddick & Hopkins (1990) report previously unpublished data from the Penn State Project indicating that family and interpersonal issues were the most frequent worries reported by 31 GAD patients and illness/health/injury the least. Family and interpersonal issues were also the most frequent worries for non-anxious controls, although in contrast to GAD clients non-anxious controls mentioned few worries. Craske et al. (1989) also note that GAD subjects differed from their non-anxious controls in reporting less control over their worrying and less success in resisting or reducing their worry.

'Worry' is central feature of GAD as defined by DSM-III-R (1987) and hence GAD patients are likely to experience excessive worry. Worry has been defined by Borkovec et al. (1983) as 'a chain of thoughts and images negatively affect-laden and relatively uncontrollable' (p. 10). Subsequent findings that worry does not have unique characteristics which separate it from somatic anxiety and depression, but contains the emotional components of both has led to its redefinition (York et al., 1987; Andrews &

Borkovec, 1988). Worry is thus defined as 'a chain of thoughts and images laden with anxious and depressed affect, and relatively uncontrollable' (Andrews & Borkovec, 1988, p. 24). The concept of worry has not been without its critics; O'Neill (1985), for example, has commented that 'it is more parsimonious to consider worry as one component of anxiety rather than as a separate phenomenon' (p. 480). Worry does, however, seem to be a useful cognitive concept with regard to general anxiety. Gross & Eifert (1990a) found worry to be the cardinal feature of generalised anxiety in a clinical sample, and further that worrying thoughts could be distinguished from intrusive thoughts (Gross & Eifert, 1990b). Mathews (1990) argues that 'worry can be seen as a special state of the cognitive system, adapted to anticipate possible future danger' (p. 456). Borkovec (1985a) suggests that 'worrisome cognitions, while they are initiated as a response to fear-producing stimuli, are response-produced stimuli and cognitive main-tainers of anxiety' (p. 481). A number of studies examining the precise nature of worry and its role in maintaining anxiety have since been reported by Borkovec and his colleagues (see reviews by Borkovec, 1985b; Borkovec, Shaddick & Hopkins, 1990; Mathews, 1990).

During induced worry, subjects exhibit greater frontal EEG activation relative to rest while worriers display greater left, relative to right, hemi-sphere activation compared to non-worriers (Carter, Johnson & Borkovec, 1986). In a comparison of self-identified worriers and non-worriers from a college population Borkovec et al. (1983) found that the induction of worry increased negative thought intrusions. The worriers experienced more difficulty stopping their worrisome thoughts. The finding that worry induces negative thoughts was replicated in two later studies (Pruzinsky & Borkovec, 1990; York et al., 1987). Of particular interest in the York et al. study was the differential effect of worry induction and somatic anxiety induction upon negative thought intrusion. The induction of a worrisome state resulted in a significantly greater increase in negative thought intrusion during a subsequent attention-focusing task in com-parison to a neutral mood induction. In contrast, although the induction of somatic anxiety produced some increase in intrusions, this was not sig-nificantly greater than for the neutral mood induction. Related to negative thought intrusion, manipulations of both state and trait worry lead to a delayed response in decision-making (Metzger et al., 1990). Tallis, Eysenck & Mathews (1991) have similarly reported significant response delays on target-absent trials of a letter search task for high worriers compared to low worriers. They argue that worry is associated with 'elevated evidence requirements', i.e. 'worriers need to be absolutely sure that they are doing "the right thing" before a response can be made' (p. 22).

Borkovec and his co-workers have recently suggested a further refinement to the nature of worry. They argue that worry is characterised predominantly by thoughts rather than images of worrying scenes (Borkovec & Inz, 1990). In a test of this supposition 13 GAD patients and non-anxious controls were asked to judge their mental content on three occasions while relaxing and while worrying. During the relaxation phase controls showed a predominance of imagery with little thought, while GAD subjects showed about equal amounts of each. In contrast, during worry controls changed from image predominance to thought predominance, while for GAD subjects thoughts predominated over images, though non-significantly. Therapeutic intervention for the GAD subjects (ranging from relaxation to non-directive therapy) resulted in a predominance of images over thoughts during relaxation comparable to the control subjects, and a decrease in thoughts during worry, although the reduction was non-significant.

The finding that worry is predominantly characterised by thoughts has led Borkovec (Borkovec & Hu, 1990; Borkovec & Inz, 1990) to suggest that worry 'may represent the motivated avoidance of imaginal process' so that 'one way to learn to avoid somatic anxiety is to avoid imagery by increasing the generation of, or attentional focus on, conceptual activity. Worry may represent an avoidance of affect in general or emotional experience in particular' (Borkovec & Inz, 1990, pp. 157 and 158). Worry may thus play a central part in maintaining GAD. As Foa & Kozak (1986) have argued, emotional processing, the accessing of cognitive/affective fear structure stored in memory, is essential for complete fear reduction. Cognitive avoidance (i.e. strategies which impede emotional processing) has been suggested as a factor which may impede fear reduction in exposure-based treatments. Thus instructions to engage in distraction or avoid focusing upon fearful material will result in less fear reduction than instructions to attend to the phobic material (Grayson, Foa & Steketee, 1982, 1986). Worry may thus allow subjects to actively avoid thinking about the feared situation so that anxiety will be maintained. Evidence that worry can indeed fulfil such a function has been presented by Borkovec & Hu (1990) in a study with speech-anxious subjects. When the subjects engaged in worrisome thinking just prior to visualising a phobic scene they displayed significantly less heart rate response than subjects instructed to engage in neutral or relaxed thinking. However, the worry group showed significantly greater subjective fear to the images than the neutral group.

Barlow (1988), Mathews (1990) and Borkovec, Shaddick & Hopkins (1990) have reached related conclusions regarding the possibly central role of worry in maintaining generalised anxiety. It seems that the difference between pathological and non-pathological states is a sense that in the former case events are out of one's personal control. Worry may be a method of attempting to avoid feared outcomes, and indeed will be frequently reinforced by the non-occurrence of such feared events. As such it is a dysfunctional method of coping and regaining control, preventing complete processing of feared material and instead leading to increased anxiety. Further delineating the precise nature of worry in GAD and the modification of worrisome cognitions provides an important avenue for future research.

THEORETICAL PERSPECTIVES

As recently as 1987 Thyer commented that 'as yet no good theory has emerged that accounts for the etiology and maintenance of generalized anxiety disorder' (p. 117). GAD is, by definition, diffuse in its nature and cannot therefore be tied to specific triggers or specific bodily reactions. This inevitably means that models of GAD are likely to be multifaceted in nature. Barlow (1988) outlines a model which involves a complex interaction of biological, psychological and environmental events. This centres upon the notion of biological vulnerability which is activated by negative stressful life events. The events are experienced as unpredictable and uncontrollable, leading to a focusing of attention towards the worry or concern and a subsequent spiral of worry. A similar complex interaction of events is outlined by Deffenbacher & Suinn (1987), who propose that 'at some point, the combination of stressor characteristics, person variables, and environmental resources leads to the developments of a learned anxiety response' (pp. 334–335). Such models would be consistent with the multicomponent process models of emotion referred to in Chapter 1.

However, even the notion that 'worry' might be involved in maintaining GAD leads to the difficulty of ascertaining why some people are worriers and others are not; a factor often accounted for by recourse to notions of 'vulnerability'. As noted in earlier chapters, 'vulnerability' may relate to Eysenck's (1967, 1982) notion of an overly responsive nervous system, Gray's (1982, 1985) notion of a highly reactive behavioural inhibition system or the notion of Mathews and his colleagues (e.g. Mathews, 1988a, 1990; Mathews & MacLeod, 1987; Mathews & Eysenck, 1987) of a systematic bias in the cognitive input to the emotional evaluative system. As Mathews & Eysenck (1987) note, these suppositions may well not be mutually exclusive with the physiological and cognitive parameters operating at different levels in parallel, influencing each other at various points.

Selective processing of emotional stimuli

In relation to cognitive models of anxiety, a number of studies suggest that anxious individuals are more vigilant than their non-anxious counterparts to threat-related cues (see Chapter 2). Thus Mathews & MacLeod (1985) and Mogg, Mathews & Weinman (1989) found evidence for selective processing and interference from emotional stimuli. In both studies generally anxious subjects were slower at naming threat words in a Stroop colour-naming task. However, the Stroop test cannot demonstrate that attention is drawn to emotional stimuli—interference could be produced later in the processing sequence by a subsequent emotional reaction to the words.

In a further study MacLeod, Mathews & Tata (1986) displayed word pairs on a VDU and required subjects to report the appearance of a dot which subsequently appeared in one of the spaces occupied by the words. GAD subjects were faster to detect the dot if it replaced a threatening word, while non-anxious subjects were faster if it replaced a non-threatening word. GAD subjects seem more likely to shift attention towards threat words. Such findings have led Mathews and his colleagues (e.g. Mathews & MacLeod, 1987; Mathews, 1988a) to conclude that attentional bias favouring emotional stimuli maintains and intensifies anxiety by directing processing resources towards whatever potential threat cues may exist in the environment. Attentional capture by threat has also been illustrated in a further study in which subjects were required to ignore various types of distractors, and search instead for a neutral target word (Mathews et al., 1990b). In line with previous findings, when the position of the target was unknown, threat distractors slowed detection of the target by GAD subjects relative to controls. GAD subjects were slowed by all distractors (physical and social threat), whereas a group of recovered GAD patients were slowed only by physical threat distractors. This led Mathews et al. to conclude that 'selective attentional attraction to threat cues is an enduring characteristic of those vulnerable to anxiety disorders' (Mathews et al., 1990b, p. 173), vulnerability referring to sensitivity to threat associated with high trait anxiety.

However, the tasks used in the above studies do not provide any indication of whether interference or attentional vigilance arises from automatic processes outside of awareness, or whether the subjects exert voluntary control. In an investigation of this issue Mathews & MacLeod (1986) compared GAD and non-anxious controls on reaction times when shadowing neutral passages in a dichotic listening task while simultaneously exposed to threat- or non-threat-related words in the unattended channel. GAD but not control subjects were slower in performing the simultaneous reaction time task when the unattended words were threatening in content, although neither group could report or recognise the words to which they had been exposed.

In an extension of their previous studies Mathews, Richards & Eysenck (1989b) investigated the possibility that anxiety is also associated with a tendency to interpret ambiguous cues as threatening. Current and recovered GAD patients listened to homophones with spellings that correspond to either a threatening or neutral meaning. In writing down what they heard, currently anxious subjects used spellings which implied a threatening interpretation more often than control subjects, with a recovered group being intermediate.

In contrast to the consistent findings using various paradigms that GAD patients selectively attend to threatening material there is a lack of evidence for an anxious mood-congruent bias in memory for threat words. Indeed, Mogg, Mathews & Weinman (1987) found that normal controls recalled proportionally more threatening words than generally anxious patients. Mathews et al. (1989a) investigated the possibility that although voluntary retrieval may be inhibited, recall of threatening words may be more readily activated automatically. Following presentation of threat and non-threat words GAD and non-anxious controls were required to complete three-letter stems with the first word that came to mind. This priming activated stronger representations of threat for anxious compared to non-anxious subjects.

These findings provide empirical evidence for the theorising of Beck and his colleagues (e.g. Beck, Emery & Greenberg, 1985), who suggest that anxiety is maintained through the selective encoding, elaboration, storage, and retrieval of information related to personal danger. The findings do not, however, indicate whether such biases also have a causal role in the development of GAD; they may be merely secondary consequences. Given that they at least maintain anxiety, however, one might assume that the most effective form of therapeutic intervention for GAD would be one specifically aimed at identifying and modifying cognitive structures shown to be associated with anxiety. As Butler et al. (1991) note, however, progress in the development of effective treatments for GAD has been disappointing, and cognitive treatments have met with mixed results.

ASSESSMENT

Self-report measures

Only recently has an instrument been developed to measure the specific trait of worry (Meyer et al., 1990), although a variety of self-report measures of subjective anxiety have been used in both evaluation and treatment studies of GAD. Perhaps the most widely used of these is the State–Trait Anxiety Inventory (STAI; Spielberger, Gorsuch & Lushene, 1970). Other scales which have been used include the Zung self-rating anxiety scale (Zung, 1971), the Leeds scale for anxiety and depression (Snaith, Bridges & Hamilton, 1976); the Beck Anxiety Inventory (Beck et al., 1988) and the Cognitive Somatic Anxiety Questionnaire (Schwarz, Davidson & Goleman, 1978). Given that anxiety is a defining attribute of anxiety disorders it is perhaps not surprising that there is little difference between subjects from the various diagnostic groups on measures of state–trait anxiety. Simple phobic subjects tend to obtain lower scores than the other subgroups with GAD subjects scoring at the upper end of the range (Turner et al., 1986). However, measures of general anxiety do not tend to discriminate GAD from other anxiety disorders.

The recently developed Penn State Worry Questionnaire (PSWQ; Meyer et al., 1990) consists of 16 items (e.g. 'my worries overwhelm me') rated on a five-point scale indicating whether the item is 'not at all typical' or 'very typical' for the subject. The authors report that the scale, assessed with several student populations, possesses high internal consistency and good test–retest reliability. Within student populations it was also correlated with several psychological constructs related to worry (e.g. STAI) but not with psychologically unrelated constructs (e.g. locus of control). The authors also report data indicating that the measure is related to time spent worrying and number of worrying topics reported by college students. GAD patients obtained far higher scores than college students; for GAD patients the PSWQ was unrelated to more general measures of anxiety and depression and was sensitive to change as a result of cognitive therapy. These preliminary data suggest that the scale could become a useful measure of the trait of worry in both clinical and analogue populations.

Self-monitored diary records of anxiety are often recorded as a matter of course during therapy, and frequently reported in outcome studies. For example, Lindsay et al. (1987) asked subjects to rate how anxious they were each day by marking a 15 cm line ranging from no anxiety at the left of the line through three gradings of anxiety to extremely anxious at the right of the line. Barlow et al. (1987) and Borkovec & Mathews (1988) asked subjects to complete a diary on three occasions each day (at the end of the morning, afternoon and evening), rating their general anxiety level (on a 100-point scale) and entering information about any intense, acute episodes of anxiety. Lindsay et al. (1987) also specifically asked subjects to record on a daily basis 'how much time they spent worrying and thinking about their problems' on a 15 cm scale separated into four points from no time on the left to all the time on the right.

In addition to self-rating scales, clinician rating scales such as the Hamilton Anxiety Scale (HAS; Hamilton, 1959) have been used in outcome studies. The HAS is also incorporated into the ADIS (DiNardo et al., 1983) and ADIS-R (DiNardo et al., 1985). Specific questions relate to tension and anxiety with no apparent cause and anxiety related to excessive worrying about family, job performance, finances, etc. These interview schedules have been widely used in a number of studies by Barlow and his colleagues and by other researchers, for identifying DSM-III and DSM-III-R GAD in treatment studies (e.g. Barlow et al., 1984; Borkovec & Mathews, 1988) and for classifying GAD and other anxiety disorders in assessment studies (e.g. de Ruiter et al., 1989; Sanderson & Barlow, 1991 Sanderson et al., 1990).

Behavioural and physiological parameters

Behavioural parameters have rarely formed the focus of assessment and treatment in relation to GAD, reflecting the generally held opinion that avoidance behaviour is absent in GAD. Barlow et al. (1984), for example, comment that 'exposure is of little or no use to those with generalised anxiety disorder . . . since they avoid nothing to begin with' (p. 443). This may not, however, be the case. Butler et al. (1987b) report that 67% of their sample of 45 GAD patients reported avoidance of specific situations. Avoidance of parties, dating, authority and assertion is reported by GAD subjects to a degree which, though less than, does not differentiate them from, socially phobic subjects; while avoidance of meetings and public speaking is reported by GAD subjects to a degree which, though less than, does not differentiate them from, agoraphobic or panic disorder subjects (Rapee et al., 1988b). Clearly, then, in assessing GAD careful note needs to be taken of any avoidance, whether related to specific situations or somatic cues.

With the exception of biofeedback studies, which have monitored physiological responses inherent in treatment, few studies have specifically assessed physiological parameters of GAD in relation to treatment. In one of the exceptions Barlow et al. (1984) assessed frontalis EMG and heart rate during a six-minute baseline period and during relaxation and a stressor task. Responding decreased significantly from pre- to post-treatment. Given that experimentally induced worry in undergraduate subjects has been found to give rise to increases in cardiovascular activity (York et al., 1987) monitoring heart rate change in response to treatment may well be useful. As Barlow (1988) notes, however, given the inherent difficulties of assessing physiological parameters in clinical situations the utility of such measures is not always clear.

TREATMENT

> The apparent lack of any external focus for anxiety in generalised anxiety states ... has resulted in some lack of consensus about how such non-phobic anxiety disorders should be treated ... most therapists have abandoned straightforward exposure methods in favour of relaxation, anxiety management or cognitive therapy (Mathews, 1988b, p. 75).

Relaxation and biofeedback

A number of studies, mostly during the 1970s, have used biofeedback in the treatment of GAD. A number of methodological difficulties inherent in many of these studies, such as variable treatment sessions (e.g. Canter, Kondo & Knott, 1975), variable length of treatment (e.g. LeBoeuf & Lodge, 1980), large drop-out rates (e.g. Raskin, Bali & Peeke, 1980) and variable concomitant medication (e.g. Townsend, House & Addario, 1975) make it difficult to draw any firm conclusions from this work. In a review of this research Rice & Blanchard (1982) comment that 'there is a lack of any consistent support for the utility of HR or EEG alpha biofeedback ... there is more consistent evidence for differential physiological change as a result of frontal EMG biofeedback' (p. 572). Also, while some studies suggest that EMG biofeedback might be superior to muscle relaxation (e.g. Canter et al., 1975) other studies suggest little difference between relaxation and biofeedback in the treatment of chronic anxiety. Raskin et al. (1980), for example, found no significant difference between transcendental meditation, muscle biofeedback and relaxation therapy as treatment for chronic anxiety, concluding that relaxation therapies on their own have a limited place in the treatment of chronic anxiety.

In a study using procedural variants of relaxation training (Tarrier & Main, 1986) 50 patients with generalised anxiety with panic attacks were assigned to one of four treatment groups or a waiting list control. Patients were taught applied relaxation during one session either by participant demonstration, written instructions, taped instructions or a combination of all three with instructions to practise at home. At post-treatment all four treatment groups showed improvement relative to the control group. While the findings point to the usefulness of relaxation training the absence of long-term follow-up data suggests caution. Relaxation is, however, widely used in combination with both cognitively based interventions and other techniques for controlling anxiety.

Anxiety management training

Anxiety management training (AMT) (Suinn & Richardson, 1971; Suinn, 1976) was developed specifically for the treatment of pervasive or general anxiety. The actual steps of AMT involve several phases: (1) rationale and relaxation training; (2) guided rehearsal for anxiety arousal and control; (3) cue-discrimination training; (4) graduated self-control training and (5) transfer to real-life applications (Suinn, 1984). A number of studies have found that AMT is effective in reducing general anxiety in college students (e.g. Hutchings et al., 1980) and generally anxious medical outpatients (Cragan & Deffenbacher, 1984). However, it is difficult to ascertain how far these successful results can be generalised to clinical populations as there are few studies specifically using AMT with GAD patients. A clinical trial of this method with patients with persistent anxiety neurosis (Janoun, Oppenheimer & Gelder, 1982) found large therapeutic gains which persisted during three months follow-up (gains which did not occur while the patients were on the waiting list). Further studies which have incorporated cognitive treatments with relaxation training have also been described as AMT (e.g. Blowers, Cobb & Mathews, 1987). As Butler et al. (1987a) note, however, AMT focuses on patients' fears of not being able to cope; cognitive therapy makes a more ambitious attempt to alter patients' ways of thinking.

Cognitive techniques

A number of studies have used cognitive–behavioural treatments for general anxiety with mixed results. Woodward & Jones (1980) treated 27 general anxiety outpatients by either cognitive restructuring, modified systematic desensitisation, or a combined treatment comparing outcome to a no-treatment control. The combined treatment was more effective than either of the individual treatments in reducing Fear Survey Schedule scores; the cognitive treatment failed to result in any apparent improvement on the dependent variables measured. Because differences which emerged were based upon measures not necessarily central to general anxiety, and in the absence of any more than a four-week follow-up, these results should be treated with some degree of caution.

Barlow et al. (1984) compared a combined treatment for GAD consisting of relaxation training, biofeedback and cognitive therapy with a waiting list control. They report significant post-treatment gains on a number of measures for the treated group who continued to improve at follow-up. Although these results are promising they are based upon only nine subjects (five treatment and four control). In addition, the multifaceted nature of the intervention means that it is not possible to say whether the cognitive component was the effective ingredient or whether it is effective only when in combination with other treatments.

In a further study Durham & Survey (1987) randomly assigned 41 outpatients with a diagnosis of chronic anxiety of at least one year's duration to either behaviour therapy (relaxation, distraction, graded exposure) or cognitive therapy, which included 'behavioural techniques when appropriate'. Both treatments showed post-treatment improvement. At six-month follow-up there was a significant trend on a number of outcome measures for the cognitive therapy patients to maintain or improve further, while the behaviour therapy patients reverted towards their pre-treatment scores. In spite of the beneficial effects of the cognitive intervention, virtually no patients were symptom-free at follow-up.

In a further study Blowers, Cobb & Mathews (1987) compared relaxation plus brief cognitive therapy with non-directive counselling as treatments for generalised anxiety. Outcome results were compared to a waiting list control. Relaxation plus cognitive therapy was significantly more effective than the waiting list condition on a number of measures at post-treatment, although there were few differences between relaxation plus cognitive therapy and non-directive counselling either at post-treatment or at follow-up. Subsequent studies using the same treatment have met with mixed success. Borkovec et al. (1987) compared relaxation training plus cognitive therapy with relaxation plus non-directive therapy for 30 GAD patients randomly assigned to the two treatment conditions. At post-treatment both groups showed substantial reductions in anxiety with the cognitive plus relaxation group showing significantly greater improvements, although there were no group differences in anxiety at 6–12 month follow-up. In an extension of this study (Borkovec & Mathews, 1988), with more severe GAD patients, an additional coping desensitisation with relaxation treatment was compared to the cognitive and non-directive treatments used in the earlier study. All three treatment groups showed improvement at post-treatment and follow-up on a range of self-report questionnaire and diary data with little between-group difference; the superiority of the cognitive plus relaxation treatment group at post-treatment found in the previous study was not replicated in this later research. Obviously in the absence of a waiting list control group it is not possible to state with complete certainty that the results are due to the treatments per se although, as the authors note, untreated GAD patients do not tend to show change noted in the study. The lack of difference between treatments is perhaps surprising, but may well be accounted for by the common element of relaxation contained in each of the treatments.

In a further study Lindsay et al. (1987) randomly assigned 40 patients whose primary problem was anxiety to a waiting list control group or one of three treatment groups: cognitive–behaviour therapy and relaxation, anxiety management training or a drug treatment. At post-treatment both psychological treatment groups showed improvement on measures of anxiety with the most consistent and significant changes in the cognitive–behaviour therapy group, although at three-month follow-up there was no difference between the two psychological treatment groups. (Comparisons with the drug treatment group are not meaningful as treatment was tapered off in the fourth and last week of treatment due to concern with drug-dependency problems.)

In a further report Power et al. (1989) compared cognitive behaviour therapy (based upon Beck and Emery's model) with medication as treatments for GAD. Although the results are suggestive of greater treatment gains for the cognitive–behavioural intervention, as the authors themselves acknowledge, the lack of a waiting list control group means that it is not possible to ascertain whether the change over time is wholly attributable to treatment. The absence of an adequate follow-up also makes it difficult to assess treatment efficacy.

The most promising results for cognitive interventions are presented in a series of recent reports by Butler and her colleagues (Butler & Anastasiades, 1988; Butler et al., 1987a,b, 1991). The treatment, 'anxiety management', involved the elements used by the same research group in treating social phobia (Butler et al., 1984). These were a modification of anxiety management training removing image switching and adding an exposure component and 'modifying the cognitive component of treatment to place more emphasis on the identification and response to each person's specific thoughts, rather than drawing on a common set of thoughts, or single strategy, for all patients' (Butler et al., 1987a, pp. 535–537).

In a report of their 'anxiety management' treatment for GAD Butler et al. (1987a) report highly significant changes in anxiety, depression and problem ratings after treatment in comparison to a waiting list control group. These changes were replicated when the waiting list group also received treatment. The gains were maintained by both groups at six-month follow-up. In spite of these impressive results, few patients were symptom-free at the end of treatment and about 25% of patients showed relatively little improvement. Butler & Anastasiades (1988) report that a combination of three variables measured before treatment reliably predicted outcome. Thus, outcome was relatively poor if initial levels of anxiety were higher, if patients rated their depression as more disabling while at the same time depression rated by an assessor was lower.

In their most recent report, Butler et al. (1991) compared cognitive–behaviour therapy (as described by Beck, Emery & Greenberg, 1985) with behaviour therapy, involving applied relaxation and exposure, in relation to a waiting list control group as a treatment for GAD. Results showed a clear advantage for cognitive–behaviour therapy over behaviour therapy. At post-treatment the CBT differed significantly on 15 of the 16 outcome measures in comparison to a waiting list control, while the BT differed on only four measures. However, the BT group improved on all but one of the four anxiety measures during treatment, and this was maintained at follow-up. Butler *et al.* (1991) comment that cognitive interventions are more likely to be effective because they make it easier to deal with additional problems such as depression, as well as making it easier to overcome reservations about treatment and motivation; they also deal with worrisome patterns of thinking which generate anxiety. In view of theoretical advances incorporating selective processing and interference from emotional stimuli and worry as factors maintaining GAD, one might assume that cognitive interventions may well hold the key for success with GAD in the future.

SUMMARY

GAD was first referred to as a distinctive psychiatric category in DSM-III. With the advent of DSM-III-R the central diagnostic feature of GAD was specified as excessive and unrealistic worry about two or more life circumstances. Given the recent specification of GAD as a distinctive anxiety disorder it is difficult to be certain about the accuracy of prevalence rates published prior to establishing DSM-III-R criteria. However, preliminary reports suggest that generalised anxiety occurs frequently within the general population, and may be three to four times more prevalent than panic disorder. This contrasts with the finding that amongst clinic attenders, panic is far more prevalent than GAD. It seems that many with GAD manage their difficulties by self-help or GP-prescribed medication, while panic patients are more likely to seek specialist treatment. Generalised anxiety frequently co-occurs with both panic and social phobia. Questionnaire responses suggest that there is some degree of overlap between GAD and panic, although the two conditions seem to differ in onset and course. Particular differences seem to lie in the way in which bodily sensations are interpreted. Also, diffuse worry seems to characterise GAD and to play a key role in maintaining anxiety; worry may be an effective form of cognitive avoidance. By focusing upon worrying thoughts, images and thoughts of the feared situation can be avoided and hence effective emotional processing is blocked and general anxiety maintained (Borkovec, Shadick & Hopkins, 1990; Mathews, 1990).

Recent theoretical accounts of GAD have emphasised the complex interaction of biological, psychological and environmental events in line with multicomponent process models of anxiety outlined in Chapter 1. Psychological factors which seem to play a central part in at least maintaining

GAD involve the extent to which chronic worriers selectively process emotional stimuli. Empirical studies have illustrated that generally anxious subjects are characterised by their tendency to selectively attend to threat cues. While it remains to be seen whether such processing is a cause or consequence of general anxiety it is plausible to assume that certain people may be biologically and/or physiologically and/or cognitively vulnerable to anxiety. Given recent research findings concerning the cognitive basis of GAD one might assume that cognitively based interventions would be the most effective treatment. Until recently, however, there has been a lack of consensus about how to treat generalised anxiety. During the 1970s relaxation and anxiety management were widely used treatments, the latter mainly with analogue populations. However, treatment outcome studies of relaxation-based strategies have led some authors to conclude that such strategies on their own have a limited place in the treatment of chronic anxiety. Within the past few years the first evaluations of cognitive interventions for GAD have been published. These suggest mixed results, although the balance of evidence seems to favour such interventions. Given the recent theoretical emphasis on cognitive aspects of anxiety, and the possible part played by worrisome cognitions in maintaining general anxiety, cognitive interventions may well hold the key to future success in treating chronic generalised anxiety.

Chapter 7

Obsessions and Compulsions

DEFINITION AND DESCRIPTION

Clinical accounts of obsessional–compulsive disorder (OCD) have appeared in the literature for over 150 years, while attempts to formally document and describe the condition were undertaken at the beginning of this century (see Foa, Steketee & Ozarow, 1985b). DSM-III-R defines OCD as 'recurrent obsessions or compulsions sufficiently severe to cause marked distress, be time-consuming, or significantly interfere with the person's routine, occupational functioning, or with usual social activities or relationships with others' (American Psychiatric Association, APA, 1987, p. 245). Obsessions are defined as 'persistent ideas, thoughts, impulses, or images that are experienced, at least initially, as intrusive and senseless', while compulsions are defined as 'repetitive, purposeful, and intentional behaviors that are performed in response to an obsession, according to certain rules or in a stereotyped fashion' (APA, 1987, p. 245). Although there are slight modifications in the DSM-III-R definition of OCD from earlier definitions, it is essentially unchanged from DSM-I, -II and -III. The definition implies that obsessions are covert, involuntary thoughts, which increase anxiety, while compulsions are overt, voluntary behaviours which decrease anxiety. While, in many cases, this might be true, it masks the fact that compulsions can also involve covert neutralising thoughts, and that both overt and covert compulsive actions can lead to increases rather than decreases in anxiety.

Clinical observations and research findings tend to indicate that obsessions and compulsions are closely related. In a study of 150 OCD inpatients Welner *et al.* (1976) report that 69% complained of both obsessions and compulsions, 25% had obsessions only, and as few as 6% had compulsions only. In a recent review, Emmelkamp (1987) suggests that approximately 80% of OCD patients have obsessions as well as compulsions, only a minority suffer from obsessions alone while pure rituals without accompanying obsessive thoughts are rare. However, this contrasts with recent epidemiological data. Karno *et al.* (1988) found that obsessions were experienced by 55.1% of those identified as OCD, compulsions by 53.4% and both compulsions and obsessions by only 8.6%. They suggest that in their community-based sample less severe cases were encountered than might be expected in a clinical context, and that 'obsessions and compulsions aggregate separately in nonclinical populations' (p. 1098).

The content of typical obsessions involves thoughts about dirt or contamination, aggressive impulses or thoughts that are sexual in nature; obsessions may take the form of thoughts, images, impulses, fears or doubts (e.g. Akhtar *et al.*, 1975). Given the inherent difficulty of differentiating between these various forms of obsession it is perhaps not surprising that estimates of their relative frequency are variable. Thus, Reed (1985) reports that fears are the most frequent obsession (reported by 65% of 48 subjects), while Akhtar *et al.* (1975) report doubts as the most frequent obsession (reported by 75% compared to 38% in Reed's study); only 25% in Akhtar *et al.*'s study reported fears most frequently. In both these studies obsessions involving images were the least reported, with 2% (Reed, 1985) and 7% (Akhtar *et al.*, 1975). In contrast, de Silva (1986) has argued that the imagery phenomenon in obsessive–compulsive patients is far more frequent, but is underestimated both because of the lack of routine assessment of imagery in OCD patients and due to confusion between images and thoughts. He further proposes four distinct types of imagery in OCD: obsessional, compulsive, disaster and disruptive, each serving different functions. The obsessional image, like the obsessional thought, is assumed to be anxiety-inducing; the consequent compulsive image corrects or neutralises the original image and hence is anxiety-reducing. The disaster image focuses upon the consequences of the obsession or a failure to carry out the compulsion; disruptive images occur during the compulsion and hence serve to invalidate it.

Attempts have also been made to classify compulsive behaviours, with cleaning and checking rituals the most commonly identified categories. Hodgson & Rachman (1977) found that 52% of their patients had checking rituals and 48% cleaning rituals; Stern & Cobb (1978) found that 51% of their sample exhibited washing or cleaning rituals and 38% checking rituals. Rachman & Hodgson (1980) and Foa *et al.* (1983b) report that 86% and 66% respectively of their patients had washing rituals. In a systematic comparison of 36 washers and 23 checkers Steketee, Grayson & Foa (1985) found that washers' fears were triggered more by external cues while checkers' fears tended to focus upon concerns with preventing future harm. There were, however, few other substantive differences between the two groups.

In addition to washing and checking rituals, Hodgson & Rachman (1977) refer to primary obsessional slowness identified in 52% of their sample and defined as 'slow repetitive behaviour with little or no anxiety and no persistent ruminations' (p. 394).

Prevalence of OCD

Reports during the 1970s suggested that OCD was relatively rare. Estimates of patients treated in general psychiatric inpatient settings who were diagnosed as OCD in these studies ranged from 0.5% to 4.0% (Rasmussen & Tsuang, 1984). Estimates of prevalence rates within the general population also suggested that OCD was rare, occurring in less than 0.1% of the general population (Woodruff & Pitts, 1964). However, recent findings from the Epidemiological Catchment Area Programme in the USA suggest that OCD is far more common than these earlier reports indicate. One-year prevalence rates for DIS/DSM-III diagnosed OCD range from 0.8% (Los Angeles), and 1.4% (St Louis), to highs of 2.2% (Baltimore) and 2.3% (Durham) (Eaton et al., 1989). The six-month prevalence rate of 1.5% for all sites combined means that OCD occurs twice as frequently as panic (Regier et al., 1988). The lifetime prevalence rates for the five sites ranged from 1.9% to 3.3% (Karno et al., 1988) giving a combined lifetime prevalence rate of 2.5% (Regier, Burke & Burke, 1990). While there are a number of reasons why the lower figures reported in earlier studies may underestimate the incidence of OCD (e.g. the lack of available treatments when earlier epidemiological studies were conducted, the failure of people to seek treatment and the secretive nature of obsessive–compulsives) the higher figures may well overestimate the prevalence, perhaps including non-clinical cases.

Although there is a fairly equal representation of males and females with OCD, Eaton et al. (1989) and Karno et al. (1988) report a slightly higher incidence among women than men. Similar findings have been reported in earlier studies (e.g. Black, 1974; Welner et al., 1976). This parallels to some extent (although to a less marked degree) similar female overrepresentation amongst other anxiety disorders with the exception of social phobia. However, Karno et al. (1988) note that when other demographic risk factors (e.g. age, marital status, employment status) are controlled for, gender differences in prevalence rates are eliminated. Rachman & Hodgson (1980) suggest, on the basis of some interesting findings, that OCD may take gender-specific forms. In a sample of 83 patients 86% of compulsive cleaners were female, with the ratio of female to male cleaners being 6 : 1. In a further report Hoekstra, Visser & Emmelkamp (1989) found that 21 out of 29 (72%) compulsive washers were female, while 39 of 53 (73%) compulsive checkers were male. Sociocultural pressures and expectations may thus influence the development of specific types of OCD.

A number of reports suggest that as many as two-thirds of OCD patients report significant life events associated with the onset of their problem (Rachman, 1985). McKeon, Roa & Mann (1984) found that obsessive–compulsives had a higher mean life event score than control subjects in the year prior to onset of their problem, and that the incidence of life events was particularly noticeable in the six preceding months. The incidence of life events in relation to OCD is not, however, dissimilar to that noted for the anxiety disorders in general.

Age of onset

Age of onset of OCD is typically described as late adolescence or early adulthood (e.g. Rachman & Hodgson, 1980; Welner *et al.*, 1976) with data from the ECA programme suggesting a mean age of onset ranging from 20.9 to 25.4 (Karno *et al.*, 1988). Some reports cite an earlier age of onset for men than for women (15.5 versus 22.9, Rasmussen & Tsuang, 1986), although others cite similar mean age of onset (22.4 versus 23.0, Karno *et al.*, 1988). Similarly, an earlier age of onset for checking or mixed rituals in comparison to obsessions only, or cleaning rituals (18–19 versus 27), has been noted in one study (Minichiello *et al.*, 1990) but not in another (Rachman & Hodgson, 1980). Given that information regarding age of onset is obtained from patients' and/or family members' self-reports the findings are open to the criticisms inherent in any such study relying on retrospective recall.

Childhood incidence of OCD is rare but not unknown. Recent reports suggest that as many as 10% of referrals to outpatient clinics for anxiety-disordered children meet DSM-III-R criteria for OCD (Last & Strauss, 1989). Amongst such children research indicates that the peak age at onset is between 10 and 14 years, that the disorder is more common amongst boys than girls to a ratio of between 2 : 1 and 3 : 1, and that OCD in boys is more severe and with an earlier age at onset (Swedo *et al.*, 1989). Studies with childhood OCD also indicate that, as with adults, obsessions without compulsions are rare, multiple rituals are common, and that washing is the most common ritual (e.g. Flament *et al.*, 1988; Last & Strauss, 1989; Rapoport, 1986, 1989; Swedo *et al.*, 1989).

Non-clinical obsessions and compulsions

Although attempts to delineate discrete characteristics for OCD add to the precision of epidemiological and clinical findings it seems clear that OCD, like other anxiety disorders, exists along a continuum of severity. A number of studies have reported that obsessional thoughts are frequently experienced by otherwise normal subjects, and that these thoughts are identical in form and content to those experienced by clinically based obsessionals. Rachman & de Silva (1978) and Salkovskis & Harrison (1984) found that between 80% and 90% of subjects in non-clinical samples experienced obsessional thoughts and impulses. In a series of studies Frost, Sher and their colleagues report that between 10% and 15% of their college student samples obtained scores on the Maudsley Obsessional–Compulsive Inventory (MOCI—see below) within the clinical range. Those reporting high levels of everyday checking behaviour had poorer memory for prior actions, and had more difficulty distinguishing between real and imagined events, took longer to sort components of a concept into sub-categories and were more depressed and anxious than non-checkers (Frost, Sher & Green, 1986; Frost et al., 1988; Sher, Frost & Otto, 1983; Sher, Man & Frost, 1984). Indeed a number of studies suggest that impaired decision-making is a central feature of OCD. Others have argued that OCD shows similarities to, and may overlap with, other clinical conditions.

CO-MORBIDITY OF OCD WITH OTHER CONDITIONS

A number of authors have noted the presence of obsessional thinking and/or compulsive rituals in other disorders. This ranges from noting an overlap with other DSM-III-R anxiety disorders to suggesting links with depression, schizophrenia, personality disturbance, head injury, and bulimia and anorexia nervosa (Black & Noyes, 1990). Anorectic patients, for example, are characterised by specific food-related obsessions and almost ritualistic exercise and dieting programmes, while bulimic behaviour is characterised by rituals of vomiting, purging or exercise as temporary relief from anxiety (e.g. Holden, 1990). Both clearly have many parameters which overlap, although OCD is more specific in focus. Other reports in the literature have documented the presence of obsessive–compulsive symptoms during recovery from head injury (e.g. McKeon, McGuffin & Robinson, 1984) although it is unclear whether such symptoms predate the injury. There have been far more reports linking OCD with schizophrenia, although such reports are rare within the contemporary literature. Thus, although some authors have suggested a continuum of severity between OCD and psychosis (Insel & Akiskal, 1986) noting that delusions of schizophrenics can sometimes resemble obsessions (Munro, 1980), it seems to be the exception rather than the rule for OCD patients to develop schizophrenia (Rachman & Hodgson, 1980). Also while there may well be certain similarities between OCD and schizo-phrenia, there are many clear differences. In contrast to schizophrenics, OCD patients do not exhibit hallucinations or formal thought disorder, they usually recognise that their behaviour is irrational and do not report being directed by external forces (Turner & Beidel, 1988b). In commenting on the evidence Black & Noyes (1990) conclude that 'OCD and schizophrenia appear to have little relationship' (p. 307).

OCD and personality disorder

There have been frequent reports within the literature of the co-occurrence of OCD and personality disorders. For example, Mavissakalian, Hamann & Jones (1990) report that 53% of their 43 OCD patients received at least one personality disorder diagnosis. In the earlier literature the most fre-quently cited link was with obsessive–compulsive personality disorder. The latter is defined by DSM-III-R as characterised by (a) being serious, conventional and stingy, with restricted ability to express warm emotions; (b) being perfectionistic and overly concerned with details; (c) insisting that others submit to one's way of doing things, without showing concern for the feelings of others; (d) showing excessive involvement with work at the expense of pleasure and interpersonal relationships; and (e) being indecisive, being tardy, and procrastinating.

Black (1974), reviewing early studies, reports a 71% rate of compulsive personality among obsessional patients. In a more recent clinic-based report Tyrer, Casey & Gall (1983) note that seven of their eight OCD patients were also rated as having compulsive personality disorder. Other clinic-based reports and recent epidemiological studies tend to report lower figures. Thus, Rasmussen & Tsuang (1986) report a co-occurrence of 55% between OCD and compulsive personality, while Joffe, Swinson & Regan (1988) report that only one out of 23 OCD patients also exhibited obsessive–compulsive personality disorder. Comparable figures from other recent studies are six out of 96 OCD patients (Baer et al., 1990) and one out of 26 OCD patients (Steketee, 1990). In the latter study Steketee reports that one-quarter to one-third of her sample met criteria for avoi-dant, histrionic, schizotypal and dependent personality disorder; findings similar to those reported by Joffe, Swinson & Regan (1988) and Mavissaka-lian, Hamann & Jones (1990). Indeed Jenike et al. (1986) have suggested a link between OCD and schizotypal personality, a disorder characterised by many features similar to a less severe form of schizophrenia. However, estimates of co-occurrence of OCD and schizotypal personality are highly variable, ranging from 5% (Baer et al., 1990) to 30% (Jenike et al., 1986). In a further recent report Stanley, Turner & Borden (1990) note that although 28% of their sample of 25 OCD patients had schizotypal features only 8% met criteria for schizotypal personality disorder. Jenike and colleagues (e.g. Jenike, 1986; Jenike et al., 1986; Minichiello, Baer & Jenike, 1987), as well as other authors (e.g. Rasmussen & Tsuang, 1987), have suggested that patients for whom OCD is linked to personality disorder are resistant to treatment. However, Steketee (1990) found that personality diagnosis was not predictive of treatment outcome for the OCD patients in her study.

The field of personality disorders is beset with difficulties, not least that relating to the lack of consensus regarding measurement. Hyler et al. (1989) recently commented that 'no gold standard or even lead standard for personality diagnosis has yet been established'. This no doubt accounts for the variable co-occurrence of OCD and personality disorders. Additionally, the lack of consensus about the co-occurrence of OCD and personality disorder and treatment outcome questions the significance of any co-occurrence noted. Steketee (1990), for example, comments that 'the case for interference of personality disorder in behavioural treatment outcome is not compelling' (p. 12)

OCD and depression

Perhaps the most frequently reported association of OCD with another disorder is its link with depression. Reports of co-occurrence rates range from 20% (Kringlen, 1970) to 66% (Solyom et al., 1971). Others have pointed to the fact that certain physiological abnormalities and symptoms (guilt, low self-esteem, indecision, anxiety, exhaustion and sleep disturbance) are common to both depression and OCD (Insel, Zahn & Murphy, 1985). It should be kept in mind, however, that OCD frequently occurs without associated depression, and that when depression occurs it is more likely to antedate than to predate the onset of OCD. Welner et al. (1976), for example, note that in their sample of '150 inpatients in whom obsessions and compulsions were major or predominant symptoms' (p. 537) for 38% depression followed many years of severe obsessions and compulsions, while only 11% had primary depressive illness with the subsequent development of OCD. Further, the relationship between depression and OCD is not an exclusive one amongst the anxiety disorders; Sanderson et al. (1990) report an overall co-occurrence for anxiety disorders and depression of 21%. Studies also consistently show that depression and anxiety can be readily differentiated (e.g. Kendler et al., 1987; Riskind et al., 1987). Perhaps of greatest importance is the suggestion that treatment is less effective for OCD patients with significant levels of depression (Foa *et al.*, 1983a), although contrary evidence also exists (e.g. Basoglu *et al.*, 1988). Clearly the links between OCD and depression are far from 'resolved and remain a fertile area of enquiry.

The relationship between OCD and depression has led some to question whether OCD should be classified with depressive illness rather than with phobias, GAD and panic, for which anxiety is a defining feature (e.g. Insel, Zahn & Murphy, 1985). There are, however, a number of similarities between OCD and other anxiety disorders. As Baer & Jenike (1986) note: 'obsessive–compulsive disorder is categorized as an anxiety disorder . . . because the central factor seems to be anxiety and discomfort' (p. 1). Rachman & Hodgson (1980) further point out that, for both OCD and phobic patients, specific stimuli elicit subjective distress and discomfort, increased physiological reactivity and avoidance behaviour. There is also little difference between OCD and other anxiety disorder patients on measures of neuroticism, general measures of anxiety or fears, all groups obtaining elevated scores relative to normative data (Steketee, Grayson & Foa, 1987; Turner *et al.*, 1986). However, OCD patients are clearly distinguishable from other anxiety disorders by consistently obtaining higher scores on specific measures of obsessions and compulsions such as on the MOCI (e.g. Steketee, Grayson & Foa, 1987; Turner *et al.*, 1986).

OCD and anxiety disorders

In examining the symptom pattern of the anxiety disorders it is evident that there is overlap between OCD and the other anxiety disorders. Rasmussen & Eisen (1988) report that for 200 OCD patients lifetime prevalence of associated disorders was 28% for simple phobias, 26% for social phobia, 17% for separation anxiety and 15% for panic disorder. In a further study Austin *et al.* (1990) report that for 36 OCD patients five (14%) currently met DSM-III-R criteria for panic disorder, seven (19%) simple phobia and five (14%) social phobia. Sanderson *et al.* (1990) report that, of 12 DSM-III-R diagnosed OCD patients, five received an additional anxiety disorder diagnosis (one social phobia, one panic disorder and three simple phobias) although this rate of co-occurrence was lower than for the other anxiety disorders. Some reports suggest that panic attacks are not uncommon in OCD, with OCD patients reporting many of the purportedly specific panic-related symptoms (Barlow *et al.*, 1985). In contrast Cameron *et al.* (1986) found that OCD patients were least similar to other anxiety disorders on measures of panic and anxiety severity. In a further report Borkovec (1985b) notes that the persistent ideas and thoughts which characterise OCD resemble the worry component of generalised anxiety. He further suggests that because the worrier may fear the consequences of no longer worrying, as this would mean being less vigilant for possible danger, worry may well serve to maintain difficulties. Such a negative cognitive style may well be implicated in the genesis and maintenance of OCD.

INFORMATION PROCESSING

Memory processes and cognitive deficits in OCD have been described as 'perhaps the most central feature of obsessional disorder' (Reed, 1977a, p. 177) and yet there is a surprising paucity of research in this area. Kozak, Foa & McCarthy (1988) suggest that obsessive–compulsives show cognitive impairments in four major areas: indecisiveness and uncertainty, overestimating the likelihood of harm, irrational beliefs associated with harm and impairments in the organisation and integration of experience. The role of perceived threat and irrational beliefs is central in relation to cognitive theories of OCD. Empirical studies have been directed specifically at issues of uncertainty, indecisiveness and organisation and integration of experience.

With regard to questions of uncertainty a number of studies have found specific memory deficits in relation to OCD. Reed (1977a) found that patients with obsessive–compulsive personality disorders had better immediate memory span and recall for anecdotal information than did subjects with other personality disorders. He also found that obsessive–compulsives relied almost exclusively on visual imagery, while comparison subjects relied on images from all modalities. In two studies using normal subjects, high scorers on the Maudsley Obsessive Compulsive Inventory (MOCI—see below) (Sher, Frost & Otto, 1983; Sher, Mann & Frost, 1984) had poorer memory for prior actions and underestimated their ability to distinguish memories of real from imagined events compared to low scorers. This was particularly true of those scoring highly on the checking rather than the washing subscale of the MOCI. In a replication with a clinical sample Sher *et al.* (1989) also found poorer recall for recently completed actions amongst checkers relative to non-checkers.

Other studies have specifically investigated doubt and indecisiveness in OCD. Milner, Beech & Walker (1971) report that obsessive–compulsives requested more repetitions of trials when asked to distinguish auditory tones presented in white noise in comparison to depressed patients. In a further task Volans (1976) found that obsessional checkers required more information when making a decision in comparison to normals and phobics, while Sartory & Master (1984) found that obsessionals showed greater uncertainty and doubt than matched normal controls on a motor set contingent negative variation paradigm.

With regard to organisation and integration of experience a number of studies suggest that obsessive–compulsives tend to have narrow conceptual categories, employing overly strict category boundaries. This seems to relate to findings which suggest that obsessive–compulsives exhibit a general level of indecisiveness. The use of narrow conceptual categories or under-inclusive categorisation (Reed, 1977b) is illustrated by findings that subjects with obsessional personality disorder select fewer alternatives when identifying category membership (Reed, 1969a) and generate more categories in a sorting task in comparison to non-obsessionals (Reed, 1969b). In a similar vein Persons & Foa (1984) have outlined a 'complex concepts' hypothesis suggesting that obsessive–compulsives have a more involved definition of concepts, especially with regard to those of relevance to their difficulties such as contamination and danger. In a test of this hypothesis they presented subjects with four sets of cards with names of objects or descriptions of situations typed on them, so that each deck had a different defining concept: size, contamination, temperature, seriousness of mistakes. Subjects were asked to sort each set of cards into groups which 'go together'. Obsessives in comparison to non-obsessives took longer to sort the cards and used a greater number of categories; the time effect was most pronounced for the fear-relevant sets—contamination and seriousness of mistakes. This result was partially replicated in a non-clinical sample (Frost *et al.*, 1988)—non-clinical compulsives (high scorers on the MOCI) took longer to sort the cards into categories than non-compulsives, although there was no difference in the number of categories used; further, both compulsive and non-compulsive subjects took longer to sort the fear-relevant sets. As with their earlier studies (Sher, Frost & Otto, 1983; Sher, Mann & Frost, 1984) the effect was more characteristic of those obtaining high scores on the checking rather than the washing subscales of the MOCI.

Clearly the existence of cognitive deficits does not provide a sufficient account of OCD. As Marks (1987b) notes: the 'numerous "cognitive" features . . . could be as much a sign of OCD as its cause' (p. 439). It seems reasonable to assume, however, that certain cognitive styles or deficits act as vulnerability factors for the development of OCD, as emphasised in recent theoretical accounts. Cognitive formulations may be particularly useful in adding to our understanding of the psychological processes involved in the development, maintenance and treatment of intrusive thoughts, particularly when these occur in the absence of associated overt compulsive rituals.

THEORETICAL PERSPECTIVES

Behavioural models

The behavioural model most widely applied to explain the development and maintenance of OCD is Mowrer's two-stage theory of fear and avoidance (e.g. Mowrer, 1960—see Chapter 2). In the first stage a neutral stimulus acquires anxiety-evoking properties through conditioning (i.e. obsessions are conditioned stimuli). Subsequently behaviours develop which reduce the anxiety associated with this stimulus and which are reinforced due to their anxiety-reducing properties. In the case of OCD a distinction can be drawn between 'passive' avoidance (i.e. avoidance of the stimuli or situation provoking anxiety) and 'active' avoidance (i.e. performing a ritual or compulsive behaviour specifically to reduce anxiety) (Teasdale, 1974).

Although the model seems intuitively reasonable, a number of authors have noted limitations (e.g. Carr, 1974; Emmelkamp, 1982, 1987; Foa, Steketee & Ozarow, 1985b). Individuals presenting with phobias frequently cannot recall a traumatic event associated with phobia onset; recall of traumatic events seems to be even less usual for OCD. Further, OCD patients often present with a number of obsessions and rituals. Theoretically one would have to assume several traumatic episodes to account for this phenomenon, although there is no evidence that this is the case. The linking of obsessions and specific compulsions is also not always clear; some are logically related while others are seemingly acquired by chance.

In addition, the evidence that performing a ritual serves to reduce anxiety is not entirely clear-cut. A number of studies assessing both subjective and physiological indices of anxiety have found that obsessional ruminations in the absence of compulsive rituals lead to an increase in heart rate and subjective anxiety (e.g. Hodgson & Rachman, 1972) with a subsequent decrease in anxiety following the performance of an overt ritual (e.g. Roper & Rachman, 1976; Roper, Rachman & Hodgson, 1973). Other findings, particularly in the case of checkers, suggest that performance of the ritual actually results in an increase rather than a decrease in anxiety (e.g. Roper and Rachman, 1976). Indeed, compulsive rituals can become more and more complex, becoming increasingly difficult to perform and unpleasant in nature. It was largely as a result of such shortcomings that cognitive–behavioural formulations evolved during the 1970s.

Cognitive–behavioural models

The central tenet of cognitive–behavioural models is that unrealistic threat appraisals are characteristic of OCD (i.e. OCD is associated with a tendency to overestimate the probability of an unfavourable outcome— e.g. Carr, 1974). Drawing on Carr's approach McFall & Wollersheim (1979) outline a number of unreasonable beliefs and irrational patterns of thinking or 'primary appraisals' which they hypothesised would increase the likelihood of making unrealistic subjective estimates of danger; this pattern of thinking would in turn result in anxiety. Such 'primary appraisals' include the idea that one must always be competent and adequate in order to be worth while; the belief that any failure to live up to these unrealistic expectations will be punished; certain thoughts and feelings that can lead to disastrous consequences will be punished while rituals will prevent disasters.

McFall & Wollersheim further hypothesised that 'deficits' in the 'secondary appraisal' process lead obsessive–compulsive patients to devalue their ability to cope with their subjective estimates of danger. Distortions associated with secondary appraisal include beliefs that if something is or may be dangerous it will be upsetting; that rather than confronting the feelings or thoughts directly it is easier to perform a ritual; and that it is intolerable to have feelings of uncertainty and loss of control. As the authors comment, obsessionals feel unable to cope adaptively with threat and 'symptoms are *their best option* for reducing distress' (p. 336; italics in original).

While there is undoubtedly some descriptive utility in such an account there is little to suggest that these inaccuracies of cognitively mediated threat appraisals in OCD differ from those experienced in other anxiety disorders. It has further been suggested that McFall & Wollersheim's theory is 'directed at "bridging the gap" between behavioural and psychoanalytic theory, and carries with it many of the problems associated with such an enterprise' (Salkovskis, 1985, p. 571).

An alternative cognitive model for obsessions recently suggested (Salkovskis, 1985, 1989a,b,c; Salkovskis & Warwick, 1988) lies within the hypothesised framework of cognitive phenomena proposed by Beck (1967, 1976). Salkovskis (1985) argues that obsessional thoughts function as stimuli which may provoke a particular type of automatic thought. Obsessions and negative automatic thoughts differ in that the former are noticeable, perceived as irrational and experienced as intrusive, while the latter are not necessarily noticeable, are perceived as rational and not perceived as intrusive. Salkovskis further suggests that intrusive thoughts occur frequently in normal individuals but only become bothersome when they become negative automatic thoughts through interaction with the individual's belief system. As Salkovskis notes; 'In terms of Beck's model intrusions may, for some individuals on some occasions, activate pre-existing dysfunctional schemata and hence result in unpleasant automatic thoughts' (1985, p. 574). Examples of 'dysfunctional assumptions' most likely to interact with intrusive thoughts include: one could (and can) exercise control over one's thoughts; and failing to prevent (or failing to try and prevent) harm to self or others is the same as having caused the harm in the first place (p. 579). As a result of these appraisals the individual will attempt some kind of corrective action in order to neutralise the implications of his/her own thoughts. The result is that this prevents reappraisal of the true risks and hence an increase in pre-existing beliefs about responsibility. Based upon this model Salkovskis (1985) argues that 'cognitive modification of obsessions should concentrate not on modification of intrusions, which would be unlikely to have other than a transient effect on the belief system of the individual, but on the automatic thoughts consequent on the intrusions, and the beliefs which give rise to these' (p. 581). Although the derived treatment has been described in some detail (e.g. Salkovskis, 1989a) there has been little empirical evaluation to date of therapy based upon this model except for case reports (e.g. Salkovskis & Warwick, 1985). The theory itself is also not without its critics. Jakes (1989a), for example, has questioned the distinction between obsessional thoughts and the way they are evaluated (negative automatic thoughts), suggesting that the latter are not necessary to account for OCD (see also the reply by Salkovskis, 1989b and the rejoinder by Jakes, 1989b).

ASSESSMENT

A number of important issues for therapists when assessing OCD patients are discussed by Turner & Beidel (1988b). These include the secretive nature of OCD patients, their tendency to be manipulative and their ambivalence towards treatment. In view of this the clinical interview has a particularly important role. Kozak, Foa & McCarthy (1988), for example, suggest that during the clinical interview there is a need to focus upon obsessions (both external cues and non-external cues—thoughts, images or impulses—which provoke anxiety), anticipated harm from both external and non-external cues; avoidance of specific situations or objects; ritualistic behaviour including washing, cleaning, checking and repeating; and cognitive rituals such as neutralising thoughts. Similar points are raised by Turner & Beidel (1988b). In this context the completion of clinician-rated scales such as the recently developed 10-item Yale-Brown Obsessive Compulsive Scale (Y-BOCS; Goodman et al., 1989a,b) may be useful. The authors suggest that the scale has high internal consistency, discriminates between OCD and other disorders, is sensitive to drug-induced changes and 'is well suited to studies evaluating specific effects of drug treatment' (Goodman *et al.* (1989a) p. 1016). It could also provide additional information to that obtained from behavioural monitoring and self-report inventories.

Questionnaires and rating scales

A number of standardised scales have been developed to assess obsessive–compulsive symptoms, of which the Maudsley Obsessive–Compulsive Inventory is probably the most widely used.

The Maudsley Obsessive–Compulsive Inventory (MOCI; Hodgson & Rachman, 1977) is a 30-item true–false report scale which assesses cognitive–behavioural aspects of OCD. It yields a total score as well as four subscale scores for washing (11 items), checking (nine items), slowness (seven items) and doubting (seven items). Based on responses of 100 OCD patients Hodgson & Rachman (1977) report adequate reliability and validity for the total score, and good validity for the washing and checking subscales, while the doubting and slowness subscales seem less well supported. There is also evidence for the validity of the MOCI in non-clinical samples; Sternberger & Burns (1990a) found that of 11 individuals from a sample of undergraduates who scored within the top 2% on the MOCI, nine were classified as OCD on the basis of the Anxiety Disorders Interview Schedule (DiNardo *et al.*, 1983). Further analysis of the scale with a student population has shown three components very similar to the checking, cleaning and doubting components found in the case of obsessional subjects (Rachman & Hodgson, 1980). Similar components have been obtained using large samples of Italian college students (Sanavio & Vidotto, 1985), Chinese college students (Chan, 1990) and American college students (Sternberger & Burns, 1990b). A number of studies indicate that the MOCI is sensitive to treatment effects (e.g. Foa, Steketee & Grayson, 1985a; Emmelkamp, Visser & Hoekstra, 1988). The scale is brief and easy to administer and score, although it is limited to assessing ritualistic behaviours rather than obsessional ruminations.

The Leyton Obsessional Inventory (LOI) (Cooper, 1970) contained 69 items in its original form, designed to assess obsessional symptoms and obsessional traits. Also, in its original form the LOI consisted of a card sort which took a considerable length of time to administer. A revised version using a simpler and quicker to administer paper-and-pencil format was found to be reasonably correlated with the card sort version ($r = 0.72$) (Snowdon, 1980). A 20-item self-report measure (the Lynfield Obsessional/Compulsive Questionnaire), based upon questions taken from the LOI, has also been developed, although this does not distinguish reliably between OCD patients and other patient groups with obsessional symptoms (Allen & Tune, 1975). Factor analysis of the LOI with a sample of normal English and Irish subjects has revealed four components: clean and tidy, incompleteness, checking and ruminating (Cooper & Kelleher, 1973). Murray, Cooper & Smith (1979) report a similar five-factor structure for a sample of 73 obsessional patients; the factors relating to household order, personal contamination, doubting, checking and ruminations. The scale is reliable and discriminates obsessional patients from normals (Cooper, 1970; Murray, Cooper & Smith, 1979) and 'houseproud housewives' (Cooper, 1970). As Freund, Steketee & Foa (1987) note, however, the scale 'focuses heavily on compulsive personality traits rather than on behaviours and cognitions associated with obsessive–compulsive disorder' (p. 67).

The Compulsive Activity Checklist (CAC; Philpott, 1975) contained 62 items in its original form describing specific activities, each of which was rated on a four-point scale of severity. Various revised versions of the scale have since been used. Using a 37-item version Marks et al. (1980) report that the CAC was sensitive to changes in symptoms following treatment; they also report an inter-rater reliability of 0.90 between self and assessor ratings. Using a 38-item version with OCD patients Freund et al. (1987) report moderate test–retest reliability over an average of 36 days and high internal consistency. Their factor analysis revealed two subscales, washing/cleanliness and checking/repetitive acts; they also found that the CAC discriminated between washers and checkers, and that it was sensitive to treatment effects. In an assessment of a French translation of the scale with 45 OCD patients Cottraux et al. (1988) report that the CAC appears valid, sensitive to clinical change but with moderate test–retest reliability. In contrast to Freund et al. (1987), Cottraux et al. (1988) suggest a unidimensional factor structure for the CAC. In a further recent study using the 38-item version of the CAC with a large sample of American college students, Sternberger & Burns (1990b) report good internal consistency and test–retest reliability over a six- to seven-month period and three factors: washing, checking and personal hygiene.

The Padua Inventory (PI; Sanavio, 1988), a recently devised scale, consists of 60 items describing common obsessional and compulsive behaviour. In an assessment of the scale with a large sample of normal Italian subjects Sanavio reports satisfactory internal consistency and test–retest reliability at one month. Factor analysis revealed four factors: impaired control of mental activities, becoming contaminated, checking behaviours and urges, and worries of losing control over motor behaviour. The scale correlated highly with the MOCI and LOI and discriminated between 75 outpatients with OCD and a similar group of outpatients with other neurotic disorders. A very similar factor structure was obtained with a large sample of US undergraduate students; the four subscales also showing good internal consistency and close relationship with corresponding subscales of the MOCI (Sternberger & Burns, 1990c). Although further research is clearly required with this scale, initial data appear to be promising. The fact that the scale assesses both obsessions and compulsions, and the similar results obtained in the two studies to date, suggest that the scale may be a useful measure of OCD.

Self-monitoring

A number of studies have used self-monitoring diaries to obtain detailed information of OCD patients' thoughts and behaviours. For example, Foa et al. (1984) obtained details of the average daily time spent washing and cleaning, severity of rituals and urge to ritualise for 32 OCD patients. Other studies have asked patients to detail the frequency and duration of obsessional thoughts and the amount of distress such thoughts cause. Given the problem of secrecy associated with OCD, determining the accuracy of self-monitoring is clearly an important issue, and obtaining corroborative information from a family member or involved other can be useful. A further issue relates to the converse of reactivity noted in relation to self-monitoring phobias (i.e. an associated decrease in frequency of monitored behaviour). It has been suggested that obsessive–compulsives in general, and checkers in particular, actually increase their target behaviour as a result of self-monitoring (Rosenberg & Upper, 1983). Self-monitoring clearly provides important information and can highlight patterns of change; however, care needs to be exercised both in its use and interpretation.

Behavioural assessment

A few studies have observed and recorded naturally occurring rituals. Mills et al. (1973) recorded from a mechanically triggered pen the number of occasions an obsessive–compulsive inpatient approached a sink to wash. Turner et al. (1979) report behavioural observations of the frequency of rituals for three obsessive–compulsive inpatients using a number of time-sampling schedules conducted by trained nursing staff. Clearly such approaches are less viable on an outpatient basis. Other studies have used rather more contrived measures under controlled circumstances where patients are asked to approach the feared stimuli and to rate their degree of discomfort (e.g. Rachman *et al.*, 1979). Clearly, objective assessment of observed rituals presents rather less difficulty than assessment of obsessive thoughts where assessment relies upon self-report questionnaires and ratings.

Physiological assessment

A range of physiological parameters have been studied in OCD patients for purposes of standardised assessments, and for evaluating treatment response. These include heart rate and skin conductance (e.g. Boulougouris, Rabavilas & Stefanis, 1977; Grayson, Nutter & Mavissakalian, 1980; Kozak, Foa & Steketee, 1988) and pulse rate (e.g. Hodgson & Rachman, 1972). In one of the earliest assessment studies Hodgson & Rachman (1972) compared pulse rate variability of obsessive–compulsives when exposed to a neutral object, a 'contaminated' object and after hand-washing. Although there was a trend (though non-significant) towards an increase in variability on exposure to the 'contaminated' object, and a decrease after handwashing, the small sample size and lack of a comparison group mean that caution is required in interpreting these results. In fact, psychophysiological assessment studies have not always revealed differences between obsessive–compulsives and comparison groups. Thus, Hornsveld, Kraaimaat & Dam-Baggen (1979) found no difference between six patients with compulsive handwashing and 12 psychiatric controls on measures of heart rate or skin conductance during neutral exposure, contaminated exposure and handwashing, although the former group had a higher number of skin conductance spontaneous fluctuations when anticipating touching, and when actually touching, the contaminated object in comparison to the psychiatric controls.

In two outcome studies Boulougouris (1977) recorded heart rate and skin conductance before and after therapy while Kozak *et al.* (1988) recorded heart rate and skin conductance responses during treatment sessions. Boulougouris found differential responding to feared and neutral stimuli before treatment and a decreased response to feared stimuli after therapy. Kozak *et al.* (1988) found decreased responding within sessions, providing evidence of within-session habituation but no evidence for between-subject habituation (comparing peak response early in therapy with peak response at the end of treatment). Larger across-session decreases in heart rate and skin conductance were positively related to a reduction of obsessive–compulsive symptoms.

In sum, results of studies investigating psychophysiological parameters in relation to OCD are mixed. Whether reactions of obsessive–compulsives to feared and neutral stimuli can be differentiated from responses of non-patients or adequate comparison groups, or whether physiological indices provide clear outcome measures, remains to be fully explored. This has led to conflicting views about the utility of such assessments in clinical practice. For example, Turner & Beidel (1988b) comment that: 'for the practicing clinician, physiological assessment when the patient is in contact with the feared objects or situations can provide important corroborative data for the initial assessment' (p. 43) while Barlow (1988) comments that 'pending further exploration of the additive value of this type of measure in predicting clinical outcome, there does not seem to be any reason to recommend routine clinical administration at the present time' (p. 622).

TREATMENT

Until the 1960s OCD was considered to have a poor prognosis, being generally unresponsive to psychologically based treatments and with long-term hospitalisation and psychosurgery the recommended treatments. With the advent of behavioural interventions in the late 1960s and 1970s success rates increased dramatically, with successful outcomes of up to 85% reported (Foa & Goldstein, 1978). Behavioural interventions, particularly those emphasising a combination of exposure and response prevention, have thus become the treatment of choice for OCD.

Exposure treatments

The assumption behind exposure-based treatments is that compulsive rituals are maintained because they serve an anxiety-reducing function. Once obsessional cues cease to evoke anxiety, compulsive behaviour will be reduced because it will no longer be reinforced by its anxiety-reducing properties. Several variants of exposure-based treatments have been used in numerous treatment outcome studies over the past two and a half decades.

One of the first behavioural treatments to be used with OCD was systematic desensitisation, used by Cooper, Gelder & Marks (1965) to treat 10 patients, only three of whom improved. A series of single case reports provide more positive results for this method with OCD patients, but the results are far from uniformly positive (e.g. Furst & Cooper, 1970). Turner & Michelson (1984) suggest a number of reasons for the failure of systematic desensitisation with OCD, including the possibility that the exposure component might be too short to provide benefit.

A number of procedural variations of exposure-based techniques have also been employed. Although the procedures might vary, the common theoretical rationale seems to be the emphasis on exposure to anxiety-inducing stimuli. Procedures used include exposure with aversion relief (e.g. Solyom & Kingstone, 1973), prolonged exposure (e.g. McCarthy, 1972), and satiation—the verbalising of ruminations for an hour with therapist encouragement (e.g. Stern, 1978). The latter is of some interest as it involves continuous presentation of obsessional material and is based on the premise that obsessional ruminations are noxious stimuli to which the subject has difficulty habituating (Rachman, 1976b). This treatment strategy may be of particular importance in dealing with obsessional ruminations in the absence of overt compulsions. A recently studied habituation training strategy involving audiotaped exposure therapy has been used effectively in a series of single case reports (Headland & McDonald, 1987; Salkovskis, 1983; Thyer, 1985). Exposure is based on the presentation via headphones of obsessional thoughts (recordings of patients speaking their obsessional thoughts).

In summary, although some positive results have been obtained for exposure-based treatments, particularly those involving habituation training in relation to obsessional ruminations, these tend to be the exception rather than the rule. Further, many of these studies consist of single case reports which have rarely been followed up by larger-scale group comparison studies.

Response prevention

A central tenet for the maintenance of compulsive behaviour is that performance of the ritual reduces anxiety. As a converse, therefore, if the rituals become associated with an increase rather than a decrease in anxiety the rituals should tend to extinguish. A number of strategies have been based upon this assumption. Rubin and Merbaum (1971), for example, used aversion relief as treatment for OCD. This involved pairing shock with performance of the ritual and termination of the shock upon contact with the 'contaminated' object. A number of other studies have used variations of this paradigm with some degree of success. Kenny, Mowbray & Lalani (1978), for example, divided obsessions and compulsions into component steps that were then imagined by the patient, with shock accompanying each of the imagined scenes. Improvement was reported for three out of five patients. However, such strategies are rarely used as the treatment of choice.

Preventing obsessional thoughts

A strategy for preventing obsessional thoughts used widely in the 1970s is thought-stopping. The procedure involves the patient ordering thoughts from least to most disturbing and by instruction shouting 'stop' upon experiencing an intrusive thought. The premise is that the patient can learn that the thoughts can be prevented from occurring. A number of single case reports detail successful treatment of obsessions using this method (e.g. Leger, 1978) although outcome studies present a far less positive picture (e.g. Emmelkamp & Kwee, 1977). Salkovskis & Westbrook (1989), summarising four outcome studies in which 28 patients with obsessional ruminations in the absence of overt compulsions were treated by thought-stopping, note that only 13 patients (i.e. 46%) showed a 50% improvement in frequency of ruminations. In two studies reporting individual distress ratings only two out of 17 subjects showed a 50% improvement on these measures. Obsessional thoughts do not seem to respond well to treatment, particularly when these occur in the absence of overt rituals. As Emmelkamp (1987) comments 'thought-stopping has no adequate theoretical basis and its empirical strength is far from convincing' (p. 323). Referring to thought-stopping Rachman (1983b) notes that 'the main obstacle to the effective treatment of obsessions is the absence of effective techniques'; the use of habituation training by audiotaped exposure to obsessional ruminations, referred to above, suggests a way forward. Recent conceptualisations recognising the existence of cognitive rituals in conjunction with obsessional thoughts, and using audiotaped exposure to the ruminations in conjunction with prevention of the cognitive rituals, may prove to be a useful treatment strategy in the future.

Exposure and response prevention

In the 1960s Meyer (Meyer & Levy, 1973) successfully treated a series of 15 OCD patients (10 of whom were rated much improved or symptom-free and the remaining five moderately improved) by preventing rituals when the patients were exposed to conditions which would normally provoke compulsive behaviour. A number of studies have since appeared evaluating the efficacy of this treatment. In a series of earlier reports Rachman, Marks, Hodgson and their colleagues found exposure and response prevention superior to relaxation as treatment for OCD (e.g. Marks, Hodgson & Rachman, 1975; Roper, Rachman & Marks, 1975). Given that several behavioural strategies were used in these studies (modelling, exposure, response prevention) both alone and in combination as well as treatments (behavioural or relaxation) being administered sequentially over a period of weeks, it is difficult to ascertain precisely the effective treatment ingredient.

In a series of subsequent studies, many conducted by Emmelkamp, Foa and their colleagues, a number of treatment parameters have been investigated (see Emmelkamp, 1982, 1987; Foa, Steketee & Ozarow, 1985b; Steketee & Tynes, 1991); these include inpatient treatment vs treatment in the natural environment, spouse involvement vs non-involvement; imaginal vs *in vivo* exposure, prolonged vs short exposure sessions, attention vs distraction during exposure, and exposure alone vs response prevention alone vs combined treatments.

Inpatient treatment vs treatment in the natural environment. Many early studies evaluated treatments in inpatient settings involving daily exposure sessions. In contrast with this work, Emmelkamp and his colleagues report a series of studies in which patients were treated in their own homes. In their first study 15 OCD patients were treated with 15 two-hour sessions of exposure with response prevention. At the end of treatment seven were symptom-free and three showed some improvement with treatment gains maintained at follow-up (Boersma *et al.*, 1976). The maintenance of post-treatment gains is also reported in a further study in which 15 OCD patients received 10 sessions of *in vivo* exposure and response prevention in the natural environment (Emmelkamp *et al.*, 1980). There was, however, evidence of slight relapse at one-month follow-up with patients given, on average, 15 additional treatment sessions.

Other studies also suggest that outpatient treatment can be as effective as inpatient treatment (Hoogduin & Hoogduin, 1984; van den Hout *et al.*, 1988), and that treatment administered by the patient in her/his natural environment can be as effective as therapist-controlled exposure (Emmelkamp & Kraanen, 1977; Emmelkamp *et al.*, 1989; Hoogduin & Duivenvoorden, 1988). In the case of patient-controlled exposure the treatment is compiled with the patient's involvement, but then involves home practice sessions of exposure in the absence of the therapist with either discussion with the therapist after every other exposure session (Emmelkamp *et al.*, 1989) or with weekly discussion sessions (Hoogduin & Duivenvoorden, 1988). In the latter study 78% of 62 treated patients showed improvement of greater than 30% on outcome measures.

Spouse involvement vs non-involvement. A number of authors have commented on the fact that partners and families are often involved in the patient's obsessive–compulsive difficulties and that marital problems are often seen in conjunction with OCD. This raises the possibility that marital therapy or spouse involvement in treatment could have beneficial effects.

However, in one comparison of marital therapy and exposure *in vivo* for patients with both marital difficulties and OCD, while exposure improved both OCD symptoms and marital problems, marital therapy improved only the couple's relationship (Cobb *et al.*, 1980). This finding was, however, based upon a small sample, and used a very specific form of behavioural marital therapy.

Studies evaluating the impact of spouse involvement upon treatment outcome for OCD have produced mixed results. Some studies suggest that spouse involvement can have beneficial effects (e.g. Hafner, 1982). Emmelkamp & de Lange (1983), however, found that while there were beneficial effects during treatment these effects had disappeared at one-month follow-up. In a further report Emmelkamp, de Haan & Hoogduin (1990) found improvement irrespective of partner involvement in therapy. In this latter study, exposure *in vivo* with response prevention resulted in improvement irrespective of marital quality, while treatment gains led to neither deterioration of the marriage nor to adjustment problems in the partner. As the authors point out, however, as a large number of their subjects were classified as maritally distressed, corroborating findings from other studies, 'there is a clear need for studies investigating the effects of marital therapy . . . and marital relationships of these patients' (p. 59).

Imaginal vs in vivo exposure. In an early report Rabavilas, Boulougouris & Stefanis (1976) compared short and long periods of imaginal and *in vivo* exposure as treatment for 12 OCD patients. Although *in vivo* exposure was generally more effective in reducing symptoms, the limited number of sessions used (two treatment sessions) and the lack of follow-up data limit the conclusions that can be drawn. Foa *et al.* (1980c) found that the combination of 90 minutes of imaginal and 30 minutes of *in vivo* exposure was as effective as 120 minutes of *in vivo* exposure over 10 sessions. In fact at 11-month follow-up those who received the combined treatment maintained treatment gains whereas those who received *in vivo* exposure alone showed partial relapse on some of the measures. In a further report Foa, Steketee & Grayson (1985a) compared the efficacy of imaginal with *in vivo* exposure in the absence of response prevention for 19 obsessive–compulsive checkers. Both treatments were moderately effective (although less effective than other studies combining exposure with response prevention) with no difference between treatments at either post-treatment or follow-up.

Duration of exposure. Rabavilas *et al.* (1976) found that 80 minutes of continuous *in vivo* exposure time had greater treatment efficacy than eight 10-minute segments. When the treatment involved imaginal exposure then duration did not affect outcome. Given the lack of effectiveness of short exposure time used in systematic desensitisation studies, it seems that prolonged *in vivo* exposure enhances therapeutic effectiveness.

Attention vs distraction during exposure. Borkovec (1982) has suggested that even in the absence of overt avoidance behaviour functional exposure may still fail to take place if the individual fails to attend properly to the feared stimulus (cf. cognitive avoidance, Foa & Kozak, 1986). This has been illustrated in two studies by Grayson, Foa & Steketee (1982, 1986). They compared attention focusing (observing and discussing the contaminant) with distraction (playing video games) during exposure *in vivo* as treatment for OCD. In both studies heart rate response reduced substantially during attention-focusing, but remained elevated during distraction. The results of self-reported anxiety produced conflicting results between the two studies. The lack of between-sessions habituation for heart rate has been associated with poor treatment outcome for OCD (Kozak, Foa & Steketee, 1988) so that the combined findings suggest that cognitive avoidance impairs long-term habituation.

Exposure with and without response prevention. Theoretical assumptions lead to the supposition that exposure is necessary to reduce anxiety while rituals would be more affected by response prevention. Studies tend to support this notion. Foa, Steketee & Milby (1980b) compared exposure vs response prevention for obsessive–compulsive washers. Prolonged exposure reduced anxiety to contaminants more than it affected ritualistic behaviour, while response prevention affected rituals more than anxiety. Similar findings were obtained in a subsequent study (Steketee, Foa & Grayson, 1982). In a further report Foa *et al.* (1984) compared the efficacy of exposure vs response prevention with a third combined treatment group. Results from the single-treatment modalities replicated previous findings (anxiety to contaminants was reduced by exposure whereas ritualistic behaviour was affected more by the response prevention) with the combined treatment producing greater changes in anxiety and rituals than either of the single treatments alone.

Exposure and response prevention for obsessional ruminations and 'cognitive rituals'. Ruminations, particularly in the absence of overt compulsions, do not respond well to techniques such as thought-stopping, although habituation training appears to be more promising. Recent conceptualisations of obsessional ruminations in conjunction with covert 'cognitive rituals' (Robertson, Wendiggensen & Kaplan, 1983; Salkovskis & Westbrook, 1989) have led to suggestions that habituation training might be usefully employed in conjunction with training in self-directed covert response prevention (Salkovskis & Westbrook, 1989). Initial results from single cases appear promising. Given the infrequent occurrence of obsessions in the absence of overt rituals further evidence from controlled trials may not be readily forthcoming.

With regard to obsessional ruminations in conjunction with overt rituals the results of outcomes studies would seem to indicate that optimal treatment gains are obtained by prolonged *in vivo* exposure with attention focused upon the feared object in conjunction with response prevention. Similar treatment gains are obtained for outpatients with therapist support but with minimal therapist involvement during exposure sessions as for intensive therapist-guided exposure with inpatients. The role of the spouse in treatment is rather more equivocal, and clearly an area that warrants further research.

From an analysis of 50 OCD patients, who had participated in their various studies evaluating exposure and response prevention, Foa *et al.* (1983a) conclude that 58% were much improved, 38% were improved and 4% failed. Further, in a review of 18 controlled studies conducted over the past two decades in which 200 obsessive–compulsive ritualisers had been treated, Foa, Steketee & Ozarow (1985) conclude that 51% of the patients treated by this method were either symptom-free or much improved at the end of treatment, 39% were moderately improved and only 10% failed to benefit from therapy, although at follow-up the failures had increased to 24%. This led them to conclude that 'exposure and response prevention can indeed be considered the treatment of choice for obsessive–compulsive ritualisers' (p. 79) with treatment by exposure and response prevention benefiting about 75% of obsessive–compulsives who enter treatment. Although behavioural interventions have clearly revolutionised treatment of OCD, the very high success rates need to be treated with some degree of caution. They are inevitably based upon 'selected research populations, and in centres of excellence, using a team of highly trained staff in an intensive in-patient setting' (Salkovskis, 1989a, p. 51). In addition many patients refuse treatment, drop out of treatment or relapse subsequent to initial treatment gains, so that true success rates, while excellent, may be somewhat lower than the average reported. Even if the figure of 75% is accepted, this still leaves a further 25% for whom treatment is not effective. This has led both to attempts to explain treatment failures (Foa, 1979; Foa *et al.*, 1983b; Rachman, 1983b) and to suggestions that treatment failures are amenable to cognitive therapy (Salkovskis, 1988b, 1989a; Salkovskis & Warwick, 1985, 1988).

Factors affecting outcome of behavioural treatment

There is general agreement that for OCD most demographic variables are at best minimally predictive of treatment outcome (Steketee, 1988). Several studies have also failed to find a relationship between severity of symptoms and treatment outcome (e.g. Foa et al., 1983a) although severity of rituals was found to be the best predictor of poor outcome in one recent report (Basoglu et al., 1988). A number of authors have also reported that level of depression is negatively related to treatment gains (e.g. Foa, 1979; Foa, Steketee & Groves, 1979) and that antidepressant medication enhances the efficacy of exposure treatment (e.g. Marks et al., 1980). There seems to be less association between depression and longer-term treatment gains (Foa, Grayson & Steketee, 1982). Foa (1979) has argued that depression impedes the process of habituation of anxiety and hence reduces the efficacy of exposure treatment. In partial support of this notion she found a trend in the predicted direction for mean degree of habituation of subjective anxiety during exposure sessions for severely, moderately and mildly depressed patients (Foa et al., 1982). Others (e.g. Basoglu et al., 1988) have argued that depression is secondary to OCD severity and that it is not depression per se, but rather the severity of OCD, that determines response to treatment.

A further group of OCD patients who do not respond to treatment are those who are convinced that their concerns are reasonable. Unlike delusional beliefs it is assumed that those with overvalued ideations can be persuaded to recognise the irrationality of their beliefs. Four patients with overvalued ideas described by Foa (1979) showed within- but not between-session habituation. In these cases the overvalued idea itself must be dealt with before traditional behavioural interventions will be effective. It is particularly in cases such as these that cognitively based interventions might be most effective.

Cognitive techniques

Although a few reports within the past decade have advocated the use of cognitive techniques as treatment for OCD few treatment studies have appeared as yet. This is perhaps surprising, given the potentially important part played by cognitions in maintaining OCD. One of the first studies evaluating cognitive treatments for OCD investigated the utility of combining a cognitive modification with exposure in vivo (Emmelkamp et al., 1980). The cognitive modification consisted of self-instructional training in which the patients were 'trained to emit more productive self-statements . . . (1) preparing, (2) confronting, (3) coping and (4) reinforcing self-statements were practiced' (p. 63). Self-instructional training failed to add to the effectiveness of in vivo exposure, which if anything was superior to the combined approach. Whether such a cognitive strategy is the most appropriate as a treatment for OCD is, however, open to question. As Kendall (1983) points out, such patients already engage in excessive self-talk and ruminations; encouraging further self-talk may be counter-productive.

In a further report Emmelkamp, Visser & Hoekstra (1988) compared rational emotive therapy (RET) and exposure *in vivo* as treatment for 18 OCD patients randomly assigned to one of the two treatment conditions. The key elements of RET involved the patients identifying their cognitions, challenging and modifying their irrational beliefs. No significant differences between groups emerged, with both groups showing significant changes in obsessive–compulsive symptoms which were maintained at six-month follow-up.

Other suggestions for cognitive interventions for OCD have been developed by Salkovskis (1989a,b,c) based upon Beck's theorising (e.g. Beck, 1976). The central tenet is that therapy should 'concentrate not on modification of intrusions . . . but on automatic thoughts consequent on the intrusions, and on the beliefs which give rise to these' (Salkovskis, 1985, p. 581). Although Salkovskis has described the therapy in some detail, only case examples exist to date evaluating the effectiveness of this approach (e.g. Salkovskis, 1985; Salkovskis & Warwick, 1985). These suggest that such strategies might hold some promise, although in the absence of controlled evaluations initial results must inevitably be treated with some degree of caution.

SUMMARY

Obsessions have traditionally been conceptualised as covert, involuntary thoughts which increase anxiety, with compulsions as overt voluntary behaviours which decrease anxiety. Such a distinction fails to recognise the existence of covert rituals which can also be initiated by the patient in an attempt to reduce discomfort. OCD was at one time thought to be a relatively rare problem, although more recent epidemiological reports suggest that OCD identified by the DIS may be more prevalent than DIS-identified panic attacks. The common occurrence of obsessional thinking and/or compulsive rituals in relation to a number of other problems, and in relation to depression in particular, has been frequently reported. This has led some to question whether OCD should be classified with depression rather than with phobias, GAD and panic. However, the fact that depression associated with OCD tends to antedate rather than predate onset of OCD, the many similarities between OCD and the other anxiety disorders, and the central part played by anxiety in maintaining the condition seem to mitigate against such suggestions.

Recent research has emphasised the fact that obsessional thoughts and impulses are common in non-clinical samples, and that useful models can be established with such analogue populations. The latter, in particular, have focused upon the possibility of specific cognitive styles in relation to OCD. Given the inherent cognitive component in OCD the dearth of empirical research relating to cognitive deficits is perhaps surprising, and it is likely to be a fruitful avenue of future research. There is also a need for further empirical evaluation of cognitive interventions derived from this research. As Reed (1983) commented: 'the clinical remediation of obsessional problems, it is suggested, should focus upon the sufferers' thinking' (p. 179). Indeed, cognitively based interventions are likely to become the treatments of choice for ruminations in the absence of overt rituals.

Over the past two decades the treatment of choice for ruminations and associated overt rituals has been exposure with response prevention. The development of such treatment strategies has transformed the once-gloomy picture regarding prognosis, with reports suggesting that as many as 75% of OCD patients may benefit from such interventions. As many authors have noted, however, many patients refuse treatment, drop out of treatment or relapse subsequently, while even if the excellent success rates of 75% are accurate this still means that 25% fail. A number of studies have investigated factors predictive of treatment failure, with associated depression proposed as one important factor, although results of studies have been mixed. Other suggestions relate to patients with 'overvalued ideation', i.e. those with a greater conviction that their concerns are sensible. This has led some to suggest that cognitively based interventions might be more effective for such patients, possibly to complement available behavioural treatments.

Progress within the last 25 years in our understanding and treatment of OCD has been dramatic, and a once-gloomy picture is now far more promising. There are inevitably many questions that remain to be answered, and future research might usefully be directed towards further investigations of the factors predictive of treatment failure, the specific cognitive style associated with OCD, and the part to be played by cognitively based interventions in the treatment of obsessional ruminations both when they occur in isolation and when they occur with overt and/or covert rituals.

Chapter 8

Anxiety and Psychosexual Dysfunction

INTRODUCTION

Sexual dysfunctions have been defined as problems of a physiological, cognitive–affective, or behavioural nature that prevent an individual from engaging in or enjoying satisfactory sexual activity, intercourse or orgasm (Friedman & Chernen, 1987). Clinicians have frequently observed that anxiety plays a major role in the development and maintenance of such difficulties. Theorists from various backgrounds have also argued that anxiety plays a central role in the development of sexual dysfunction. Freud (1938), for example, wrote that 'intensive affective processes, even excitements of a terrifying nature encroach upon sexuality' (p. 601). From a different perspective, Wolpe (1958) conceptualised sexual dysfunction as a conditioned anxiety response to the sexual situation. The efficacy of relaxation and systematic desensitisation procedures based upon this theoretical stance has been evaluated in a number of treatment studies. Other influential writers such as Kaplan (1974, 1981, 1988) emphasise fear of failure as a central factor maintaining sexual dysfunction with sexual anxiety also influenced by performance demand and the need to please one's partner. Anxiety is seen as the critical mechanism that prevents physiological sexual arousal through disruption of autonomic nervous system functioning. Masters & Johnson (1970) also emphasise the importance of specific performance fears in the genesis and maintenance of sexual dysfunctions, describing anxiety as the greatest known deterrent to sexual arousal because it interferes with the reception of sexual stimuli and hence has an inhibitory effect upon physiological responsivity.

Numerous experimental studies have also been conducted investigating the role of anxiety in psychosexual dysfunction. Results from such studies are mixed with findings suggesting that experimentally induced anxiety can either impede or facilitate sexual arousal. This may be due in part to various interpretations of anxiety used within different studies. Many have emphasised relatively general fears while others have emphasised particular cognitive aspects of anxiety such as worries over performance (Masters & Johnson, 1970) or fears about loss of control (Kaplan, 1981). With regard to the specific cognitive aspects of anxiety implicated in relation to sexual dysfunction Beck & Barlow (1984) suggest that these involve a high frequency of distracting, intrusive thoughts that draw the sexually dysfunctional person's attention away from arousing cognitions and fantasies. The effect of anxiety and cognitive distraction of interference has been reviewed in a number of reports (Barlow, 1986, 1988; Beck, 1986; Beck & Barlow, 1984; Dekker & Everaerd, 1989; Everaerd, 1989; Norton & Jehu, 1984; Rosen & Beck, 1988).

The notion of control over sexual responding via cognitive strategies parallels the emphasis on cognitive factors in determining emotional state incorporated into recent theories of emotion discussed in Chapter 1 (e.g. Lazarus, Kanner & Folkman, 1980; Leventhal & Mosbach, 1983). Indeed, some writers have specifically stated that they view sexual arousal as an emotion (e.g. Dekker & Everaerd, 1988, p. 53). This creates the possibility of the complex pattern of cognitive, physiological and behavioural parameters associated with anxiety interacting with similar parameters associated with sexual arousal. In the same way that the components of an anxiety response may be discordant so may components of sexual responding (e.g. Morokoff & Heiman, 1980; Palace & Gorzalka, 1990). Interference may thus occur between various combinations of the components of anxiety and sexual arousal. The interactive effect will inevitably be complex.

In addition to anxiety, it is recognised that a wide range of biological factors (such as illness, hormonal disorders and neural impairment) and psychosocial factors (such as attitudes towards sexual activities, emotional reactions including anger, guilt and shame in addition to sexual skills) can influence human sexual responding. It is not the aim of the present chapter to address the wide range of emotional or other correlates of sexual behaviour, or to examine the various parameters of sexual response or assessments of these components, or to present a detailed discussion of sex therapy, but to focus explicitly on the role played by anxiety in causing and maintaining sexual dysfunctions and on treatments which focus explicitly on the modification of anxiety. Although terms will be defined, and the incidence of sexual dysfunction discussed, these will be covered only briefly. For more detailed accounts of the broader issues the reader is referred to Bancroft (1983), Kaplan (1981), LoPiccolo & LoPiccolo (1979) and Rosen & Beck (1988), amongst the many texts available in this area.

DEFINITIONS

Until the 1980s the problem of the lack of consensus and precision in the use of terms and in the classification of sexual dysfunction was a major obstacle to precise research in this area. Terms such as frigidity often encompassed all sexual dysfunctions in women, this particular term having been described as 'poor slang' by Masters & Johnson (1970). Similarly the term impotence has often been used to refer to lack of sexual interest in general in males, as well as being used to refer to erectile failure or erectile dysfunction in particular. Use of the term impotence has been criticised by Kaplan (1974) because of its pejorative connotations. In her 1974 and 1979 texts Kaplan classified sexual dysfunctions into those involving inhibited sexual excitement and orgasmic difficulties while later adding disorders of desire. This tripartite distinction formed the basis for the DSM-III (1980) classification of sexual dysfunction and the subsequent DSM-III-R (1987). The former included diagnoses of inhibited sexual desire, inhibited sexual excitement and three diagnoses for problems of sexual orgasm (inhibited female orgasm, inhibited male orgasm and premature ejaculation) with additional categories for dyspareunia and vaginismus. The assumption of these diagnostic categorisation systems is that the problem cannot be attributed entirely to organic factors, or to other difficulties such as depression or to inadequate sexual stimulation.

The DSM-III-R categories vary only slightly from DSM-III with distinctions made between sexual aversion and lack of desire (previously subsumed under inhibited sexual desire) and the terms erectile/arousal problems replacing inhibited sexual excitement. Like its predecessor the DSM-III-R categories reflect problems of sexual desire, orgasm and pain, and can be primary, occurring under all situations, or secondary, occurring in some circumstances and not others; each is described briefly below.

Hypoactive sexual desire disorder, defined as: persistently or recurrently deficient or absent sexual fantasies and desire for sexual activity. The judgement of deficiency or absence is made by the clinician taking into account factors that affect sexual functioning, such as age, sex and the context of the person's life (APA, DSM-III-R, 1987, p. 293).

Sexual aversion disorder, defined as: persistent or recurrent extreme aversion to, avoidance of all, or almost all, genital sexual contact with a sexual partner (p. 293).

Male erectile disorder, referring to either (1) persistent or recurrent partial or complete failure in a male to attain or maintain erection until completion of the sexual activity or (2) persistent or recurrent lack of a subjective sense of sexual excitement and pleasure in a male during sexual activity (p. 294).

Female sexual arousal disorder, referring to (1) persistent or recurrent partial or complete failure to attain or maintain the lubrication-swelling response of sexual excitement until completion of the sexual activity or (2) persistent or recurrent lack of subjective sense of sexual excitement and pleasure in the female during sexual activity (p. 294).

Inhibited female orgasm, refers to persistent or recurrent delay in, or absence of, orgasm in a female following a normal sexual excitement phase during sexual activity that the clinician judges to be adequate in focus, intensity or duration (p. 294).

Inhibited male orgasm refers to persistent or recurrent delay in, or absence of, orgasm in the male following a normal sexual excitement phase during sexual activity that the clinician, taking into account the person's age, judges to be adequate in focus, intensity and duration. This failure to achieve orgasm is usually restricted to an inability to reach orgasm in the vagina, with orgasm possible with other types of stimulation such as masturbation (p. 295).

Premature ejaculation refers to persistent or recurrent ejaculation with minimal sexual stimulation or before, upon, or shortly after penetration and before the person wishes it. The clinician must take into account factors that affect duration of the excitement phase, such as age, novelty of the sexual partner or situation, and frequency of sexual activity (p. 295).

Dyspareunia refers to recurrent and persistent genital pain in either male or female before, during or after sexual intercourse (p. 295). This must not be due to purely physical reasons or lack of lubrication or vaginismus.

Vaginismus refers to recurrent and persistent involuntary spasm of the outer third of the vagina that interferes with coitus (p. 295).

PREVALENCE

In a recent review Spector & Carey (1990) refer to 23 studies published within the past 50 years which have assessed the incidence and/or prevalence rates of sexual dysfunction. For females, inhibited orgasm is the most common presenting difficulty in sex therapy clinics, although sexual arousal disorder is also frequently reported. Renshaw (1988), for example, refers to orgasmic dysfunction rates of 32.2% amongst sex clinic attenders. In their pioneering community-based survey Kinsey *et al.* (1953) report that 10% of married women never experienced orgasm during intercourse. Hite (1976) also identified 10% of the female population as non-orgasmic, while Frank, Anderson & Rubinstein (1978) found that, in a sample of 100 'normal happily married couples', 63 of the women reported a history of arousal or orgasmic difficulty.

For males, erectile disorder and premature ejaculation are common presenting complaints in sex therapy clinics. Bancroft & Cole (1976) found that 40% of males presenting for sex therapy had erectile disorder as their primary complaint while for 22% their concern was premature ejaculation. In their community-based survey Kinsey, Pomeroy & Martin (1948) report the incidence of erectile failure as less than 1% amongst those aged less than 19, increasing to 25% by age 75. Frank, Anderson & Rubinstein (1978) found that 45 males from a sample of 100 'normal happily married couples' reported a history of erectile or ejaculatory dysfunction. Inhibited male orgasm is less common both in community and clinical settings.

As Spector & Carey (1990) note, prevalence rates are highly variable across studies, and reflect the range of methodologies, sampling and assessment procedures used and the differing definitions adopted. While reports suggest a high level of dysfunction within relationships more precise figures have yet to be obtained.

ASSESSMENT

Assessment of psychosexual dysfunction, as with assessment of the anxiety disorders, has focused on three different domains: self-report, behavioural and physiological. These various methods of assessment have been reviewed in detail elsewhere (e.g. Conte, 1983, 1986; Davis, Yarber & Davis, 1988; McConaghy, 1988). Self-reports involve diagnostic interviews (see Kaplan, 1983 for a discussion of this), standardised questionnaires and self-report records of sexual behaviour. For obvious reasons, direct behavioural observation has rarely been used even in laboratory-based studies. In contrast, physiological parameters have been increasingly assessed over the past two decades. These include nocturnal penile tumescence (see Karacan, 1982, for a description) for assessing erectile difficulties and various vaginal plethysmographs for assessing vaginal blood volume and vaginal pulse amplitude (Hoon, 1979) as measures of sexual arousal in females.

Although there are a wide range of questionnaires for assessing psychosexual dysfunction these tend to be directed towards sexual satisfaction and functioning rather than specifically assessing sexual anxiety (see Davis et al., 1988). The lack of objective measures of sexual anxiety has meant that researchers have either developed their own measure for use in one specific study (e.g. Obler, 1973) or adapted existing inventories or used card sorts or single-item rating scales. The Bentler scale (1968a,b), which lists 21 items relating to heterosexual behaviour, has been adapted in a number of studies by asking clients to rate how much anxiety they experience in each of the specified activities and situations (e.g. Everaerd & Dekker, 1982; Nemetz, Craig & Reith, 1978; Spence, 1985). A number of studies have also used card sorts of anxiety-based items (e.g. Caird & Wincze, 1974; Nemetz et al., 1978). Nemetz et al., for example, used 25 cards, each describing various sexual behaviours, which were sorted by the client according to the levels of anxiety induced if they were to engage in the behaviours depicted. The validity and reliability of these measures have rarely been assessed, and the variety of measures used inevitably makes it difficult to evaluate assessment procedures and treatment efficacy across studies. Also, many treatment studies, using procedures specifically designed to reduce sexually related anxiety, have assessed the marital and sexual relationship rather than anxiety both before treatment and for evaluating treatment outcome. In the absence of an assessment of anxiety it is not possible to ascertain whether anxiety (rather than lack of knowledge or skills or relationship difficulties, etc.) should form the focus of intervention.

ANXIETY AND PSYCHOSEXUAL DYSFUNCTION

As indicated in the introduction to this chapter the role of anxiety in the aetiology of sexual dysfunction has been advanced by a number of theorists. Masters & Johnson (1970) have commented, with regard to factors maintaining sexual dysfunction, that 'the prevalent roadblock is one of fear. Fear can prevent erection just as fear can increase the respiratory rate or lead to diarrhea or vomiting' (p. 196). They have also referred to an anxiety-associated cognitive set, or performance demand which inhibits or disrupts sexual arousal. Wolpe's (1958) theory of reciprocal inhibition proposed that human emotional states characterised by parasympathetic arousal (including sexual arousal) would interfere with sympathetic arousal produced by anxiety, that is, sympathetic and parasympathetic arousal are mutually inhibitory. Anxiety would thus interfere with sexual arousal, being implicated in the aetiology of erectile failure in particular. Hence interventions (relaxation and systematic desensitisation) aimed at reducing anxiety would counteract this particular sexual dysfunction. This proposition has been investigated in a number of experimental studies (e.g. Hoon, Wincze & Hoon, 1977; Barlow, Salkeim & Beck, 1983b) as well as providing the basis for many intervention studies.

The role of anxiety in the aetiology of sexual dysfunctions other than erectile failure is less evident. Wolpe (1973) also discusses the role of anxiety in the development of premature ejaculation, proposing that as ejaculation is sympathetically mediated it will be facilitated by anxiety which is also sympathetically mediated. However, evidence from studies investigating the neurophysiology of the ejaculatory response suggests that ejaculation is both sympathetically and parasympathetically mediated. Shiloh, Paz & Homannai (1984) note that the sympathetic nervous system is responsible for emission of semen into the posterior urethra while the parasympathetic nervous system elicits the actual delivery of the ejaculate. Further, a recent experimental study reports that while premature ejaculators had a shorter ejaculatory latency than non-premature ejaculators the two groups did not differ in self-reported anxiety (Strassberg et al., 1990). These authors suggest that some individuals may have a very low somatic vulnerability and require little, if any, anxiety in order to manifest their low orgasmic threshold. The role of anxiety in orgasmic dysfunction in women, or retarded ejaculation in men, is even less clear. Anxiety has also been implicated in the aetiology of vaginismus (Kaplan, 1974) and as being responsible for inhibiting lubrication, hence leading to pain (dyspareunia) during intercourse (Masters & Johnson, 1970) and in problems of hypoactive sexual desire (Kaplan, 1983). Kaplan conceptualises hypoactive sexual desire as a result of emotional conflicts involving both anxiety and anger. Bozman & Beck (1991) have recently conducted an empirical investigation of this hypothesis which partially supports Kaplan's model. Male subjects were presented with three audiotapes containing sexual content and statements by the participants that were designed to evoke anger or anxiety, or that were situationally appropriate (control condition). Reported sexual desire was decreased most by anger but was also decreased by anxiety relative to the control condition. Sexual arousal assessed by penile tumescence was decreased by anger but not anxiety.

Evidence concerning the role of anxiety in the aetiology of sexual dysfunction has thus been derived from clinically based evaluations and observations, as well as laboratory-based studies. Some studies have specifically investigated the role of anxiety in sexual responding using sexually functional subjects, while others have compared sexually functional and dysfunctional subjects. Many of these studies have been concerned specifically with sexually dysfunctional males (most usually erectile dysfunction), thus limiting any conclusions which can be drawn. As more research emerges the complex interaction between anxiety-related cognitions and physiological arousal has become apparent.

Clinical and other observations

In one of the earliest studies Cooper (1969) asked male patients with a sexual dysfunction (erectile failure and ejaculatory incompetence) to rate their anxiety related to coitus. Coital anxiety was defined as anxiety related temporarily to the act of coitus or sexual overtures and stimulations short of intercourse that could culminate in a coital attempt. Of the dysfunctional men 94% experienced recognisable anxiety during intercourse, with 'fear of failure' and a generalised feeling of inadequacy being the most frequently cited examples of specific anxieties experienced. Cooper notes, however, that for only 14% of the patients could anxiety be 'confidently indicted as a specific cause' (p. 146). The usual onset pattern involved failure engendering anxiety followed by a further loss of confidence in a vicious circle of anxiety.

In a further study Kockott et al. (1980) compared 32 psychogenic sexually dysfunctional males (erectile dysfunction, $N = 16$ and premature ejaculation, $N = 16$) with organically dysfunctional males (diabetes-related erectile dysfunction) and normal controls on a measure of sexual anxiety. The psychogenic sexually dysfunctional males reported the highest levels of sexual anxiety and seemed to overestimate their partner's sexual interest. Within the premature ejaculation group two subgroups were identifiable similar to those reported by Cooper (1969), one group with high sexual anxiety scores and a second who obtained lower (but nevertheless elevated) sexual anxiety scores. For the former group premature ejaculation seemed to be an expression of sexual inhibitions and anxiety; for the second group premature ejaculation was recognised as a problem only following comment by their partners, hence anxiety was subsequent to initial difficulties. In a further report Munjack, Kano & Oziel (1978) found that males with retarded ejaculation scored higher than non-dysfunctional males on five out of eight measures of anxiety, while premature ejaculators scored higher on two out of eight measures of anxiety. In summary, these studies suggest that elevated anxiety is related to psychosexual dysfunction; further this anxiety may be in part a cause rather than a consequence of psychosexual dysfunction.

By way of contrast, other reports suggest that, far from inhibiting sexual arousal, anxiety serves to increase arousal. Ramsey (1943), in a survey of adolescent boys, reported that approximately 50% noted erections in situations involving fear or excitement of a non-sexual nature. In a further report Sarrel & Masters (1982) provide descriptions of men accosted by gangs of women and threatened at knife-point or with other weapons to perform sexually. The men were able to attain an erection and to perform repeatedly although, given the number subsequently seeking clinical help, clearly suffering distress. The likely anxiety engendered by these attacks did not inhibit arousal in the men concerned. Psychosexual dysfunction may well be related to some specific aspects of anxiety, but anxiety *per se* may increase as well as inhibit sexual arousal.

Laboratory studies

A number of studies have investigated the effects of experimentally induced anxiety upon arousal in sexually functional subjects. Lange *et al.* (1981) induced 'clinical anxiety' by injecting subjects with epinephrine hydrochloride, after which the subjects viewed erotic stimuli. Epinephrine hydrochloride increased subjects' ratings of anxiety and decreased penile tumescence levels in the post-film period, but not during the sexual-stimulus presentation itself.

In one of the first studies to examine the effects of experimentally induced anxiety upon sexual arousal, Hoon, Wincze & Hoon (1977) specifically addressed Wolpe's theory of reciprocal inhibition. Sexually functional women were exposed to either neutral or anxiety-provoking films (either a travelogue or scenes of traffic accidents) followed by an erotic film, and vice versa. Consistent with reciprocal inhibition theory, sexual arousal induced by pre-exposure to the erotic film diminished more rapidly when subsequent exposure was to the anxiety stimulus than to the control stimulus. Contrary to reciprocal inhibition theory, however, prior exposure to the anxiety-evoking film resulted in significantly greater arousal during the erotic film. In a partial replication of this study with sexually functional males a similar increase in arousal during an erotic film was obtained following exposure to an anxiety-inducing film (threatened amputation) (Wolchik *et al.*, 1980).

A number of specific points relating to these studies are worthy of brief mention. Hoon *et al.* do not report any pre-testing of the 'anxiety'-inducing nature of the accident scenes, and hence there is no certainty that anxiety was actually induced (Wolchik *et al.* report a pilot study in which the same scenes were found to be anger-inducing in males). In addition, as Wolpe (1978b) points out, the reciprocal inhibition premise assumes the simultaneous presence of anxiety-inducing and sexual arousal stimuli. In both the Hoon *et al.* and Wolchik *et al.* studies the anxiety and erotic stimuli were successive and hence the increase in sexual arousal might be due to an anxiety relief or contrast effect, rather than being due to a facilitatory effect of anxiety.

In view of this Barlow, Sakheim & Beck (1983b) simultaneously manipulated both performance anxiety and generalised anxiety, via threat of receiving a shock (although no shock was actually administered), in addition to manipulating arousal (viewing an erotic film). In the two experimental groups, subjects were either told there was a 60% chance of a shock if they did not achieve adequate arousal (contingent threat—performance anxiety group) or that the chance of shock was unrelated to their arousal or any other response (non-contingent shock—generalised anxiety group). Arousal, measured by penile circumference, for the two experimental groups was compared with a no-shock control group. Both shock conditions showed greater arousal than the no-shock condition with the performance demand (contingent threat) group producing highest overall sexual arousal. Thus, not only did anxiety increase arousal but, contrary to predictions, performance demand, as specified in this study, served to increase arousal even more.

In these experimental studies, then, anxiety seems to facilitate arousal in sexually functional subjects. A recent report has, however, produced contrary results which are in line with the contention that anxiety reduces sexual arousal (Hale & Strassberg, 1990). Fifty-four sexually functional male volunteers viewed a series of erotic videotapes after receiving one of three sets of instructions: neutral feedback; feedback indicating that they would be receiving a painful electric shock (physical threat); and feedback indicating that their level of sexual arousal during baseline measurement was subnormal (self-threat). Both the physical threat and self-threat resulted in a significant reduction in sexual arousal (penile tumescence) compared to the neutral condition. Contrary to their predictions the self-threat (designed to create concern about sexual performance) was no more disruptive to sexual arousal than the physical threat. The authors suggest a number of methodological reasons for the difference between their results and those of Barlow et al. (1983b). First, Barlow et al.'s subjects were exposed to an actual shock prior to the experimental phase potentially reducing anticipatory anxiety; second, Barlow et al.'s subjects expected a 50% chance of receiving a shock, whereas Hale & Strassberg's subjects believed they were guaranteed to receive a shock, potentially increasing anxiety in the second study. Although Hale & Strassberg's finding that anxiety interferes with sexual arousal is in line with clinical assumptions, this is one of the few studies to find such an effect. The balance of evidence seems to suggest that for functional subjects anxiety facilitates sexual arousal, although it must be borne in mind that the experimental induction of anxiety and 'performance demand' will have different properties from those experienced within the context of a relationship.

As Beck & Barlow (1984) point out, however, if anxiety facilitates arousal it cannot also maintain arousal difficulties. It is possible, however, that while there is a general facilitatory effect of anxiety upon arousal for functional subjects a different pattern of responding is evident for sexually dysfunctional subjects. One explanation for the general finding that anxiety increases arousal in functional subjects is that they misattribute general arousal as sexual arousal (Beggs, Calhoun & Wolchik, 1987). It is possible that dysfunctionals make different interpretations (Norton & Jehu, 1984). However, in one recent study anxiety pre-exposure enhanced the rate and magnitude of genital arousal and self-reported autonomic arousal for both sexually functional and dysfunctional women (Palace &

Gorzalka, 1990). That anxiety facilitates arousal in functional women is consistent with research findings with sexually functional males. The finding that anxiety also facilitates arousal for dysfunctional women is, however, contrary to a number of studies which have found an inhibitory effect of anxiety upon sexual arousal in dysfunctional men (see below). Clearly the pattern of responding may be very different for dysfunctional men and women. For example, Palace & Gorzalka found that although both groups of women exhibited an increased physiological response they reported less subjective sexual arousal after anxiety pre-exposure. This desynchrony of sexual response for women differs from the synchrony generally noted for men (Rosen & Beck, 1988). Palace & Gorzalka argue that their findings suggest that 'anxiety may enhance sexual arousal through the direct instigation and facilitation of sympathetic activation . . . which serves to prepare the person for sexual arousal. Cognitive expectancy may provide a secondary effect that further increases or decreases the physiological effect elicited by sympathetic nervous system activation' (pp. 409–410). Cognitive parameters, such as attentional focus, may interfere with or enhance anxiety-induced arousal; this has been investigated in a number of laboratory studies.

Attentional focus

It is clear from a range of reports that sexual responding can be influenced by cognitive factors. Dekker & Everaerd (1988) found an increased sexual response in both men and women instructed to attend to images of sexual situations, actions and responses in comparison to men and women instructed to attend only to those images involving situations and actions. In addition, when instructed to do so both male and female subjects can suppress sexual arousal (e.g. Abel *et al.*, 1975; Cerny, 1978) presumably either by focusing attention on some non-arousing activity or by distracting thoughts away from arousal content (Barlow, 1986). A number of experimental studies have investigated the effect of distraction upon sexual arousal.

Geer & Fuhr (1976) presented sexually functional male subjects with a dichotic listening task consisting of a distractor (arithmetical tasks of varying complexity) and an erotic audiotape. As the complexity of the distractor task increased, arousal, as measured by penile tumescence, decreased. In a similar study evaluating the effect of distraction (presentation of tones) on arousal induced by visual erotic stimuli, Farkas, Sine & Evans (1979) found a marked effect of distraction on penile response, but not upon subjectively reported arousal. It is interesting to note that in both these studies audiotaped distraction reduced arousal (penile response) irrespective of the modality of presentation of the erotic stimuli

ANXIETY AND PSYCHOSEXUAL DYSFUNCTION

(auditory or visual). In a further report Przybyla & Byrne (1984) found that as complexity of an audiotaped distractor increased, males who viewed erotic films did not report less arousal, while males who listened to audiotaped erotic material did so. Thus, while there might be some modality differences it seems that distraction inhibits physiological if not subjective sexual arousal in experimental investigations with sexually functional males. A comparable study designed to assess the effects of cognitive distraction (visually presented addition tasks) on female sexual arousal (induced by audiotape presentation of erotic material) found significant decreases in both subjective and physiological measures of arousal (Adams, Haynes & Brayer, 1985).

It is, of course, of interest to know if these findings generalise to sexually dysfunctional subjects. Such an investigation comparing sexually functional with sexually dysfunctional males (10 subjects with erectile dysfunction) is reported by Abrahamson et al. (1985b). They found that distraction (listening to an audiotaped reading of a novel) while viewing erotic videotapes resulted in decreased arousal for sexually functional males (as measured by penile circumference), while sexually dysfunctional subjects were unaffected by distraction. Dysfunctional subjects, however, continuously underestimated arousal on a simultaneously recorded continuous measure of subjective arousal.

While distracting stimuli unrelated to sexual performance may not inhibit arousal in dysfunctional males one possibility is that, for such individuals, sexually related performance demand may generate sexually disruptive cognitive interference. Two studies (Beck, Barlow & Sakheim, 1983; Abrahamson et al., 1985a) have specifically investigated such performance demand. The effect of attentional focus (self-focus versus partner focus) and level of partner responsiveness (high, low, ambiguous) were investigated. The manipulations consisted of instructional priming given to male subjects just prior to watching an erotic videotape or listening to an erotic audiotape. Comparing responses of sexually functional and dysfunctional males watching an erotic videotape, Beck et al. (1983) found that partner focus resulted in high levels of tumescence for functional subjects when the partner displayed high sexual arousal while under these circumstances dysfunctional subjects' arousal was inhibited. Both this study and the Abrahamson et al. (1985a) report using audiotaped erotic stimuli found that for sexually functional subjects under conditions of high partner responsiveness, partner focus produced significantly higher tumescence than did self-focus. Beck et al. (1983) report that post-session interviews revealed that functional males concentrated on partner arousal while dysfunctional subjects concentrated on performance-related cues, thus providing some *post-hoc* evidence that distraction plays a part in dysfunctional subjects' difficulties.

The possibility that sexually related performance demand is specifically responsible for dysfunctionals' responses was investigated in a further study by Barlow and his colleagues (Abrahamson, Barlow & Abrahamson, 1989). They compared the effect of performance-related distraction and neutral distraction cues to a no-distraction control condition on arousal for 10 functional and 10 dysfunctional males. In the performance distraction condition subjects viewed video feedback of their genital response and were asked to estimate percentage of full erection; in the neutral distraction condition subjects estimated the length and width of a line appearing on another monitor. For dysfunctionals, only performance-related distraction resulted in decreased arousal relative to the no-distraction control; conversely, functional subjects showed elevated arousal during the performance-related distraction but lower arousal during neutral distraction relative to the no-distraction control condition. The lack of effect of neutral distraction upon sexual arousal in dysfunctional males is contrary to findings reported by Abrahamson et al. (1985a) and Geer & Fuhr (1976), although this may be due to the greater complexity of the neutral distractor employed in the latter two studies. Abrahamson, Barlow & Abrahamson (1989) suggest that the differential responding of functional and dysfunctional subjects under conditions of performance demand is due to the sense of control and positive affect for the former in contrast to the sense of uncontrollability concerning sexual responding and negative affect for the latter. The latter are thus distracted from erotic cues.

Similar disruptive effects on focusing upon sexual and performance-related cues are reported for dysfunctional subjects by Heiman & Rowland (1983). They instructed functional and dysfunctional men either to focus on pleasurable internal sensations (sensate focus) or to get an erection as quickly as possible (performance demand) prior to exposure to an erotic audiotape. Functional subjects in general showed greater physiological and subjective arousal and less anxiety than the dysfunctional subjects. In addition the sexually functional subjects showed stronger penile responses under the demand condition while dysfunctional subjects had the strongest genital response during sensate focus instructions. Sexually functional and sexually dysfunctional subjects seem, then, to react differently to both neutral and sexually related distractors. Performance-related concerns seem to inhibit arousal in dysfunctional males while neutral distractors seem to have little effect; in contrast neutral distractors inhibit sexual arousal in functional subjects whose arousal is enhanced by sexual performance demand. Clearly the issue is far from simple, and is complicated further by the fact that physiological aspects of anxiety and cognitive distractors can have an interactive as well as a differential effect for functional and dysfunctional subjects.

Anxiety and cognitive interference

A number of studies have investigated the interaction of sexual anxiety and distraction. Beck *et al.* (1987) presented 16 sexually functional males with brief erotic audiotapes simultaneously with four levels of shock threat (no shock, half tolerance, tolerance and twice tolerance). Following presentation of the stimuli, subjects completed a sentence-recognition task to check attention to the audiotapes. Shock threat lowered penile tumescence particularly during half tolerance and tolerance, while during twice tolerance penile response was almost equal to no shock threat. Performance on the sentence-completion task showed almost the reverse pattern: improved performance during half tolerance and tolerance, deteriorated performance during twice tolerance. The decrease in tumescence in relation to shock threat contrasts with previous reports with sexually functional subjects (e.g. Barlow, Sakheim & Beck, 1983b) although it is consistent with other studies involving additional experimental manipulations of attentional focus (Beck & Barlow, 1986a).

Beck & Barlow (1986a,b) compared physiological, cognitive and affective responses of 12 sexually functional and 12 sexually dysfunctional males under conditions of shock threat and no shock threat, and self-focus or partner focus, during exposure to erotic films. As with the Beck *et al.* (1987) study shock threat diminished tumescence for sexually functional subjects while dysfunctional subjects showed a trend towards elevated responding during shock threat under spectator focus instructions. Dysfunctional subjects reported a higher frequency of thoughts involving non-evaluative spectator focus, more attention to internal thoughts, sensations and feelings and greater misperception of actual physiological response. Beck & Barlow (1986b) conclude that 'excessive cognitive attention to performance is a cardinal feature of sexual dysfunction, coupled with affective blunting' (p. 26).

In a further intriguing report Beggs, Calhoun & Wolchick (1987) asked functional women to describe a sexual anxiety experience or fantasy, and a pleasurable sexual experience or fantasy. Measures of arousal taken while subjects subsequently listened to narratives extracted from their reports showed that levels of both genital and subjective arousal increased significantly in response to both sexual anxiety and sexual pleasure. However, increases in the pleasure condition were significantly greater than in the anxiety condition. As the authors point out, more meaningful results might be obtained from studies like their own, where the stimuli used are specifically relevant to the subjects. As Dekker & Everaerd (1989) note, however, because of the nature of the stimuli used, other variables correlated with the anxiety/pleasure dimension may have caused the results.

Both Barlow (1986) and Dekker & Everaerd (1989), in summarising the research findings dealing with the interrelationship between anxiety and sexual arousal, suggest that (a) cognitive distraction (usually with regard to neutral stimuli) reduces sexual arousal in functional subjects but has no effect on dysfunctional subjects; (b) performance demand and anxiety induction alone either have no effect or increase sexual arousal in functional males while in dysfunctional men they decrease sexual arousal; (c) dysfunctional subjects clearly experience negative affect in sexual relations while sexually functional subjects experience more positive affect; (d) sexually dysfunctional subjects tend to under-report sexual arousal in relation to physiological indices. Clearly the interaction between anxiety, distraction and presence or absence of sexual problems is complex. While experimental studies have offered a number of pointers, a number of concerns can be raised regarding the studies conducted to date, and a number of issues remain to be investigated. While investigating the relationship between anxiety and sexual dysfunction is no easy matter there may well be a limit to the extent to which findings from laboratory studies using shock threat, erotic stimuli and imagined others can be generalised to real-life situations. Further, the majority of studies have collected data from men with erectile difficulties, and the extent to which these findings apply both to other difficulties and to women remains to be seen (similar findings for males and females have been reported in some studies, e.g. Hoon et al., 1977, although differences have also been observed, e.g. Palace & Gorzalka, 1990).

Given the theoretical emphasis on performance demands and spectatoring, and the overall weight of experimental findings that performance demand and anxiety decrease sexual arousal in dysfunctional subjects, treatments focusing on cognitive change and attentional focus in addition to anxiety reduction may become increasingly important. Clearly, however, ascertaining the precise effects of anxiety upon sexual arousal is essential. Given their finding that anxiety may enhance sexual arousal through facilitation of sympathetic arousal in both functional and dysfunctional women Palace and Gorzalka (1990) comment that 'treatment of sexually dysfunctional women directed towards extinguishing anxiety and increasing parasympathetic response may be counterproductive to the physiological elicitation of sexual arousal' (p. 410). Anxiety reduction is, nevertheless, a common component of treatment.

TREATMENT

Until the 1960s psychoanalytically oriented therapies were the treatment of choice for sexual dysfunction, although there was little evidence that these were effective. Interventions based upon learning theories were introduced in the late 1950s drawing on Wolpe's (1958) assumption that sexual dysfunction was a conditioned anxiety response to the sexual situation. Such dysfunctions were thus treated by relaxation or systematic desensitisation, with the emphasis upon the reduction of anxiety. There are numerous single-case reports demonstrating the efficacy of this approach, but fewer controlled studies—the latter will be discussed below. The aim of other behavioural interventions, such as assertiveness and communication training, has been to provide the couple with appropriate behavioural and communication skills within the context of a sexual relationship. While these interventions may well serve to reduce sexual anxiety this is clearly not their main focus.

In the 1960s several cognitively based interventions, such as rational emotive therapy, which often included an element of anxiety reduction and skills training, were applied to the treatment of sexual dysfunction. Again the lack of controlled studies makes it difficult to evaluate the efficacy of such approaches.

The major breakthrough in the treatment of sexual dysfunction was in the 1970s following Masters & Johnson's (1970) innovative work. The role played by anxiety was clearly central to their conceptualisation and treatment of sexual dysfunction, although treatment was not directed specifically towards this. Their central assumption was that sexual difficulties were the result of informational and communication deficits and performance anxiety. The result of this is 'spectatoring' where the partner (most usually the male) focuses attention on his sexual functioning, watching for signs of failure. Therapy is usually short-term, involving a graduated series of sexual tasks for couples as homework assignments, in conjunction with a ban on sexual intercourse primarily to reduce performance anxiety. The tasks begin with 'sensate focus', the primary aim of which is to reduce anxiety and eliminate 'spectatoring'. The couple are encouraged to concentrate on their own sexual sensations and to provide feedback about their feelings to their partner.

Clearly facets of treatment such as the banning of intercourse, and the focus upon enjoyment, make the elimination of performance anxiety a central goal of sex therapy. As sex therapy involves a series of graduated exercises relating to bodily exploration with the focus on pleasurable sensations, there are also clear parallels with systematic desensitisation. Anxiety reduction thus plays a varying role in the treatments of sexual dysfunction. However, it is the primary objective of only systematic desensitisation. This has been used in the treatment of inhibited female orgasm (see reviews by Anderson, 1983; Kilmann, 1978) and erectile difficulties (see reviews by Reynolds, 1977; Kilmann & Auerbach, 1979; Mohr & Beutler, 1990) and in the treatment of premature ejaculation (see review by Ruff & St Lawrence, 1985). The comments in the following sections will be directed specifically towards those studies in which the emphasis in treatment has been the reduction of anxiety.

Treatment of male sexual dysfunction

Systematic desensitisation has been widely used in the treatment of erectile difficulties and premature ejaculation. A number of reviews published during the 1970s suggest that treatment of male sexual dysfunction with systematic desensitisation can improve sexual functioning (e.g. Shusterman, 1973; Laughran & Kass, 1975; Reynolds, 1977; Kilmann & Auerbach, 1979). In their review, Kilmann & Auerbach (1979) note the positive outcome of various single-case studies but also note, at the time of their report, a lack of group comparison studies. In his review Reynolds (1977) refers to seven successful single-case reports and two single-treatment group studies reporting successful treatment with systematic desensitisation for 14 out of 17 men with erectile or ejaculatory problems. He also details two group comparison studies, one of which suggests that systematic desensitisation is more effective than interpretive group therapy while the second (Kockott, Dittmar & Nusselt, 1975) found little difference in clinical outcome between systematic desensitisation, a routine therapy group or a waiting list control. In this latter study, however, subjects in the desensitisation group, in comparison to subjects in the other two treatment groups, reported that their feelings in sexual situations were associated with less anxiety.

In a more recent report Everaerd & Dekker (1985) compared systematic desensitisation with an adaptation of Masters & Johnson's sex therapy as treatment for 22 males with at least a 1-year history of psychogenic sexual dysfunction. Patients were assigned at random to treatments (20 of the patients had erectile difficulties and two premature ejaculation). The authors report that both treatments led to significant improvements in sexual functioning with no differences between treatments. Sexual anxiety was not assessed in this study. In general, then, systematic desensitisation seems to be helpful in alleviating erectile difficulties, although as there has been little attempt to evaluate anxiety as well as sexual functioning it is difficult to know whether anxiety reduction *per se* is the mechanism by which treatment operates.

Inhibited male orgasm has received very little attention in the therapeutic literature. Clinical case studies suggest a range of aetiological factors, including anxiety, but there is little supporting empirical research (see review by Shull & Sprenkle, 1980). Indeed, one of the few clinical studies (Cooper, 1969) found only a weak relationship between anxiety and inhibited male orgasm. However, the major treatment elements for inhibited male orgasm remain reduction of performance anxiety and increasing physical stimulation (LoPiccolo & Stock, 1985).

Treatment of female sexual dysfunction

A number of studies report the use of systematic desensitisation both in combination with other treatments and as the sole treatment for both primary and secondary orgasmic dysfunction in women (DSM-III-R equivalent: inhibited female orgasm) (see Kilmann, 1978). Lobitz and LoPiccolo (1972), for example, used a combination of sexual skills training, sexual re-education, couple communication training and systematic desensitisation as treatment for both primary and secondary orgasmic dysfunction. It is obviously impossible to deduce from these studies the relative contribution of anxiety reduction *per se* to treatment success. Also these studies tend to use sexual and marital adjustment as outcome criteria without evaluating sexual anxiety.

In her review of primary orgasmic dysfunction in women Anderson (1983) refers to 12 single-case and group treatment studies involving 140 patients treated by more than a dozen therapists using systematic desensitisation. There was a wide variation across these studies in the length of sessions (10 minutes to 1 hour) and treatment duration (2 weeks to 6 months), as well as measures used. Further, some of the studies involved individual treatment while others evaluated group-based systematic desensitisation. In addition some studies involved the spouse while some used video desensitisation (modelling). Anderson notes that across studies subjects uniformly reported reductions in sexual anxiety, and on occasion increases in such behaviour as coital frequency. In terms of anxiety reduction, video presentation appeared to be as effective as verbal presentation, while involvement of the partner had either neutral or positive impact. Change in orgasmic status is often not observed in these studies; in single-case reports most subjects experienced orgasm either during treatment or shortly afterwards, although group comparison studies suggest either no change in orgasmic status or only insignificant to moderate gains.

The utility of systematic desensitisation has also been investigated in relation to secondary orgasmic dysfunction. There is, however, even less controlled evaluative research than in relation to primary orgasmic dysfunction. The majority of reports have been single-case studies, or have included a variety of sexual disorders within the treated population. Long-term follow-ups have also rarely been reported. Some studies suggest that treatments focusing upon anxiety reduction are less successful in achieving orgasm in coitus with secondary orgasmic dysfunction than with primary (e.g. McGovern, Stewart & LoPiccolo, 1975). This apparent lack of success is often assumed to be due to the fact that secondary orgasmic dysfunction is more likely to be associated with a disturbed marital relationship, although there is little evidence to support this notion. In fact, some studies suggest that desensitisation is equally effective for both secondary and primary orgasmic dysfunction (e.g. Sotile & Kilmann, 1978).

In one report specifically focusing upon secondary orgasmic dysfunction, Everaerd & Dekker (1982) randomly assigned subjects to a waiting list control or one of three treatment groups (systematic desensitisation, an adapted version of Masters & Johnson's method or a combination of these two methods). At follow-up both methods used alone resulted in improved satisfaction with the total relationship, while desensitisation additionally reduced sexual anxiety (these changes were small in comparison to the control group). Surprisingly the combined treatment produced poor results which the authors attribute to the lack of time available to develop either treatment. No measure of attainment of orgasm was taken in this study. As with male sexual dysfunction, systematic desensitisation seems to be helpful in alleviating orgasmic difficulties in women although again, as there has been little attempt to evaluate anxiety as well as sexual functioning, it is difficult to know whether anxiety reduction *per se* is the mechanism by which treatment operates. Indeed, as noted, Palace & Gorzalka's (1990) research suggests that anxiety might enhance arousal in dysfunctional women and hence anxiety reduction may be counterproductive. Both the interaction between physiological and cognitive responses and the implications of this for treatment warrant further investigation.

Mixed populations

A number of studies have included both males and females with sexual dysfunctions within their treatment groups. Obler (1973) compared systematic desensitisation with group therapy and a no-treatment control. Subjects were 37 females with orgasmic dysfunction and 27 males with erectile and ejaculatory difficulties. Those treated by systematic desensitisation were more likely to be sexually functional after treatment and at follow-up, as well as showing reduced social and sexual anxiety. Mathews *et al.* (1976a) compared systematic desensitisation plus counselling with Masters & Johnson's sex therapy plus counselling and the same treatment with minimal therapist contact. The 36 couples were evenly divided between male and female dysfunctions. Although there was a trend towards the

Masters & Johnson sex therapy plus counselling obtaining better results, the three methods did not differ significantly in their effects on sexual functioning or the marital relationship. Anxiety was not specifically assessed in this study.

Taken overall, systematic desensitisation seems to be effective as a treatment for erectile difficulties and inhibited female orgasm. Whether improvement in sexual functioning is specifically related to anxiety reduction has been suggested by only very few studies, and the mechanism by which systematic desensitisation operates remains unclear. The possibility that dysfunctional males and females exhibit different reaction patterns warrants further investigation; at present the theoretical rationale for anxiety reduction with the latter remains equivocal.

SUMMARY

Reports suggest that sexual dysfunction is common within relationships, although prevalence rates are highly variable across studies and reflect the range of definitions, methodologies, sampling and assessment procedures used. A range of environmental, social and biological factors have been implicated in the aetiology of sexual dysfunction. In addition, the suggestion that anxiety plays a major role in the development and maintenance of psychosexual difficulties has frequently been noted by clinicians, as well as being advanced by theorists from a variety of backgrounds (Freud, 1938; Kaplan, 1974, 1981; Masters & Johnson, 1970; Wolpe, 1958). Treatment studies, specifically based on the premise that anxiety plays a major role in the aetiology of sexual dysfunction, have been applied for more than two decades. Indeed the application of such methods preceded the experimental investigation of the role of anxiety in sexual arousal by more than a decade.

Some of these experimental studies have specifically investigated the role of anxiety in sexual responding using sexually functional subjects, while others have compared sexually functional and dysfunctional subjects. Many of these studies have been concerned specifically with sexually dysfunctional males (most usually erectile dysfunction), thus limiting any conclusions which can be drawn. As more research emerges it is clear that there is a complex interaction between anxiety-related cognitions and physiological arousal. Cognitive distraction involving non-sexually related stimuli seems to reduce sexual arousal in functional subjects but has no effect on dysfunctional subjects. In contrast performance demand and anxiety induction alone either have no effect or increase sexual arousal in functional males, while in dysfunctional men they decrease sexual arousal.

While investigating the relationship between anxiety and sexual dysfunction is no easy matter, it is unlikely that findings from laboratory studies using shock threat, erotic stimuli and imagined others can be directly transferable to real-life situations. Furthermore, the majority of studies have collected data from men with erectile difficulties, and the extent to which these findings apply both to women and to other difficulties remains to be seen. Indeed, one recent study suggests that anxiety enhances physiological arousal for both dysfunctional and functional women during subsequent exposure to erotic stimuli; this contrasts with the inhibitory effect for anxiety with dysfunctional males.

A number of facets of treatment from Masters & Johnson's sex therapy, such as the banning of intercourse and the focus upon enjoyment, make anxiety reduction a central goal. Further, the use of a series of graduated exercises relating to bodily exploration suggest clear parallels with systematic desensitisation. Anxiety reduction thus plays a varying role in the treatments of sexual dysfunction, although it is only in systematic desensitisation that anxiety reduction is the primary objective. Systematic desensitisation seems to be helpful in alleviating both erectile difficulties in men and orgasmic difficulties in women. There has, however, been little attempt to evaluate anxiety as well as sexual functioning, making it difficult to ascertain whether anxiety reduction *per se* is the mechanism by which treatment operates. Further, quesionnaires for assessing sexual dysfunction are rarely directed specifically to assessing sexual anxiety. The lack of objective measures of sexual anxiety has meant that researchers have either developed their own measure for use in one specific study or adapted existing inventories, or used card sorts or single-item rating scales, making it difficult to compare results across studies.

The interrelationship between cognitive and physiological parameters of sexual arousal with cognitive and physiological parameters of anxiety is clearly complex. Much can be gained from drawing parallels with the multicomponent models of emotion discussed in Chapter 1. In view of the anxiety reduction component inherent in many sex therapies, unravelling the part played by anxiety in the aetiology of sexual dysfunction will provide a clearer rationale for using such interventions.

Chapter 9

Preoperative Anxiety and Preparation for Surgery

INTRODUCTION

The prospect of undergoing an unpleasant medical procedure may be anxiety-provoking for a number of reasons: patients might be concerned about the pain and discomfort they expect to experience; they may be unfamiliar with the procedure and they may have concerns about the diagnosis and prognosis. Within the past three decades there has been an accumulating research literature concerning psychological techniques designed to prepare patients, both adults and children, for invasive surgical procedures. Numerous reviews of this work have appeared within the past decade or so (e.g. Anderson & Masur, 1983; Cohen & Lazarus, 1979; Gill, 1984; Ludwick-Rosenthal & Neufeld, 1988; MacDonald & Kuiper, 1983; Mathews & Ridgeway, 1984; Melamed, Siegel & Ridley-Johnson, 1988; Mumford, Schlesinger & Glass, 1982; Peterson, 1989; Reading, 1979; Rogers & Reich, 1986; Saile, Burgmeier & Schmidt, 1988; Schultheis, Peterson & Selby, 1987; Wilson-Barnett, 1984). Outcome studies surveyed have employed a range of techniques, including informative, psychotherapeutic, modelling, behavioural, cognitive–behavioural and/or hypnotic procedures whose aim has been to reduce one or more of preoperative anxiety, complications during surgery, postoperative distress and recovery time. In general this research suggests that these approaches can be effective, although variations in sample characteristics and outcome measures mitigate against uncritical generalisation of these results. Interventions have been broadly based upon three main theoretical perspectives: Janis's (1958) emotional-drive theory; Leventhal & Johnson's (1983) self-regulation theory and Lazarus & Folkman's (1984) cognitive appraisal/coping model. Each model inevitably offers a differing rationale about the relationship of anxiety to noxious medical procedures, and for the applicability and utility of certain interventions in reducing preoperative anxiety and postoperative distress.

THEORETICAL ASSUMPTIONS

Emotional-drive theory

A frequent assumption behind preparation for surgery is that excessive levels of presurgical fear are detrimental to postoperative recovery. Interventions have thus been aimed at reducing patients' preoperative anxiety and fear by such techniques as information provision, preoperative relaxation training and/or preoperative supportive counselling. However, the precise relationship between preoperative fear and postoperative adjustment remains unclear. Janis (1958), one of the first investigators to examine the link, proposed that the relationship was curvilinear. He argued that patients with a moderate amount of preoperative anxiety would show best adjustment, whereas patients with low or high presurgical anxiety, or fear, would show the poorest adjustment. He argued that moderate levels of preoperative fear motivated the patient to do the necessary 'work of worry'. Such patients, on receiving information about the event, will mentally rehearse the event and mobilise appropriate coping techniques. Highly anxious patients, while they may undoubtedly worry about the event, will be submerged in worry-related cognitions rather than being motivated to mobilise coping resources. Patients with low levels of anxiety are not sufficiently prompted to engage in the mental activity necessary to prepare themselves for the distressing event.

Rather than finding a curvilinear relationship, subsequent research using broader samples and more varied outcome measures has tended to find small but significant linear relationships between anticipatory fear and subsequent recovery, with high-fear patients showing the least favourable outcome (e.g. Johnson, Leventhal & Dabbs, 1971; Sime, 1976). Sime (1976), for example, found that patients high in preoperative fear required longer hospital stays, greater analgesic and sedative use and showed more postoperative negative affect than patients with either moderate or low levels of preoperative fear.

Information provision approaches, which were the first psychological preparations for surgery to be evaluated, were largely based upon Janis's work (i.e. information provision creates accurate expectations and hence induces moderate levels of anxiety, thereby promoting the work of worry). The rationale frequently offered for this approach in contemporary work is that information influences cognitive factors such as the individual's expectations, hence allowing them to enhance their own sense of control as suggested by self-regulation and appraisal/coping models.

Self-regulation theory

A central concept of self-regulation theory involves variations in the extent to which patients perceive, focus upon and process information (i.e. the schema they form of impending events; Leventhal & Johnson, 1983). 'Schemata guide the organization of incoming information, retrieval of stored information, goal directed behaviour, and focus of attention' (Johnson, Lauver & Nail, 1989, p. 359). Leventhal and Johnson have argued that information provision influences the composition of the schema the patient forms of the impending experience and helps in the facilitation of coping strategies. In their recent report Johnson, Lauver & Nail (1989) argue that provision of concrete information that is accurate, clear and unambiguous can not only focus a patient's attention away from emotional features but can also facilitate the processing of incoming information. Attention focused away from emotional aspects of an experience is assumed to be associated with less distress. In a review of avoidant and non-avoidant coping strategies Suls & Fletcher (1985) conclude that avoidance strategies tend to be more beneficial than attention in the short term unless the attention entails the monitoring of sensory rather than threatening aspects of the situation. As reviewed below it does seem that sensory information, either alone or in conjunction with procedural information, is more beneficial in terms of reducing anxiety and discomfort in relation to surgical procedures than procedural information alone. It also seems that the individual's own habitual coping style will influence the effectiveness of avoidance or attention-enhancing strategies.

Cognitive appraisal/coping

A third theoretical conception is based upon Lazarus & Folkman's (1984) cognitive appraisal model. In this model the coping process is conceptualised as consisting of two broad categories: problem-focused and emotion-focused coping. Problem-focused coping involves actions directed towards the modification, avoidance or minimisation of the impact of the problem encountered, or attempts to control the situation. Accordingly, problem-focused interventions will include those designed to provide accurate details of sensory and procedural information allied with instructions which foster problem-solving activity. Emotion-focused coping entails attempts to regulate the emotional distress by relaxation and attention redirection, or by denial or wishful thinking to avoid direct confrontation with the problem. The assumption is that patients who are poorly prepared, or who use maladaptive coping strategies, will become anxious, angry and depressed in coping with illness (Cohen & Lazarus, 1979). A further assumption is that those who habitually adopt an information-seeking style (variously referred to as copers, sensitisers, monitors and internals) will benefit from information provision or problem-focused interventions. In contrast those who habitually seek to distract themselves or avoid anxiety-provoking information (variously referred to as avoiders, repressors, blunters and externals) will not benefit from information provision but may benefit from more emotion-focused interventions.

Coping has thus been used to refer to both physical behaviours, including relaxation training and breathing exercises which the person actively engages in, as well as cognitive strategies, such as calming self-talk or distraction which can alter the person's evaluation of the event. Others have used a combination of coping techniques or packages such as stress inoculation training (Meichenbaum & Cameron, 1983). Training in the use of adaptive coping skills should therefore decrease negative post-operative affect, and hence improve patient recovery as long as it is tailored to the patient's habitual coping style.

One interlinking feature of all three models is the central part played by perceptions of control in reducing psychological distress (Janis, 1958; Lazarus, 1966). Providing coping techniques could serve to generate such perceptions of control. Information provision could operate in a similar manner—given time people may use information to develop their own ways of controlling events. Indeed, notions of control have formed the central tenet of various explanations for the effectiveness of information provision in anxiety reduction. These suggest that individuals should show less arousal with information because they can (1) discriminate safe from unsafe periods (safety-signal theory; Seligman, Maier & Solomon, 1971); (2) make a well-timed preparatory response (preparatory-response theory; Perkins, 1955, 1968); and (3) reduce uncertainty and conflict (information-seeking theory; Berlyne, 1960). However, as is clear from the various studies reviewed, information provision is not always effective in reducing anxiety, and the role of individual differences in determining who will benefit from a particular type of intervention cannot be ignored.

ANXIETY REDUCTION

Information provision

Provision of information was one of the earliest forms of intervention for patients undergoing stressful medical procedures. Much of this work was based upon Janis's (1958) conceptualisation that some optimal level of such preparatory communication is effective because it results in a moderate level of anticipatory fear, which in turn leads to constructive 'work of worrying'. Too much or too little fear was thought to be detrimental.

Two types of information are discussed in the literature: procedural, involving a description of the medical event, when and where it will take place, etc., and sensory, giving the patient an expectation of the sensations that are likely to be felt during and/or after the procedure. Some studies have investigated the efficacy of each procedure in isolation, others have examined a combination of sensory and procedural information in relation to other interventions, while more recent studies have investigated the interaction between information provision and individual difference variables such as the patient's coping style. Most recent reviews of this literature suggest that preoperative information provides benefits to individuals undergoing stressful medical procedures, and that sensory or combined sensory and procedural information has the most beneficial effects (Johnson, 1984; Reading, 1979; Suls & Wan, 1989; Taylor & Clarke, 1986).

Procedural or sensory information

In their review of this literature Anderson & Masur (1983) refer to five studies, while Taylor & Clark (1986) refer to 10 studies which have examined the effects of procedural information alone. Vernon & Bigelow (1974), for example, investigated the efficacy of procedural information in reducing the anxiety of male patients hospitalised for the repair of inguinal hernias. The intervention consisted of information, given two days prior to surgery, concerning the medical events and the rationale for each. Analyses of the patients' anxiety, as measured by an adjective checklist, revealed few significant differences between information and no-information groups, although the former were more likely to express favourable postoperative attitudes such as greater confidence in their nurses. In their review of the effects of procedural information Taylor & Clark (1986) conclude that eight of 10 studies indicated at least some positive impact on some indices of adjustment while only two studies found virtually no effects. However, the effects were in general small and information provision had little effect on many variables examined. Indeed, providing procedural information alone seems to have little impact on indices of postoperative recovery.

Further studies such as those by Johnson and her colleagues (Johnson *et al.*, 1978a,b; Johnson, Morrissey & Leventhal, 1973; Johnson & Leventhal, 1974), have compared the relative impact of the provision of procedural or sensory information. Johnson *et al.* (1973) divided 99 gastrointestinal endoscopy patients into three groups, two of whom received an audiotaped message consisting of either sensory or procedural information while the third control group received only routine explanation. Less medication was required by both information groups in comparison to the controls, while the sensory information patients exhibited fewer tension-related movements. However, information groups showed no differences in measures of tranquilliser use, gagging, heart rate or restlessness. Unfortunately no measures of anxiety were taken. Johnson & Leventhal (1974), in the same setting, also compared procedural and sensory information provision in comparison to a group receiving behavioural skills training. There were few group differences on tension-related arm movements or heart rate, although sensory information reduced the number of patients who gagged during the procedure.

Johnson and her colleagues (Fuller, Endress & Johnson, 1978; Johnson, 1984; Johnson et al., 1978b) have also evaluated the relative effects of procedural or sensory information in comparison with a relaxation procedure involving instruction in deep breathing, coughing, leg exercises and ways of moving to reduce pain or a combination of these treatments as a preparation for various patient groups. The results of the studies are contradictory. In the first of two studies Johnson et al. (1978b) found that for female cholecystectomy patients all interventions had some positive benefits, with relaxation in particular reducing the use of analgesics and increasing ambulation while provision of sensory information specifically increased the rate of recovery from surgery. In the second study reported in this paper, using the same interventions but with male herniorrhaphy patients, there were no effects of any of the interventions upon postoperative recovery. In a subsequent study with women undergoing a routine pelvic examination Fuller et al. (1978) found no significant effects for relaxation but significantly less distress, as indicated by overt behaviours and pulse rate, for those receiving sensory information. The differential results between these studies are no doubt due in part to the fact that patient groups in the studies differ both in terms of severity of complaint (cholecystectomy vs herniorrhaphy vs pelvic examination) and gender of sample; cell sizes are also small, particularly in the latter study ($N = 6$) and many of the effect sizes are small. It should also be kept in mind that any attempt to compare sensory and procedural information is clouded by the fact that provision of the former inevitably involves some degree of provision of the latter. A number of studies have thus specifically investigated the combined effects or procedural and sensory information provision.

Combined sensory and procedural information

The efficacy of sensory plus procedural information has been investigated either in relation to low information or alternative information, or in comparison to alternative interventions. In one such study, Kendall *et al.* (1979) randomly assigned 44 patients having to undergo cardiac catheterisation to either an information group, a cognitive–behavioural intervention group or one or two control groups (an attention placebo or standard hospital procedure control). The information group were taught about heart disease and the catheterisation procedure, and were provided with written information describing sensory and procedural aspects. The information group demonstrated better behavioural ratings of adjustment and lower anxiety during the catheterisation than either of the two control groups. Given that the majority of subjects had previously experienced the procedure, and were already knowledgeable about the events, one might assume an even greater effect of information provision in less knowledgeable patients. In a more recent report Johnson, Lauver & Nail (1989) compared the effectiveness of sensory/procedural information intervention for patients undergoing radiation therapy for prostate cancer with a no-information comparison group. The preparatory intervention reduced the extent to which recreation and pastime activities were disrupted, but did not alter negative mood.

Kendall *et al.*'s and Johnson *et al.*'s findings are, however, contrary to some previous findings comparing information with attention placebo controls. Langer, Janis & Wolfer (1975), for example, in a study of general surgical patients, found no significant differences between the group that received information and support and an attention placebo control group. Indeed, information in this case had the initial effect of making the impending operation more anxiety-arousing. Heightened distress was also reported by Miller & Mangan (1983) for a group given a great deal of information in comparison to a minimal-information group. It seems inevitable that a range of factors such as the medical procedure involved, individual difference variables or the outcome measures taken will influence the extent to which information provision is shown to be beneficial.

Several other studies have combined information provision with additional treatment components such as emotional support (e.g. Langer *et al.*, 1975; Leigh, Walker & Janaganathan, 1977). Although these tend to suggest positive effects for information provision it is difficult to ascertain the extent to which this is due to information *per se* rather than to other components of the treatment programme.

As well as presenting different types of information to a variety of patient groups, mode of presentation has varied between studies. Wallace (1984), using a detailed information booklet, found a range of benefits for laparoscopy patients in comparison to patients receiving a placebo booklet or routine care. Other studies have obtained beneficial results from videotaped (Anderson, 1987), audiotaped (Wilson, 1981) or verbal presentation of information (Langer *et al.*, 1975). In addition, studies have used a variety of outcome measures, including days to discharge and number of postoperative medications (Andrew, 1970), attitude, mood and ward adjustment (Vernon & Bigelow, 1974), anxiety self-report, state anxiety, self-statement, adjustment and attitude (Kendall *et al.*, 1979). Some studies have compared treatment groups with control groups receiving standard care (e.g. Vernon & Bigelow, 1974) (which one might assume would have some beneficial effects) or have used an attention placebo control group (e.g. Langer *et al.*, 1975).

Given these between-study variations, it is perhaps not surprising that some reviews suggest that preoperative information alone can have beneficial effects on outcome (e.g. Mumford *et al.*, 1982; Anderson & Masur, 1983; Taylor & Clarke, 1986) with a combination of procedural and sensory information being most effective (e.g. Anderson & Masur, 1983), whilst others suggest that only moderate support for the efficacy of information provision appears in the literature (e.g. Kendall, 1983; Ludwick-Rosenthal & Neufeld, 1988). In their meta-analytic review of 21 studies published between 1967 and 1984 Suls & Wan (1989) conclude that sensory information, but not procedural information, has significant benefits over no instruction, but that combined sensory–procedural preparation yields the strongest and most consistent benefits in terms of reduced negative affect, pain reports and other-rated distress. Only studies which specifically compared sensory, procedural, combined sensory/procedural and/or no instruction were included in their comparison with studies providing information in conjunction with other techniques or multicomponent packages excluded.

With regard to anxiety in particular Anderson & Masur (1983), in summarising 24 studies investigating provision of information, note that half took specific measures of patients' anxiety (a further three studies recording parental anxiety) and that in all but three cases the information intervention successfully reduced anxiety. In general, however, self-reports of anxiety are less affected than behavioural ratings of adjustment and discomfort. Information provision may facilitate ability to cope, or may at least modify apparent, observable coping ability rather than being an effective way to reduce anxiety. Physiological parameters of anxiety have rarely been assessed and self-report instruments may not be sufficiently sensitive to detect modest changes in anxiety (Ludwick-Rosenthal & Neufeld, 1988).

In addition, a number of authors have pointed out that it is erroneous to assume that all patients will respond to any psychological procedure in a uniform manner, so that varying amounts of information or changing its specificity may enhance effectiveness. With regard to individual differences, locus of control and coping style in particular have been investigated.

Individual differences and information provision

The literature provides several examples of how patients' coping style interacts with information provision in the reduction of stress (e.g. Andrew, 1970; Cohen & Lazarus, 1973; Miller & Mangan, 1983; Shipley et al., 1978; Shipley, Butt & Horowitz, 1979; Wilson et al., 1982). Cohen & Lazarus (1973), for example, found that while some patients actively sought information prior to surgery, others actively avoided it. In fact those who avoided information spent fewer days in hospital and had fewer post-surgical complications than those who sought information.

In an early study (Andrew, 1970) minor surgery patients were divided into three groups on the basis of their preferred coping styles: avoiders, who were more likely to deny or distance themselves from feelings; sensitisers, who readily acknowledged their feelings; and neutrals, who showed no preference for either avoidance or sensitised coping style. One half of the patients were given surgery-related information, while the other half received no information. Neutrals who received the information spent fewer days in the hospital and required less medication, sensitisers showed no significant difference between information and no-information groups, but negative effects were seen in avoiders who received information—they required more medication.

Two further reports by Auerbach and his colleagues (Auerbach et al., 1976; Auerbach, Martelli & Mercuri, 1983) investigated individual differences in locus of control and receptivity to health-care information in relation to the efficacy of information provision. In the earlier report procedural and sensory information was provided to a group of patients prior to tooth extraction and self-reported anxiety and observed behaviour compared with a general-information comparison group. The internal locus of the control group who received specific information had better behavioural adjustment ratings than internals who received general information, with the pattern reversed for the external group. This pattern was not, however, mirrored by anxiety ratings. In the latter report similar procedural and sensory or general information was again provided to dental patients, who this time were differentiated on the basis of individual differences in receptivity to health-care information as well as locus of control. Patients in the high-information condition who had a high preference for information showed better behavioural adjustment than high-information-preference patients in the low-information condition. The reverse pattern (though non-significant) was observed for patients with a low preference for information. The pattern found for locus of control in the earlier study was not replicated in this latter report; also neither study assessed anxiety during the procedure either by retrospective self-report or by physiological measures.

Heart rate during the procedure was specifically assessed by Wilson *et al.* (1982) in an evaluation of psychological preparation of patients for gastroendoscopy. Patients who were assigned to either procedural and sensory information, muscle relaxation or a control group were also assessed on a coping-styles questionnaire to measure aspects of avoidance, emotional control, arousability and independence. Both interventions produced beneficial results while for the information group those low on the dimension of independence had less change in heart rate. As Ludwick-Rosenthal & Neufeld (1988) note, however, the small sample size (as few as seven subjects in some cases) and the numerous correlations reported by Wilson *et al.* make meaningful interpretation of the results difficult.

In a further study Miller & Mangan (1983) divided gynaecological patients at risk from cervical cancer and about to undergo a diagnostic procedure (colposcopy), into information-seekers (monitors) and information-avoiders (blunters). Half of each group were provided with voluminous information (a 20-minute visual and verbal presentation about both procedural and sensory details), the other half were provided with low-level information. Pre- and post-treatment assessment of pulse rate and self-report ratings of anxiety in addition to other measures were taken. Overall, low-information patients expressed less subjective tension/anxiety than high-information patients, and blunters showed less subjective and behavioural anxiety than monitors. In addition, blunters showed less physiological arousal with low information and monitors less physiological arousal with high information.

Information seems to be most effective when its provision is congruent with coping style. Blunters/avoiders prefer to attempt to cope with threat by not dealing with it, hence the absence of information or the provision of general non-threatening information is most effective for this group. Monitors/sensitisers in contrast seek information, and hence information provision is likely to be more effective for this group. It would seem, then, that intervention strategies are likely to be maximally effective when individual coping styles are considered and when the intervention and individual styles are congruent. Successful interventions should thus mesh with and reinforce the patient's own coping style. Although this is the most consistent finding some studies have not found the expected interaction between individual difference variables and treatment. Further, behavioural indices rather than anxiety *per se* are more likely to be affected by information provision; indeed, anxiety is not always assessed.

Sounding a rather more cautionary note than many empirical studies and earlier reviews, Ludwick-Rosenthal & Neufeld (1988) comment that 'the overall clinical significance of information provision as a preparatory intervention may be open to question, given that reductions in subjective anxiety, a major goal of the intervention, are not apparent' (p. 331).

Relaxation and behavioural coping preparations

Relaxation has been used both as a behavioural preparatory approach aimed at anxiety reduction and as a coping preparation to provide training in a specific skill or behaviour to facilitate recovery. Deep-breathing and coughing exercises have also been used in conjunction with relaxation. Several research studies suggest that relaxation as a preparatory procedure has generally positive results. For example, Aiken & Henrichs (1971) report fewer psychotic episodes following surgery for cardiac patients, and Flaherty & Fitzpatrick (1978) less incisional pain and distress and less medication for elective surgery patients trained in relaxation. In neither of these studies, however, were there adequate control groups. The former study also combined supportive counselling with relaxation, making it impossible to attribute treatment effects to relaxation alone. Nevertheless a number of other studies support the contention that relaxation may be effective in various settings, although this may be related to their coping use rather than to anxiety reduction *per se*.

In a study which pioneered the use of psychological preparations (Egbert *et al.*, 1964), the intervention consisted of a combination of information regarding pain during recovery and instruction in a breathing training relaxation technique for use as a coping strategy. Patients who received the intervention required significantly fewer analgesics and had significantly shorter postoperative hospitalisations relative to a control group given only procedural information by an anaesthetist. Given the combined treatment it is not possible to judge the relative efficacy of the relaxation procedure. However, a number of studies have investigated relaxation procedures as coping strategies either using relaxation alone or in conjunction with breathing or movement exercises or cognitively based strategies.

A series of studies by Corah and his associates (Corah, Gale & Illig, 1979a,b; Corah *et al.*, 1981) evaluated the effectiveness of relaxation as preparation for patients undergoing dental surgery. In their first report relaxation was compared to perceived control, distraction or a non-intervention control group. Relaxation reduced both self-rated and dentist-rated discomfort for highly anxious patients although these effects were also observed in the distraction group. Similar beneficial effects of relaxation were found in their subsequent replication study with the additional finding that the relaxation group reported the greatest decrease in anxiety. As Ludwick-Rosenthal & Neufeld (1988) note, in both these studies the absence of measures of muscle tension or subjective reports of relaxation does not allow for any evaluation of the extent to which relaxation may have served to distract patients rather than reduce muscle tension or relax patients *per se*. In their subsequent study Corah *et al.* (1981) did employ such ratings. However, although the relaxation group found the relaxation tape more relaxing than distracting, Corah *et al.* report that, in contrast to their previous findings, there were no differences between the relaxation and control patients in terms of anxiety or self-ratings of discomfort.

A series of studies by Johnson and her colleagues (Fuller, Endress & Johnson, 1978; Johnson, 1984; Johnson *et al.*, 1978b), referred to previously, compared relaxation-based procedures with information provision or a combination of these treatments, although the studies provide conflicting results. Johnson *et al.* (1978b) found that both relaxation and information reduced hospitalisation with relaxation additionally reducing reports of pain, while Fuller *et al.* (1978) found no significant effects for relaxation. As noted previously, however, the patient groups differed between studies, and the sample size in the Fuller *et al.* study was small.

In a recent report, Anderson (1987) compared information-only and information plus coping preparations with a contact control group. The coping preparation consisted of a sound/slide show outlining a postoperative exercise regimen which showed a therapist guiding a patient through coughing, deep-breathing and leg exercises, and other movements designed to reduce muscle stiffness. Both preparations were equally successful in reducing psychological distress and improving recovery relative to the control group. Similar relaxation and deep-breathing exercise preparations have been shown to reduce anxiety, discomfort and physiological measures of arousal in children undergoing dental surgery (e.g. Siegel & Petersen, 1980). As with information provision, however, it seems likely that the relative effectiveness of relaxation procedures will depend in part on their degree of congruence with the individual's current coping style.

Individual differences and relaxation effectiveness

In an attempt to unravel the efficacy of relaxation dependent upon initial fear levels and coping style two studies by Wilson and colleagues are noteworthy. Wilson (1981) looked at the relative effects of relaxation, information provision or a combination of these treatments in relation to routine hospital care for elective surgery patients. The information treatment included taped information concerning the surgical preparation and process, as well as information related to specific sensations of discomfort to be experienced during recovery. The relaxation preparation consisted of a 20-minute taped exercise in autogenic relaxation, which was to be used once before, and as often as desired after, surgery. The relaxation and combined groups used less medication and had shorter hospital stays in comparison to the control group. The extent to which compliance with relaxation was a central factor is unclear (it is reported that 45% of patients used the tape at least once a day) but one possibility is that it enhanced patients' perceived coping capacity. However, this was only the case for low-fear subjects; relaxation was not sufficient for initially high-fear patients. In a further study (Wilson *et al.*, 1982), gastrointestinal patients were either informed about expected sensations, trained in systematic muscle relaxation, or received normal hospital care. Both preparations reduced arousal while relaxation additionally increased positive mood change following the procedure. As with information provision, recovery measures suggested that patients benefited most from the preparation that matched their preferred coping style, although there was no detrimental effect of preparations which did not match their preferred style. As noted above, however, the small sample size and numerous correlations reported make meaningful interpretation of the results difficult.

In a recent study directed towards the same issue, Martelli *et al.* (1987) provided prosthetic oral surgery patients with either a problem-focused, emotion-focused or mixed-focus stress management intervention. The problem-focused intervention was largely information-based with instructions to facilitate rational analysis of this information. The emotion-focused intervention involved instruction in the use of brief relaxation procedures and cognitive techniques aimed at enhancing their use. The mixed-focus intervention produced the best overall response to surgery, while the emotion-focused intervention produced the lowest adjustment levels. Subjects were also classified into high- and low-information preference groups. Better adjustment and satisfaction and lower self-reported pain were obtained when high-information preference subjects were given a problem-focused intervention and when low-information preference subjects were given an emotion-focused intervention. As with information-based studies this emphasises that most benefits are obtained when treatment conditions or interventions are congruent with attention/avoidance coping tendencies.

Although relatively few studies have evaluated relaxation training without additional procedures such as coughing, deep breathing or exercises it does seem that relaxation is effective in reducing anxiety and improving adjustment. Whether the observed benefits are due solely to relaxation training, or to some other non-specific factors such as distraction or some other facets of the programme such as deep breathing which provide the patient with coping resources, is unclear. The interaction between individual patient characteristics such as coping style has not revealed any consistent pattern, although emotion-focused subjects seem to gain the most benefit from relaxation training. Individual differences clearly need to be considered in determining who might benefit from specific treatments.

Modelling approaches

A large body of research suggests that exposure to a coping model, demonstrating initial fear and stress followed by successful coping, can help to reduce patients' (particularly children's) distress (e.g. Ferguson, 1979; Melamed & Siegel, 1975; Klingman et al., 1984; Peterson et al., 1984; Pinto & Hollandsworth, 1989), although a recent review (Saile, Burgmeier & Schmidt, 1988) suggests that modelling techniques may not be as effective in preparing children for hospitalisation as originally suggested (however, see the commentary and critique of this paper by Eiser, 1988).

Modelling can operate in three ways (Bandura, 1969): first by observational learning effects whereby the person acquires new coping strategies not initially present in his or her available repertoire of behaviours; second by response facilitation effects whereby strategies which are already available to the individual are enhanced; and third by inhibition effects whereby behaviours which promote positive consequences are encouraged while those resulting in negative consequences are discouraged or inhibited. Bandura's later theorising (1977b) has emphasised the effect that modelling can have upon self-efficacy outcomes and anticipated outcomes; i.e. modelling alters people's expectations regarding their ability to perform certain actions and their expectations regarding the likely consequences of performing such actions.

Modelling as preparation for surgery with children

In their review of psychological preparation of children for aversive medical procedures Saile, Burgmeier & Schmidt (1988) identify 56 treatment comparisons (of a total of 125 carried out in 75 studies) using modelling procedures. In 80% of these cases the model was presented by film, in 9% by dolls and in 2% by live models. In 41% of the cases the film showed the model in a setting comparable to that experienced by the children. On average the modelling was presented 45 minutes prior to the medical procedure and lasted for approximately 19 minutes. In the majority of cases (70%) the intervention was directed specifically towards the child, although in a number of cases (20%) both mother and child were present.

In one early study (Melamed & Siegel, 1975) four- to 12-year-old children who viewed a film depicting a peer coping with surgery demonstrated better pre- and postoperative adjustment on both anxiety and behavioural measures in comparison to children who only viewed a control film. Other studies by Melamed and her colleagues (e.g. Melamed *et al.*, 1975) also indicate positive effects from a filmed model procedure. In a further report Peterson *et al.* (1984) compared children undergoing oral surgery who saw either one of two filmed models of a child patient (one accurate, the other partially inaccurate) or a puppet model, or who were in a routine hospital care group. All three modelling conditions were equally as effective in reducing anxiety and distress compared to the control group.

In a more recent report Pinto & Hollandsworth (1989) randomly assigned 60 children undergoing first-time elective surgery to either an adult-narrated videotape, a peer-rated videotape or a no-videotape control group viewed either with their parents or on their own. Children who viewed the videotape exhibited less arousal, less self-reported anxiety, and less behaviourally rated anxiety in comparison to children who did not view the videotape. There was no difference between patients who viewed the adult or peer-narrated version, but patients who viewed the videotape with their parents exhibited less preoperative arousal than children who viewed it alone. In addition, parents who viewed the videotape showed less arousal prior to the operation in comparison to parents who did not view the videotape.

In contrast to these positive findings other studies have failed to find beneficial effects. For example, Zachary *et al.* (1985) found no benefit on indices of anxiety and behavioural compliance for children observing a filmed model prior to restorative dental treatment (although this lack of effect may be due to initially low levels of distress experienced by the children in the sample). Indeed, Saile *et al.* (1988), commenting on the outcome effects for different treatments and methods used to prepare children for surgery, note that 'among the preparation method classified as behaviour therapy, techniques based on the modeling paradigm were below the average of all preparation methods evaluated in this study' (p. 116). They further note, when commenting upon non-specific effects that 'preparations using coping-modelling films . . . result in only minimal effects when these non-specific factors are controlled by placebo-attention control groups' (p. 124). As Eiser (1988) points out, however, there are a number of methodological difficulties inherent in the inclusion of all available studies in Saile *et al.*'s meta-analysis. A number of reviews have noted the methodological limitations of many early studies conducted on the preparation of children for hospitalisation (e.g. Elkins & Roberts,

1983); including these together with unpublished reports and dissertations inevitably draws into question any findings based upon these data. In addition studies have varied widely in terms of subject populations and aims and outcome measures used.

A further issue, noted by Saile *et al.* (1988), and consistent with previous research, is that the effectiveness of modelling is dependent on a number of moderating variables. For example, Elkins & Roberts (1985) found that although viewing an audiovisual peer-modelling procedure decreased medical fears for highly fearful non-patient children no changes were found for low-fearful children. Other studies comparing experienced children with inexperienced children have found very different patterns of response to preparation. Klorman *et al.* (1980) found that modelling reduced uncooperative behaviour in inexperienced paediatric dental patients, but had little effect on children with prior restorative dental treatment. Further, modelling has been found to increase arousal and self-reported medical concerns in young, experienced paediatric surgery patients (e.g. Faust & Malamed, 1984; Melamed, Dearborn & Hermecz, 1983). One possibility is that experienced children are reminded about prior aversive experiences whereas inexperienced patients may focus rather more on the coping behaviour of the model. In a further study Klingman *et al.* (1984) found that participant modelling (children encouraged to practise the modelled techniques as they watched the filmed model) was more effective than merely watching a videotaped model (symbolic modelling) in reducing disruptive behaviour and physiological arousal (though non-significantly) during dental treatment. While many studies attest to the efficacy of modelling procedures in preparing children for hospitalisation, results are far from uniformly positive and are influenced by a number of moderating variables. Initial optimism has been replaced by a more realistic yet still generally positive view of the efficacy of modelling procedures.

Modelling as preparation for surgery with adults

There are surprisingly few studies using modelling as preparation with adults. Shipley *et al.* (1978) examined anxiety during endoscopy as a function of repression–sensitisation coping style and the number of prior viewings of an explicit preparation videotape. Subjects viewed a videotaped endoscopy either zero, one, or three times. Subjects also received procedural and sensory information independently. The stress of the endoscopy was reduced as a function of the number of viewings of the videotape for sensitisers, while repressors showed an inverted-U-shaped function with one viewing producing the highest heart rate change. Employing similar procedures, Shipley, Butt & Horwitz (1979) report that when coping style was ignored the intervention had no effect, but when subjects' coping styles were taken into account a significant reduction in anxiety was found for the sensitisers. Whether these effects are due to information received or due to exposure to the model is difficult to ascertain in the absence of an information-only comparison group.

In a more recent report Allen, Danforth & Drabman (1989) randomly assigned 11 patients referred for hyperbaric oxygen therapy to a combined videotaped coping model intervention or a standard hospital care comparison group. The intervention group were more relaxed and completed significantly more of their prescribed treatment sessions. Given the small subject numbers the results should inevitably be treated with some degree of caution. Also, as the model specifically described several strategies (relaxation, cognitive coping statements, imagery) it is not possible to ascertain whether there was one specifically salient component or if they operated in combination. The authors provide anecdotal evidence that problem-focused coping statements were used more by the intervention group, suggesting that a cognitively based intervention rather than modelling *per se* might be effective.

Overall, then, modelling seems to have beneficial effects but this is by no means a universal finding and many factors may serve to moderate overall efficacy of this procedure. Further, in many of the modelling procedures used, information relating to the medical procedure is also inevitably available so that it is not possible to ascertain whether treatment effects are due to information provision or modelling. A few studies have attempted to separate the effect of viewing a model from the effect of receiving information by providing either procedural information with or without a model present. Melamed *et al.* (1978), for example, randomly allocated 80 children to five groups receiving different combinations of modelling or procedural information. Those children exposed to the model showed less self-reported fear and less disruptive behaviour than those viewing the demonstration in the absence of a model. A further issue concerns the specific features of the model (coping vs mastery vs fearful) required to obtain optimal effects. Most research suggests that a coping model is likely to produce more beneficial effects than either a mastery or fearful model (Anderson & Masur, 1983) but this is a question which remains to be fully explored.

Cognitive approaches

The rationale for cognitive interventions is that the patient's perception and appraisal of the invasive event help to determine the anxiety and distress they experience. Thus distraction, attention focusing and the use of positive self-statements, as well as multiple strategy packages (e.g. stress inoculation training; Meichenbaum & Cameron, 1983), have been used in an attempt to alter the patient's perception and appraisal of the situation and hence reduce operative anxiety. A number of studies have now evaluated the efficacy of such techniques, either in relation to standard hospital care (Wells et al., 1986) in comparison to relaxation procedures (Pickett & Clum, 1982) or in comparison to information provision (Langer, Janis & Wolfer, 1975; Ridgeway & Mathews, 1982; Kendall et al., 1979).

Corah and his colleagues have used distraction-based techniques as one of their interventions in a number of studies with dental patients (Corah et al., 1979a,b, 1981; Seyrek, Corah & Pace, 1984). These studies suggest that distraction results in decreased anxiety, distress and discomfort, although some distraction tasks result in increased physiological arousal (possibly due to the cognitive effort expended towards the task).

In a further report with sigmoidoscopy patients, Kaplan, Atkins & Lenhard (1982) compared two cognitively based interventions emphasising self-statements with a no-treatment control. The two cognitive groups were either provided with model-generated self-statements to supplement their own or were taught self-statements which emphasised the doctor's capability. Half of each of the two treatment and control groups also received relaxation training. Patients in the two treatment groups reported less anxiety and better adjustment on behavioural and verbal measures than the control group. Relaxation training seemed to enhance these effects. Although it seems that both the cognitive interventions were effective, the absence of baseline anxiety ratings means that the differences could be attributable to increased anxiety in the control group (who were advised to control their anxiety but were not told how to do so) rather than to decreases for the treated subjects.

In a more recent study, Wells et al. (1986) randomly assigned 24 elective surgery patients to either a stress inoculation or standard hospital care group. The stress inoculation involved an information phase, a skills acquisition phase (monitoring cognitive cues, deep breathing, relaxation, induction of pleasant images, use of coping and reinforcing self-statements) and an application phase involving rehearsing and applying the procedure. The treatment group showed reduced levels of self-reported anxiety and pain, reduced medication use and faster recovery. The use of a multiple-strategy package inevitably draws into question the precise elements of the package which might be effective. The package used by Wells et al. involved information provision and relaxation, both of which have been shown to have some effect on anxiety levels. Whether the availability of more than one strategy has an additive impact on anxiety reduction is obviously a matter of interest. Also, it is unclear whether subjects actively used more than one element of the treatment programme.

In a study of gallbladder surgery patients Pickett & Clum (1982) randomly assigned patients to either relaxation training, relaxation instructions, cognitive distraction or a no-treatment control. The cognitive technique significantly reduced anxiety relative to the other interventions. In two further studies (Langer, Janis & Wolfer, 1975; Ridgeway & Mathews, 1982) a cognitive intervention involving calming self-talk and distraction was compared with procedural information, a combined approach and routine care. (In the Ridgeway & Mathews study no combined group was used.) In the Langer et al. study patients who received the cognitive intervention had superior outcomes to those who received procedural information on postoperative anxiety, medication use and length of hospitalisation. In the Ridgeway & Mathews study the group means suggest that the results favoured the cognitive intervention, although the range and magnitude of support are less than that reported by Langer et al.

A cognitive intervention was also superior to information provision for a population that included patients with prior experience with an invasive procedure (Kendall et al., 1979; Kendall, 1983). Patients in the cognitive treatment received individual training in the identification of those aspects of the hospitalisation that aroused distress and the application of their own cognitive coping strategies to lessen their anxiety. Patients receiving this treatment reported less anxiety during a catheterisation procedure.

Cognitively based interventions have also been used with children with varying degrees of success. Siegel & Peterson (1980) randomly assigned 42 children attending for dental treatment to one of three conditions: self-control coping skills (relaxation, deep and regular breathing, imagery and calming self-talk), sensory information or a no-treatment control. Although both treatments were effective in reducing disruptive behaviour, ratings of anxiety and discomfort and physiological arousal there were no differences in effectiveness between the two treatment groups. In a further report Peterson & Shigetomi (1981) randomly assigned 66 children scheduled for tonsillectomies to either an information group, a filmed model, a coping skills group (relaxation, imagery and self-talk) or a combination of modelling and coping skills. Although both groups involving coping skills tended to show less distress, these results were largely based on parental reports and there were minimal between-group differences on any measures obtained from the patients themselves.

In a more recent report Dahlquist et al. (1986) randomly assigned 79 paediatric outpatients to one of five preparation conditions: training in coping skills (deep breathing and positive self-talk), sensory information, combined sensory information and coping skills training, attention control (discussion of a non-medical topic with an adult) and a no-treatment control. The interventions seemed to provide a certain protective function. Children with previous negative medical experiences became more distressed as a result of discussing the non-medical topic with an adult, while children with neutral or positive past medical experiences were unaffected by the preparation they received. There was little difference in outcome between the treatments.

Although results are mixed, research findings for cognitive–behavioural interventions are generally promising. The inclusion of multiple strategies (relaxation, breathing, imagery, self-talk) makes it difficult to ascertain the efficacy of specific treatment components. Evaluating separate contributions of each of these preparatory techniques would provide valuable information and address the extent to which benefits are obtained from behaviourally focused interventions such as relaxation or cognitively based strategies such as self-talk. The process by which procedures operate, whether calming, controlling or coping, could also then be delineated. Individual differences have also rarely been addressed in studies using cognitive interventions, although clearly such factors are likely to be of importance.

Methodological concerns

From the above review it seems that there is general agreement within the literature that several types of intervention technique, most notably informational, modelling and cognitive–behavioural, are effective in minimising negative outcome from surgery. However, in any review of the literature on preparation for surgery it is clear that conclusions must of necessity be treated with caution given the numerous variations between studies. Many studies have compared treatments to a 'routine hospital care' control group but have failed to include a placebo group to control for the effects of contact alone. The viability of a placebo control is itself questionable for as Auerbach (1989) suggests, the rapport established in an attention placebo condition is likely to stimulate emotion-focused coping rather than being theoretically inert; hence comparative studies using treatments that are operationally and theoretically distinctive would perhaps be more informative.

A further difficulty is that preparations within the same rubric have varied greatly between studies (e.g. information may consist of a standard package, video presentation, etc.). Also, treatments are often used in combination, making it difficult to ascertain the efficacy of each treatment component. A variety of different outcome measures have been used across studies so that divergent findings may partly reflect the broad range of responses measured. In addition, process measures are frequently ignored so that it is often not clear whether patients trained in a particular skill actually use it. Further, the homogeneity of patient groups varies widely across studies. Many studies have placed patients undergoing various types of surgery into the same group without taking into account variations in the seriousness of the procedure. Similarly, within a given category of invasive procedure, little attempt is made to control for variations in the severity of the patient's medical condition.

A further concern relates to the significance of individual differences in influencing the impact of psychological preparations. This may range from a failure to control for differences in previous experience with the medical procedures to a failure to take account of the role of individual differences in anxiety or coping disposition. Thus Boeke *et al.* (1991), in a study of 58 cholecystectomy patients, found longer periods of hospitalisation for patients with high state anxiety measured on the third day postoperatively, particularly if the patients were male, had undergone more previous operations and had postoperative complications. In their review of the earlier literature Mathews & Ridgeway (1981) concluded that there was reasonable evidence that individuals high in neuroticism or trait anxiety were subject to more post-surgery complications and slower recovery from surgery in comparison to those with lower neuroticism or anxiety. Auerbach (1989) has further noted that 'high trait anxiety appears to be a useful characteristic for identifying patients who are likely to experience poorer surgical outcome' (p. 391).

In addition, a number of intervention studies have evaluated the interaction between preparation and coping style, with the general finding that information seekers respond more positively to information provision prior to the medical procedure in contrast to avoiders. In non-intervention studies it seems that an avoidant coping strategy is associated with less distress. Thus George *et al.* (1980), in a study of oral surgery patients, found that patients with a vigilant coping style were more likely to complain of pain, to have a slower recovery and more interference with daily living in comparison to patients with an avoidant style. In a similar vein two other non-treatment studies with volunteer blood donors (Kaloupek, White & Wong, 1984; Kaloupek & Stoupakis, 1985) found that avoidant coping was associated with lower anticipatory anxiety. Clearly, implementation of intervention strategies should be allied to assessment of dispositional coping style, although this is hindered by differing conceptualisations of coping and varying assessment instruments.

SUMMARY

There is evidence that information provision, relaxation, modelling and cognitive-preparatory interventions all have some beneficial effects in reducing distress associated with noxious medical procedures, although the mechanism by which this might operate is far from clear. One assumption is that preparation improves recovery by reducing preoperative anxiety, although this seems unlikely to provide the full explanation. It seems more likely that, in addition to reducing anxiety, preparatory interventions provide patients either directly or indirectly with active coping strategies.

Although there have been numerous evaluations of psychological interventions for noxious surgical procedures in the past 30 years, the many reviews of this work which have appeared within the past decade have all referred to methodological deficiencies which prevent any firm conclusions being drawn. Problems include the frequent failure to include adequate control groups; a failure to ascertain whether the specific intervention provided is actually being used by the patients concerned; the use of packages of treatments making it difficult to ascertain whether there is one effective treatment ingredient; idiosyncratic measures across studies making meaningful comparisons difficult; heterogeneous subject populations both in terms of medical conditions and individual differences in terms of previous experience with those conditions and dispositional factors. With regard to assessment parameters, although some studies have recognised the need to assess cognitive, behavioural and physio-logical parameters there is little consensus on the specific measurement devices to employ within each sphere. In relation to individual differences it is clearly important to ascertain which patients are more likely to experience negative outcomes from noxious medical procedures in the absence of psychological preparation (high trait anxiety, neuroticism and a coping style emphasising information need seem possible identifying character-istics) and which characteristics are most likely to identify those who will respond most favourably to which intervention (sensitisers seem to respond favourably to information provision and avoiders to distraction or relaxation strategies).

Of the four approaches reviewed, modelling has yielded the widest range of positive effects on behavioural as well as self-report indices, particularly with children. However, Saile, Burgmeier & Schmidt (1988), in reviewing the evidence, paint a less positive, but probably more realistic picture, than expressed in some empirical reports. Cognitive–behavioural interventions also seem to offer promise, but there are less evaluative studies using this approach and there is a tendency to use multicompo-nent packages. Not only do these often supply subjects indirectly with procedural or sensory information, but may often involve relaxation in addition to cognitive self-control strategies. It would clearly be useful to determine which approach provides most benefit to which population, and for which medical procedure.

Chapter 10

Health Anxiety and Medical Avoidance

INTRODUCTION

Two broad areas of health concern will be discussed in this chapter: anxiety related to perceived symptoms and anxiety related to expected treatments or investigations. The first section addresses the question of health anxiety in relation to illness phobia and hypochondriasis. This includes concerns about specific illnesses in the absence of diagnosable pathology, such as a fear of sexually transmitted diseases (venerophobia) including the more recently reported 'pseudo-AIDS' relating to acquired immune deficiency syndrome (AIDS), as well as a preoccupation with more diffuse and non-specific symptoms. Two features characterise patients with such concerns: a lack of organic pathology for their symptoms and an unreasonable amount of concern about symptoms which persist despite medical reassurance.

Clearly care needs to be exercised in identifying such patients. While ruling out organic pathology will, in many instances, involve relatively straightforward diagnostic procedures, there will inevitably be certain cases where a diagnosis of 'no detectable organic pathology' is based upon current knowledge and investigative procedures; as medical knowledge advances and new investigative procedures are developed organic pathology may be detected in cases previously designated as 'no known cause'. Additionally, many patients with symptoms may not present for treatment. A good exemplar of these issues involves irritable bowel syndrome (IBS), which is characterised by abdominal pain and changed bowel habits in the absence of known organic pathology. Some have argued that there are biological markers for IBS (see Shabsin & Whitehead, 1988) while others have pointed out that IBS is common within the community but that most people with IBS do not seek health care; IBS clinic presenters obtain higher hypochondriasis scores on psychometric tests in comparison to IBS sufferers who do not present at clinics (e.g. Drossman *et al.*, 1988).

As such IBS is more than just a hypochondriacal health concern, and will be considered in the following chapter together with gastrointestinal conditions of known organic pathology. Hypochondriacal or illness phobic patients are thus characterised by excessive health anxiety. Their presenting symptoms have no identifiable organic basis and they frequently persist in seeking medical help despite repeated medical reassurance. Not only are such patients a drain on medical resources, they are also inevitably difficult to treat; medical treatment is not appropriate and yet such patients may be resistant to psychological treatment, insisting that their symptoms are medically related.

The second section of this chapter addresses the converse problem, fear-induced health avoidance. The specific question of blood/injury fears, including dental fears are discussed, together with their relationship to avoidance of medical treatment. Marks (1988) comments that 'some patients with blood–injury phobia avoid urgent medical procedures that could save their lives: those who become diabetic may eschew insulin injections, and those who develop cancer may shun surgery . . . blood–injury phobia leads some women to avoid becoming pregnant because pregnancy and childbirth are associated with blood and medical procedures' (p. 1208). The extent of such medical avoidance is, however, not known; as Kleinknecht & Lenz (1989) point out, 'although it is readily acknowledged that blood/injury is one of the more prevalent phobias, relatively little is known of the extent to which this phobia results in or is associated with avoidance of medical treatment . . . the data on dental fear and avoidance are relatively more voluminous (pp. 537, 538).

ILLNESS PHOBIA, HEALTH ANXIETY AND HYPOCHONDRIASIS

Definitions

Illness phobia refers to an intense fear of dying and a fear of specific illnesses such as cancer, heart disease and more recently AIDS. Indeed, a number of authors have pointed to the fact that 'topical' disorders such as AIDS, which are widely publicised, tend to form the focus of unnecessary concerns (e.g. Miller, Acton & Hedge, 1988; Warwick, 1989). The avoidance of disease reminders, such as articles in the media, as well as frequent checking for signs of illness and requests for examination and reassurance from doctors, are typical of such cases. The delineation and description of such fears have long history, illness phobia sometimes being encapsulated within the category blood–injury–illness phobia.

However, blood–injury phobia is classified as a distinctive focal or simple phobia within DSM-III-R, and has a specific cardiovascular reaction (see below) which is not evident in illness phobia (Marks, 1987b, 1988). Also, illness and blood–injury phobias are characterised by different patterns of avoidance: while illness phobia is characterised by repeated health-care attendance and avoidance of disease reminders, blood–injury phobia is characterised by avoidance of medical situations. Blood–injury phobia is thus considered separately in the second half of this chapter.

Others have attempted to differentiate between illness phobia and hypochondriasis. From a questionnaire study of 100 hypochondriacal and 100 control subjects Pilowsky (1967) derived three dimensions of hypochondriasis: bodily preoccupations, disease phobia and the conviction of the presence of disease with a non-response to reassurance. Marks (1987b) suggests that 'illness phobia can be regarded as a form of focused hypochondriasis. In hypochondriasis the fears are diffuse and not of any particular malady' (p. 297); 'when the fear persistently focuses on a simple syndrome or illness in the absence of another psychiatric disorder, the term illness phobia is appropriate; it is a focal form of hypochondriasis' (p. 410). This does not, however, match the DSM-III-R definition of hypochondriasis as a preoccupation with the fear of having a specific and serious physical disease without identifiable organic pathology, with the fear persisting in spite of medical reassurance. Others suggest definitions encompassing both the general and the specific. Barsky & Klerman (1983), for example, suggest that the physical complaints associated with hypochondriasis are usually vague and variable, with pain the most common symptom and bowel and cardiorespiratory symptoms frequent presenting complaints. Kellner (1985) argues that research findings identify two components of hypochondriasis: an unrealistic fear of disease, disease phobia or nosophobia and the conviction of having a disease. As Costa & McCrae (1985) point out, hypochondriasis is frequently used in a more general sense to refer to the tendency to make unfounded medical complaints. As they further state: 'categorisation of a patient as a hypochondriac is generally informal, based not on validated tests and procedures, but on the physician's conviction that complaints are exaggerated and unfounded' (p. 20).

Within DSM-III-R, complaints of bodily symptoms suggesting a physical dysfunction, but for which no physiological basis can be identified, are referred to as somatoform disorders. Somatoform disorders have for long been thought to be associated with anxiety. The International Classification of Diseases (ICD-9), for example, identifies hypochondriasis as one category in which anxiety is a contributory defining feature. DSM-III-R proposes five such disorders including hypochondriasis. The remaining categories are: conversion disorder (impaired musculature or sensory functions), Briquet's syndrome (multiple somatic complaints with no apparent physical cause), somatoform pain disorder (pain with no apparent physical cause), and body dysmorphic disorder (preoccupation with an imagined or exaggerated defect in appearance). However, such distinctions are often blurred.

Rather than assuming that hypochondriasis is qualitatively different from everyday health concerns, Salkovskis & Warwick (1986) argue that health concerns follow a continuum from those with mild concerns about some unusual bodily sensation to those who are preoccupied with and fearful of bodily symptoms to the extent that all thoughts and activities centre on their illness. They describe this continuum as reflecting dimensions of 'health preoccupation' with 'morbid health preoccupation' representing the extreme end of the continuum with such behaviours typical of hypochondriacal patients. A similar dimensional perspective is advocated by Costa & McCrae (1985), supported by Barsky & Klerman's (1983) contention that some people are prone to transient hypochondriacal concerns and by Garfield et al.'s (1976) reference to the 'worried well'. This quantitative difference in health-related worries receives some support from a study by Kellner et al. (1987a) who compared 21 patients meeting DSM-III criteria for hypochondriasis with matched family practice patients, non-patient employees and non-hypochondriacal psychiatric patients. Although all groups reported some level of fear about disease, death, etc., hypochondriacal patients reported more fears of, and false beliefs about, disease, attended more to bodily sensations, had more fears about death and distrusted physicians' judgements more, yet sought more medical care than other subjects.

The need to constantly seek reassurance from physician, family and friends, as well as being preoccupied with bodily health, has been noted by a number of authors (Baker & Mersky, 1983; Barsky & Klerman, 1983). Salkovskis & Warwick (1986) illustrate with two case examples the way in which reassurance provides an immediate but transient reduction in anxiety leading to further reassurance-seeking so that provision of reassurance unwittingly reinforces the patient's condition. This notion forms a central tenet of Salkovskis & Warwick's recent theoretical conceptualisation of hypochondriasis.

Prevalence

Given the varying definition of hypochondriasis and illness phobia, it is perhaps not surprising that estimates of prevalence rates are highly variable and the true rates are unknown. Estimates of the prevalence of hypochondriasis are frequently based upon the number of patients for whom no known medical cause can be found for their presenting symptoms; clearly not all such patients would be considered hypochondriacal. As an example, it is estimated that between 30 000 and 120 000 patients undergoing coronary angiography for chest pain in the USA each year have either normal or minimally diseased arteries (Marchandise *et al.*, 1978). Given that many such patients may be unable to work as a result of their symptoms (51% of a sample of 57 patients described by Ockene *et al.*, 1980) and many continue to believe they have coronary artery disease (44% of 57 reported by Ockene *et al.*) it is possible that a significant number of these might be identified as hypochondriacal. Estimates of the proportion of patients who seek medical help for which no organic cause can be found range from 20% to 84% although these clearly include a high number of 'worried well' (estimated as 12% of patients in one large group practice; Garfield *et al.*, 1976) and those not excessively concerned about their symptoms. When a narrower definition of hypochondriasis is used prevalence figures range from 3% to 13% (Kellner, 1985).

Specific estimates of DSM-III somatisation disorder identified by the Diagnostic Interview Schedule as part of the ECA programme suggest that this condition is relatively rare, occurring in less than one in 500 persons in each of three study sites (New Haven, Baltimore and St Louis) (Robins *et al.*, 1984). Also, it was found only in women, occurred most frequently in those under 44 and not at all in those over 65 years (Myers *et al.*, 1984). Similarly low prevalence rates and the absence of male cases are reported in a later ECA analysis of one-month prevalence rates for DIS/DSM-III-identified somatisation disorder from five sites (New Haven, Baltimore, St Louis, Durham NC and Los Angeles) (Regier *et al.*, 1988). Somatisation disorder is defined as the tendency to experience and communicate psychological distress in the form of somatic symptoms that the patient misinterprets as signifying serious physical illness, and tends to be characterised by multiple unfounded somatic complaints. Such a precisely defined condition will clearly not include the majority of people preoccupied by health and symptoms or the 'worried well'.

The prevalence of illness phobia is also difficult to estimate. Among psychiatric outpatient clinic attenders Marks (1969) estimates that 15% of all phobics were illness phobics, while Raguram & Bhude (1985) quote a comparable figure of 24% from a sample of psychiatric outpatients in India. Agras, Sylvester & Oliveau (1969) give an estimated prevalence of 34% for injury/illness phobia from a sample of 50 subjects identified as phobic from a larger general population sample. With regard to specific illness fears Beunderman & Duyvis (1990) refer to estimates of between 2% and 5% of cardiac phobia within the general population, and suggest that 10% of general practitioner lists and 40% of cardiologists' practices are made up of such patients.

Co-morbidity with other disorders

The co-morbidity of anxiety, depression and OCD with hypochondriasis has been noted by a number of authors, (e.g. Kellner, 1983, 1990; Kenyon, 1965) while a previous psychiatric history, most notably anxiety and depressive disorders, has been noted in relation to AIDS-related fears (Miller, Acton & Hedge, 1988). Within a psychiatric framework this has led some to suggest the hypochondriasis is secondary to another syndrome, usually an affective one (e.g. Kenyon, 1965). Other studies of hypochondriacal patients identify approximately equal numbers of primary and secondary hypochondriasis (e.g. Pilowsky, 1970). A number of authors thus assert that primary hypochondriasis is a viable and valid diagnostic entity (e.g. Kellner, 1986). Kellner (1985) suggests a complex relationship between anxiety and hypochondriasis, arguing that irrational beliefs about illness may be due to anxiety in some instances while in other instances anxiety may be a consequence of irrational beliefs about symptoms. Others have pointed to the possibility that the noted co-occurrence of hypochondriasis with anxiety and depression may reflect the fact that the majority of studies report findings based upon patients seen in psychiatric clinics. As Bridges & Goldberg (1985) note, the majority of hypochondriacal patients are likely to be treated in non-psychiatric contexts, so that findings from psychiatric clinics may not be representative of hypochondriacal patients as a whole. The issue of primary and secondary hypochondriasis can be evaluated fully only by examining the chronological development of hypochondriacal and depressive symptoms (Warwick & Salkovskis, 1990).

A number of additional studies suggest that general somatic symptoms are more prevalent in patients who are anxious (Tyrer, 1976), that high symptom reporters are generally more anxious (Pennebaker, 1982), that hypochondriacal beliefs and attitudes are associated with anxiety (Kellner et al., 1986) and that somatic concerns are related to neuroticism (Costa & McCrae, 1980; McCrae, Bartone & Costa, 1976; Ryle & Hamilton, 1962). Costa & McCrae (1980) have argued that chronic worriers, in contrast to temperamentally calm individuals, may be more likely to interpret benign symptoms as a cause of concern. They report data from a sample of 912 men aged between 17 and 98 years showing a relationship between neuroticism and each of 12 somatic sections of the Cornell Medical Index. Individuals high in neuroticism reported two to three times as many symptoms as those at the lower end of the neuroticism range.

Other symptom co-occurrences have been reported by Bianchi (1971), who found that agoraphobia was more common in disease phobics than matched controls. Conversely, Buglass et al. (1977) report that 16 out of 39 agoraphobics had persistent health-related worries when not in phobic situations in comparison to no control subjects. Others have noted that hypochondriacal concerns are common within panic disorder patients (Noyes *et al.*, 1986), while several reports refer to the similarities between patients with persistent chest pain of non-organic origin and patients with panic disorder (e.g. Mukerji *et al.* 1987). Drawing on such findings Warwick & Salkovskis (1990) suggest a potentially important link between panic and hypochondriasis and the misinterpretation of bodily sensations.

Theoretical assumptions

Early theoretical overviews of the genesis of illness phobias (e.g. Bianchi, 1971) and more recent reviews of predisposing factors for hypochondriasis (Kellner, 1985) emphasise the probable multiplicity of factors involved. These include awareness of familial history of specific diseases, thus sensitising the individual to specific symptoms, specific traumatic events or as a reflection of guilt about other behaviours. Such factors may serve to influence the patients' beliefs about health so that health-related stimuli are perceived inaccurately. Such a faulty perception of health-related stimuli forms the central focus within the cognitive–behavioural approach to hypochondriasis and health anxiety suggested by Barsky & Klerman (1983) and Kellner (1985, 1986), and more recently detailed by Salkovskis and Warwick (e.g. Salkovskis, 1989d; Salkovskis & Warwick, 1986; Warwick, 1989; Warwick & Salkovskis, 1989, 1990).

Drawing analogies with cognitive formulations of panic the starting point in health-related fears is the misinterpretation of bodily symptoms as signs of illness. Warwick & Salkovskis (1990) point out there are two broad differences between the way panic and hypochondriacal patients interpret symptoms. First, panic patients are more likely to misinterpret autonomic symptoms with anxiety rapidly escalating; in hypochondriacal problems the symptom misinterpretation is less likely to involve such direct amplification, and is more likely to be of lumps and blemishes. In this context there is no evidence that hypochondriacal patients misinterpret normal bodily sensations. Tyrer, Lee & Alexander (1980) found little difference between hypochondriacal and anxiety neurosis patients in awareness of pulse rate, although both were more aware than phobic anxiety patients. Interestingly, a specific subgroup of patients with cardiac concerns showed highest awareness of pulse rate. Although there may be commonalities in the cognitive misinterpretations involved in panic and hypochondriasis the bodily signs forming the focus of concerns may differ, the closest relationship being between panic patients and those with cardiac concerns. A number of reports suggest a close relationship between chest pain without coronary artery disease and panic disorder (e.g. Mukerji *et al.*, 1987; Beitman *et al.*, 1987; Beck *et al.*, 1989, 1990). A consistent finding in these studies is the absence of catastrophic ideation concerning panic-related somatic sensations among chest pain patients. Beck *et al.* (1990) note that the only cognitive or affective symptom which chest pain patients reported was fear of a heart attack suggesting that, although these patients may report anxiety, their focus of concern is more specific than for panic disorder patients. Similar symptom focusing may occur in other potentially hypochondriacal groups both in a broad sense and in those with a specific symptom focus (e.g. gastrointestinal).

A second issue raised by Warwick & Salkovskis (1990) is that the time scale for feared catastrophes differs, with panic occurring rapidly while hypochondriasis has a more insidious course. Kellner (1985) suggests that most people experience one functional somatic symptom each day, and it is only when there is inaccurate or biased perception of this symptom that it will be interpreted as other than innocuous or irrelevant. Factors influencing the likelihood that bodily symptoms will be interpreted as more dangerous than they actually are, as well as determining which symptom(s) will form the focal concern in vulnerable individuals, include previous experience with illness in oneself or one's family, previous experience with unsatisfactory medical management and media-induced concerns as in AIDS-related fears (Warwick & Salkovskis, 1990).

Warwick & Salkovskis further suggest that various attentional factors will then serve to maintain anxiety. Barsky & Klerman (1983) suggest three perceptual or cognitive styles which lead to the development of hypochondriasis: the amplification and augmentation of normal bodily sensations; the incorrect assessment and misinterpretation of somatic symptoms of emotional arousal and of normal bodily function; and the predisposition to think and perceive in physical and concrete terms rather than in emotional and subjective terms. The likely result of misinterpretations of bodily symptoms as illness is the repeated checking of these symptoms, medical information seeking and reassurance.

The role of reassurance seeking plays a particularly important part in this formulation (Marks, 1987b; Salkovskis & Warwick, 1986; Warwick & Salkovskis, 1990). These authors have argued that reassurance seeking in hypochondriasis functions in a similar way to compulsive behaviour in OCD, i.e. short-term anxiety reduction with anxiety rapidly returning to pre-reassurance/compulsive ritual levels. Functionally reassurance then serves to maintain the health-related preoccupation. A similar short-lived reduction in anxiety as a result of reassurance in relation to cardiac phobia is described by Beunderman & Duyvis (1990). The elimination of reassurance is central to recent suggestions for treatment of excessive health anxiety.

Assessment issues

A number of self-rating scales have been published that measure somatic symptoms and hypochondriasis (see Kellner, 1986, Chapter 7); these have been largely used as research measures rather than for diagnostic purposes. Although illness fears may be more readily identifiable than hypochondriacal concerns *per se*, few detailed descriptions of the psychological assessment of such patients appear in the literature.

Hypochondriasis

A number of studies have used the MMPI Hypochondriasis Scale (McKinley & Hathaway, 1940) to assess somatic symptoms. The scale discriminates between hypochondriacal and non-hypochondriacal patients, although there is marked overlap in scores; in addition, the scale does not assess hypochondriacal attitudes and beliefs *per se*. Rather, it provides an assessment of actual somatic complaints and not the discrepancy between objective and subjective health that typifies hypochondriasis. Thus studies often report that patients with similar symptoms, one group of whom have a known organic pathology while the other group do not, obtain similar MMPI hypochondriasis subscale scores with both groups obtaining elevated scores relative to healthy controls. Talley *et al.* (1990), for example, report such a finding for organic gastrointestinal disease patients compared to irritable bowel syndrome patients with similar symptoms but no known organic pathology. They do, however, report that a further group of patients with somatoform disorder (described as psychiatric referrals presenting with chronic symptoms usually affecting multiple systems but with no organic basis), obtained markedly elevated hypochondriasis subscale scores relative to both the other two patient groups and the healthy controls. Findings of elevated MMPI hypochondriasis scores have also been reported for patients with severe headache and low back pain, although again the pattern appears to hold regardless of whether the pain has a known organic cause (e.g. Rappaport *et al.*, 1987; Rosen *et al.*, 1987).

The Illness Attitude Scale (IAS; Kellner, 1986) was developed specifically to measure psychopathology associated with hypochondriasis and abnormal illness behaviour. The IAS was constructed from statements made by patients diagnosed as having hypochondriacal concerns or showing abnormal illness behaviour. Eight factors were derived from subsequent analysis, each consisting of three questions each, rated on a five-point scale from 'no' to 'most of the time'. The eight scales are worry about illness, concerns about pain, health habits, hypochondriacal beliefs, thanatophobia, disease phobia, bodily preoccupations and treatment experience. Kellner reports the use of the scale in several studies (e.g. Kellner, 1986; Kellner et al., 1987) and suggests that the scale is reliable and has good construct validity as a measure of hypochondriacal concerns. Kellner (1986) reports several studies in which the IAS discriminates between hypochondriacal (as defined by DSM-III) and other patients, and notes that hypochondriacal patients obtain high scores on either the hypochondriacal beliefs and/or disease phobia subscales, responses which are rare in other patients. Although the IAS appears a valid and reliable measure of hypochondriacal beliefs and attitudes, and correlates with clinical diagnosis, as Kellner notes, 'by themselves they are not adequate to make a diagnosis' (Kellner, 1986, p. 321).

Illness phobia

Identifying illness phobic patients clearly involves the necessary elimination of organic pathology coupled with the observation that patients persistently present symptoms and seek reassurance in a manner which suggests a morbid anxiety regarding their health. Few detailed descriptions of samples of patients with fear of a given disease appear in the literature. Fears relating to sexually transmitted diseases, cancer and heart disease appear to be the most prevalent. MacAlpine (1967) describes 24 'syphilophobics', all of whom had been investigated repeatedly for syphilis, one having received 22 negative tests within a year. More recently Miller et al. (1985) have described two 'pseudo-AIDS' patients for whom the degree of concern had reached such levels that they exhibited marked signs of anxiety and depression. Both patients had had extensive negative investigations and received reassurance from a senior venereologist, but persistently misinterpreted minor symptoms as confirmation that they had AIDS since some of the symptoms appeared superficially similar. A series of 19 similar worried-well patients with AIDS-related fears are presented by Miller, Acton & Hedge (1988). They comment that 'almost all subjects showed an unshakeable and anxiety-laden conviction that they had HIV infection or disease, as indicated to them by the presence of anxiety-based physical features which they had misinterpreted as signs of HIV disease' (p. 159). They further suggest that such patients can best be understood in relation to a hypochondriasis/health preoccupation model. Green (1989) has also characterised such individuals as 'expressing hypochondriacal health worries' (p. 117).

In an earlier report Ryle (1948) describes 31 cases of cancer phobia of whom 12 had lost a near relative or friend from cancer. Finally Bianchi (1971) describes 30 disease-phobic patients, 14 of whom feared cancer and 10 of whom feared heart disease. Sixteen of the patients reported such illnesses in relatives.

Treatment

By their very nature patients identified as illness phobic or hypochondriacal will present on numerous occasions at medical outpatients for treatment and may well expect referral to medical specialists rather than to a psychologist. They may adamantly reject any suggestion of a psychological contribution to their problems (Barsky, Geringer & Wool, 1988) and may thus not accept psychological treatment. As Warwick & Salkovskis (1990) note: 'The principal obstacle to the treatment of hypochondriacal patients is their reluctance to view their problems as being caused by anything other than a medical condition. Psychological treatment therefore depends on persuading the patient to engage in treatment' (p. 114). Indeed there is a general sparsity of psychological treatment studies relating to hypochondriasis or illness phobia within the literature. Early reports refer to a variety of treatments including pharmacological, electro-convulsive therapy and psychoanalytic therapies. Studies also detail the treatment of depression as the primary condition, the assumption being that secondary hypochondriacal symptoms will improve subsequently. The general conclusion from these reports is that the prognosis from treatments for hypochondriasis is generally poor (see Kellner, 1985, 1986; Warwick & Salkovskis, 1990). More recently, initial reports of cognitive–behavioural treatments suggest encouraging results.

Salkovskis & Warwick (1986) describe two cases in which treatment was specifically directed at the elimination of reassurance. As noted, providing reassurance produces an immediate but only transient reduction in anxiety, the assumption being that reassurance seeking functions as a compulsive ritual in relation to health preoccupation operating like the compulsive rituals in OCD. One central aim of treatment is thus to prevent inappropriate reassurance seeking. This is achieved by demonstrating to the patients that reassurance produces only transient anxiety reduction while, on some measures, resulting in long-term worsening. Eliminating reassurance is then intended to facilitate self-directed exposure and cognitive change. Using such a treatment procedure Salkovskis & Warwick found that ratings of health anxiety were considerably reduced at three months follow-up in both cases.

Warwick & Marks (1988) report the treatment of 16 patients whose main problem was an abnormal concern about health and who had an International Classification of Diseases (ICD-9) diagnosis of illness phobia or hypochondriasis. Six patients feared heart attacks, one rabies, one haemorrhoids and two ill-health in general, while the remaining patients complained of symptoms which they regarded as a sign of current disease or death. Treatment involved live exposure to feared stimuli, such as visiting hospital and reading literature relating to the feared illness; satiation, involving repeatedly writing down detailed accounts of their fears; paradox, such as exercising to 'bring on a heart attack'; and the banning of reassurance seeking. There was a significant reduction in problem severity subsequent to treatment and a postal follow-up one to eight years later suggested that six of the 13 cases which could be traced had no further health anxiety. Although these results are clearly promising, as the authors themselves note the sample was small, and may not be representative of health anxiety in general. As they further note, the lack of a comparison group and detailed follow-up data mean that the results should be treated with some degree of caution.

Using a similar approach Miller, Acton & Hedge (1988) describe the treatment of 19 patients with an anxiety-laden conviction that they had HIV infection or disease. The primary aims of the intervention were to encourage patients to reinterpret their symptomatology in terms of anxiety rather than manifestations of HIV, and to train patients in appropriate strategies for coping with their concerns. A significant reduction in state anxiety was evident at three-month follow-up although there was wide variation across patients.

In a further report Fiegenbaum (1986) describes the long-term efficacy of exposure *in vivo* with or without additional group therapy, as treatment for cardiac phobia. Prior cognitive preparation is described as a central component of treatment to facilitate patients' control of their 'hypochondriacal self-observation of cardiac sensations'. It should be noted, however, that although the 31 patients treated were referred for cardiac phobia (defined as recurrent anxiety attacks in conjunction with the patient's unrealistic fear of suffering from cardiac disease) they were also all identified as suffering from agoraphobia with panic attacks. In this context it is unclear from the report whether exposure was directed towards cardiac or agoraphobic fears or both, although all patients are described, both at post-treatment and at three years follow-up, as having significantly reduced cardiac anxiety.

Summary

Hypochondriacal or illness fears are characterised by the presentation of symptoms in the absence of identifiable organic pathology, with patients repeatedly seeking medical help in spite of reassurance. Health-related anxieties are clearly widespread, although such patients may be referred for psychological help relatively infrequently and may be reluctant to accept a psychological explanation for their difficulties. Indeed, psychology has not had a great deal to offer such patients until recently, when cognitive–behavioural explanations have provided a clearer psychological framework in which to understand and treat such difficulties. The notions that certain vulnerable patients are prone to focus upon and misinterpret bodily sensations as signs of illness, and that the repeated seeking of reassurance for their symptoms has the paradoxical effect of immediate anxiety relief followed by its longer-term return and increased reassurance seeking, provides the framework for psychological intervention. Although initial treatment reports involving the elimination of reassurance in conjunction with exposure to feared stimuli provide promising results, these are based upon only a small number of cases. In the absence of larger controlled studies with detailed follow-up data the results should be treated with cautious optimism; cognitive–behavioural treatments clearly require further evaluation. In addition the factors prompting certain people to focus upon and misinterpret certain specific bodily symptoms need to be unravelled, as well as the process involved in such misinterpretation. The way in which differing assumptions and experiences prompt some people to constantly seek medical assistance, while others endeavour to avoid medical contact even when this may be detrimental to their general well-being, also needs to be explored.

BLOOD–INJURY FEAR AND MEDICAL AVOIDANCE

Definitions and prevalence

As noted, blood–injury phobia is classified as a simple phobia within DSM-III-R, and hence defined as a persistent fear of a circumscribed stimulus without agoraphobia/panic or social phobia. In some cases the fear may concern not blood but needles, injections, or medical or dental procedures. As Marks (1988) notes, 'whether these should all be lumped into a single category is unclear and needs further study' (p. 1209). Given that both minor medical procedures such as injections and dental procedures are similarly invasive, and both may involve by-products such as blood, for present purposes blood–injury and dental fears will be considered together, although they are often dealt with separately in the literature.

Mild fears of blood are common in children, being noted in 44% of six- to eight-year-olds and 27% of nine- to 12-year-olds (Lapouse & Monk, 1959), mild dental fears are also common. Intense fear is less frequent in both children and adults, although fear of blood, injuries and mutilation is one of the most prevalent fears within community samples. Agras, Sylvester & Oliveau (1969) report a figure of 31/1000 for blood–injury fears, while Milgrom et al. (1988) report high dental fear for 20% of a community sample. Blood–injury fears are more frequently reported by females in some studies (Kleinknecht, 1987, 1988), although not in others (Thyer, Himle & Curtis, 1985a); dental fears are more commonly reported in females (Kleinknecht, Klepac & Alexander, 1973; Milgrom *et al.*, 1988; Wardle, 1982).

Reported figures relating to age of onset for blood–injury fears suggest a mean age of about seven to nine years (Öst, 1987; Öst & Hugdahl, 1985; Öst, Sterner & Lindahl, 1984c; Thyer *et al.*, 1985a) although the average age at presentation for treatment is 31 years (Ost *et al.*, 1984b). Mean age of onset for dental fears is marginally older at 12 years (Öst, 1987; Öst & Hugdahl, 1985). There is also evidence that a large proportion of dental phobics are likely to report previous aversive dental experiences (Bernstein, Kleinknecht & Alexander, 1979; Kleinknecht, Klepac & Alexander, 1973; Lautch, 1971; Öst & Hugdahl, 1985). Lautch (1971) describes 34 dental phobics all of whom reported one or more traumatic experiences of dental treatment, while Öst & Hugdahl (1985) report a figure of 69% for their sample of 51 dental phobics. Almost half (10 out of 22) of their sample of blood phobia subjects also reported previous aversive experiences in medical situations. A number of reports also refer to the fact that blood–injury fearful people are particularly prone to fainting, with at least 80% of blood–injury phobics fainting when exposed to blood–injury stimuli (Öst *et al.*, 1984c; Thyer *et al.*, 1985a) (see below).

There seems to be some evidence for a family history of blood–injury fears and fainting. Thyer *et al.* (1985a) report that 27% of their blood–injury phobic patients had a family history of the problem while Öst *et al.* (1984b) report that 67% of their sample of 18 patients with phobias of blood, wounds and injuries had members of their biological family who were also blood phobics (Öst & Hugdahl, 1985 report 68% or 22 such patients). Kleinknecht (1987, 1988) reports in two studies that 35% and 32% of people who reported fainting to blood–injury stimuli reported having family members who fainted, compared to 13% and 11% of non-fainters respectively. In a further report Kleinknecht & Lenz (1989) found 66% of a group of blood–injury fainters had at least one parent who also reported a history of fainting to blood–injury stimuli. This has led some to suggest a possible hereditary component to the tendency to react to blood–injury stimuli with the diphasic physiological response resulting in fainting (see below) (Öst & Hugdahl, 1985; Kleinknecht & Lenz, 1989).

Medical avoidance

In the absence of systematic studies the extent and correlates of medical avoidance due to blood–injury fears are unknown. There are, however, a number of single case studies which document such avoidance. Lloyd & Deakin (1975) describe a 51-year-old woman with a long-standing history of fear of hospitals and medical procedures who avoided hospital in spite of a four-year history of illness eventually diagnosed as uterine carcinoma. Behavioural treatment of her fears eventually allowed for medical intervention for the carcinoma. Curtis & Thyer (1983) also describe a patient who 'sought [psychological] treatment because he was avoiding needed medical and dental treatment' (p. 771). In their review of 15 cases of blood–injury phobics Thyer et al. (1985a) comment that avoidance of medical care was common. An indication of how widespread such medical avoidance might be is suggested by data from Kleinknecht & Lenz (1989). They report that one-third of a sample of 68 undergraduates, identified as having fainted in response to blood–injury stimuli and who were either phobic or fearful of such stimuli, avoided both medical and dental treatment. Given that the rather more voluminous data on fear of dentistry and its frequent results, avoidance of dental care, suggests that it is a pervasive problem one might assume from Kleinknecht & Lenz's data that avoidance of medical treatment is a similarly pervasive problem. Kleinknecht & Lenz further note that the extent to which medical situations are subsequently avoided is a joint function of the number of past faints and the subject's prediction of likelihood of fainting in the presence of blood–injury stimuli in the future.

Studies investigating dental fear (see Lindsay, 1983) estimate that 20% of patients avoid visits to the dentist due to such fear (Milgrom et al., 1988) and that 40% of adults delay or avoid visits to the dentist unless suffering from toothache, fractured teeth or gum disease, and that about 5% are identifiable as dental phobics (Kleinknecht, Klepac & Alexander, 1973). Given the number of people avoiding dental treatment due to their fears, the comparative extent of medical avoidance clearly requires investigation; many people may unnecessarily delay medical treatment until a readily treatable symptom becomes a life-threatening condition. The increasing emphasis upon preventive medicine means that it is important to identify not only those at risk of illness but also those who may be at risk of avoiding treatment.

Fainting

As noted, fainting is common in blood–injury phobics when exposed to blood–injury stimuli. Unlike the typical phobic response (an increase in heart rate, respiration, skin conductance, etc.) in which associated feelings of faintness are common but actual fainting rare, a large number of people fearful of blood, injury or related stimuli show bradycardia, decreased blood pressure and faint or become dizzy or nauseous in their presence (Connolly, Hallam & Marks, 1976; Steptoe & Wardle, 1988; Thyer *et al.*, 1985a; Öst *et al.*, 1984c; Kleinknecht, 1987). Fainting has been noted during dental procedures (Edmonson *et al.*, 1978), reported in as many as 19% of blood–injury fearful college students (Kleinknecht, 1987) and in approximately 80% of blood–injury phobics seeking treatment for their fear (Öst *et al.*, 1984b).

Several studies suggest that those who faint in response to blood–injury stimuli are more anxious than non-fainters (e.g. Kaloupek, Scott & Khatami, 1985) and are more frightened by, and dysfunctional in, stressful situations. Some studies suggest that females report a higher prevalence of fainting to blood–injury stimuli (e.g. Kleinknecht, 1987) while others report that males are more likely to faint (Engel, 1978). Kleinknecht (1987, 1988) reports a mean age of 13 and a lower age of six years for the first blood–injury-related fainting reported by subjects.

The typical reaction on exposure to blood–injury stimuli seems to be a biphasic response, the first phase of which is sympathetic arousal followed rapidly by a switch to a parasympathetic response. Thus Öst *et al.* (1984c) documented an initial increase in heart rate and blood pressure followed within a few seconds or minutes by a marked drop in these parameters in blood phobics exposed to phobic stimuli. A similar diphasic response was noted by Steptoe & Wardle (1988) for a group of volunteers prone to fainting, but not in a non-fainting group, when viewing a film depicting open-heart surgery. However, these authors note marked individual differences in response; indeed the biphasic pattern is not invariant as blood–injury fear and fainting seem to be partially independent. Some blood–injury phobics do not exhibit the diphasic pattern (Öst *et al.*, 1984c) while some non-fearful persons faint at the sight of blood–injury stimuli. Graham (1961), for example, reports fainting in as many as 15% of blood donors.

Two explanations for fainting in blood–injury phobia have been suggested (Graham, 1961; Engel, 1978). Both implicate anxiety over perceived threat as the first phase but differ in their analysis of the mechanisms which trigger the second phase. Graham (1961) suggests that the first phase results from anxiety arousal in the face of threat, with the second phase being activated by 'relief' when the threat is removed either by the passage of time, or by the carrying out of the threatening procedure; i.e. this provides an explanation for fainting that occurs after the threat has passed. Engel (1978) suggests that fainting results from the activation of two simultaneous escape mechanisms: the sympathetically mediated 'fight or flight' response and the parasympathetically mediated 'conservation–withdrawal' response. In situations where escape or flight is not possible the second phase is initiated abruptly by a sense of 'unresolved uncertainty' over how to respond or a 'giving-up' which constitutes the 'conservation–withdrawal' response; i.e. this provides an explanation for fainting which occurs during an aversive procedure.

A number of other authors have suggested similar explanations to Engel's. Vingerhoets (1985) and Vingerhoets & Schomaker (1989), for example, propose that, following an initial threat, the extent to which the individual is prone to a passive versus active response will determine parasympathetic versus sympathetic nervous system activity respectively. He further suggests that the adoption of a passive stance and associated parasympathetic nervous system activity is an adaptive process adopted by a threatened organism. This suggestion parallels Mark's (1988) discussion of the possibility that emotional fainting has some commonality with 'playing dead' (tonic immobility) which occurs in some animal species when threatened with attack.

As Kleinknecht et al. (1990) point out, however, Graham's proposal does not account for fainting in anticipation of, or during, trauma, whilst Engel's does not explain fainting when the immediate threat has passed. As they further note, many fainters are non-anxious and thus not dealt with by the Engel, Graham or Vingerhoets models. Their finding that parental fainting history seems to be particularly noticeable in the case of non-anxious fainters leads them to suggest the possibility that such individuals are genetically predisposed to respond to blood–injury stimuli with only a monophasic parasympathetic nervous system response. Avoidance of medically related situations is far less marked in non-fearful fainters (Kleinknecht & Lenz, 1989).

Assessment

There are a number of self-report instruments covering a diversity of commonly feared stimuli which contain a dimension relating specifically to blood–injury fears, e.g. the Fear Survey Schedule (FSS; Wolpe & Lang, 1964) and Fear Questionnaire (FQ; Marks & Mathews, 1979). Other questionnaires are designed with the express purpose of assessing blood–injury fears, e.g. the Mutilation Questionnaire (MQ) (Klorman et al., 1974) or a particular stimulus class such as dentistry, e.g. the Dental Fear Survey (DFS; Kleinknecht, Klepac & Alexander, 1973) and the Dental Anxiety Scale (DAS; Corah, 1969). Some salient features of these measures will be briefly reviewed.

The FQ consists of three factor-analytically derived scales (agoraphobia, social phobia and blood–injury phobia), each consisting of five items rated on an eight-point scale of severity. Marks & Mathews (1979) suggest that the scale has satisfactory test–retest reliability and is sensitive to clinical change. Arrindell, Emmelkamp & van der Ende (1984) report that the factor structure of the scale is replicable with a wide range of populations across a variety of cultures, and that all the subscales have acceptable temporal stability across a long time interval. In reviewing this scale Arrindell *et al.* (1984) comment that its use should be restricted to phobic patients which, as they note, was one of the reasons for its introduction. They further comment that, in contrast to the FQ, the FSS, while useful for clinical purposes, is particularly useful for selecting analogue populations.

The FSS has been widely used as a measure of a range of feared stimuli. There are a number of reviews of factor-analytic studies of the FSS, although these are largely based upon student samples. From one such review Tasto (1977) concludes that the scale has fairly good factor stability with one of the four factors concerning fears associated with death, physical pain and surgery. There are fewer factor-analytic studies with phobic samples, although in one such large-scale study with 703 subjects Arrindell (1980) reports five factors of which one concerned fears related to bodily injury, death and illness. Factor analysis of the scale with a wide range of populations across a variety of cultures has also produced a factor relating to bodily injury, illness or death (Arrindel *et al.*, 1984). This factor correlates highly (0.75) with the Mutilation Questionnaire (MQ), another widely used measure of blood–injury fears (Kleinknecht & Thorndike, 1990).

The MQ is a 30-item true–false measure of blood–injury or mutilation fear with evidence of good internal consistency (Klorman *et al.*, 1974; Kleinknecht & Thorndike, 1990). However, factor analysis of the scale does not appear to identify a clear unitary construct of mutilation fear, a recent analysis resulting in 11 factors. The first two factors described the components typically associated with blood–injury fear (fear of bodily harm and revulsion and avoidance of related stimuli) but these two factors accounted for only 19% and 7% of the variance respectively (Kleinknecht & Thorndike, 1990). These authors also comment that while the MQ may serve as an adequate instrument for a broad screening of blood–injury fearful subjects it does not reliably distinguish between fainters and non-fainters.

The DAS (Corah, 1969) is a brief, four-item self-report scale with reasonable internal consistency and test–retest reliability. Corah reports that scores on the scale have low but significant correlations with dentists' ratings of patients' anxiety. Although the limited number of questions in the scale restricts the range of situations, fear stimuli and reactions which can be assessed, it has been widely used in research.

The DFS (Kleinknecht *et al.*, 1973) is a self-report inventory with 20 items relating to potentially fearful aspects of the dental situation rated on a five-point Likert scale. Three stable and reliable factors have been obtained from four diverse population groups. The first factor pertains to specific dental stimuli (e.g. sight and sound of the drill), the second to physiological response to dental treatment (e.g. heart rate increase and nausea) and the third to fear associated with anxious anticipation of dental treatment (e.g. making an appointment) (Kleinknecht *et al.*, 1984). The scale also appears to have construct validity, high scorers being more likely than low scorers to cancel dental appointments and report pain during treatment (Kleinknecht & Bernstein, 1978).

Treatment

Blood–injury phobia

A number of studies have successfully used variants of exposure-based methods as treatment for blood–injury phobias. These include desensitisation in imagination, *in vivo* exposure, relaxation training with gradual *in vivo* exposure, and *in vivo* systematic desensitisation with modelling (reviewed by Marks, 1988 and Thyer, Himle & Curtis, 1985a). As Marks (1988) notes, fainting can be potentially problematic, so that from a practical point of view treatment of blood–injury phobia by *in vivo* exposure should begin with the patient reclining.

There are several case reports of blood–injury phobia treated successfully by exposure-based methods (e.g. Curtis & Thyer, 1983; Elmore, Wildman & Westefeld, 1980; Wardle & Jarvis, 1981; Yule & Fernando, 1980). Curtis & Thyer (1983) report two patients with phobias for medical procedures who were also prone to fainting and who were treated successfully with graded exposure. Eleven-month follow-up for one patient, and four months for the other, showed that reductions in anxiety were maintained; both patients had received injections without fainting during that time. Wardle & Jarvis (1981) combined exposure *in vivo* with cognitive restructuring in the treatment of a 25-year-old male. The patient was reported to be much improved after five sessions. Yule & Fernando (1980) combined exposure *in vivo* and systematic desensitisation in the treatment of a 16-year-old boy. He was reported to be completely recovered after five sessions, a state maintained at five-year follow-up. Finally, Elmore *et al.* (1980) treated a 28-year-old male with 11 sessions of desensitisation in imagery and with slides, combined with 16 sessions of self-desensitisation. He was reported to be much improved at the end of treatment and at eight months follow-up.

Although these case reports are clearly promising there are few controlled studies. In one such study Öst *et al.* (1984b) randomly assigned 18 patients with phobia for blood, wounds and injuries to one of two treatment conditions: either exposure *in vivo* or applied relaxation. Patients were treated individually for nine weekly sessions. Both groups improved significantly on most of the measures, improvements which were sustained at six-month follow-up. Interestingly 10 of the 16 patients who completed the treatment programme went on to become blood donors. Between-treatment comparisons showed that while exposure had a more beneficial effect on three self-report measures at post-treatment this difference was not apparent at follow-up, nor was there any between-treatment difference on behavioural or physiological measures. Clearly, the extent to which exposure can benefit blood–injury phobics warrants further controlled investigation.

Dental anxiety

Two areas of work pertain to the treatment of dental anxiety. The first deals with the preparation of patients for dental treatment and is thus not restricted to avoidant patients. The second deals with interventions for dental phobic patients or those who avoid dental treatment.

A number of studies involving a wide range of interventions have been used to prepare people for dental surgery; these have been reviewed in the preceding chapter and merit only a brief summary comment here. Studies investigating the relative efficacy of sensory and procedural information with adult dental patients (Auerbach *et al.*, 1976; Auerbach, Martelli & Mercuri, 1983) indicate the need to take individual differences into account when evaluating the efficacy of information provision. Siegel & Peterson (1980) found that both information provision and training in coping skills were equally effective in reducing disruptive behaviour, anxiety and discomfort in children attending for dental treatment. Corah and his colleagues (Corah, Gale & Illig, 1979a,b; Corah *et al.*, 1981) found in their earlier, but not subsequent study, that relaxation reduced both self-rated and dentist-rated discomfort for highly anxious patients; in these studies distraction also decreased anxiety, distress and discomfort. Modelling as preparation for children undergoing dental treatment has been investigated in a series of studies by Melamed and her colleagues. For example, Melamed *et al.* (1975) demonstrated reduced behaviour management problems in school-age children who viewed a cooperative peer model compared with children who either drew pictures or saw a non-threatening film unrelated to dentistry. Klingman *et al.* (1984) report greater reductions in dental anxiety for children highly fearful of dentists who engaged in participant modelling rather than symbolic modelling. However, the effects are not always positive. Some studies suggest no beneficial effects for filmed modelling viewed by children prior to restorative dental treatment (Zachary *et al.*, 1985); others suggest that modelling reduces uncooperative behaviour in inexperienced but not experienced children awaiting dental treatment (Klorman et al., 1980); while other studies suggest a sensitising effect for young experienced paediatric surgery patients (although these were not all specifically dental surgery patients), e.g. Faust & Melamed, 1984. In reducing distress associated with dental procedures, information provision, relaxation and modelling all have some beneficial effects.

With regard to dental avoidance there are several case reports of the effective reduction of dental fear and the promotion of regular dental visits in adults by desensitisation either used alone (e.g. Klepac, 1975) or in combination with modelling (e.g. Kleinknecht & Bernstein, 1978). There are also several controlled studies of behavioural interventions with adult dental phobics. Miller, Murphy & Miller (1978) found that a self-relaxation control was as effective as EMG biofeedback and progressive relaxation in reducing EMG level, scores on the Dental Anxiety Scale and state anxiety. Gatchel (1980) compared group-administered systematic desensitisation to an education and discussion group and a non-treatment control. Both treatments were equally effective in reducing dental fear (as measured by number of dental appointments made and adhered to) and dental anxiety (as measured by the Dental Anxiety Scale), although the desensitisation treatment was marginally more effective in reducing anxiety. Bernstein & Kleinknecht (1982) assigned 33 patients who had avoided dental treatment for between one and 10 years to either participant modelling, symbolic modelling, graduated exposure, an attention-placebo or an unaided effort control. There were no between-treatment differences although both treatments resulted in reductions in state anxiety and expected pain relative to the control group; the attention-placebo group almost equalled the results of the treatment group. Berggren & Linde (1984) report that dentistry was completed more often and with less anxiety (as measured by the Dental Anxiety Scale) by those treated behaviourally (systematic desensitisation in combination with biofeedback training) in comparison to those who had dental procedures under general anaesthetic. Gauthier et al. (1985) compared flooding with coping skills training in a crossover design as treatment for 29 dental fearful patients; each patient received two sessions of flooding and two of coping skills training. Although no differential effects were found on any of the measures used, follow-up assessment of dental contact revealed that 100% of patients made and kept appointments in the coping followed by flooding group, while only 42.8% did so in the flooding followed by coping group, emphasising the importance of allowing patients to practise coping skills.

In the most detailed investigation to date, Jerremalm, Jansson & Öst (1986b) assigned 37 dental phobics, on the basis of detailed assessment, to one of two groups: cognitive reactors ($N = 20$; negative thought content but low physiological reaction) or physiological reactors ($N = 17$; high physiological reaction but positive thought content). Half of each group were then randomly assigned to either applied relaxation (i.e. appropriate for the physiological reactors but not the cognitive reactors) or self-instructional training (appropriate for the cognitive reactors but not the physiological reactors). Both treatments yielded significant improvements on most measures. One problem with this study is that both treatments involved some similar elements (self-instructions, rehearsal of images) so that the two treatments may not have been completely dissimilar and may have facilitated the development of general coping skills. Further, in the absence of a control group it is not possible to ascertain whether change was due specifically to the treatment; as noted above in the study by Bernstein & Kleinknecht (1982) the attention-placebo produced effects almost equivalent to the treatment groups. Jerremalm *et al*. note, however, that at nine to 12 months follow-up only one patient had failed to go through a full dental treatment and both self-reported anxiety and dentists' ratings of fear remained low.

Taken overall it seems that most treatment methods, whether exposure-based, involving relaxation training or modelling, reduce dental phobic patients' self-reported anxiety and dental avoidance. However, such positive treatment effects have been obtained from studies which have generally used volunteer dental-fearful subjects rather than referrals from special dental clinics or dentists. Such volunteers may be more receptive to psychological intervention. Further, few studies have included a control group to assess the effects of non-specific factors. The fact that in Bernstein & Kleinknecht's (1982) study the attention-placebo group almost equalled the results of the treatment group suggests that caution is required in interpreting positive treatment results, and further evaluative studies would be useful.

Summary

Blood–injury fear, defined as fear of blood, needles, injections or medical and dental treatments, is one of the most prevalent fears within community samples. In the absence of systematic studies, the extent to which medical situations are avoided as a result of such concerns is unknown. However, given our knowledge of the extent of dental avoidance, one might assume that avoidance of medical treatment is a similarly pervasive problem. A specific feature of blood–injury fears is the likelihood of fainting when exposed to blood–injury stimuli. A biphasic response of sympathetic arousal followed rapidly by parasympathetic arousal differentiates blood–injury phobics' reactions from the reactions associated with exposure to other phobic stimuli. Some have argued (e.g. Marks, 1988; Vingerhoets, 1985) that such a reaction is an adaptive response by a threatened organism possibly paralleling the tonic immobility which occurs in some animal species when threatened with attack. A number of single case studies suggest that both blood–injury and dental fears can be effectively treated by exposure-based methods. However, there are few studies which have compared treatments with no-treatment controls, suggesting that although initial results are promising further evaluative studies would be useful. In addition, with the exception of a few single case studies, little attention has been directed towards the identification and treatment of medical avoidance. Given the increasing emphasis upon preventive medicine it is important to identify not only those at risk of illness but also those likely to avoid treatment. Through fear, many people may leave untreated a readily treatable illness until it becomes life-threatening. As Marks (1988) comments: 'Blood–injury phobia can threaten life through causing avoidance of medical and surgical procedures and can prevent patients from undertaking careers or raising children' (p. 1212).

Chapter 11

Anxiety and Disease

INTRODUCTION

The recognition that psychological processes are implicated in the experience of health and illness has a long history, dating back to at least ancient Greece. In modern times the first medical discipline to acknowledge the influence of psychological processes in disease was psychosomatic medicine (Lipowski, 1977). From the 1930s to 1950s psychoanalytically based theories of psychosomatic medicine promoted the notion that 'certain personality characteristics, certain interpersonal conflicts and characteristic responses to these conflicts were causative factors in the origin of specific somatic illnesses' (Kaptein & van Rooijen, 1990, p. 6). Asthma, neurodermatitis, duodenal ulcers, ulcerative colitis, rheumatoid arthritis, essential hypertension and diabetes were supposed to be psychosomatic illnesses.

During the 1960s psychosomatic medicine took a broader perspective concerned with the interrelationship between psychological and social factors, biological and physiological functions, and the development and course of all illnesses (Lipowski, 1976). The 1970s saw the emergence of behavioural medicine and subsequently health psychology. Behavioural medicine was concerned with 'the development and integration of behavioral and biomedical science knowledge and techniques relevant to health and illness and the application of this knowledge and techniques to prevention, diagnosis, and rehabilitation' (Schwartz & Weiss, 1978, p. 250). Health psychology invited a broader interdisciplinary perspective to 'the promotion and maintenance of health, the prevention and treatment of illness, the identification of etiologic and diagnostic correlates of health, illness and related dysfunction' (Matarazzo, 1982, p. 4).

Broome (1989, p. xii) has identified seven major developments within health psychology, two of which are of particular relevance to the present discussion: the interplay between personality, stress and vulnerability in ill-health and the identification of high levels of psychological reactions that relate to medical problems. The present chapter will evaluate these two facets in relation to asthma, gastrointestinal disease and cardio-vascular disease. These have been selected to illustrate illnesses included within traditional psychosomatic domains, for which there is uncertainty about the specific biological mechanism implicated (e.g. asthma) as well as those with clear organic damage (e.g. myocardial infarction). In each case the part played by dispositional anxiety as a vulnerability factor in the development of these diseases will be discussed, in addition to the extent to which certain aspects of the illness are in themselves anxiety-provoking (e.g. gasping for air associated with asthma; unclear prospects for the future following myocardial infarction).

With regard to personality, stress and vulnerability, two hypotheses linking psychological variables and illness have been suggested: genera-lised susceptibility and specific illness risks (Cohen, 1979). There is broad empirical support for the generalised susceptibility hypothesis which pro-poses that psychological factors such as stressful life events, and how one appraises and adapts to these events, increases the overall risk of illness (e.g. Lazarus & Folkman, 1984); the notion of a 'disease-prone' personality (Friedman & Booth-Kewley, 1987) is incorporated within the generalised susceptibility hypothesis. There is less general support for the specific illness hypothesis which proposes that certain psychological factors are linked to the increased risk of developing specific illness (such as Type A behaviour and coronary disease).

While life events can be assumed to be potential 'stressors' the extent to which these are appraised as stressful will inevitably be influenced by per-sonality, behaviour and coping resources with the subsequent reaction modified by social reactions and personal resources. The relationship between personality and disease has generated a great deal of controversy since its popularisation with the advent of psychosomatic medicine (see Friedman, 1990 for a recent review). Recent systematic evaluation by Friedman & Booth-Kewley (1987) has placed such suggestions on a firmer footing. Indeed, Friedman (1990) has commented that 'there should be little doubt that personality, stress, and health are interrelated. There is solid evidence for associations among individual personality differences, emotional reactions, health related behaviors, physiological responses and diseases' (p. 283). Dispositional anxiety and neuroticism have frequently been evaluated as personality factors which increase vulnerability to disease (Friedman & Booth-Kewley, 1987). Others have interpreted the data rather more cautiously, suggesting that while personality factors may be predictive of somatic complaints or health care utilisation they are not necessarily associated as causal agents in organic disease (e.g. Costa & McCrae, 1987; Stone & Costa, 1990).

Less controversy is associated with theoretical assumptions and research findings that specific psychological reactions, including anxiety, occur as a response to disease. Such formulations have led some to emphasise the need to direct psychological interventions towards such reactions. Unfortunately, however, there is not always a clear rationale for such interventions and outcome results have been mixed. The present discussion will thus focus upon anxiety as a vulnerability factor for disease and as a specific response to ill-health.

ASTHMA

Asthma has been described by the American Thoracic Society (1962) as: 'a disease characterised by an increased responsiveness of the airways to various stimuli and manifested by slowing of forced expiration which changes in severity either spontaneously or as a result of therapy' (p. 763). Diagnosis was at one time made simply on the evidence of wheezing while today, in addition to observable symptoms, diagnosis is made on the basis of pulmonary physiology, blood counts, skin tests and the detection of elevated levels of specific antibodies. Because asthma is viewed as a disorder associated with airway abnormality it is bracketed together with other respiratory disorders such as bronchitis, emphysema, bronchiolitis and chronic obstructive pulmonary disease (COPD). Emphysema and bronchiolitis are identified on the basis of anatomical evidence while identification of both COPD and asthma owe rather more to clinical judgement. COPD is a respiratory disease of unknown aetiology that is characterised by persistent slowing of airflow during forced expiration. Asthma is definable in functional terms, although a precise definition which does not involve some overlap with other conditions (e.g. chronic bronchitis) has proved elusive (Creer, 1988).

Differing definitions have inevitably led to differing diagnostic criteria between clinics, and hence to highly variable prevalence rates. Gregg (1983), in an analysis of several epidemiological studies, primarily with adults in Europe and the USA, reports prevalence rates ranging from 0.9% to 6.2%. Most reports suggest that rates are higher for children, especially boys, than for adults, with over three-quarters of asthmatics experiencing their first attack by the time they are five years old. Asthma then declines with age, with between 25% and 50% of children who experience asthma in childhood no longer experiencing it in adulthood (Cluss & Fireman, 1985).

A number of mechanisms have been proposed to account for asthma, with some combination of the following factors likely to be responsible: specific allergic reactions to pollens and moulds, dust or food additives; a reaction to non-specific irritants (e.g. inhalation of cold, dry air), due to infections of the airways in addition to psychosocial factors such as stress and emotional state. Attacks are thus likely to be triggered by a combination of physical and psychological factors, sometimes the former predominating, sometimes the latter.

A number of authors have implicated psychological factors both as precipitants and as factors influencing the course of the disease. Much early research concentrated on attempting to isolate psychological factors which might trigger asthma attacks. As Creer (1988) notes 'in the case of emotional reactions that may trigger asthma there has been more confusion than enlightenment' (p. 233). More recent research has concentrated on examining specific dispositional factors which may make some asthmatics more vulnerable to attacks, as well as those psychological factors which may serve to maintain or exacerbate an attack. Anxiety has frequently been assumed to play a central role.

Dispositional anxiety

In a review of the relationship between several theoretically important and commonly studied aspects of personality in relation to disease Friedman & Booth-Kewley (1987) include 11 studies published between 1945 and 1984 specifically focusing on general anxiety and asthma. The authors conclude that anxiety, depression, anger, hostility and aggression are reliably and positively associated with the disease. As similar personality characteristics were associated with other diseases in their view it seems that there is a general rather than an illness-specific disease-prone personality.

The possibility that personality may act as a predisposing factor for asthma is also highlighted in the work of Dirks, Kinsman and their colleagues on psychomaintenance, i.e. the psychological and behavioural perpetuation and exacerbation of physical illness (e.g. Kinsman, Dirks & Jones, 1982). Their research has been specifically directed towards identifying basic, predisposing personality styles in relation to asthma which may interact with the patients' attitudes and subjective experience of their illness to maintain and exacerbate their condition. Using the Panic–Fear personality scale (Dirks, Jones & Kinsman, 1977), developed specifically for research relating to asthma illness behaviour, they identify high panic–fear asthmatics who are dispositionally anxious, dependent, tend to feel helpless, emphasise their distress and tend to give up in many situations. Such patients lack confidence in their ability to cope with their asthma and are more likely to be rehospitalised than patients with moderate levels of anxiety. For inpatients hospitalised in an asthma centre Dirks & Kinsman (1981) found that a panic–fear disposition was related to length of hospitalisation, medication at discharge and rehospitalisation rates. In earlier reports they note that twice as many high panic–fear asthmatics are rehospitalised at six months and again at 12 months following intensive treatment compared with moderate anxiety patients. A similar relationship is reported by Kaptein (1982), who found that asthma patients admitted to a general hospital, and who had a disposition to anxiety and neuroticism, had a worse prognosis. High panic–fear patients may thus exaggerate asthmatic symptom reporting. As Steptoe (1985) notes, however, most patients studied have been severe chronic asthmatics so that there is no indication as to whether the pattern is universal; further, whether panic–fear scores reflect differential responses to asthma rather than enduring personality traits predating asthma which relate aetiologically to onset cannot be inferred from current research.

Illness-related anxiety

In addition to assessing specific personality styles Dirks and Kinsman have also assessed subjective experiences and symptoms during an asthma attack using the Asthma Symptom Checklist (Kinsman et al., 1977). This has been used to identify patterns of low, moderate and high panic–fear symptomatology (also referred to as disregarding, typical or vigilant responding). Thus patients may differ both in specific personality styles in relation to asthma and in the degree to which they attend to asthma symptoms. Vigilant responders are specifically attuned to illness-focused anxiety. If this is allied to a disposition towards anxiety, and hence a doubt about their ability to cope, such asthmatics may panic. Such a style of reacting serves to maintain asthma, increasing the frequency of hospitalisation and medication use (Kinsman et al., 1982). A number of other authors have also noted that panic attacks are frequently associated with asthma attacks, with panic interacting with the asthma and so worsening the attack (e.g. Creer, 1982; Creer & Wigal, 1989).

However, symptom-directed anxiety is not of itself maladaptive as it is associated with some necessary degree of vigilance. Low panic–fear patients may show such a lack of concern about their condition that they fail to take necessary immediate remedial action (Kinsman et al., 1977). Moderate levels of anxiety may thus be related to an optimal degree of responsivity.

Anxiety reduction as treatment for asthma

The treatment of asthma by relaxation and systematic desensitisation has been reported in a number of single case and group comparison studies (e.g. Moore, 1965; Sirota & Mahoney, 1974; Yorkston *et al.*, 1974). Single case reports suggest some beneficial effects for relaxation, although the absence of comparison or control subjects means that the results must of necessity be treated with a certain degree of caution. When evaluating group comparison studies it seems that, on the whole, these interventions have little effect on respiratory functioning as such, but clearly reduce anxiety which may precipitate or exacerbate an attack.

In one of the first studies to use relaxation as a treatment for asthma, Alexander, Miklich & Hershkoff (1972) assigned 32 children to either a relaxation group or a control group. Lung function, assessed before and after each session, showed that only children trained in relaxation had a statistically significant improvement. Further studies by the same group (e.g. Alexander, Cropp & Chai, 1979) also suggest a small but significant change in respiratory volume as a result of relaxation. Although statistically significant, however, the changes reported were not clinically significant; although lung function changed as a result of relaxation it was still not within the normal range predicted for the patients' sex, age, height and weight subsequent to treatment. This has led Alexander and his colleagues to conclude that relaxation is not clinically beneficial for children with asthma (Alexander & Solanch, 1980).

Systematic desensitisation has also been used as a treatment for asthma. The rationale for such a treatment is based on the assumption that a conditioned fear response develops to the initial symptoms of wheezing which is then partially responsible for the development of a full asthmatic attack. Alexander (1977) reports a case study of a child who experienced anxiety when he wheezed even slightly, treated successfully by *in vivo* desensitisation. The child was taught relaxation, which was then applied in response to wheezing while the bronchodilator was withheld for increasing periods of time.

In a review of eight controlled studies using either relaxation or systematic desensitisation as treatment for 134 asthma patients Richter & Dahme (1982) conclude that the results of controlled studies with behaviour therapy are not very convincing. In only two out of seven groups treated by relaxation was there an improvement in lung function, although two of three groups treated by systematic desensitisation showed an improvement. A number of methodological issues also suggest that the results of behavioural interventions should be treated with caution. Thus, the incidental recording of lung function reported in many studies does not measure the course of asthma; further, lung function assessment requires maximum effort from the patient and thus may be unreliable. Other authors have noted a heterogeneous response to anxiety reduction procedures with asthmatics, which is no doubt due to the heterogeneous nature of asthma (e.g. Kinsman *et al.*, 1980). As Creer

(1988) notes, frequency of asthmatic episodes varies from patient to patient and, for any given patient, from time to time. In addition severity is highly variable so that medication regimes may be altered during the course of the psychological intervention. Further, as Everaerd, Vromans & van der Elst (1990) note, relaxation treatment can be meaningful only when tension and anxiety play an important role in relation to the respiratory difficulties. Given these issues Creer (1988) has reasonably concluded that conducting psychological treatment research with asthma, and interpreting outcome data gathered from such investigations, is no easy matter. With detailed assessment it should be possible to provide a maximally effective intervention incorporating both biological and psychological parameters as appropriate.

GASTROINTESTINAL DISORDERS

Psychological factors have traditionally been implicated in many gastrointestinal disorders. With increased understanding of physiological mechanisms the contribution of psychological factors in the aetiology and treatment of such diseases has become clearer. This is particularly true of functional gastrointestinal disorders, those conditions involving abdominal symptoms but in the absence of evident organic pathology. Following a brief description of the main gastrointestinal disorders the role of anxiety in the aetiology and maintenance of these conditions and psychological interventions specifically aiming to reduce anxiety will be discussed (for a full review of the anatomy, physiology and psychology of gastrointestinal disorders see Whitehead & Schuster, 1985).

Both ulcers and inflammatory bowel disease (IBD) are illnesses which involve lesions in the digestive tract and which frequently cause pain and bleeding. Ulcers occur in the stomach and the duodenum, or upper part of the small intestine. Although mainly occurring in adults, children and adolescents may also suffer. Stomach ulcers are thought to be produced by excess gastric juices eroding the stomach lining, although they have also been found in people with very low levels of stomach acid. Stomach ulcers affect approximately 10% of the population at some stage of their life (Whitehead & Schuster, 1985).

IBD refers to two related diseases: Crohn's disease and ulcerative colitis. Crohn's disease affects the outer layers of the intestinal wall, and may occur anywhere in the gastrointestinal tract. Scarring and constriction of the bowel may occur with bowel resection or removal sometimes necessary. Ulcerative colitis results from inflammation and ulceration of the mucosa, or inner lining, of the colon. It may affect just the rectum or sigmoid colon, or may extend to the entire colon. In severe cases removal of the large bowel is necessary. Prevalence rates are estimated to be between 36 and 70 per 100 000 for ulcerative colitis and between 20 and 40 per 100 000 for Crohn's disease (Mendeloff, 1975).

In contrast to the above, many individuals with abdominal symptoms have no evidence of organic pathology and are diagnosed as having functional gastrointestinal disorders. The most commonly diagnosed of such conditions is irritable bowel syndrome (IBS) characterised by abdominal pain and changes in bowel habit in the absence of organic disease. Although IBS is the term most frequently used to describe this condition, other terms which have been used in the literature include spastic colitis, mucous colitis and irritable colon. A further functional gastrointestinal disease frequently encountered is dyspepsia of unknown origin (DUO), also known as non-ulcer dyspepsia, pseudo-ulcer syndrome, or non-organic dyspepsia. There are surprisingly few studies examining the association of psychological factors with DUO (see Morris, 1991 for a recent review). However, there is some evidence that patients with DUO have neuroticism levels elevated relative to general populations, but that they show little difference from other patient groups (Talley & Piper, 1986). It has also been reported that DUO patients are more anxious than patients with similar physical symptoms of organic origin (i.e. peptic ulcer disease) (Langeluddecke, Goulston & Tennant, 1990). Given the sparsity of research it is difficult to draw conclusions from the evidence to date; further discussion of gastrointestinal disorders without identifiable organic pathology will focus specifically upon IBS.

Irritable bowel syndrome

A number of explanations have been suggested for IBS: these include those emphasising aspects of dietary intake. Others have emphasised the primary role of physiological factors, suggesting that greater contractile activity of the large intestine and myoelectric activity of the colon occurs in IBS patients. Any associated psychological symptoms are thus viewed as a consequence of the suffering engendered by such physiological differences. An alternative explanation is to emphasise the predominant role of psychological factors which result in short-term or long-term alteration of gastrointestinal functioning. Because its symptoms are characteristic of a number of organic diseases that may affect the gastrointestinal tract IBS is difficult to diagnose (Shabsin & Whitehead, 1988). Prevalence rates thus tend to be highly variable; estimates in both the UK and USA suggest that between 40% and 70% of all referrals to gastroenterology clinics have functional gastrointestinal disorders, of which three-quarters are IBS (Fielding, 1977; Mitchell & Drossman, 1987).

Is anxiety a distinguishing feature of IBS patients?

A number of studies report higher levels of anxiety, depression and hypochondriasis, as indicated by standard personality measures, in IBS patients in comparison to either the general population or matched controls having physical disorders (Bergeron & Monto, 1985; Esler & Goulston, 1973; Richter *et al.*, 1986; Palmer *et al.*, 1974; Ryan, Kelly & Fielding, 1983; Talley *et al.*, 1990; Whitehead, Engel & Schuster, 1980; see also reviews by Blanchard, Schwarz & Radnitz, 1987; Langeluddecke, 1985). The general conclusions from this work are that IBS sufferers are more psychologically abnormal or distressed than comparison groups, with depression and anxiety the two most commonly observed psychological features. As discussed below, however, studies are often methodologically weak and results contradictory. Whether psychological states represent predisposing factors or are reactions to the illness is also unclear (Blanchard *et al.*, 1987; Sammons & Karoly, 1987).

In an early study, Esler & Goulston (1973) found higher anxiety and neuroticism scores in a subgroup of irritable-colon patients with pain-free diarrhoea as their predominant symptom, in comparison to ulcerative colitis patients and general medical outpatients. A subgroup of irritable-colon patients with abdominal pain as their predominant symptom did not differ from the latter two comparison groups. However, differences between IBS subgroups were not found in further studies by Talley *et al.* (1990) and Whitehead *et al.* (1980), both of whom report a similar psychological profile for diarrhoea- and constipation-predominant IBS subjects. In the latter report the IBS group as a whole scored significantly higher than normal controls on measures of somatisation of affect, interpersonal sensitivity, depression, anxiety and hostility. Severity of psychological symptoms was not, however, related to severity of IBS symptoms. In a further study Palmer *et al.* (1974) report higher neuroticism scores for 41 IBS patients compared with normative data, but lower scores than a matched group of anxious outpatients without gastrointestinal complaints. Ryan *et al.* (1983) also report significantly higher levels of free-floating and somatic anxiety in an IBS group compared with a group of matched controls. Similar findings of higher somatic anxiety in association with IBS compared to medical patients and healthy controls are reported by Richter *et al.* (1986). These authors report similar heightened somatic anxiety for IBS patients and patients with recurrent non-cardiac chest pain, although IBS patients obtained higher scores on general measures of anxiety and depression.

In contrast to these reports, Cook, van Eeden & Collins (1987) report one of the few studies finding no differences on measures of neuroticism, trait anxiety and state anxiety between IBS patients, patients with Crohn's disease and healthy controls. In a further study Talley *et al.* (1990) report that although IBS patients obtained significantly higher hypochondriasis scores than controls, the absolute differences were small and hence of possibly minimal clinical significance. The lack of clinical significance indicated by the often small but statistically significant differences between IBS populations, patients with physical disorders and healthy controls is further suggested by the fact that in many studies there is marked overlap between scores obtained from such groups.

As many authors note (e.g. Barsky, 1987; Bennett, 1989), IBS is not uncommon in community samples who do not present at clinics. Yet studies suggesting anxiety in IBS patients are based on research findings evaluating patients seen in hospitals; such a self-selected group may show unusually high anxiety. In an attempt to circumvent this problem Welch, Hillman & Pomare (1985) compared IBS outpatients with an IBS population who were non-reporters of their condition (consecutive blood donors screened for disorders of gastrointestinal function) and normal controls. They found no differences between the groups on general feelings of distress (one component of which was anxiety) although both IBS groups showed more somatic distress (concern about bodily symptoms) than the control group. One difficulty in interpreting the results is that the IBS clinic attenders obtained lower anxiety scores than reported for a similar population in other studies. Two more recent studies (Whitehead et al., 1988; Drossman et al., 1988) do, however, suggest that it is only those individuals with IBS who also seek medical help for their problem who show evidence of psychological distress in relation to controls.

Thus, Drossman et al. (1988) report that IBS patients obtained significantly higher scores than both IBS non-patients and normal controls for MMPI scales assessing hypochondriasis and depression although they found no difference on MMPI-assessed anxiety. They also note that IBS patients obtained significantly higher health worry scores on a scale designed to assess subjective perceptions of illness in comparison to normal controls; IBS patients and IBS non-patients obtained similar scores on this measure. Whitehead et al. (1988) also report that IBS patients obtained significantly more symptoms of psychological distress than either IBS non-patients or normal controls. It could therefore be argued that help-seeking behaviour *per se*, rather than the bowel symptoms which define IBS, is the crucial factor related to anxiety and distress in these reports. Indeed a recent study by Smith et al. (1990) found that 148 attenders at a gastroenterology clinic presenting with at least one month of continuous or intermittent abdominal distress, altered bowel habits or both, obtained anxiety scores elevated relative to a normal control population irrespective of whether they were subsequently diagnosed with IBS or organic disease. These authors conclude that psychological, health care-seeking behaviours are present in patients with both organic and non-organic disease. However, another recent study by Blanchard *et al.* (1990) showed elevated anxiety scores for IBS in relation to IBD patients, with patients in both groups actively seeking medical help.

Concurrent psychopathology has also frequently been noted in IBS patients. Only a minority of the early studies used structured psychiatric interviews, and there is a tendency for these to report that a large proportion (averaging 79%) of IBS patients have diagnosable psychopathology. The commonest co-occurring psychiatric diagnoses approximated from a range of studies are hysteria (20%), depression (20%) and anxiety neurosis (14%) (Whitehead & Schuster, 1985). In contrast a recent report by Blanchard *et al.* (1990), using the Revised Anxiety Disorders Interview Schedule, found that anxiety disorders predominated in their sample of 62 IBS patients (39.7% anxiety disorders) with rather less identified as mood disordered (12%). The proportion of patients with diagnosable psycho-pathology was also lower (56%) than reported in the earlier literature, although significantly greater than the rate for IBD patients (25% of a sample of 44) or non-patients controls (18% of a sample of 38).

An alternative approach to investigating the incidence of anxiety in IBS is to compare colonic response in IBS patients with non-IBS anxious controls. Latimer *et al.* (1981) found that IBS patients could not be distinguished in their colonic responses from a group of patients who were equally anxious, neurotic and depressed but who did not have IBS. This led Latimer to suggest a direct link between anxiety and IBS (Latimer, 1981). His basic supposition is that there is a clear overlap between neuroticism and IBS. He further suggests that the symptoms of IBS and anxiety result from a common underlying autonomic reactivity, with the resulting symptom choice determined by vicarious learning (e.g. that symptoms of IBS are a socially acceptable sign of distress) and maintained by environmental contingencies (e.g. a diagnosis of medical illness and prescribed treatment). The studies detailed above show only a degree of consistency with Latimer's contention. Indeed, while anxiety is associated with IBS it is unclear whether this is (a) related to health care-seeking behaviour rather than IBS *per se* or (b) a reaction to symptoms rather than a causal factor.

Anxiety reduction and IBS

One implication of Latimer's model is that treatments designed to reduce anxiety will also reduce IBS symptomatology. Although there are many studies suggesting the efficacy of psychological interventions for IBS most of these are single case studies or lack adequate control groups, see Blanchard, Schwarz & Radnitz, 1987; Creed & Guthrie, 1989). There is, however, some indication that strategies such as progressive muscular relaxation, used as part of a multicomponent treatment package, reduce IBS symptomatology in both the short and long term (e.g. Neff & Blanchard, 1987; Schwartz et al., 1990). The latter study, for example, showed reductions in abdominal pain/tenderness, diarrhoea, nausea and flatulence at four years follow-up.

Although the monitoring of abdominal pain and discomfort suggests that physical symptomatology may be reduced by such strategies, rarely have attempts been made to additionally assess psychological parameters. It is thus not possible to ascertain the extent to which anxiety reduction per se plays a role in such treatment. Indeed, the few studies which have monitored both physical and psychological parameters have produced mixed results. Svedlund et al. (1983) treated IBS patients either with medication plus dynamically oriented short-term individual psycho- therapy which focused on ways of coping with stress and emotional problems, or with medication alone. Assessments were taken of both 'mental symptoms' (a total score obtained for an 'asthenic–depressive syndrome' and an 'anxiety syndrome') in addition to 'physical symptoms' (somatic complaints, abdominal pain and bowel dysfunction). Both groups showed improvements in measures of abdominal pain at three months, with the psychological treatment group showing continued improvement at 15 months. Those receiving medication regressed towards initial severity of their symptoms at the 15-month follow-up. Both groups showed improvements on psychological symptoms at three months, although there were no between-group differences in psychological symptoms at either three or 15 months.

In a further study Bennett & Wilkinson (1985) randomly assigned 24 IBS patients to either a combined stress management and operant approach or a standard medical treatment following a no-treatment control period. After eight weeks of intervention both treatment groups showed improve- ments in bowel movement, abdominal pain and discomfort, while only the psychological intervention group had significant reductions in anxiety. Unfortunately, no follow-up data are reported, suggesting that a degree of caution is required in interpreting these results; many drug trials with IBS suggest short-term symptom improvement which is not maintained, while there is also evidence from controlled drug trials of a large placebo response (Whitehead, 1985).

In sum, while there is evidence for elevated anxiety in IBS clinic attenders, there is a strong case for arguing that this is more related to help-seeking behaviour than to the bowel symptoms which define IBS. The balance of evidence does not support the view that anxiety and IBS come from a common autonomic reactivity as suggested by Latimer (1981). Nevertheless a number of treatment studies have been guided by such suggestions. These studies, frequently using relaxation as part of their treatment package, highlight the success of such strategies in reducing abdominal symptoms. Few studies have additionally monitored anxiety, so that it remains to be seen whether anxiety reduction plays a central part in such treatment success.

Stomach ulcers

A large body of research has implicated stress and anxiety in the aetiology and maintenance of ulcers. In an early report Minski & Desai (1955) suggested that anxiety characterised duodenal ulcer patients. More recent reports also suggest that ulcer patients, when compared to healthy or hospitalised controls, are low achievers, more anxious, emotionally unstable, hypochondriacal and lacking in assertiveness (Christodoulou, Alevisos & Konstantakakis, 1983; Feldman et al., 1986; Lyketsos et al., 1982; McIntosh et al., 1983). This relationship is borne out by the findings from Friedman & Booth-Kewley's (1987) meta-analytic review of the 'disease-prone personality'. They cite seven studies published between 1945 and 1984 examining the relationship between anxiety and ulcers, and conclude that anxiety is reliably and positively associated with the occurrence of ulcers.

Studies not included or published more recently than those included in Friedman & Booth-Kewley's review provide further evidence of elevated anxiety in ulcer patients. McIntosh et al. (1983) compared gastric ulcer and duodenal ulcer patients with a community control group and a patient control group on 16 PF scores. In comparison to both control groups the female ulcer patients obtained higher scores on emotional instability, tension and anxiety, while the male ulcer patients obtained higher scores on components of neuroticism. Christodoulou et al. (1983) also report elevated neuroticism scores for peptic ulcer patients in relation to healthy controls, and higher general and trait anxiety scores for the peptic ulcer group in relation to patients hospitalised for illnesses unrelated to their gastrointestinal tract. Feldman et al. (1986) report that peptic ulcer patients obtained higher hypochondriasis scores and were more depressed, anxious and worried than control groups of kidney stone patients and healthy volunteers. As with the IBS studies, these findings are generally based upon patients seeking medical help, and so may be biased towards those who are likely to be more anxious, although this would not necessarily explain differences between peptic ulcer patients and hospitalised controls. In this regard, however, Sandberg & Bilding (1976) found no association between ulcers and psychopathology in non-hospital clinic attenders, and note that patients with ulcers attending hospital clinics were more anxious than non-clinic attenders. On balance, however, the evidence seems to suggest that elevated anxiety is not unusual in ulcer patients, although whether this is a causal rather than a consequential factor is less clear. Friedman & Booth-Kewley (1987) suggest that 'the accumulated evidence is definitely not inconsistent with a causal role for personality' (p. 551); anxiety may be an important component of a broader personality style acting as a vulnerability factor in the aetiology of ulcers.

Anxiety reduction and ulcers

The possibility that anxiety characterises those with stomach ulcers has prompted some to design treatment programmes specifically aimed at managing anxiety in such patients. Brooks & Richardson (1980) randomly assigned 22 patients with diagnosed uncomplicated duodenal ulcer to either a psychological treatment programme consisting of anxiety manage-ment training and assertiveness training or an attention placebo control. Training consisted of eight sessions over a two-week period. At 60 days follow-up the trained group reported less severe ulcer symptomatology and lower anxiety, although this was evident only for those patients who were initially highly anxious. At three-year follow-up a review of the medical records revealed a significantly lower rate of ulcer recurrence for the treated group. Anxiety scores were not assessed at this time. On bal-ance, the limited available evidence suggests that there is a relationship between anxiety and ulcers, and that anxiety reduction is accompanied by more rapid medical recovery. Future research could usefully be directed towards examining the extent of this relationship and whether the beneficial effects of anxiety reduction can be replicated in further treatment outcome studies.

Inflammatory bowel disease

A variety of uncontrolled and single case studies since the 1940s and, more recently, a number of retrospective reports have implicated psychological factors in the aetiology of IBD. However, results from these studies have been far from consistent. A similar set of conflicting results emerge from studies investigating psychometrically assessed anxiety and neuroticism or levels of psychopathology in relation to Crohn's disease and IBD (see Schwarz & Blanchard, 1990). Thus, Tarter et al. (1987) compared ulcerative colitis, Crohn's disease and normal controls using the Diagnostic Interview Schedule. While the ulcerative colitis patients were similar to the normal controls, Crohn's disease was more likely to be associated with anxiety disorder, panic disorder and depression. The authors report that panic disorder had an excess prevalence in Crohn's disease patients prior to disease onset. These results are, however, based upon retrospective recall and must be treated cautiously; in addition, as the authors themselves note, the results may be an artefact of the number of statistical comparisons performed. Indeed, other studies report no difference between Crohn's disease and ulcerative colitis patients for prevalence of psychopathology (e.g. Andrews, Barczak & Allen, 1987).

In one of the first studies using standardised psychometric assessments, Sheffield & Carney (1976) administered the Taylor Manifest Anxiety scale to 28 outpatients with Crohn's disease, 17 patients deemed to have a chronic illness (e.g. chronic heart disease and chronic gastrointestinal and renal disorders) and 43 patients deemed to have psychosomatic illnesses (e.g. asthma and diabetes but also including duodenal ulcer and ulcerative colitis). Scores for the Crohn's group were elevated relative to normative data and the scores of the chronic illness group but comparable to the psychosomatic group. The inclusion of patients with gastrointestinal disorders in both comparison groups, and the specific inclusion of patients with ulcers and ulcerative colitis in the psychosomatic comparison group, clearly makes it difficult to interpret the results meaningfully.

Indeed, contrasting findings have been reported in other studies. Esler & Goulston (1973) administered the Eysenck Personality Inventory and IPAT anxiety scale to 16 patients with ulcerative colitis, 40 general medical outpatients and 31 patients with irritable-colon syndrome (cf. irritable bowel disease), 15 of whom had abdominal pain and 16 of whom had painless diarrhoea as their predominant symptom. Both the ulcerative colitis and abdominal pain subgroup of irritable-colon patients obtained scores on both scales comparable to the general medical outpatients. In a further study Helzer et al. (1982) report no differences in neuroticism scores for a sample of ulcerative colitis patients and a matched control sample with chronic non-gastrointestinal medical illnesses (hypertension, diabetes and various cardiac illnesses). In a recent study Blanchard et al. (1990) also report no difference in anxiety between IBD patients and non-patient controls. In contrast to research findings relating to peptic ulcers, studies to date concerned with IBD provide little evidence of elevated neuroticism or anxiety in such patients. Indeed, when elevated anxiety is reported in a few studies this may reflect a reaction to the disease rather than being a causal factor. As Schwarz & Blanchard (1990) comment, 'the disease and its symptoms, especially during exacerbations or "flares", is probably a major life stressor and probably leads to an increase in psychological distress such as anxiety and depression' (p. 103). Longitudinal evaluations would shed light on this issue.

Anxiety reduction and IBD

Although a number of psychological interventions have been used as treatment for IBD (supportive psychotherapy, relaxation and hypnosis), with a few exceptions these have assessed pain, medication or symptom severity rather than assessing these in addition to more general psychological change (see Schwarz & Blanchard, 1990). In one early single case report, Mitchell (1978) reports decreases in muscle tension and frequency of worry and other negative thoughts, as well as reduced colitis attacks, in a 37-year-old man instructed in muscle relaxation and cognitive control techniques. In a further report, Freyberger *et al.* (1985) randomly assigned 38 ulcerative colitis patients to either a brief psychotherapy group or a no-treatment control condition. The treatment, but not the control group, showed significant improvements in state anxiety as well as depression and mood. Unfortunately the authors did not monitor change in physical symptomatology or report any follow-up assessment. In a recently published report Schwarz & Blanchard (1991) randomly assigned 21 IBD patients to either a stress management group (consisting of a combination of progressive muscular relaxation, thermal biofeedback, training in cognitive coping strategies and education relating to IBD symptomatology) or a control group. Both groups completed daily symptom diaries. At the end of treatment and at three-month follow-up both groups showed slight but non-significant decreases in anxiety; however, the control group showed a greater reduction in total physical symptoms than the treated group. In fact when the control subjects subsequently completed the treatment regime their physical symptoms increased. To date there is thus little evidence to suggest that psychological interventions may be beneficial in alleviating the physical symptoms of IBD, although clearly more research is required. Given the seeming lack of relationship between anxiety and IBD it seems unlikely that any treatment success in terms of physical symptom reduction would be due to anxiety reduction *per se*, although such a link may be present in high-anxiety patients.

CORONARY HEART DISEASE

Coronary heart disease involves narrowing or blocking of the coronary arteries. If blockage of oxygenated blood to the heart is partial, or brief, the person may experience a sharp pain in the chest or arm, referred to as angina pectoris. If the blockage is severe, muscle tissue of the heart may be destroyed with the individual experiencing a myocardial infarction or heart attack. Hypertension, or consistently high blood pressure, is a major risk factor for coronary heart disease, stroke and kidney disease. Although some cases of hypertension are secondary to disorders of other bodily organs, the majority of cases are classified as primary or essential hypertension. In these cases there is no identifiable biological cause with psychosocial risk factors (obesity, diet, lack of exercise, family history) playing a predominant part. In addition to hypertension, epidemiological research suggests a number of risk factors known to contribute to coronary heart disease including age, sex, obesity, smoking, Type A behaviour and stress. Coronary heart disease causes one-third of all deaths in men under 65 and 28% of all deaths, and is one of the major causes of death amongst men in the UK and USA.

Anxiety as a causal factor in coronary heart disease

Coronary artery disease is frequently associated with anxiety, but whether this is implicated as a cause rather than a consequence is a matter of some controversy. Some reports suggest that while trait anxiety and neuroticism are associated with the development of angina (e.g. Medalie & Goldbourt, 1976) they are less likely to be implicated in myocardial infarction. Jenkins (1983), for example, notes that anxiety and neuroticism—amongst other variables such as depression, hypochondriasis, life dissatisfaction and interpersonal discord—have been found to be associated with the presence of one or more forms of coronary heart disease. However, in reviewing over 45 studies of behavioural risk factors in coronary artery disease he notes that the variables of anxiety and neuroticism are more consistently related to angina pectoris than to myocardial infarction (Jenkins, 1976). Razin (1982) similarly suggests that life-stress events, anxiety, depression and Type A behaviour show relatively consistent associations with coronary artery disease; while further suggesting that life-stress events and neuroticism are linked to general morbidity while anxiety, depression and life dissatisfaction are linked more specifically with angina.

The link between anxiety and angina pectoris is questioned by Costa (1986), who argues that while neuroticism is related to symptom reporting (i.e. pseudo-angina) it is unrelated or inversely related to actual angina pectoris or other aspects of the disease process. Assuming this line of reasoning is correct, then the association of anxiety or neuroticism with angina could be an artefact of symptom reporting by those who, when investigated, do not have diseased arteries. As noted previously, a number of recent reports suggest that individuals with chest pain but normal coronary arteries share symptom complaints with individuals with panic disorder (e.g. Beck et al., 1989; Mukerji et al., 1987) and that such patients also obtain significantly elevated anxiety scores relative to normal controls (Beck et al., 1990).

The possibility that anxiety is a causal factor in coronary heart disease is, however, suggested by Booth-Kewley & Friedman's (1987) meta-analytic review of the literature investigating personality variables and coronary heart disease. They cite 15 published reports specifically investigating anxiety, and conclude that higher levels of anxiety—as well as higher levels of depression, anger, hostility, aggression and extraversion—are associated with a greater likelihood of heart disease. In addition, the combined effect sizes for anxiety, anger/hostility, anger/hostility/ aggression and depression were of a similar magnitude to that observed between Type A behaviour and coronary heart disease. Type A behaviour—characterised by competitiveness, striving for achievement and a hasty, impatient, impulsive, hyperalert and tense manner—has long been implicated as a possible causal factor in coronary heart disease. Certainly research suggests that among healthy individuals Type A behaviour can predict the likelihood of subsequent coronary heart disease (Matthews & Haynes, 1986). Friedman & Booth-Kewley (1987) argue that other personality factors including anxiety may be as important as Type A behaviour in predicting heart disease. However, Stone & Costa (1990), in a critique of this review, suggest that when only prospective studies are examined the notion of a 'disease-prone' personality in relation to coronary heart disease is not supported.

Jenkins (1988) also adds a note of caution to the supposition that personality is a causal factor in coronary heart disease by pointing out that

> the relation of measures of anxiety, depression and neuroticism to angina pectoris and cardiac death has been consistently positive for studies conducted in many nations, regardless of whether the study has been prospective or retrospective. In contrast, these chronic troubling emotions are not associated prospectively with future incidence of myocardial infarction. The only positive relation between these variables and myocardial infarction has been found in retrospective case control studies and, in those instances, the emotional states may have developed after the clinical appearance of the disease (p. 329).

Anxiety following myocardial infarction

A number of authors have argued that anxiety plays a key part during the convalescence phase following myocardial infarction, and that anxiety is negatively related to many post-recovery variables such as return to work. Razin (1982), for example, suggests that long-term emotional distress occurs in a significant minority (perhaps 25%) of recovering coronary artery disease patients, and that this tends to peak just after discharge from hospital. It should be noted that many other reports suggest far lower figures for severe anxiety. Taylor et al. (1986a), for example, found severe anxiety in only 3% of a sample of 210 post-myocardial infarction patients, pointing out that this is no greater than in the population at large. However, moderate anxiety is frequently reported, and Doehrman (1977) and Wiklund et al. (1985) cite a number of studies which suggest that the high levels of anxiety common in the first few days post-infarction decline after five or six days, although remaining elevated relative to normative data for months and sometimes years.

Anxiety and/or depression are thus not unusual responses in post-myocardial infarction patients. This is illustrated in a report by Crisp, Queenan & D'Souza (1984), who compared 26 men with severe myocardial infarction, 15 of whom had been assessed prior to the infarction while the remaining 11 had been assessed subsequently, to 235 comparison subjects on measures of free-floating anxiety, phobic anxiety, obsessionality, functional somatic complaints, depression and hysteria. Prior to infarction, coronary patients reported more somatic complaints and greater depression than the comparison group. However, higher levels of anxiety, greater depression, social avoidance and introversion were the most marked changes in psychological status post-infarction.

High levels of anxiety persist at least while patients are hospitalised. Serial measurements of anxiety in coronary patients admitted to hospital suggest that anxiety is highest on admission to the coronary care unit and immediately after transfer to the ward, falling rapidly over the following week, rising just prior to discharge and falling to the lowest level at four months (e.g. Billing et al., 1980; Cay et al., 1972a,b; Dellipiani et al., 1976; Philip et al., 1979; Thompson et al., 1987). Level of anxiety seems to be unrelated to age (Billing et al., 1980) or severity of the infarct (e.g. Cay et al., 1972a; Dellipiani et al., 1976). Specific sources of anxiety, both while hospitalised and at six weeks post-discharge, involve the myocardial infarction itself in addition to concerns about returning to work, the future and possible complications (Thompson et al., 1987).

In contrast to the range of findings which suggest that anxiety declines post-discharge, a recent report of a large sample of hospitalised myocardial infarction patients (Havik & Maeland, 1990) found stable levels of anxiety during the in-hospital period with anxiety increasing markedly at one to two weeks discharge and remaining constant at these higher levels at four subsequent assessments conducted one to two weeks, six weeks, six months and three to five years post-discharge. Other reports suggest that anxiety peaks at around two months when patients have just returned to work or are anticipating doing so (Trelawny-Ross & Russell, 1987). Differing results are no doubt due to the fact that studies take assessments at different times, using a variety of measures, rarely making comparisons with other hospitalised subjects and rarely assessing the focus of any anxiety experienced.

Certainly, findings do seem to indicate that where the medical prognosis is good, anxiety declines in the subsequent year or two post-infarction for the majority of cases. However, episodes of angina pectoris may occur for many months or even years subsequent to discharge, provoking further anxiety both for patients and their families (Langosch, 1984). Factors relating to poorer emotional adjustment reported in the study by Havik & Maeland (1990) were previous angina pectoris, previous hospitalisation due to heart disease and higher levels of pre-myocardial infarction physical limitations in daily activity.

Another factor interacting with the level of reported anxiety post-infarction is the use of denial as a coping strategy. Denial is frequently employed in such circumstances, and has been found to be an effective strategy for reducing anxiety immediately post-infarction. By about day four, however, anxiety levels for deniers and non-deniers are about the same and elevated relative to normative data (Froese et al., 1974). Havik & Maeland (1990) note that myocardial infarction patients who showed least emotional upset, both in the short and long term, were those who had high levels of denial of impact assessed while hospitalised. Although denial might reduce anxiety in the short term, longer-term denial may result in the minimising of symptoms and poorer compliance. The effect is interactive, however, as elevated anxiety may also be a sign of poor adaptation, which also results in less than optimum compliance with a rehabilitation regime (lifestyle change, exercise and stress management) with subsequent deterioration in the patient's condition (Doehrman, 1977). Indeed, high levels of anxiety and depression have been found to be important factors impeding recovery from myocardial infarction and subsequent return to work (Nagle, Gangola & Picton-Robinson, 1971).

In one report, Smith, Follick & Korr (1984) found that neuroticism was related to a tendency to avoid activity because of the possibility of eliciting angina symptoms in post-myocardial infarction patients. They further suggest that neuroticism may account for some of the variation in activity levels of post-myocardial infarction patients with equivalent levels of disease.

Rehabilitation and anxiety reduction following myocardial infarction

A number of studies have evaluated the efficacy of physical exercise, information provision, counselling and structured psychological interventions during both the acute phase and longer-term rehabilitation phase following myocardial infarction (see, for example, reviews by Blumenthal & Emery, 1988; Johnston, 1985; Wiklund et al., 1985). Anxiety has often been assessed as one of the outcome measures in such intervention studies.

Acute-phase intervention The few studies which have investigated the efficacy of in-hospital intervention suggest that specifically dealing with patients' fears and anxieties during the acute coronary care phase can have a beneficial outcome on both psychological and medical parameters. In one of the earliest such studies, Gruen (1975) randomly divided 70 myocardial infarction patients into two groups. The experimental group, who were seen almost daily for 30 minutes individual psychotherapy during hospitalisation (average 23 days), were given support and reinforcement as well as reassurance that reactions such as fear, anxiety and depression were acceptable. The control group received standard hospital care. Those receiving brief therapy fared better on a number of measures (e.g. days hospitalised) in comparison to the control group while hospitalised, although there was a general lack of difference on measures of anxiety. As the author notes, however, there was a tendency for the anxiety scores of the treated group to cluster around an average anxiety score while the scores for the control group showed a very wide range. At a four-month follow-up interview the anxiety ratings of the treated group were significantly lower.

In a further study, Young *et al.* (1982) compared 100 post-myocardial infarction inpatients provided with a comprehensive educational, training and counselling rehabilitation package with 100 controls on a range of physical and psychological parameters. At three months the rehabilitation group showed improvements on a range of physical measures, although there was little difference between rehabilitation and controls at one-year follow-up. An anxiety questionnaire administered 18 months following discharge from hospital suggested a trend towards lower anxiety scores for the rehabilitation group. A similar information/counselling programme was evaluated by Oldenberg, Perkins & Andrews (1985). They allocated patients to two treatment groups or a control group. One of the treatment groups, a counselled group, received information about their condition and treatment, training in relaxation, and counselling for their fears and anxieties while they were still in hospital. The other treatment group, an education group, received education and relaxation only. Although anxiety was assessed separately it was combined in a factor including Type A, psychiatric morbidity and attitudes towards illness, and termed psychological dysfunction as an outcome measure. Follow-up at three, six and 12 months showed that patients in both intervention groups fared better on this measure of psychosocial adjustment than patients receiving standard care.

In a further study Langosch *et al.* (1982) compared stress management with relaxation training and a no-treatment control for 90 male post-myocardial infarction inpatients. At six-month follow-up more of the treatment group patients had returned to work, were more confident and less socially anxious in comparison to the controls.

In a more recent report Thompson & Meddis (1990) randomly assigned 60 male patients admitted to a coronary care unit with a first-time acute myocardial infarction to either a treatment group receiving in-hospital counselling in addition to routine care, or a control group which received routine care only. The patient's spouse was included in the intervention, which was provided by a nurse counsellor over four 30-minute sessions during the patient's hospital stay. The intervention consisted of a structured support and education package focusing upon the patient's illness and recovery. Patients who received in-hospital counselling reported significantly less anxiety and depression in comparison to the routine care group, an effect which was maintained at six-month follow-up. Taken together, the few studies of in-hospital counselling conducted to date provide generally favourable results. This has led Thompson & Meddis (1990) to suggest that 'such simple intervention in the acute phase is therapeutically beneficial, efficient and economic, and should be offered routinely to patients who have suffered a first MI' (p. 247).

Rehabilitation after myocardial infarction A number of studies have evaluated physical rehabilitation, longer-term counselling or psychological treatment programmes subsequent to hospital discharge. Studies evaluating physical cardiac rehabilitation programmes suggest that while there is a tendency for patients to show increased subjective anxiety in response to such treatment, there is evidence for the beneficial effects of such programmes as assessed by other outcome measures. Stern & Cleary (1981), for example, found that physical rehabilitation for 748 post-myocardial infarction patients decreased feelings of depression and increased sexual activity whilst simultaneously increasing feelings of anxiety. Similarly van Dixhoorn, de Loos & Duivenvoorden (1983) found that post-myocardial patients treated with physical training in combination with relaxation exercises showed increased well-being and decreased perceptions of themselves as disabled, whilst also showing increases in anxiety. A plausible explanation for such results is suggested by Stern & Cleary (1981), who argue that anxiety is a natural response in post-myocardial infarction patients engaging in increased physical exercise.

However, these findings can be contrasted with those from three further reports. Mayou (1983) found no differences at three months on measures of anxiety, depression or physical activity for groups of post-myocardial infarction patients treated with either standard cardiological aftercare, physical rehabilitation in addition to aftercare or psychosocial advice in addition to aftercare. In a further report Taylor *et al.* (1986a) report a significantly greater decrease in anxiety at six-month follow-up for post-myocardial infarction patients receiving supervised gym exercise training in comparison to a non-trained control group. The decreases in anxiety were not, however, significantly greater than the decreases in anxiety reported for groups receiving home exercise training and treadmill testing but not specific exercise training. This finding led the authors to suggest that the modest benefits might be due to greater nurse contact rather than exercise *per se*. In a more recent report van Dixhoorn *et al.* (1990) randomly assigned 156 myocardial infarction patients to either an exercise plus relaxation and breathing therapy programme or to exercise training only. The former group showed improvements on three out of eight psychological measures, including anxiety, while no such improvements were seen for the exercise alone; there were not, however, any significant differences between the treatments. About half the patients in each condition showed improvement in physical fitness while negative outcomes in physical terms occurred less frequently when exercise was combined with relaxation.

Overall, then, while graded exercise programmes may be beneficial in terms of physical rehabilitation, results are mixed. Further, anxiety is likely to be a natural response to the associated increased heart rate and it seems important to provide the patient with adequate cognitive or physiological techniques to control adverse responses to such natural heart rate increases.

Reports also suggest that providing post-myocardial infarction patients and their families with adequate counselling and information about physical and psychological risk factors reduces anxiety, particularly for highly anxious patients. In this context Naismith *et al.* (1979) found that psychological counselling from a nurse counsellor had little effect, apart from increasing social independence six months after myocardial infarction, except for highly neurotic patients who were more likely to have a good outcome if they received counselling. Unfortunately, the high anxious patients are also the ones most likely to drop out of treatment (Theorell, 1983).

Other studies suggest that counselling subsequent to hospital discharge does have a generally beneficial effect both on physical and psychological indices. In one study, Fielding (1980) provided behavioural counselling subsequent to hospital discharge. Ten myocardial infarction patients were assigned to either a behavioural counselling/relaxation training group or non-intervention control. The intervention group showed reduced muscle tension and decreased anxiety, and returned to work sooner, although the small sample means the results should be treated with caution.

In a further study Burgess *et al.* (1987) randomly assigned 180 post-myocardial infarction patients to either a cardiac rehabilitation programme consisting of cognitive–behavioural counselling or standard cardiological aftercare. At three months the cardiac rehabilitation group reported less distress, anxiety and depression than the control group (the difference was significant only in the case of depression). Although the cardiac rehabilitation group had similarly lower scores at 13 months follow-up none of the differences was significant. However, Burgess *et al.* argue for the need to adopt an integrative approach to cardiac rehabilitation, intervening at multiple levels: psychological, social, occupational and physical. Certainly taking account of the possible anxiety-inducing effects of physical rehabilitation programmes, where naturally increased heart rates can be misinterpreted as a catastrophic reaction, the addition of cognitive–behavioural interventions to rehabilitation programmes could be particularly important in limiting the patients' psychological distress.

SUMMARY

This chapter has examined two aspects of anxiety in relation to asthma, gastrointestinal disorders and coronary artery disease. Firstly the extent to which dispositional anxiety increases vulnerability to disease and secondly the extent to which anxiety as a response to disease increases symptomatology or impedes recovery. Although the search for personality variables related to specific illnesses has had a long history this has often been a poorly defined and ill-researched area, with little evidence to support such a notion. In contrast, the view that there is a broad 'disease-prone' personality rather than illness-specific personality dispositions has received some recent support, with anxiety included as a dispositional characteristic of some importance (Friedman & Booth-Kewley, 1987). Whether anxiety is related to illness complaints rather than to illness *per se*, however, remains a matter of some controversy (Stone & Costa, 1990). As Friedman (1990) notes, though, even if the former case applies this does not mean that anxiety or other dispositional characteristics 'cannot also play a true causal role in disease' (p. 287). Clearly this is an issue for future research to attempt to unravel.

The impact of anxiety upon symptomatology and recovery has been more clearly articulated. A number of authors have noted that anxiety and panic are frequently associated with asthma attacks in an interactive fashion, so worsening the attack. Similarly anxiety as a response to myocardial infarction is not uncommon, with heightened anxiety frequently negatively related to many post-recovery variables. However, the results of psychological interventions in relation to physical illness, while reducing anxiety when this has been assessed, have produced mixed results in relation to physical functioning. Both relaxation and systematic desensitisation have been evaluated as treatments for asthma. Alexander & Solanch (1980) have concluded that results for the former have not been promising, while Richter & Dahme (1982) suggest that results from the latter are not very convincing. Indeed anxiety-reduction techniques are likely to be beneficial only in those cases where anxiety plays an important role in maintaining respiratory difficulties and anxiety is not necessarily monitored in intervention studies. A similar situation arises with regard to IBS, where anxiety-management strategies have frequently been shown to reduce abdominal symptoms although few studies have additionally monitored anxiety. Perhaps the most promising aspect of psychological intervention in relation to physical symptoms and anxiety reduction relates to the efficacy of acute-phase intervention subsequent to myocardial infarction. The promising results of inpatient counselling in reducing anxiety and depression and enhancing recovery have led Thompson & Meddis (1990) to suggest that such intervention should be offered routinely to patients who have suffered a first myocardial infarction.

The links between anxiety and disease provide an exciting area for future research. One issue relates to attempting to unravel the implications of anxiety for symptom reporting, as reviewed in the previous chapter or as a vulnerability factor for disease. The extent to which anxiety as a response to illness exacerbates symptoms or impedes recovery warrants further investigation. Finally, the rationale for employing specific psychological treatments for specific diseases needs to be clearly specified, and the extent to which reductions in anxiety relate to reductions in physical symptoms ascertained.

References

Abel, G. G., Barlow, D. H., Blanchard, E. B. & Mavissakalian, M. (1975). Measurement of sexual arousal in male homosexuals: Effects of instructions and stimulus modality. *Archives of Sexual Behavior*, **4**, 623–630.

Abrahamson, D. J., Barlow, D. H. & Abrahamson, D. H. (1989). Differential effects of performance demand and distraction on sexually functional and dysfunctional males. *Journal of Abnormal Psychology*, **98**, 241–247.

Abrahamson, D. J., Barlow, D. H., Beck, J. G., Sakheim, D. K. & Kelly, J. P. (1985a). The effects of attentional focus and partner responsiveness on sexual responding: replication and extension. *Archives of Sexual Behavior*, **14**, 361–371.

Abrahamson, D. J., Barlow, D. H., Sakheim, D. K., Beck, J. G. & Athanasiou, R. (1985b). Effects of distraction on sexual responding in functional and dysfunctional men. *Behavior Therapy*, **16**, 503–515.

Adams, A. E., Haynes, S. N. & Brayer, M. A. (1985). Cognitive distraction in female sexual arousal. *Psychophysiology*, **22**, 689–696.

Adler, C., Craske, M. G. & Barlow, D. H. (1987). Relaxation induced panic: when resting isn't peaceful. *Journal of Integrative Psychiatry*, **5**, 94–112.

Agras, W. S., Leitenberg, H. & Barlow, D. H. (1968). Social reinforcement in the modification of agoraphobia. *Archives of General Psychiatry*, **19**, 423–427.

Agras, W. S., Sylvester, D. & Oliveau, D. (1969). The epidemiology of common fears and phobia. *Comprehensive Psychiatry*, **10**, 151–161.

Aiken, H. S. & Henrichs, T. F. (1971). Systematic relaxation as a nursing intervention technique with open heart surgery patients. *Nursing Research*, **20**, 212–217.

Akhtar, S., Wig, N. N., Verma, V. K., Pershad, D. & Verma, S. K. (1975). A phenomenological analysis of symptoms in obsessive–compulsive neurosis. *British Journal of Psychiatry*, **127**, 342–348.

Alexander, A. B. (1977). Behavioral methods in the clinical management of asthma. In W. D. Gentry & R. B. Williams (Eds), *Behavioral Approaches to Medical Practice*. Cambridge, MA: Ballinger.

Alexander, A. B. & Solanch, L. S. (1980). Psychological aspects in the understanding and treatment of bronchial asthma. In J. Ferguson & C. B. Taylor (Eds), *Advances in Behavioral Medicine*. New York: Spectrum.

Alexander, A. B., Cropp, G. J. A. & Chai, H. (1979). Effects of relaxation training on pulmonary mechanics in children with asthma. *Journal of Applied Behavior Analysis*, **12**, 27–35.

Alexander, A. B., Miklich, D. R. & Hershkoff, H. (1972). The immediate effects of systematic relaxation training on peak expiratory flow rates in asthmatic children. *Psychosomatic Medicine*, **34**, 388–394.

Allen, J. J. & Tune, G. S. (1975). The Lynfield Obsessional/Compulsive Questionnaire. *Scottish Medical Journal*, **20**, 21–24.

Allen, K. D., Danforth, J. S. & Drabman, R. S. (1989). Videotaped modeling and film distraction for fear reduction in adults undergoing hyperbaric oxygen therapy. *Journal of Consulting and Clinical Psychology*, **57**, 554–558.

Alstrom, J. E., Nordlund, C. L., Persson, G., Harding, M. & Ljungqvist, C. (1984). Effects of four treatment methods on social phobia patients not suitable for insight-oriented psychotherapy. *Acta Psychiatrica Scandinavica*, **70**, 97–110.

American Psychiatric Association (1975). *A Psychiatric Glossary*. Washington, DC: American Psychiatric Association.

American Psychiatric Association (1980). *Diagnostic and Statistical Manual of Mental Disorders*, 3rd edn. Washington, DC: American Psychiatric Association.

American Psychiatric Association (1987). *Diagnostic and Statistical Manual of Mental Disorders*, 3rd edn rev. Washington, DC: American Psychiatric Association.

American Thoracic Society Committee on Diagnostic Standards for Non Tuberculous Disease (1962). Definitions and classifications of chronic bronchitis, asthma and pulmonary emphysema. *American Review of Respiratory Disease*, **85**, 762–768.

Amies, P. L., Gelder, M. G. & Shaw, P. M. (1983). Social phobia: A comparative clinical study. *British Journal of Psychiatry*, **142**, 174–179.

Anderson, B. (1983). Primary orgasmic dysfunction. *Psychological Bulletin*, **43**, 105–136.

Anderson, D. J., Noyes, R. & Crowe, R. R. (1984). A comparison of panic disorder and generalized anxiety disorder. *American Journal of Psychiatry*, **14**, 572–575.

Anderson, E. A. (1987). Preoperative preparation for cardiac surgery facilitates recovery, reduces psychological distress, and reduces the influence of acute postoperative hypertension. *Journal of Consulting and Clinical Psychology*, **55**, 513–520.

Anderson, K. O. & Masur, F. T. (1983). Psychological preparation for invasive medical and dental procedures. *Journal of Behavioral Medicine*, **6**, 1–40.

Andrew, J. M. (1970). Recovery from surgery, with and without preparatory instructions, for three coping styles. *Journal of Personality and Social Psychology*, **40**, 264–271.

Andrews, H., Barczak, P. & Allen, R. N. (1987). Psychiatric illness in patients with inflammatory-bowel disease. *Gut*, **28**, 1600–1604.

Andrews, V. H. & Borkovec, T. D. (1988). The differential effects of inductions of worry, somatic anxiety, and depression on emotional experience. *Journal of Behavior Therapy and Experimental Psychiatry*, **19**, 21–26.

Argyle, N. (1988). The nature of cognitions in panic disorder. *Behaviour Research and Therapy*, **26**, 261–264.

Arkowitz, H., Lichtenstein, E., McGovern, K. & Hines, P. (1975). The behavioral assessment of social competence in males. *Behavior Therapy*, **6**, 3–13.

Arkowitz, H., Hinton, R., Perl, J. & Himadi, W. (1978). Treatment strategies for dating anxiety in college men based on real-life practice. *Counselling Psychologist*, **7**, 41–46.

Arnkoff, D. B. & Glass, C. R. (1989). Cognitive assessment in social anxiety and social phobia. *Clinical Psychology Review*, **9**, 61–74.

Arnow, B. A., Taylor, C. B., Argras, W. S. & Telch, M. J. (1985). Enhancing agoraphobia treatment outcome by changing couple communications patterns. *Behavior Therapy*, **16**, 452–467.

Aronson, T. A. (1987). Is panic disorder a distinct diagnostic entity? *Journal of Nervous and Mental Disease,* **175**, 584–594.

Aronson, T. A. & Logue, C. M. (1987). On the longitudinal course of panic disorder: Developmental history and predictors of phobic avoidance. *Comprehensive Psychiatry,* **28**, 344–355.

Arrindell, W. A. (1980). Dimensional structure and psychopathology correlates of the Fear Survey Schedule (FSS-III) in a phobic population: A factorial definition of agoraphobia. *Behaviour Research and Therapy,* **18**, 229–242.

Arrindell, W. A. & Emmelkamp, P. M. G. (1986). Marital adjustment, intimacy and needs in female agoraphobics and their partners: A controlled study. *British Journal of Psychiatry,* **149**, 592–602.

Arrindell, W. A. & Emmelkamp, P. M. G. (1987). Psychological states and traits in female agoraphobics: A controlled study. *Journal of Psychopathology and Behavioral Assessment,* **9**, 237–253.

Arrindell, W. A., Emmelkamp, P. M. G., Monsma, A. & Brilman, E. (1983). The role of perceived parental rearing practices in the aetiology of phobic disorders: A controlled study. *British Journal of Psychiatry,* **143**, 183–187.

Arrindell, W. A., Emmelkamp, P. M. G. & van der Ende, J. (1984). Phobic dimensions: I. Reliability and generalizability across samples, gender and nations. *Advances in Behaviour Research and Therapy,* **6**, 207–254.

Arrindell, W. A., Emmelkamp, P. M. G. & Sanderman, R. (1986). Marital quality and general life adjustment in relation to treatment outcome in agoraphobia. *Advances in Behaviour Research and Therapy,* **8**, 139–185.

Arrindell, W. A., Kwee, M. G. T., Methorst, G. J., van der Ende, J., Pol, E. & Moritz, B. J. M. (1989). Perceived parental rearing styles of agoraphobic and socially phobic patients. *British Journal of Psychiatry,* **155**, 526–535.

Auerbach, S. M. (1989). Stress management and coping research in a health care setting: An overview and methodological commentary. *Journal of Consulting and Clinical Psychology,* **57**, 388–395.

Auerbach, S. M., Kendall, P. C., Cuttler, H. F. & Levitt, N. R. (1976). Anxiety, locus of control, type of preparatory information, and adjustment to dental surgery. *Journal of Consulting and Clinical Psychology,* **44**, 809–818.

Auerbach, S. M., Martelli, M. F. & Mercuri, L. G. (1983). Anxiety, information, interpersonal impacts, and adjustment to a stressful health care situation. *Journal of Personality and Social Psychology,* **44**, 1284–1296.

Austin, L. S., Lydiard, R. B., Fossey, M. D., Zealberg, J. J., Laraia, M. T. & Ballenger, J. C. (1990). Panic and phobic disorders in patients with obsessive compulsive disorder. *Journal of Clinical Psychiatry,* **51**, 456–458.

Baer, L. & Jenike, M. A. (1986). Introduction. In M. A. Jenike, L. Baer & W. E. Minichiello (Eds), *Obsessive–Compulsive Disorders: Theory and Management.* Littleton, MA: PSG.

Baer, L., Jenike, M. A., Ricciardi, J. N., Holland, A. D., Seymour, R. J., Minichiello, W. E. & Buttolph, M. L. (1990). Standardized assessment of personality disorders in obsessive–compulsive disorder. *Archives of General Psychiatry,* **47**, 826–830.

Baker, B. & Mersky, H. (1983). Classification and associations of hypochondriasis in patients from a psychiatric hospital. *Canadian Journal of Psychiatry,* **28**, 629–634.

Baker, R. (1989) (Ed.) *Panic Disorder: Theory, Research and Therapy.* Chichester: Wiley.

Ballinger, J. C., Burrows, G. D., DuPont, Jr, R. L., Lesser, I. M., Noyes, Jr, R., Pecknold, J. C., Rifkin, A. & Swinson, R. P. (1988). Alprazolam in panic disorder

and agoraphobia: Results from a multicenter trial. 1. Efficacy of short-term treatment. *Archives of General Psychiatry*, **45**, 413–423.
Bancroft, J. (1983). *Human Sexuality and its Problems*. New York: Churchill-Livingstone.
Bancroft, J. & Cole, L. (1976). Three years' experience in a sexual problems clinic. *British Medical Journal*, **1**, 1575–1577.
Bandura, A. (1969). *Principles of Behavior Modification*. New York: Holt, Rinehart & Winston.
Bandura, A. (Ed.) (1971). *Psychological Modeling: Conflicting Theories*. Chicago, IL: Aldine-Atherton.
Bandura, A. (1977a). *Social Learning Theory*. Englewood Cliffs, NJ: Prentice-Hall.
Bandura, A. (1977b). Self-efficacy: Towards a unifying theory of behavior change. *Psychological Review*, **84**, 191–215.
Bandura, A. & Menlove, F. (1968). Factors determining vicarious extinction of avoidance behavior through symbolic modelling. *Journal of Personality and Social Psychology*, **8**, 99–108.
Bandura, A., Adams, N. E. & Beyer, J. (1977). Cognitive processes mediating behavior change. *Journal of Personality and Social Psychology*, **35**, 125–139.
Bandura, A., Adams, N. E., Hardy, A. & Howells, G. (1980). Tests of the generality of self-efficacy theory. *Cognitive Therapy and Research*, **4**, 19–66.
Barlow, D. H. (1985). The dimensions of anxiety disorders. In A. H. Tuma & J. D. Maser (Eds), *Anxiety and the Anxiety Disorders*. Hillsdale, NJ: Erlbaum.
Barlow, D. H. (1986). Causes of sexual dysfunction: The role of anxiety and cognitive interference. *Journal of Consulting and Clinical Psychology*, **54**, 140–148.
Barlow, D. H. (1988). *Anxiety and its Disorders*. New York: Guildford Press.
Barlow, D. H. (1990). Long-term outcome for patients with panic disorder treated with cognitive–behavioral therapy. *Journal of Clinical Psychiatry*, **51**, 12 (Suppl. A), 17–23.
Barlow, D. H. & Cerny, J. A. (1988). *Psychological Treatment of Panic*. New York: Guildford Press.
Barlow, D. H. & Craske, M. G. (1988). The phenomenology of panic. In S. Rachman & J. D. Maser (Eds), *Panic. Psychological Perspectives*. Hillsdale, NJ: Erlbaum.
Barlow, D. H. & Wolfe, B. E. (1981). Behavioral approaches to anxiety disorders: A report on the NIMH–SUNY Albany research conference. *Journal of Consulting and Clinical Psychology*, **49**, 448–454.
Barlow, D. H., Mavissakalian, M. & Hay, L. R. (1981). Couples treatment of agoraphobia. *Behaviour Research and Therapy*, **19**, 245–255.
Barlow, D. H., Mavissakalian, M. R. & Schofield, L. D. (1980). Patterns of desynchrony in agoraphobia: A preliminary report. *Behaviour Research and Therapy*, **18**, 441–448.
Barlow, D. H., O'Brien, G. T. & Last, C. G. (1984). Couple treatment of agoraphobia. *Behavior Therapy*, **15**, 41–58.
Barlow, D. H., Sakheim, D. K. & Beck, J. G. (1983b). Anxiety increases sexual arousal. *Journal of Abnormal Psychology*, **92**, 49–54.
Barlow, D. H., O'Brien, G. T., Last, C. G. & Holden, A. E. (1983a). Couples treatment of agoraphobia: Initial outcome. In K. D. Craig & R. J. McMahon (Eds), *Advances in Clinical Behavior Therapy*. New York: Brunner Mazel.
Barlow, D. H., Cohen, A. S., Waddell, M. T., Vermilyea, B. B., Klosko, J. S., Blanchard, E. B. & DiNardo, P. A. (1984). Panic and generalized anxiety disorders: Nature and treatment. *Behavior Therapy*, **15**, 431–449.

Barlow, D. H., Vermilyea, J., Blanchard, E. B., Vermilyea, B. B., DiNardo, P. A. & Cerny, J. A. (1985). The phenomenon of panic. *Journal of Abnormal Psychology*, **94**, 320–328.

Barlow, D. H., Blanchard, E. B., Vermilyea, J. A., Vermilyea, B. B. & DiNardo, P. A. (1986a). Generalized anxiety and generalized anxiety disorder: Description and reconceptualization. *American Journal of Psychiatry*, **143**, 40–44.

Barlow, D. H., DiNardo, P. A., Vermilyea, J. A., Vermilyea, B. B. & Blanchard, E. B. (1986b). Co-morbidity and depression among the anxiety disorders: Issues in diagnosis and classification. *Journal of Nervous and Mental Disease*, **174**, 63–72.

Barlow, D. H., Craske, M. G., Cerny, J. A. & Klosko, J. S. (1989). Behavioral treatment of panic disorder. *Behavior Therapy*, **20**, 261–282.

Barsky, A. J. (1987). Investigating the psychological aspects of irritable bowel syndrome. *Gastroenterology*, **93**, 902–904.

Barsky, A. J. & Klerman, G. L. (1983). Overview: Hypochondriasis, bodily complaints, and somatic styles. *American Journal of Psychiatry*, **140**, 273–283.

Barksy, A. J., Geringer, E. & Wool, C. A. (1988). A cognitive–educational treatment for hypochondriasis. *General Hospital Psychiatry*, **10**, 322–327.

Basoglu, M., Lax, T., Kasvikis, Y. & Marks, I. M. (1988). Predictors of improvement in obsessive–compulsive disorder. *Journal of Anxiety Disorders*, **2**, 299–317.

Beck, A. T. (1967). *Depression: Clinical, Experimental and Theoretical Aspects*. (Reprinted as: *Depression: Causes and Treatment*. Philadelphia, PA: University of Pennsylvania Press.)

Beck, A. T. (1976). *Cognitive Therapy and the Emotional Disorders*. New York: International University Press.

Beck, A. T. (1988). Cognitive approaches to panic disorder: Theory and therapy. In S. Rachman & J. D. Maser (Eds), *Panic. Psychological Perspectives*. Hillsdale, NJ: Erlbaum.

Beck, A. T. & Emery, G. (1979). *Cognitive Therapy of Anxiety and Phobic Disorders*. Philadelphia, PA: Center for Cognitive Therapy.

Beck, A. T., Emery, G. & Greenberg, R. L. (1985). *Anxiety Disorders and Phobias: A Cognitive Perspective*. New York: Basic Books.

Beck, A. T., Brown, G., Epstein, N. & Steer, R. A. (1988). An inventory for measuring clinical anxiety. *Journal of Consulting and Clinical Psychology*, **56**, 893–897.

Beck, J. G. (1986). Self-generated distraction in erectile dysfunction: The role of attentional processes. *Advances in Behaviour Research and Therapy*, **8**, 205–221.

Beck, J. G. & Barlow, D. H. (1984). Current conceptualisation of sexual dysfunction: A review and an alternative perspective. *Clinical Psychology Review*, **4**, 363–378.

Beck, J. G. & Barlow, D. H. (1986a). The effects of anxiety and attentional focus on sexual responding—I. Physiological patterns in erectile dysfunction. *Behaviour Research and Therapy*, **24**, 9–17.

Beck, J. G. & Barlow, D. H. (1986b). The effects of anxiety and attentional focus on sexual responding—II. Cognitive and affective patterns in erectile dysfunction. *Behaviour Research and Therapy*, **24**, 19–26.

Beck, J. G. & Scott, S. K. (1988). Physiological and symptom responses to hyperventilation: A comparison of frequent and infrequent panickers. *Journal of Psychopathology and Behavioral Assessment*, **10**, 117–127.

Beck, J. G., Barlow, D. H. & Sakheim, D. K. (1983). The effects of attentional focus and partner arousal on sexual responding in functional and dysfunctional men. *Behaviour Research and Therapy*, **21**, 1–8.

Beck, J. G., Barlow, D. H., Sakheim, D. K. & Abrahamson, D. J. (1987). Shock threat and sexual arousal: The role of selective attention, thought content, and affective states. *Psychophysiology*, **24**, 165–172.

Beck, J. G., Taegtmeyer, M. A., Berisford, M. A. & Bennett, A. (1989). Chest pain without coronary artery disease: An exploratory comparison with panic disorder. *Journal of Psychopathology and Behavioral Assessment*, **11**, 209–220.

Beck, J. G., Berisford, A., Taegtmeyer, H. & Bennett, A. (1990). Panic symptoms in chest pain without coronary artery disease: A comparison with panic disorder. *Behavior Therapy*, **21**, 241–252.

Beecroft, R. S. (1966). *Classical Conditioning*. Goleta, CA: Psychonomic Press.

Beggs, V. E., Calhoun, K. S. & Wolchick, S. A. (1987). Sexual anxiety and female sexual arousal: A comparison of arousal during sexual anxiety stimuli and sexual pleasure stimuli. *Archives of Sexual Behavior*, **16**, 311–319.

Beidel, D. C., Turner, S. M. & Dancu, C. V. (1985). Physiological, cognitive and behavioural aspects of social anxiety. *Behaviour Research and Therapy*, **23**, 109–117.

Beidel, D. C., Turner, S. M., Stanley, M. A. & Dancu, A. V. (1989). The social phobia and anxiety inventory: Concurrent and external validity. *Behavior Therapy*, **20**, 417–427.

Beitman, B. D., Lamberti, J. W., Mukerji, V., DeRosear, L., Basha, I. & Schmidt, L. (1987). Panic disorder in chest pain patients with angiographically normal coronary arteries: A pilot study. *Psychosomatics*, **28**, 480–484.

Bellack, A. S. & Hersen, M. (1979). *Research and Practice in Social Skills Training*. New York: Plenum Press.

Bellack, A. S., Hersen, M. & Lamparski, D. (1979). Role-play tests for assessing social skills: Are they valid? Are they useful? *Journal of Consulting and Clinical Psychology*, **47**, 335–342.

Bennett, P. (1989). Gastroenterology. In A. K. Broome (Ed.), *Health Psychology. Processes and Applications*. London: Chapman & Hall.

Bennett, P. & Wilkinson, S. (1985). A comparison of psychological and medical treatment of the irritable bowel syndrome. *British Journal of Clinical Psychology*, **24**, 215–216.

Bentler, P. M. (1968a). Heterosexual behaviour assessment. I. Males. *Behaviour Research and Therapy*, **6**, 21–25.

Bentler, P. M. (1968b). Heterosexual behaviour assessment. II. Females. *Behaviour Research and Therapy*, **6**, 27–30.

Bergeron, C. M. & Monto, G. L. (1985). Personality patterns seen in irritable bowel syndrome patients. *American Journal of Gastroenterology*, **80**, 448–451.

Berggren, U. & Linde, A. (1984). Dental fear and avoidance: Two modes of treatment. *Journal of Dental Research*, **63**, 1223–1227.

Berlyne, D. (1960). *Conflict, Arousal and Curiosity*. New York: McGraw-Hill.

Bernstein, D. A. & Kleinknecht, R. A. (1982). Multiple approaches to the reduction of dental fear. *Journal of Behavior Therapy and Experimental Psychiatry*, **13**, 287–292.

Bernstein, D. A., Kleinknecht, R. A. & Alexander, L. D. (1979). Antecedents of dental fear. *Journal of Public Health Dentistry*, **39**, 113–124.

Bersh, P. J. (1980). Eysenck's theory of incubation: A critical analysis. *Behaviour Research and Therapy*, **18**, 11–17.

Beunderman, R. & Duyvis, D. J. (1990). Cardiac phobia. In A. A. Kaptein, H. M. van der Ploeg, B. Garssen, P. J. G. Schreurs & R. Beunderman (Eds), *Behavioural Medicine. Psychological Treatments of Somatic Disorders*. Chichester: Wiley.

Bianchi, G. N. (1971). The origins of disease phobia. *Australian and New Zealand Journal of Psychiatry*, 5, 241–257.

Billing, E., Lindell, B., Sederholm, M. & Theorell, T. (1980). Denial, anxiety, and depression following myocardial infarction. *Psychosomatics*, 21, 639–645.

Biran, M., Augusto, F. & Wilson, G. T. (1981). In vivo exposure vs. cognitive restructuring in the treatment of scriptophobia. *Behaviour Research and Therapy*, 19, 525–532.

Black, A. (1974). The natural history of obsessional neurosis. In H. R. Beech (Ed.), *Obsessional States*. London: Methuen.

Black, D. W. & Noyes, R. (1990). Comorbidity and obsessive–compulsive disorder. In J. D. Maser & C. R. Cloninger (Eds), *Comorbidity of Mood and Anxiety Disorders*. Washington, DC: American Psychiatric Press.

Blanchard, E. B., Schwarz, S. P. & Radnitz, C. (1987). Psychological assessment and treatment of irritable bowel syndrome. *Behavior Modification*, 12, 31–38.

Blanchard, E. B., Scharff, L., Schwarz, S. P., Suls, J. M. & Barlow, D. H. (1990). The role of anxiety and depression in the irritable bowel syndrome. *Behaviour Research and Therapy*, 28, 401–405.

Bland, K. & Hallam, R. S. (1981). Relationship between response to graded exposure and marital satisfaction in agoraphobics. *Behaviour Research and Therapy*, 19, 335–338.

Blowers, C., Cobb, J. & Mathews, A. (1987). Generalised anxiety: A controlled treatment study. *Behaviour Research and Therapy*, 25, 493–502.

Blumenthal, J. A. & Emery, C. F. (1988). Rehabilitation of patients following myocardial infarction. *Journal of Consulting and Clinical Psychology*, 56, 374–381.

Boeke, S., Stronks, D., Verhage, F. & Zwaveling, A. (1991). Psychological variables as predictors of the length of post-operative hospitalization. *Journal of Psychosomatic Research*, 35, 281–288.

Boersma, K., Den Hengst, S., Dekker, J. & Emmelkamp, P. M. G. (1976). Exposure and response prevention in the natural environment: A comparison with obsessive–compulsive patients. *Behaviour Research and Therapy*, 14, 19–24.

Bonn, J. A., Readhead, C. P. A. & Timmons, B. H. (1984). Enhanced adaptive behavioural response in agoraphobic patients pretreated with breathing retraining. *Lancet*, 2, 665–669.

Booth-Kewley, S. & Friedman, H. S. (1987). Psychological predictors of heart disease: A quantitative review. *Psychological Bulletin*, 101, 343–362.

Borden, J. W. & Turner, S. M. (1989). Is panic a unique emotional experience? *Behaviour Research and Therapy*, 27, 263–268.

Borkovec, T. D. (1982). Facilitation and inhibition of functional CS exposure in the treatment of phobias. In J. Boulougouris (Ed.), *Learning Theory Approaches to Psychiatry*. New York: Wiley.

Borkovec, T. D. (1985a). Worry: A potentially valuable concept. *Behaviour Research and Therapy*, 4, 481–482.

Borkovec, T. D. (1985b). The role of cognitive and somatic cues in anxiety and anxiety disorders: Worry and relaxation-induced anxiety. In A. H. Tuma & J. Maser (Eds), *Anxiety and the Anxiety Disorders*. Hillsdale, NJ: Erlbaum.

Borkovec, T. D. & Hu, S. (1990). The effect of worry on cardiovascular response to phobic imagery. *Behaviour Therapy and Research*, 28, 69–73.

Borkovec, T. D. & Inz, J. (1990). The nature of worry in generalized anxiety disorder: A predominance of thought activity. *Behaviour Research and Therapy*, 28, 153–158.

Borkovec, T. D. & Mathews, A. M. (1988). Treatment of nonphobic anxiety disorders: A comparison of nondirective, cognitive, and coping desensitization therapy. *Journal of Consulting and Clinical Psychology*, **56**, 877–884.

Borkovec, T. D., Shaddick, R. & Hopkins, M. (1990). The nature of normal and pathological worry. In D. H. Barlow & R. Rapee (Eds), *Chronic Anxiety and Generalized Anxiety Disorder*. New York: Guildford Press.

Borkovec, T. D., Weerts, T. C. & Bernstein, D. A. (1977). Assessment of anxiety. In A. R. Ciminero, K. S. Calhoun & H. E. Adams (Eds), *Handbook of Behavioral Assessment*. New York: Wiley.

Borkovec, T. D., Robinson, E., Pruzinsky, T. & Depree, J. A. (1983). Preliminary exploration of worry: Some characteristics and processes. *Behaviour Research and Therapy*, **21**, 9–16.

Borkovec, T. D., Mathews, A. M., Chambers, A., Ebrahimi, S., Lytle, R. & Nelson, R. (1987). The effects of relaxation training with cognitive or nondirective therapy and the role of relaxation-induced anxiety in the treatment of generalized anxiety. *Journal of Consulting and Clinical Psychology*, **55**, 883–888.

Boulougouris, J. C. (1977). Variables affecting the behavior modification of obsessive–compulsive patients treated by flooding. In J. C. Boulougouris & A. D. Rabavilas (Eds), *The Treatment of Phobic and Obsessive–Compulsive Disorders*. New York: Pergamon Press.

Boulougouris, J. C., Rabavilas, A. O. & Stefanis, C. (1977). Psychophysiological responses in obsessive–compulsive patients. *Behaviour Research and Therapy*, **15**, 221–230.

Bourdon, K. H., Boyd, J. H., Rae, D. S., Burns, B. J., Thompson, J. W. & Locke, B. Z. (1988). Gender differences in phobias: Results of the ECA community survey. *Journal of Anxiety Disorders*, **2**, 227–241.

Bower, G. H. (1981). Mood and memory. *American Psychologist*, **36**, 129–148.

Bower, G. H. (1987). Commentary on mood and memory. *Behaviour Research and Therapy*, **25**, 443–455.

Boyd, J. H., Burke, J. D., Gruenberg, E., Holzer, C. E., Rae, D. S., George, L. K., Karno, M., Stoltzman, R., McEvoy, L. & Nestadt, G. (1984). Exclusion criteria of DSM-III: A study of co-occurrence of hierarchy-free syndromes. *Archives of General Psychiatry*, **41**, 983–989.

Boyd, J. H., Rae, D. S., Thompson, J. W., Burns, B. J., Boudoun, K., Locke, B. Z. & Regier, D. A. (1990). Phobia: Prevalence and risk factors. *Social Psychiatry and Psychiatric Epidemiology*, **25**, 314–323.

Bozman, A. W. & Beck, J. G. (1991). Covariation of sexual desire and sexual arousal: The effects of anger and anxiety. *Archives of Sexual Behavior*, **20**, 47–60.

Brady, J. P. (1984a). Social skills training for psychiatric patients: I. Concepts, methods and clinical results. *American Journal of Psychiatry*, **141**, 333–340.

Brady, J. P. (1984b). Socials skills training for psychiatric patients: II. Clinical outcome studies. *American Journal of Psychiatry*, **141**, 491–498.

Bregman, E. O. (1934). An attempt to modify the emotional attitudes of infants by the conditioned response technique. *Journal of Genetic Psychology*, **45**, 169–198.

Breslau, N. & Davis, G. C. (1985). Further evidence on the doubtful validity of generalized anxiety disorder. *Psychiatry Research*, **16**, 177.

Brewin, C. R. (1988). *Cognitive Foundations of Clinical Psychology*. London: Erlbaum.

Bridges, K. W. & Goldberg, D. P. (1985). Somatic presentation of DSM-III psychiatric disorders in primary care. *Journal of Psychosomatic Research*, **29**, 563–569.

Brier, A., Charney, D. S. & Heninger, G. R. (1985). The diagnostic utility of anxiety disorders and their relationship to depressive disorders. *American Journal of Psychiatry*, **142**, 787–797.

Broadbent, D. & Broadbent, M. (1988). Anxiety and attentional bias: State and trait. *Cognition and Emotion*, **2**, 165–183.

Brooks, G. R. & Richardson, F. C. (1980). Emotional skills training: A treatment program for duodenal ulcer. *Behavior Therapy*, **11**, 198–207.

Broome, A. K. (1989). *Health Psychology: Process and Applications*. London: Chapman & Hall.

Brown, T. A. & Cash, T. F. (1989). The phenomenon of panic in nonclinical populations: Further evidence and methodological considerations. *Journal of Anxiety Disorders*, **3**, 139–148.

Brown, T. A. & Cash, T. F. (1990). The phenomenon of nonclinical panic: Parameters of panic, fear, and avoidance. *Journal of Anxiety Disorders*, **4**, 15–29.

Bryant, B. & Trower, P. E. (1974). Social difficulty in a student sample. *British Journal of Educational Psychology*, **44**, 13–21.

Buck, R. (1980). Nonverbal behavior and the theory of emotion: The facial feedback hypothesis. *Journal of Personality and Social Psychology*, **38**, 811–824.

Buck, R. (1988). *Human Motivation and Emotion*, 2nd Edn. New York: Wiley.

Buglass, D., Clarke, J., Henderson, A. S., Kreitman, N. & Presley, A. S. (1977). A study of agoraphobic housewives. *Psychological Medicine*, **7**, 73–86.

Burgess, A. W., Lerner, D. J., D'Agostino, R. B., Vokanas, P. S., Hartman, C. R. & Gaccione, P. (1987). A randomised control trial of cardiac rehabilitation. *Social Science and Medicine*, **24**, 359–370.

Burgess, I. S., Jones, L. M., Robertson, S. A., Radcliffe, W. N. & Emerson, E. (1981). The degree of control exerted by phobic and non-phobic verbal stimuli over the recognition behavior of phobic and non-phobic subjects. *Behaviour Research and Therapy*, **19**, 233–243.

Burns, B. J. & Thorpe, G. L. (1977). The epidemiology of fears and phobias (with particular reference to the National Survey of Agoraphobics). *Journal of International Medical Research*, **5**, 1–7.

Buss, A. H. (1980). *Self-consciousness and Social Anxiety*. San Francisco, CA: W. H. Freeman.

Butler, G. (1985). Exposure as a treatment for social phobia: Some instructive difficulties. *Behaviour Research and Therapy*, **23**, 651–657.

Butler, G. & Anastasiades, P. (1988). Predicting response to anxiety management in patients with generalised anxiety disorder. *Behaviour Research and Therapy*, **26**, 531–534.

Butler, G., Cullington, A., Munby, M., Amies, P. & Gelder, M. (1984). Exposure and anxiety management in the treatment of social phobia. *Journal of Consulting and Clinical Psychology*, **52**, 642–650.

Butler, G., Cullington, A., Hibbert, G., Klimes, I. & Gelder, M. (1987a). Anxiety management for persistent generalised anxiety. *British Journal of Psychiatry*, **151**, 535–542.

Butler, G., Gelder, M., Hibbert, G., Cullington, A. & Klimes, I. (1987b). Anxiety management: Developing effective strategies. *Behaviour Research and Therapy*, **25**, 517–522.

Butler, G., Fennell, M., Robson, P. & Gelder, M. (1991). Comparison of behavior therapy and cognitive behavior therapy in the treatment of generalized anxiety disorder. *Journal of Consulting and Clinical Psychology*, **59**, 167–175.

Cacioppo, J. T., Glass, C. R. & Merluzzi, T. V. (1979). Self-statements and self-evaluations: A cognitive-response analysis of heterosocial anxiety. *Cognitive Therapy and Research*, **3**, 249–262.

Caird, W. K. & Wincze, J. P. (1974). Videotaped desensitisation of frigidity. *Journal of Behavior Therapy and Experimental Psychiatry*, **5**, 175–178.

Cameron, O. G., Thyer, B. A., Nesse, R. M. & Curtis, G. C. (1986). Symptom profile of patients with DSM-III anxiety disorders. *American Journal of Psychiatry*, **143**, 1133–1137.

Cannon, W. B. (1927). The James–Lange theory of emotion: A critical examination and an alternative theory. *American Journal of Psychology*, **39**, 106–124. Reprinted in M. Arnold (Ed.), *The Nature of Emotion*. Harmondsworth: Penguin, 1968.

Canter, A., Kondo, C. Y. & Knott, J. R. (1975). A comparison of EMG feedback and progressive muscle relaxation training in anxiety neurosis. *British Journal of Psychiatry*, **127**, 470–477.

Carr, A. T. (1974). Compulsive neurosis: A review of the literature. *Psychological Bulletin*, **81**, 311–318.

Carr, A. T. (1979). The psychopathology of fear. In W. Sluckin (Ed.), *Fear in Animals and Man*. New York: Van Nostrand Reinhold.

Carter, W. R., Johnson, M. C. & Borkovec, T. D. (1986). Worry: An electrocortical analysis. *Advances in Behaviour Research and Therapy*, **8**, 193–204.

Cattell, R. B. & Scheier, I. H. (1961). *The Meaning and Measurement of Neuroticism and Anxiety*. New York: Ronald Press.

Cay, E. L., Vetter, N. J., Philip, A. E. & Dugard, P. (1972a). Psychological status during recovery from an acute heart attack. *Journal of Psychosomatic Research*, **16**, 425–435.

Cay, E. L., Vetter, N. J., Philip, A. E. & Dugard, P. (1972b). Psychological reactions to a Coronary Care Unit. *Journal of Psychosomatic Research*, **16**, 437–447.

Cerny, J. A. (1978). Biofeedback and the voluntary control of sexual arousal in women. *Behavior Therapy*, **9**, 847–855.

Cerny, J. A., Himadi, W. G. & Barlow, D. H. (1984). Issues in diagnosing anxiety disorders. *Journal of Behavioral Assessment*, **6**, 301–330.

Cerny, J. A., Barlow, D. H., Craske, M. & Himadi, W. G. (1987). Couples treatment of agoraphobia: A two-year follow-up. *Behavior Therapy*, **18**, 401–415.

Chambless, D. L. (1982). Characteristics of agoraphobia. In D. L. Chambless & A. J. Goldstein (Eds), *Agoraphobia*. New York: Wiley.

Chambless, D. L. (1991). Spacing of exposure sessions in treatment of agoraphobia and simple phobia. *Behavior Therapy*, **21**, 217–229.

Chambless, D. L. & Goldstein, A. J. (1981). Clinical treatment of agoraphobia. In M. Mavissakalian & D. H. Barlow (Eds), *Phobia. Psychological and Pharmacological Treatment*. New York: Guildford Press.

Chambless, D. L. & Goldstein, A. J. (Eds) (1982). *Agoraphobia*. New York: Wiley.

Chambless, D. L. & Gracely, E. J. (1988). Prediction of outcome following *in vivo* exposure treatment of agoraphobia. In I. Hand & H-U. Wittchen (Eds), *Panic and Phobias. 2. Treatment and Variables Affecting Course and Outcome*. Berlin: Springer-Verlag.

Chambless, D. L. & Gracely, E. J. (1989). Fear of fear and the anxiety disorders. *Cognitive Therapy and Research*, **13**, 9–20.

Chambless, D. L., Caputo, C., Bright, P. & Gallagher, R. (1984). Assessment of fear of fear in agoraphobics: The Body Sensation Questionnaire and the Agoraphobic Cognitions Questionnaire. *Journal of Consulting and Clinical Psychology*, **62**, 1090–1097.

Chambless, D. L., Caputo, C., Jasin, S., Gracely, E. & Williams, C. (1985). The mobility inventory for agoraphobia. *Behaviour Research and Therapy*, **23**, 35–44.

Chambless, D. L., Beck, A. T., Gracely, E. J. & Bibb, J. L. (1990). The relationship of cognition to fear of somatic symptoms: A test of the cognitive theory of panic (unpublished manuscript).

Chan, D. W. (1990). The Maudsley Obsessional–Compulsive Inventory: A psychometric investigation on Chinese normal subjects. *Behaviour Research and Therapy*, **28**, 413–420.

Charney, D. S., Heninger, G. R. & Breier, A. (1984). Noradrenergic function in panic anxiety. *Archives of General Psychiatry*, **41**, 751.

Charney, D. S., Heninger, G. R. & Jatlow, P. I. (1985). Increased anxiogenic effects of caffeine in panic disorders. *Archives of General Psychiatry*, **42**, 233–243.

Cheek, J. M. & Buss, A. H. (1981). Shyness and sociability. *Journal of Personality and Social Psychology*, **41**, 330–339.

Christodoulou, G. N., Alevizos, B. H. & Konstantakakis, E. (1983). Peptic ulcer in adults. Psychopathological, environmental, characterological and hereditary factors. *Psychotherapy and Psychosomatics*, **39**, 55–62.

Clark, D. M. (1986). A cognitive approach to panic. *Behaviour Research and Therapy*, **24**, 461–470.

Clark, D. M. (1988). A cognitive model of panic attacks. In S. Rachman & J. D. Maser (Eds), *Panic. Psychological Perspectives*. Hillsdale, NJ: Erlbaum.

Clark, D. M. & Hemsely, D. R. (1982). The effects of hyperventilation: Individual variability and its relation to personality. *Journal of Behavior Therapy and Experimental Psychiatry*, **13**, 41–47.

Clark, D. M. & Salkovskis, P. M. (1991). *Cognitive Therapy for Panic and Hypochondriasis*. New York: Pergamon Press.

Clark, D. M., Salkovskis, P. M. & Chalkley, A. J. (1985). Respiratory control as a treatment for panic attacks. *Journal of Behavior Therapy and Experimental Psychiatry*, **16**, 23–30.

Clark, D. M., Salkovskis, P. M., Gelder, M., Koehler, C., Martin, M., Anastasiades, P., Hackmann, A., Middleton, H. & Jeavons, A. (1988). Tests of a cognitive theory of panic. In I. Hand & H.-U. Wittchen (Eds), *Panic and Phobias. 2. Treatment and Variables Affecting Course and Outcome*. Berlin: Springer-Verlag.

Clark, J. V. & Arkowitz, H. (1975). Social anxiety and self-evaluation of interpersonal performance. *Psychological Reports*, **36**, 211–221.

Cloninger, C. R., Martin, R. L., Clayton, P. & Guze, J. B. (1981). A blind follow-up and family study of anxiety neurosis: Preliminary analysis of the St Louis 500. In D. F. Klein & J. Rabkin (Eds), *Anxiety: New Research and Changing Concepts*. New York: Raven Press.

Clum, G. A. (1989). Psychological interventions vs drugs in the treatment of panic. *Behavior Therapy*, **20**, 429–457.

Clum, G. A., Broyles, S., Borden, J. & Watkins, P. L. (1990). Validity and reliability of the panic attack symptoms and cognitions questionnaire. *Journal of Psychopathology and Behavioral Assessment*, **12**, 233–247.

Cluss, P. A. & Fireman, P. (1985). Recent trends in asthma research. *Annals of Behavioral Medicine*, **7**, 11–16.

Cobb, J., McDonald, R., Marks, I. M. & Stern, R. (1980). Marital versus exposure therapy: Psychological treatments of existing marital and phobic obsessive problems. *Behavioural Analysis and Modification*, **4**, 3–16.

Cobb, J. P., Mathews, A. M., Childs-Clarke, A. & Blowers, C. M. (1984). The spouse as co-therapist in the treatment of agoraphobia. *British Journal of Psychiatry*, **144**, 282–287.

Cohen, A. S., Barlow, D. H. & Blanchard, E. B. (1985). Psychophysiology of relaxation-associated panic attacks. *Journal of Abnormal Psychology*, **94**, 96–101.

Cohen, F. (1979). Personality, stress, and the development of physical illness. In G. C. Stone, F. Cohen & N. E. Adler (Eds), *Health Psychology*. San Francisco, CA: Jossey-Bass.

Cohen, F. & Lazarus, R. S. (1973). Active coping processes, coping dispositions, and recovery from surgery. *Psychosomatic Medicine*, **35**, 375–389.

Cohen, F. & Lazarus, R. S. (1979). Coping with the stresses of illness. In G. C. Stone, F. Cohen & N. E. Adler (Eds), *Health Psychology: A Handbook*. San Francisco, CA: Jossey-Bass.

Cohen, S. D., Monteiro, W. & Marks, I. (1984). Two-year follow-up of agoraphobics after exposure and imipramine. *British Journal of Psychiatry*, **144**, 276–281.

Cone, J. D. (1979). Confounded comparisons in triple response mode assessment research. *Behavioral Assessment*, **1**, 85–95.

Connolly, J., Hallam, R. S. & Marks, I. M. (1976). Selective association of fainting with blood–injury–illness fear. *Behavior Therapy*, **7**, 8–13.

Conte, H. R. (1983). Development and use of self-report techniques for assessing sexual functioning: A review and critique. *Archives of Sexual Behavior*, **12**, 555–576.

Conte, H. R. (1986). Multivariate assessment of sexual dysfunction. *Journal of Consulting and Clinical Psychology*, **54**, 149–157.

Cook, I. J., van Eeden, A. & Collins, S. M. (1987). Patients with irritable bowel syndrome have greater pain tolerance than normal subjects. *Gastroenterology*, **93**, 727–733.

Cook, M. & Mineka, S. (1989). Observational conditioning of fear to fear-relevant versus fear-irrelevant stimuli in rhesus monkeys. *Journal of Abnormal Psychology*, **98**, 448–459.

Cook, M., Mineka, S., Wolkenstein, B. & Laitsch, K. (1985). Observational conditioning of snake fear in unrelated rhesus monkeys. *Journal of Abnormal Psychology*, **94**, 591–610.

Cooper, A. J. (1969). A clinical study of 'coital anxiety' in male potency disorders. *Journal of Psychosomatic Research*, **13**, 143–147.

Cooper, J. (1970). The Leyton Obsessional Inventory. *Psychological Medicine*, **1**, 48–64.

Cooper, J. & Kelleher, M. (1973). The Leyton Obsessional Inventory: A principal component analysis on normal subjects. *Psychological Medicine*, **3**, 204–208.

Cooper, J. E., Gelder, M. G. & Marks, I. (1965). Results of behaviour therapy in 77 psychiatric patients. *British Medical Journal*, **i**, 1222–1225.

Corah, N. L. (1969). Development of a dental anxiety scale. *Journal of Dental Research*, **48**, 196.

Corah, N. L., Gale, E. N. & Illig, S. J. (1979a). Psychological stress reduction during dental procedures. *Journal of Dental Research*, **58**, 1347–1351.

Corah, N. L., Gale, E. N. & Illig, S. J. (1979b). The use of relaxation and distraction to reduce psychological stress during dental procedures. *Journal of the American Dental Association*, **98**, 390–394.

Corah, N. L., Gale, E. N., Pace, L. F. & Seyrek, S. K. (1981). Relaxation and musical programming as a means of reducing psychological stress during dental procedures. *Journal of the American Dental Association*, **103**, 232–234.

Costa, P. T. Jr (1986). Is neuroticism a risk factor for CAD? Is Type A a measure of neuroticism? In T. H. Schmidt, T. M. Dembroski & G. Blumchen (Eds), *Biological and Psychological Factors in Cardiovascular Disease*. Berlin: Springer-Verlag.

Costa, P. T. Jr & McCrae, R. R. (1980). Somatic complaints in males as a function of age and neuroticism: A longitudinal analysis. *Journal of Behavioral Medicine*, **3**, 245–257.

Costa, P. T. Jr & McCrae, R. R. (1985). Hypochondriasis, neuroticism and aging. When are somatic complaints unfounded? *American Psychologist*, **40**, 19–28.

Costa, P. T. Jr & McCrae, R. R. (1987). Neuroticism, somatic complaints, and disease: Is the bark worse than the bite? *Journal of Personality*, **55**, 299–316.

Costello, C. G., Devins, G. M. & Ward, K. W. (1988). The prevalence of fears, phobias and anxiety disorders and their relationship with depression in women attending family physicians. *Behaviour Research and Therapy*, **26**, 311–320.

Cottraux, J., Bouvard, M., Defayolle, M. & Messy, P. (1988). Validity and factor structure of the Compulsive Activity Checklist. *Behavior Therapy*, **19**, 45–53.

Cowan, G. S., Conger, J. C. & Conger, A. J. (1989). Social competency and social perceptivity in self and others. *Journal of Psychopathology and Behavioral Assessment*, **11**, 129–142.

Cox, B. J., Endler, N. S. & Swinson, R. P. (1991). Clinical and nonclinical panic attacks: An empirical test of a panic–anxiety continuum. *Journal of Anxiety Disorders*, **5**, 21–34.

Cox, D. J., Freundlich, A. & Meyer, R. G. (1975). Differential effectiveness of electromyographic feedback, verbal relaxation instructions, and medication placebo with tension headaches. *Journal of Consulting and Clinical Psychology*, **43**, 892–898.

Cragan, M. & Deffenbacher, J. (1984). Anxiety management training and relaxation as self-control in the treatment of generalized anxiety in medical outpatients. *Journal of Counseling Psychology*, **31**, 123–131.

Craske, M. G. & Barlow, D. H. (1988). A review of the relationship between panic and avoidance. *Clinical Psychology Review*, **8**, 667–685.

Craske, M. & Barlow, D. H. (1989). Nocturnal panic. *Journal of Nervous and Mental Disease*, **177**, 160–168.

Craske, M. G. & Barlow, D. H. (1990). Nocturnal panic: Response to hyperventilation and carbon dioxide challenge. *Journal of Abnormal Psychology*, **99**, 302–307.

Craske, M. G. & Krueger, M. T. (1990). Prevalence of nocturnal panic in a college population. *Journal of Anxiety Disorders*, **4**, 125–139.

Craske, M. G., Brown, T. A. & Barlow, D. H. (1991). Behavioral treatment of panic disorder: A two-year follow-up. *Behavior Therapy* (in press).

Craske, M. G., Rachman, S. J. & Tallman, K. (1986). Mobility, cognitions and panic. *Journal of Psychopathology and Behavioral Assessment*, **25**, 117–122.

Craske, M. G., Sanderson, W. C. & Barlow, D. H. (1987). How do synchronous response systems relate to the treatment of agoraphobia: A follow-up evaluation. *Behaviour Research and Therapy*, **25**, 117–122.

Craske, M. G., Rapee, R. M., Jackel, L. & Barlow, D. H. (1989). Qualitative dimensions of worry in DSM-III-R generalized anxiety disorder subjects and nonanxious controls. *Behaviour Research and Therapy*, **27**, 397–402.

Craske, M. G., Miller, P. P., Rotunda, R. & Barlow, D. H. (1990). A descriptive report of features of initial unexpected panic attacks in minimal and extensive avoiders. *Behaviour Research and Therapy*, **28**, 395–400.

Creed, F. H. & Guthrie, E. (1989). Psychological treatment in the irritable bowel syndrome: A review. *Gut*, **30**, 1601–1609.

Creer, T. L. (1982). Asthma. *Journal of Consulting and Clinical Psychology*, **50**, 912–921.

Creer, T. L. (1988). Asthma. In W. Linden (Ed.), *Biological Barriers in Behavioral Medicine*. New York: Plenum.

Creer, T. L. & Wigal, J. K. (1989). Respiratory disorders. In S. Pearce & J. Wardle (Eds), *The Practice of Behavioural Medicine*. Oxford: Oxford University Press/BPS Books.

Crisp, A. H., Queenan, M. & D'Souza, M. F. (1984). Myocardial infarction and the emotional climate. *Lancet*, 17 March, pp. 616–619.

Crow, R. R., Noyes, R., Pauls, D. L. & Slymen, D. J. (1983). A family study of panic disorder. *Archives of General Psychiatry*, **40**, 1065–1069.

Curran, J. P. (1975). Social skills training and systematic desensitization in reducing dating anxiety. *Behaviour Research and Therapy*, **13**, 65–68.

Curran, J. P. (1977). Skills training as an approach to the treatment of heterosexual–social anxiety: A review. *Psychological Bulletin*, **54**, 140–157.

Curran, J. P. (1982). A procedure for assessing social skills: The Simulated Social Interaction Test. In J. P. Curran & P. M. Monti (Eds), *Social Skills Training: A Practical Handbook for Assessment and Treatment*. New York: Guildford Press.

Curran, J. P., Miller, T. W., Zwick, W. R., Monti, P. M. & Stout, R. L. (1980a). The social inadequate patient: Incidence rates, demographic and clinical features, and hospital and posthospital functioning. *Journal of Consulting and Clinical Psychology*, **48**, 375–382.

Curran, J. P., Monti, P. M., Corriveau, D. P., Hay, L. R., Hagerman, S., Zwick, Q. R. & Farrell, A. D. (1980b). The generalizability of a procedure for assessing social skills and social anxiety in a psychiatric population. *Behavioral Assessment*, **2**, 389–401.

Curran, J. P., Wallander, J. L. & Fischetti, M. (1980c). The importance of behavioral and cognitive factors in heterosexual–social anxiety. *Journal of Personality*, **48**, 285–292.

Curtis, G. & Thyer, B. (1983). Fainting on exposure to phobic stimuli. *American Journal of Psychiatry*, **140**, 771–774.

Dahlquist, L. M., Gil, K. M., Armstrong, F. D., DeLawyer, D. D., Greene, P. & Wuori, D. (1986). Preparing children for medical examinations: The importance of previous medical experience. *Health Psychology*, **5**, 249–259.

Dalgleish, T. & Watts, F. (1990). Biases of attention and memory in disorders of anxiety and depression. *Clinical Psychology Review*, **10**, 589–604.

Daly, S. (1978). Behavioural correlates of social anxiety. *British Journal of Social and Clinical Psychology*, **17**, 117–120.

Darwin, C. (1873). *The Expression of Emotion in Man and Animals*, London: Murray. (Reprinted University of Chicago Press, Chicago, 1965.)

Davey, G. C. L. (Ed.) (1987). *Cognitive Processes and Pavlovian Conditioning in Humans*. New York: Wiley.

Davis, C. M., Yarber, W. L. & Davis, S. L. (1988). *Sexuality-related Measures: A Compendium*. Lake Mills, IO: Graphic Publishing.

Deffenbacher, J. L. (1980). Worry and emotionality. In I. G. Sarason (Ed.), *Test Anxiety: Theory, Research and Applications*. Hillsdale, NJ: Erlbaum.

Deffenbacher, J. L. & Suinn, R. M. (1987). Generalized anxiety syndrome. In L. Michelson & L. M. Ascher (Eds), *Anxiety and Stress Disorders. Cognitive– Behavioral Assessment and Treatment*. New York: Guildford Press.

Dekker, J. & Everaerd, W. (1988). Attentional effects on sexual arousal. *Psychophysiology*, **25**, 45–54.

Dekker, J. & Everaerd, W. (1989). Psychological determinants of sexual arousal: A review. *Behaviour Research and Therapy*, **27**, 353–364.

Dellipiani, A. W., Cay, E. L., Philip, A. E., Vetter, N. J., Colling, W. A., Donaldson, R. J. & McCormack, P. (1976). Anxiety after a heart attack. *British Medical Journal*, **38**, 752–757.

Delprato, D. J. (1980). Hereditary determinants of fears and phobias: A critical review. *Behavior Therapy*, **11**, 79–103.

Delprato, D. J. & McGlynn, F. D. (1984). Behavioral theories of anxiety disorders.

In S. M. Turner (Ed.), *Behavioral Theories and Treatment of Anxiety*. New York: Plenum Press.

Deltito, J. A., Argyle, N., Buller, R., Nutzinger, D., Ottosson, J-O., Brandon, S., Mellegard, M. & Shera, D. (1991). The sequence of improvement of the symptoms encountered in patients with panic disorder. *Comprehensive Psychiatry*, **32**, 120–129.

de Ruiter, C., Garssen, B., Rijken, H. & Kraaimaat, F. (1989a). The hyperventilation syndrome in panic disorder, agoraphobia and generalized anxiety disorder. *Behaviour Research and Therapy*, **27**, 447–452.

de Ruiter, C., Rijken, H., Garssen, B. & Kraaimaat, F. (1989b). Breathing retraining, exposure and a combination of both, in the treatment of panic disorder with agoraphobia. *Behaviour Research and Therapy*, **27**, 647–655.

de Ruiter, C., Rijken, H., Garssen, B., Schaik van, A. & Kraaimaat, F. (1989c). Comorbidity among the anxiety disorders. *Journal of Anxiety Disorders*, **3**, 57–68.

de Silva, P. (1986). Obsessive–compulsive imagery. *Behaviour Research and Therapy*, **24**, 333–350.

de Silva, P. & Rachman, S. (1984). Does escape behaviour strengthen agoraphobic avoidance? A preliminary study. *Behaviour Research and Therapy*, **22**, 87–91.

de Silva, P., Rachman, S. & Seligman, M. E. P. (1977). Prepared phobias and obsessions: therapeutic outcome. *Behaviour Research and Therapy*, **15**, 65–77.

Dewey, D. & Hunsley, J. (1990). The effects of marital adjustment and spouse involvement on the behavioral treatment of agoraphobia: A meta-analytic review. *Anxiety Research*, **2**, 69–83.

Dimburg, U. (1987). Facial reactions, autonomic activity, and experienced emotion: A three component model of emotional conditioning. *Biological Psychology*, **24**, 105–122.

DiNardo, P. A. & Barlow, D. H. (1990). Syndrome and symptom co-occurrence in the anxiety disorders. In J. D. Maser & C. R. Cloninger (Eds), *Comorbidity of Mood and Anxiety Disorders*. Washington, DC: American Psychiatric Press.

DiNardo, P. A., Guzy, L. T. & Bak, R. M. (1988a). Anxiety response patterns and etiological factors in dog-fearful and non-fearful subjects. *Behaviour Research and Therapy*, **26**, 245–251.

DiNardo, P. A., O'Brien, G. T., Barlow, D. H., Waddell, M. & Blanchard, E. B. (1983). Reliability of DSM-III anxiety disorder categories using a new structured interview. *Archives of General Psychiatry*, **40**, 1070–1074.

DiNardo, P. A., Barlow, D. H., Cerny, J. A., Vermilyea, B. B., Himadi, W. G. & Waddell, M. T. (1985). *Anxiety Disorders Interview Schedule Revised (ADIS-R)*. Albany, NY: Center for Stress and Anxiety Disorders.

DiNardo, P. A., Guzy, L. T., Jenkins, J. A., Bak, R. M., Tomasi, S. F. & Copland, M. (1988b). Etiology and maintenance of dog fears. *Behaviour Research and Therapy*, **26**, 241–244.

Dirks, J. F. & Kinsman, R. A. (1981). Clinical prediction of medical rehospitalisation: Psychological assessment with the battery of Asthma Illness Behavior. *Journal of Personality Assessment*, **45**, 608–613.

Dirks, J. F., Jones, N. F. & Kinsman, R. A. (1977). Panic fear: A personality dimension related to intractability in asthma. *Psychosomatic Medicine*, **39**, 120–126.

Dixhoorn, van A., De Loos, J. & Duivenvoorden, H. J. (1983). Contribution of relaxation technique training to the rehabilitation of myocardial infarction patients. *Psychotherapy and Psychosomatics*, **40**, 137–147.

Dixhoorn, van A., Duivenvoorden, H. J., Pool, J. & Verhage, F. (1990). Psychic effects of physical training and relaxation therapy after myocardial infarction. *Journal of Psychosomatic Research*, **34**, 327–337.

Dixon, N. F. (1981). *Preconscious Processing*. Chichester: Wiley.

Dodge, C. S., Hope, D. A., Heimberg, R. G. & Becker, R. E. (1988). Evaluation of the social interaction self-statement test with a social phobic population. *Cognitive Therapy and Research*, **12**, 211–222.

Doehrman, S. R. (1977). Psychosocial aspects of recovery from coronary heart disease: A review. *Social Science and Medicine*, **11**, 199–218.

Dollard, J. & Miller, N. E. (1950). *Personality and Psychotherapy: An Analysis in Terms of Learning, Thinking and Culture*. New York: McGraw-Hill.

Donnell, C. D. & McNally, R. J. (1989). Anxiety sensitivity and history of panic as predictors of response to hyperventilation. *Behaviour Research and Therapy*, **27**, 325–332.

Donnell, C. D. & McNally, R. J. (1990). Anxiety sensitivity and panic attacks in a nonclinical population. *Behaviour Research and Therapy*, **28**, 83–85.

Drossman, D. A., McKee, D. C., Sandler, R. S., Mitchell, C. M., Cramer, E. M., Lowman, B. R. & Burger, A. L. (1988). Psychosocial factors in the irritable bowel syndrome: A multivariate study of patients and non-patients with irritable bowel syndrome. *Gastroenterology*, **95**, 701–708.

Dube, S., Jones, D. A., Bell, J., Davies, A., Ross, E. & Sitaram, N. (1986). Interface of panic and depression: Clinical and sleep EEG correlates. *Psychiatry Research*, **19**, 119–133.

Durham, R. C. & Turvey, A. A. (1987). Cognitive therapy vs behaviour therapy in the treatment of chronic general anxiety. *Behaviour Research and Therapy*, **25**, 229–234.

Duval, S. & Wicklund, R. A. (1972). *A Therapy of Objective Self-Awareness*. New York: Academic Press.

Eaton, W. W. & Keyl, P. M. (1990). Risk factors for the onset of diagnostic interview schedule DSM-III agoraphobia in a prospective, population-based study. *Archives of General Psychiatry*, **47**, 819–824.

Eaton, W. W., Kramer, M., Anthony, J. C., Dryman, A., Shapiro, S. & Locke, B. Z. (1989). The incidence of specific DIS/DSM-III mental disorders: Data from the NIMH Epidemiologic Catchment Area Program. *Acta Psychiatrica Scandinavica*, **79**, 163–178.

Edelmann, R. J. (1985a). Dealing with embarrassing events: Socially anxious and non-socially anxious groups compared. *British Journal of Clinical Psychology*, **24**, 281–288.

Edelmann, R. J. (1985b). Individual differences in embarrassment: Self-consciousness, self-monitoring and embarrassibility. *Personality and Individual Differences*, **6**, 223–230.

Edelmann, R. J. (1987). *The Psychology of Embarrassment*. Chichester: Wiley.

Edelmann, R. J. (1990a). Chronic blushing, self-consciousness and social anxiety. *Journal of Psychopathology and Behavioral Assessment*, **12**, 119–127.

Edelmann, R. J. (1990b). *Coping with Blushing*. London: Sheldon Press.

Edelmann, R. J. (1991). Correlates of chronic blushing. *British Journal of Clinical Psychology*, **30**, 177–178.

Edelmann, R. J. & McCusker, G. (1986). Introversion, neuroticism, empathy and embarrassibility. *Personality and Individual Differences*, **7**, 133–140.

Edmonson, H. D., Gordon, P. H., Lloyd, J. M., Meesan, J. E. & Whitehead, F. I. H. (1978). Vasovagal episodes in the dental surgery. *Journal of Dentistry*, **6**, 189–195.

Egbert, L. D., Battit, G. E., Welch, C. E. & Bartlett, M. K. (1964). Reduction of postoperative pain by encouragement and instruction of patients. *The New England Journal of Medicine*, **270**, 825–827.

Ehlers, A. & Margraf, J. (1989). The psychophysiological model of panic attacks, In P. M. G. Emmelkamp, W. T. A. M. Everaerd, F. Kraaimaat & M. J. M. von Son (Eds), *Fresh Perspectives on Anxiety Disorders.* Amsterdam: Swets & Zeitlinger.

Ehlers, A., Margraf, J. & Roth, W. T. (1986). Experimental induction of panic attacks. In I. Hand & H.-U. Wittchen (Eds), *Panic and Phobias.* Berlin: Springer-Verlag.

Ehlers, A., Margraf, J. & Roth, W. T. (1988b). Selective information processing, interoception, and panic attacks. In I. Hand & H.-U. Wittchen (Eds), *Panic and Phobias 2. Treatment and Variables Affecting Course and Outcome.* Berlin: Springer-Verlag.

Ehlers, A., Margraf, J., Davies, S. & Roth, W. T. (1988a). Selective processing of threat cues in subjects with panic attacks. *Cognition and Emotion,* **2**, 201–219.

Eifert, G. H. (1990). The acquisition and cognitive–behavioral therapy of phobic anxiety. In G. H. Eifert & I. M. Evans (Eds), *Unifying Behavior Therapy: Contributions of Paradigmatic Behaviorism.* New York: Springer-Verlag.

Eiser, C. (1988). Do children benefit from psychological preparation for hospitalization? *Psychology and Health,* **2**, 133–138.

Ekman, P., Friesen, W. V. & Ellsworth, P. (1982). What emotion categories or dimensions can observers judge from facial behavior? In P. Ekman (Ed.), *Emotions in the Human Face,* 2nd edn. Cambridge: Cambridge University Press.

Elkins, P. D. & Roberts, M. C. (1983). Psychological preparation for pediatric hospitalization. *Clinical Psychology Review,* **3**, 275–295.

Elkins, P. D. & Roberts, M. C. (1985). Reducing medical fears in a general population of children: A comparison of three audio-visual modeling procedures. *Journal of Pediatric Psychology,* **10**, 67–75.

Ellis, A. (1962). *Reason and Emotion in Psychotherapy.* New York: Lyle Stuart.

Ellis, A. (1979). The theory of rational–emotive therapy. In A. Ellis & J. M. Whitely (Eds), *Theoretical and Empirical Foundations of Rational Emotive Therapy.* Monterey, CA: Brooks/Cole.

Ellis, A. & Harper, R. A. (1975). *A New Guide to Rational Living.* Englewood Cliffs, NJ: Prentice-Hall.

Elmore, R., Wildman, R. & Westefeld, J. (1980). The use of systematic desensitization in the treatment of blood phobia. *Journal of Behavior Therapy and Experimental Psychiatry,* **11**, 277–279.

Emmelkamp, P. M. G. (1974). Self-observation vs flooding in the treatment of agoraphobia. *Behaviour Research and Therapy,* **12**, 229–237.

Emmelkamp, P. M. G. (1980). Agoraphobics' interpersonal problems. *Archives of General Psychiatry,* **37**, 1303–1306.

Emmelkamp, P. M. G. (1982). *Phobic and Obsessive–Compulsive Disorders: Theory, Research and Practice.* New York: Plenum Press.

Emmelkamp, P. M. G. (1987). Obsessive–compulsive disorders. In L. Michelson & L. M. Ascher (Eds), *Anxiety and Stress Disorders. Cognitive–Behavioral Assessment and Treatment.* New York: Guildford Press.

Emmelkamp, P. M. G. (1988). Phobic disorders. In C. G. Last & M. Hersen (Eds), *Handbook of Anxiety Disorders.* New York: Pergamon Press.

Emmelkamp, P. M. G. & Emmelkamp-Benner, A. (1975). Modelling and group treatment with self-observation in agoraphobics. *Behaviour Research and Therapy,* **13**, 135–139.

Emmelkamp, P. M. G. & Kraanen, J. (1977). Therapist controlled exposure *in vivo* versus self-controlled exposure *in vivo*: A comparison with obsessive–compulsive patients. *Behaviour Research and Therapy,* **15**, 491–495.

Emmelkamp, P. M. G. & Kuipers, A. C. M. (1979). Agoraphobia: A follow-up study four years after treatment. *British Journal of Psychiatry*, **134**, 352–355.

Emmelkamp, P. M. G. & Kwee, K. G. (1977). Obsessional ruminations: A comparison between thought stopping and prolonged exposure in imagination. *Behaviour Research and Therapy*, **15**, 441–444.

Emmelkamp, P. M. G. & de Lange, I. (1983). Spouse involvement in the treatment of obsessive–compulsive patients. *Behaviour Research and Therapy*, **21**, 341–346.

Emmelkamp, P. M. G. & Mersch, P. P. (1982). Cognition and exposure *in vivo* in the treatment of agoraphobia: Short term and delayed effects. *Cognitive Therapy and Research*, **6**, 77–88.

Emmelkamp, P. M. G. & Ultee, K. A. (1974). A comparison of 'successive approximation' and 'self-observation' in the treatment of agoraphobia. *Behavior Therapy*, **5**, 606–613.

Emmelkamp, P. M. G. & Wessels, H. (1975). Flooding in imagination vs. flooding *in vivo*: A comparison with agoraphobics. *Behaviour Research and Therapy*, **13**, 7–15.

Emmelkamp, P. M. G., de Haan, E. & Hoogduin, C. A. L. (1990). Marital adjustment and obsessive–compulsive disorder. *British Journal of Psychiatry*, **156**, 55–60.

Emmelkamp, P. M. G., Kuipers, A. C. M. & Eggeraat, J. G. (1978). Cognitive modification versus prolonged exposure *in vivo*: A comparison with agoraphobics as subject. *Behaviour Research and Therapy*, **16**, 33–41.

Emmelkamp, P. M. G., Visser, S. & Hoekstra, R. J. (1988). Cognitive therapy vs exposure *in vivo* in the treatment of obsessive–compulsives. *Cognitive Therapy and Research*, **12**, 103–114.

Emmelkamp, P. M. G., van de Helm, M., van Zanten, B. & Plochg, I. (1980). Contributions of self-instructional training to the effectiveness of exposure *in vivo*: A comparison with obsessive–compulsive patients. *Behaviour Research and Therapy*, **18**, 61–66.

Emmelkamp, P. M. G., Mersch, P. P., Vissia, E. & van der Helm, M. (1985). Social phobia: A comparative evaluation of cognitive and behavioural interventions. *Behaviour Research and Therapy*, **23**, 365–369.

Emmelkamp, P. M. G., Brilman, E., Kuiper, H. & Mersch, P. P. (1986). The treatment of agoraphobia: A comparison of self-instructional training, rational emotive therapy and exposure *in vivo*. *Behavior Modification*, **10**, 37–53.

Emmelkamp, P. M. G., van Linden van den Heuvell, C., Ruphan, M. & Sanderman, R. (1989). Home-based treatment of obsessive–compulsive patients: intersession interval and therapist involvement. *Behaviour Research and Therapy*, **27**, 89–93.

Engel, G. (1978). Psychologic stress, vasodepressor (vasovagal) syncope and sudden death. *Annals of Internal Medicine*, **89**, 403–412.

English, H. B. (1929). Three cases of the 'conditioned fear response'. *Journal of Abnormal and Social Psychology*, **24**, 221–225.

Esler, D. M. & Goulston, K. J. (1973). Levels of anxiety in colonic disorders. *New England Journal of Medicine*, **288**, 16–20.

Everaerd, W. T. A. M. (1989). Sexual anxiety. In P. M. G. Emmelkamp, W. T. A. M. Everaerd, F. Kraaimaat & M. J. M. van Son (Eds), *Fresh Perspectives on Anxiety Disorders*. Amsterdam: Swets & Zeitlinger.

Everaerd, W. & Dekker, J. (1982). Treatment of secondary orgasmic dysfunction: a comparison of systematic desensitisation and sex therapy. *Behaviour Research and Therapy*, **20**, 269–274.

Everaerd, W. & Dekker, J. (1985). Treatment of male sexual dysfunction: Sex therapy compared with systematic desensitization and Rational Emotive Therapy. *Behaviour Research and Therapy*, **23**, 13–25.

Everaerd, W. T., Rijken, H. M. & Emmelkamp, P. M. G. (1973). Successive approximation and self-observation in the treatment of agoraphobia. *Behaviour Research and Therapy*, **11**, 105–117.

Everaerd, W., Vromans, I. S. Y. & van der Elst, A. M. C. (1990). Asthma. In A. A. Kaptein, H. M. van der Ploeg, B. Garssen, P. J. G. Schreurs & R. Beunderman (Eds), *Behavioural Medicine. Psychological Treatment of Somatic Disorders*. Chichester: Wiley.

Eysenck, H. J. (1967). *The Biological Basis of Personality*. Springfield, IL: Charles C. Thomas.

Eysenck, H. J. (1968). A theory of the incubation of anxiety/fear responses. *Behaviour Research and Therapy*, **6**, 309–321.

Eysenck, H. J. (1975). A note on backward conditioning. *Behaviour Research and Therapy*, **13**, 201–202.

Eysenck, H. J. (1976). The learning theory model of neurosis—a new approach. *Behaviour Research and Therapy*, **14**, 251–267.

Eysenck, H. J. (1979). The conditioning model of neurosis. *Behavioral and Brain Sciences*, **2**, 155–199.

Eysenck, H. J. (1981). *A Model for Personality*. New York: Springer-Verlag.

Eysenck, H. J. (1982). Neobehaviorist (S-R) theory. In G. T. Wilson & C. M. Franks (Eds), *Contemporary Behavior Therapy*. New York: Guildford Press.

Eysenck, H. J. (1985). Incubation theory of fear/anxiety. In S. Reiss & R. R. Bootzin (Eds), *Theoretical Issue in Behavior Therapy*. New York: Academic Press.

Eysenck, H. J. (1987). Behavior Therapy. In H. J. Eysenck & I. Martin (Eds), *Theoretical Foundations of Behavior Therapy*. New York: Plenum Press.

Eysenck, H. J. & Eysenck, M. W. (1985). *Personality and Individual Differences*. New York: Plenum Press.

Eysenck, H. J. & Rachman, S. (1965). *Causes and Cures of Neurosis*. London: Routledge & Kegan Paul.

Eysenck, M. W., MacLeod, C. & Mathews, A. (1987). Cognitive functioning and anxiety. *Psychological Research*, **49**, 189–195.

Falloon, I. R. H., Lindley, P., McDonald, R. & Marks, I. (1977). Social skills training of outpatient groups: A controlled study of rehearsal and homework. *British Journal of Psychiatry*, **131**, 610–615.

Falloon, I. R. H., Lloyd, G. G. & Harpin, R. E. (1981). The treatment of social phobia: Real-life rehearsal with nonprofessional therapists. *Journal of Nervous and Mental Disease*, **169**, 180–184.

Farkas, G. M., Sine, L. F. & Evans, I. M. (1979). The effects of distraction, performance demand, stimulus explicitness and personality on objective and subjective measures of male sexual arousal. *Behaviour Research and Therapy*, **17**, 25–32.

Farrell, A. D., Mariotto, M. J., Conger, A. J., Curran, J. P. & Wallander, J. L. (1979). Self-ratings and judges' ratings of heterosexual social anxiety and skill: A generalizability study. *Journal of Consulting and Clinical Psychology*, **43**, 522–527.

Farrell, A. D., Curran, J. P., Zwick, W. R. & Monti, P. M. (1983). Generalizability and discriminant validity of anxiety and social skills ratings in two populations. *Behavioral Assessment*, **6**, 1–14.

Faust, J. & Melamed, B. G. (1984). Influence of arousal, previous experience, and age on surgery preparation of some day of surgery and in-hospital pediatric patients. *Journal of Consulting and Clinical Psychology*, **52**, 359–365.

Fava, G. A., Grandi, S. & Canestrari, R. (1989). Treatment of social phobia by homework exposure. *Psychotherapy and Psychosomatics*, **52**, 209–213.

Feldman, M., Walker, P., Green, J. L. & Weingarden K. (1986). Life events stress and psychosocial factors in men with peptic ulcer disease: A multidimensional case-controlled study. *Gastroenterology*, **91**, 1370–1379.

Fenigstein, A. (1979). Self-consciousness, self-attention, and social interaction. *Journal of Personality and Social Psychology*, **37**, 75–86.

Fenigstein, A. & Carver, C. S. (1978). Self-focusing effects of heartbeat feedback. *Journal of Personality and Social Psychology*, **36**, 1241–1250.

Fenigstein, A., Scheier, M. F. & Buss, A. H. (1975). Public and private self-consciousness: Assessment and theory. *Journal of Consulting and Clinical Psychology*, **43**, 522–527.

Ferguson, B. F. (1979). Preparing your children for hospitalisation: A comparison of two methods. *Pediatrics*, **64**, 656–664.

Fiegenbaum, W. (1986). Longterm efficacy of exposure *in vivo* for cardiac phobia. In I. Hand & H.-U. Wittchen (Eds), *Panic and Phobias*. Berlin: Springer-Verlag.

Fiegenbaum, W. (1988). Long-term efficacy of ungraded versus graded massed exposure in agoraphobics. In I. Hand & H.-U. Wittchen (Eds), *Panic and Phobias. 2. Treatment and Variables Affecting Course and Outcome*. Berlin: Springer-Verlag.

Fielding, J. F. (1977). A year in out-patients with the irritable bowel syndrome. *Irish Journal of Medical Science*, **146**, 162–166.

Fielding, R. (1980). A note on behavioural treatment in the rehabilitation of myocardial infarction patients. *British Journal of Social and Clinical Psychology*, **19**, 157–161.

Fischer, M., Hand, I., Angenendt, J., Buttner-Westphal, H. & Manecke, C. (1988). Failures in exposure treatment of agoraphobia: Evaluation and prediction. In I. Hand & H.-U. Wittchen (Eds), *Panic and Phobias 2. Treatment and Variables Affecting Course and Outcome*. Berlin: Springer-Verlag.

Fischetti, M., Curran, J. P. & Wessberg, H. W. (1977). Sense of timing: A skill deficit in heterosexual–socially anxious males. *Behavior Modification*, **1**, 179–194.

Fisher, L. M. & Wilson, G. T. (1985). A study of the psychology of agoraphobia. *Behaviour Research and Therapy*, **23**, 97–107.

Flaherty, G. C. & Fitzpatrick, J. J. (1978). Relaxation techniques to increase comfort level of postoperative patients: A preliminary study. *Nursing Research*, **27**, 352–355.

Flament, M. F., Whitaker, A., Rapoport, J. L., Davies, M., Berg, C. Z., Kalikow, K., Sceery, W. & Shaffer, D. (1988). Obsessive–compulsive disorder in adolescence: An epidemiological study. *Journal of the American Academy of Child and Adolescent Psychiatry*, **27**, 764–771.

Fleming, B. & Faulk, A. (1989). Discriminating factors in panic disorder with and without agoraphobia. *Journal of Anxiety Disorders*, **3**, 209–219.

Floderus-Myrhed, B., Pedersen, N. & Rasmussen, I. (1980). Assessment of heritability for personality based on a short form of the Eysenck Personality Inventory. *Behavior Genetics*, **10**, 153–162.

Foa, E. B. (1979). Failure in treating obsessive–compulsives. *Behaviour Research and Therapy*, **17**, 169–176.

Foa, E. B. & Golstein, A. (1978). Continuous exposure and complete response prevention in the treatment of obsessive–compulsive neurosis. *Behavior Therapy*, **9**, 821–829.

Foa, E. B. & Kozak, M. J. (1986). Emotional processing and fear: Exposure to corrective information. *Psychological Bulletin*, **99**, 20–35.

Foa, E. B. & McNally, R. J. (1986). Sensitivity to feared stimuli in obsessive–compulsives: A dichotic listening analysis. *Cognitive Therapy and Research*, **10**, 477–485.

Foa, E. B., Grayson, J. B. & Steketee, G. S. (1982). Depression, habituation and treatment outcome in obsessive–compulsives. In J. C. Boulougouris (Ed.), *Practical Applications of Learning Theories in Psychiatry*. New York: Wiley.

Foa, E. B., McNally, R. J. & Murdoch, T. B. (1989). Anxious mood and memory. *Behaviour Research and Therapy*, **27**, 141–147.

Foa, E. B., Steketee, G. & Grayson, J. B. (1985a). Imaginal and *in vivo* exposure: A comparison with obsessive–compulsive checkers. *Behavior Therapy*, **16**, 292–302.

Foa, E. B., Steketee, G. S. & Groves, G. A. (1979). Use of behavioral therapy and imipramine: A case of obsessive–compulsive neurosis with severe depression. *Behavior Modification*, **3**, 419–430.

Foa, E. B., Steketee, G. & Milby, J. B. (1980b). Differential effects of exposure and response prevention in obsessive–compulsive washers. *Journal of Consulting and Clinical Psychology*, **48**, 71–79.

Foa, E. B., Steketee, G. & Ozarow, B. J. (1985b). Behavior therapy with obsessive–compulsives. From theory to treatment. In M. Mavissakalian, S. M. Turner & L. Michelson (Eds), *Obsessive–Compulsive Disorder. Psychological and Pharmacological Treatment*. New York: Plenum.

Foa, E. B., Steketee, G. & Young, M. C. (1984). Agoraphobia: Phenomenological aspects, associated characteristics, and theoretical considerations. *Clinical Psychology Review*, **4**, 431–457.

Foa, E. B., Jameson, J. S., Turner, R. M. & Payne, L. L. (1980a). Massed vs. spaced exposure sessions in the treatment of agoraphobia. *Behaviour Research and Therapy*, **18**, 333–338.

Foa, E. B., Steketee, G., Turner, R. M. & Fischer, S. C. (1980c). Effects of imaginal exposure to feared disasters in obsessive–compulsive checkers. *Behaviour Research and Therapy*, **18**, 1–7.

Foa, E. B., Grayson, J. B., Steketee, G. S., Doppelt, H. G., Turner, R. M. & Latimer, P. R. (1983a). Success and failure in the behavioral treatment of obsessive–compulsives. *Journal of Consulting and Clinical Psychology*, **51**, 287–297.

Foa, E. B., Steketee, G. S., Grayson, J. B. & Doppelt, H. G. (1983b). Treatment of obsessive–compulsives: When do we fail? In E. B. Foa & P. M. G. Emmelkamp (Eds), *Failures in Behavior Therapy*. New York: Wiley.

Foa, E. B., Steketee, G., Grayson, J. B., Turner, R. M. & Latimer, P. R. (1984). Deliberate exposure and blocking of obsessive–compulsive rituals: Immediate and long-term effects. *Behavior Therapy*, **15**, 450–472.

Fodor, I. G. (1974). The phobic syndrome in women. In V. Franks & V. Burtle (Eds), *Women in Therapy*. New York: Brunner Mazel.

Frank, E., Anderson, C. & Rubinstein, P. (1978). Frequency of sexual dysfunction in 'normal' couples. *New England Journal of Medicine*, **299**, 111–115.

Freedman, R. R. (1989). Ambulatory monitoring findings on panic. In R. B. Baker (Ed.), *Panic Disorder: Research and Therapy*. Chichester: Wiley.

Freeman, R. R., Ianni, P., Ettedgui, E. & Puthezhath, N. (1985). Ambulatory monitoring of panic disorder. *Archives of General Psychiatry*, **42**, 244–248.

Fremouw, W. J. & Zitter, R. E. (1978). A comparison of skills training and cognitive restructuring–relaxation for the treatment of speech anxiety. *Behavior Therapy*, **9**, 248–254.

Freud, S. (1894). On the grounds for detaching a particular syndrome from Neorasthenia under the description 'Anxiety Neurosis'. In J. Strachey (Ed.), *The Standard Edition of the Complete Works of Sigmund Freud*, Vol. XX. London: Hogarth.

Freud, S. (1938). Three contributions to the theory of sexuality. In A. A. Brill (translated and edited), *The Basic Writings of Sigmund Freud*. New York: Modern Library.

Freud, S. (1959). Inhibitions, symptoms and anxiety. In *Standard Edition*, Vol. 20. London: Hogarth (first published in 1926).

Freud, S. (1969). *A General Introduction to Psychoanalysis*. New York: Simon & Schuster.

Freund, B., Steketee, G. S. & Foa, E. B. (1987). Compulsive Activity Checklist (CAC): Psychometric analysis with obsessive–compulsive disorder. *Behavioral Assessment*, **9**, 67–79.

Freyberger, H., Kunsebeck, H.-W., Lempa, W., Wellman, W. & Avenarius, H.-J. (1985). Psychotherapeutic intervention in alexithymic patients with special regard to ulcerative colitis and Crohn patients. *Psychotherapy and Psychosomatics*, **44**, 72–81.

Friedman, H. S. (Ed.) (1990). *Personality and Disease*. New York: Wiley.

Friedman, H. S. & Booth-Kewley, S. (1987). The 'disease-prone personality': A meta-analytic review of the construct. *American Psychologist*, **42**, 539–555.

Friedman, J. M. & Chernen, L. (1987). Sexual dysfunction. In L. Michelson & L. M. Ascher (Eds), *Anxiety and Stress Disorders. Cognitive Behavioral Assessment and Treatment*. New York: Guildford Press.

Froese, A., Hackett, T. P., Cassem, N. H. & Silverberg, E. L. (1974). Trajectories of anxiety and depression in denying and non-denying acute myocardial infarction patients during hospitalization. *Journal of Psychosomatic Research*, **18**, 413–420.

Frost, R. O., Sher, K. J. & Geen, T. (1986). Psychopathology and personality characteristics of nonclinical compulsive checkers. *Behaviour Research and Therapy*, **24**, 133–143.

Frost, R. O., Lehart, C. M., Dugas, K. M. & Sher, K. J. (1988). Information processing among non-clinical compulsives. *Behaviour Research and Therapy*, **26**, 275–277.

Fry, W. F. (1962). The marital context of an anxiety syndrome. *Family Process*, **4**, 245–252.

Fuller, S. S., Endress, M. P. & Johnson, J. E. (1978). The effects of cognitive and behavioral control on coping with an aversive health examination. *Journal of Human Stress*, **4**, 18–25.

Furst, J. B. & Cooper, A. (1970). Failure of systematic desensitization in two cases of obsessive–compulsive neurosis marked by fear of insecticide. *Behaviour Research and Therapy*, **8**, 203–206.

Fyer, A., Liebowitz, M., Gorman, J., Compeas, R., Levin, A., Davies, S., Goetz, D. & Klein, D. (1987). Discontinuation of alprazolam treatment in panic patients. *American Journal of Psychiatry*, **144**, 303–308.

Garfield, S. R., Collen, M. F., Feldman, R., Soghikian, K., Richart, H. & Duncan, J. H. (1976). Evaluation of an ambulatory medical care delivery system. *New England Journal of Medicine*, **294**, 426–431.

Garvey, M. J. & Tuason, V. B. (1984). The relationship of panic disorder to agoraphobia. *Comprehensive Psychiatry*, **25**, 529–531.

Gatchel, R. J. (1980). Effectiveness of two procedures for reducing dental fear: Group-administered desensitization and group education and discussion. *Journal of the American Dental Association*, **101**, 634–637.

Gauthier, J., Savard, F., Halle, J-P. & Dufour, L. (1985). Flooding and coping skills training in the management of dental fear. *Scandinavian Journal of Behaviour Therapy*, **14**, 3–15.

Geer, J. & Fuhr, R. (1976). Cognitive factors in sexual arousal: The role of distraction. *Journal of Consulting and Clinical Psychology*, **44**, 238–243.

Gelder, M. G. & Marks, I. M. (1966). Severe agoraphobia: A controlled prospective trial of behaviour therapy. *British Journal of Psychiatry*, **112**, 309–319.

Gelder, M. G., Bancroft, J., Gath, D., Johnston, D., Mathews, A. & Shaw, P. (1973). Specific and non-specific factors in behaviour therapy. *British Journal of Psychiatry*, **123**, 445–462.

George, J. M., Scott, D. S., Turner, S. P. & Gregg, J. M. (1980). The effects of psychological factors and physical trauma on recovery from oral surgery. *Journal of Behavioral Medicine*, **3**, 291–310.

George, L. K., Hughes, D. C. & Blazer, D. G. (1986). Urban/rural differences in the prevalence of anxiety disorders. *American Journal of Social Psychiatry*, **6**, 249–258.

Gill, K. M. (1984). Coping effectively with invasive medical procedures: A descriptive model. *Clinical Psychology Review*, **4**, 339–362.

Gitlin, B., Martin, J., Shear, M. K., Frances, A., Ball, G. & Josephson, S. (1985). Behavior therapy for panic disorder. *Journal of Nervous and Mental Disease*, **173**, 742–743.

Glasgow, R. & Arkowitz, H. (1975). The behavioral assessment of male and female social competence in dyadic heterosexual interactions. *Behavior Therapy*, **6**, 488–498.

Glass, C. R. & Arnkoff, C. B. (1989). Behavioral assessment of social anxiety and social phobia. *Clinical Psychology Review*, **9**, 75–90.

Glass, C. R. & Furlong, M. (1990). Cognitive assessment of social anxiety: Affective and behavioral correlates. *Cognitive Therapy and Research*, **14**, 365–384.

Glass, C. R., Merluzzi, T. V., Biever, J. L. & Larsen, K. H. (1982). Cognitive assessment of social anxiety: Development and validation of a self-statement questionnaire. *Cognitive Therapy and Research*, **6**, 37–56.

Goldfried, M. R. (1971). Systematic desensitization as training in self-control. *Journal of Consulting and Clinical Psychology*, **37**, 228–235.

Goldfried, M. R. & D'Zurilla, T. J. (1969). A behavioral–analytic model for assessing competence. In C. D. Spielberger (Ed.), *Current Topics in Clinical and Community Psychology*, Vol. 1. New York: Academic Press.

Goldfried, M. R. & Goldfried, A. P. (1975). Cognitive change methods. In F. H. Kanfer & A. P. Goldstein (Eds), *Helping People Change*. New York: Pergamon Press.

Goldfried, M. R. & Goldfried, A. P. (1980). Cognitive change methods. In F. H. Kanfer & A. P. Goldstein (Eds), *Helping People Change*, 2nd edn. New York: Pergamon Press.

Goldfried, M. R. & Robbins, C. (1983). Self-schema, cognitive bias, and the processing of therapeutic experiences. In P. C. Kendall (Ed.), *Advances in Cognitive–Behavioral Research and Therapy*, Vol. 2. New York: Academic Press.

Goldstein, A. J. & Chambless, D. L. (1978). A reanalysis of agoraphobia. *Behavior Therapy*, **9**, 47–59.

Goldstein, A. J. & Chambless, D. L. (1980). The treatment of agoraphobia. In A. J. Goldstein & E. G. Foa (Eds), *Handbook of Behavioral Interventions*. New York: Wiley.

Goldstein, A. P., Sprafkin, R. P. & Gershaw, N. J. (1976). *Skills Training for Community Living*. Oxford: Pergamon Press.

Goodman, W. K., Price, L. H., Rasmussen, S. A., Mazure, C., Delgado, P., Heninger, G. R. & Charney, D. S. (1989a). The Yale-Brown Obsessive Compulsive Scale. II. Validity. *Archives of General Psychiatry*, **46**, 1012–1018.

Goodman, W. K., Price, L. H., Rasmussen, S. A., Mazure, C., Fleischman, R. L., Hill, C. L., Heninger, G. R. & Charney, D. S. (1989b). The Yale-Brown Obsessive Compulsive Scale. I. Development, use and reliability. *Archives of General Psychiatry*, **46**, 1006–1011.

Gorman, J. M. & Gorman, L. K. (1987). Drug treatment of social phobia. *Journal of Affective Disorders*, **13**, 183–192.

Gorman, J. M., Askenazi, J., Liebowitz, M. R., Fyer, A. J., Stein, J., Kinney, J. M. & Klein, D. F. (1984). Response to hyperventilation in a group of patients with panic disorder. *American Journal of Psychiatry*, **141**, 857–861.

Gournay, K. (1989). The behavioral treatment of agoraphobia: The impact of sex role. In P. M. G. Emmelkamp, W. T. A. M. Everaerd, F. W. Kraaimaat & W. J. M. van Son (Eds), *Fresh Perspectives on Anxiety Disorders*. Amsterdam: Swets & Zeitlinger.

Graham, D. (1961). Predictions of fainting in blood donors. *Circulation*, **23**, 901–906.

Gray, J. A. (1971). *The Psychology of Fear and Stress*. London: World University Library.

Gray, J. A. (1975). *Elements of a Two-process Theory of Learning*. London: Academic Press.

Gray, J. A. (1982). *The Neuropsychology of Anxiety: An Enquiry into the Functions of the Septo-hippocampal System*. Oxford: Oxford University Press.

Gray, J. A. (1985). Issues in the neuropsychology of anxiety. In A. H. Tuma & J. D. Maser (Eds), *Anxiety and the Anxiety Disorders*. Hillsdale, NJ: Erlbaum.

Grayson, J. B., Foa, E. B. & Steketee, G. S. (1982). Habituation during exposure treatment: Distraction vs attention-focusing. *Behaviour Research and Therapy*, **20**, 323–328.

Grayson, J. B., Foa, E. B. & Steketee, G. S. (1986). Exposure *in vivo* of obsessive–compulsives under distraction and attention-focusing conditions: Replication and extension. *Behaviour Research and Therapy*, **24**, 475–479.

Grayson, J. B., Nutter, D. & Mavissakalian, M. (1980). Psychophysiological assessment of imagery in obsessive–compulsives: A pilot study. *Behaviour Research and Therapy*, **18**, 580–593.

Green, J. (1989). Counselling in HIV infection and AIDS. In S. Pearce & J. Wardle (Eds), *The Practice of Behavioural Medicine*. Oxford: Oxford University Press/BPS Books.

Greenberg, L. & Safran, J. D. (1984a). Integrating affect and cognition: A perspective on the process of therapeutic change. *Cognitive Therapy and Research*, **8**, 559–578.

Greenberg, L. & Safran, J. D. (1984b). Hot cognition—emotion coming in from the cold: A reply to Rachman. *Cognitive Therapy and Research*, **8**, 591–598.

Gregg, I. (1983). Epidemiologic aspects. In T. J. H. Clark & S. Godfrey (Eds), *Asthma*, 2nd edn. London: Chapman & Hall.

Greist, J. H., Marks, I. M., Berlin, F., Gourney, K. & Noshirvani, H. (1980). Avoidance versus confrontation of fear. *Behavior Therapy*, **11**, 1–14.

Griez, E. & van den Hout, M. A. (1983). Treatment of phobophobia by exposure to CO_2 induced anxiety symptoms. *Journal of Nervous and Mental Disease*, **171**, 506–508.

Griez, E. & van den Hout, M. A. (1986). CO_2 inhalation in the treatment of panic attacks. *Behaviour Research and Therapy*, **24**, 145–150.

Gross, P. R. & Eifert, G. H. (1990a). Components of generalised anxiety: The role of intrusive thoughts vs worry. *Behaviour Research and Therapy*, **28**, 421–428.

Gross, P. R. & Eifert, G. H. (1990b). Delineating generalized anxiety: A preliminary investigation. *Journal of Psychopathology and Behavioral Assessment*, **12**, 345–357.

Gross, P. R., Oei, T. P. S. & Evans, L. (1989). Generalized anxiety symptoms in phobic disorders and anxiety states: A test of the worry hypothesis. *Journal of Anxiety Disorders*, **3**, 159–169.

Gruen, W. (1975). Effects of brief psychotherapy during the hospitalization period on the recovery process in heart attacks. *Journal of Consulting and Clinical Psychology*, **43**, 223–232.

Hafner, R. J. (1977a). The husbands of agoraphobic women: Assortive mating or pathogenic interaction? *British Journal of Psychiatry*, **130**, 233–239.

Hafner, R. J. (1977b). The husbands of agoraphobic women and their influence on treatment outcome. *British Journal of Psychiatry*, **131**, 289–294.

Hafner, R. J. (1982). Marital interaction in persisting obsessive–compulsive disorders. *Australian and New Zealand Journal of Psychiatry*, **16**, 171–178.

Hafner, R. J. (1984). The marital repercussions of behavior therapy for agoraphobia. *Psychotherapy*, **14**, 530–542.

Hafner, R. J. & Marks, I. M. (1976). Exposure *in vivo* of agoraphobics: Contributions of diazepam, group exposure and anxiety evocation. *Psychological Medicine*, **6**, 71–88.

Hafner, R. J. & Ross, M. M. (1983). Predicting the outcome of behaviour therapy for agoraphobia. *Behaviour Research and Therapy*, **21**, 375–382.

Hale, V. E. & Strassberg, D. S. (1990). Role of anxiety on sexual arousal. *Archives of Sexual Behavior*, **19**, 569–582.

Halford, K. & Foddy, M. (1982). Cognitive and social correlates of social anxiety. *British Journal of Clinical Psychology*, **21**, 17–28.

Hall, R. & Goldberg, D. (1977). The role of social anxiety in interaction difficulties. *British Journal of Psychiatry*, **131**, 610–615.

Hallam, R. S. (1985). *Anxiety: Psychological Perspectives on Panic and Agoraphobia*. New York: Academic Press.

Hallam, R. S. (1989). Classification and research into panic. In Baker, R. (Ed.), *Panic Disorder: Theory, Research and Therapy*. Chichester: Wiley.

Hamann, M. S. & Mavissakalian, M. (1988). Discrete dimensions in agoraphobia: A factor analytic study. *British Journal of Clinical Psychology*, **27**, 137–144.

Hamilton, M. (1959). The assessment of anxiety states by rating. *British Journal of Medical Psychology*, **32**, 50–55.

Hand, I., Lamontagne, Y. & Marks, I. M. (1974). Group exposure (flooding) *in vivo* for agoraphobics. *British Journal of Psychiatry*, **124**, 588–602.

Hand, I., Angenendt, J., Fischer, M. & Wilke, C. (1986). Exposure *in vivo* with panic management for agoraphobia: Treatment rationale and long-term outcome. In I. Hand & H.-U. Wittchen (Eds), *Panic and Phobias*. Berlin: Springer-Verlag.

Hauri, P. J., Friedman, M., Ravaris, R. L. & Fisher, J. (1985). Sleep in agoraphobia with panic attacks. In M. H. Chafe, D. J. McGinty & R. Wilder-Jones (Eds), *Sleep Research*. Los Angeles, CA: BIS/BRS.

Havik, O. E. & Maeland, J. G. (1990). Patterns of emotional reactions after myocardial infarction. *Journal of Psychosomatic Research*, **34**, 271–285.

Hayes, B. J. & Marshall, W. L. (1984). Generalization of treatment effects in training public speakers. *Behaviour Research and Therapy*, **22**, 519–533.

Headland, K. & McDonald, R. (1987). Rapid audiotape treatment of obsessional ruminations: A case report. *Behavioural Psychotherapy*, **15**, 188–192.

Heide, F. J. & Borkovec, T. D. (1983). Relaxation-induced anxiety: Paradoxical anxiety enhancement due to relaxation training. *Journal of Consulting and Clinical Psychology*, **51**, 171–182.

Heide, F. J. & Borkovec, T. D. (1984). Relaxation-induced anxiety: Mechanisms and theoretical implications. *Behaviour Research and Therapy*, **22**, 1–12.

Heiman, J. R. & Rowland, D. L. (1983). Affective and physiological sexual patterns: The effects of instructions on sexually functional and dysfunctional men. *Journal of Psychosomatic Research*, **27**, 105–116.

Heimberg, R. G. (1989). Cognitive and behavioral treatments for social phobia: A critical analysis. *Clinical Psychology Review*, **9**, 107–128.

Heimberg, R. G. & Barlow, D. H. (1988). Psychosocial treatments for social phobia. *Psychosomatics*, **29**, 27–37.

Heimberg, R. G., Dodge, C. S. & Becker, R. E. (1987). Social phobia. In L. Michelson & M. Ascher (Eds), *Anxiety and Stress Disorders: Cognitive–Behavioral Assessment and Treatment*. New York: Guildford Press.

Heimberg, R. G., Keller, K. E. & Peca-Baker, T. (1986). Cognitive assessment of social-evaluative anxiety in the job interview: The job interview self-statement schedule. *Journal of Counseling Psychology*, **33**, 190–195.

Heimberg, R. G., Becker, R. E., Goldfinger, K. & Vermilyea, J. A. (1985). Treatment of social phobia by exposure, cognitive restructuring, and homework assignments. *Journal of Nervous and Mental Disease*, **173**, 236–245.

Heimberg, R. G., Hope, D. A., Rapee, R. M. & Bruch, M. A. (1988). The validity of the social avoidance and distress scale and fear of negative evaluation scale with social phobic patients. *Behaviour Research and Therapy*, **26**, 407–410.

Heimberg, R. G., Bruch, M. A., Hope, D. A. & Dombeck, M. (1990a). Evaluating the states of mind model: Comparison to an alternative model and effects of method of cognitive assessment. *Cognitive Therapy and Research*, **14**, 543–557.

Heimberg, R. G., Dodge, C. S., Hope, D. A., Kennedy, C. R. & Zolla, L. J. (1990b). Cognitive behavioral group treatment for social phobia: Comparison with a credible placebo control. *Cognitive Therapy and Research*, **14**, 1–23.

Heimberg, R. G., Hope, D. A., Dodge, C. S. & Becker, R. E. (1990c). DSM-III-R subtypes of social phobia: Comparison of generalised social phobics with public speaking phobics. *Journal of Nervous and Mental Disease*, **178**, 172–179.

Hekmat, H. (1987). Origins and development of human fear reactions. *Journal of Anxiety Disorders*, **1**, 197–218.

Helzer, J. E., Stillings, W. A., Chammas, S., Norland, C. L. & Alpers, D. H. (1982). A controlled study of the association between ulcerative colitis and psychiatric diagnosis. *Digestive Diseases and Sciences*, **27**, 513–518.

Hibbert, G. A. (1984). Ideational components of anxiety: Their origin and content. *British Journal of Psychiatry*, **144**, 618–624.

Hibbert, G. A. & Chan, M. (1989). Respiratory control: Its contribution to the treatment of panic attacks. A controlled study. *British Journal of Psychiatry*, **154**, 232–236.

Higgins, R. L., Frisch, M. B. & Smith, D. (1983). A comparison of role-played and natural responses to identical circumstances. *Behavior Therapy*, **14**, 158–169.

Himadi, W. G. (1987). Safety signals and agoraphobia. *Journal of Anxiety Disorders*, **1**, 345–360.

Himadi, W. G., Boice, R. & Barlow, D. H. (1985). Assessment of agoraphobia: Triple response measurement. *Behaviour Research and Therapy*, **23**, 311–323.

Himadi, W. G., Cerny, J. A., Barlow, D. H., Cohen, S. & O'Brien, G. T. (1986).

The relationship of marital adjustment to agoraphobia treatment outcome. *Behaviour Research and Therapy*, **24**, 107–115.

Hite, S. (1976). *The Hite Report*. New York: Macmillan.

Hodgson, R. & Rachman, S. (1972). The effects of contamination and washing in obsessional patients. *Behaviour Research and Therapy*, **10**, 111–117.

Hodgson, R. & Rachman, S. (1974). Desynchrony in measures of fear. *Behaviour Research and Therapy*, **12**, 319–326.

Hodgson, R. & Rachman, S. (1977). Obsessional–compulsive complaints. *Behaviour Research and Therapy*, **15**, 389–395.

Hoehn-Saric, R. (1982). Comparison of generalized anxiety disorder with panic disorder patients. *Psychopharmacological Bulletin*, **18**, 104–108.

Hoehn-Saric, R. & McLeod, D. R. (1988). The peripheral sympathetic nervous system: Its role in normal and pathologic anxiety. *Psychiatric Clinics of North America*, **11**, 375–386.

Hoekstra, R. J., Visser, S. & Emmelkamp, P. M. G. (1989). A social learning formulation of the etiology of obsessive–compulsive disorders. In P. M. G. Emmelkamp, W. T. A. M. Everaerd, F. Kraaimaat & M. J. M. van Son (Eds), *Fresh Perspectives on Anxiety Disorders*. Amsterdam: Swets & Zeitlinger.

Hohmann, G. W. (1966). Some effects of spinal cord lesions on experienced emotional feelings. *Psychophysiology*, **3**, 143–156.

Holden, A. E. & Barlow, D. H. (1986). Heart rate and heart rate variability recorded *in vivo* in agoraphobics and nonphobics. *Behavior Therapy*, **17**, 26–42.

Holden, A. E., O'Brien, G. T., Barlow, D. H., Stetson, D. & Infantino, A. (1983). Self-help manual for agoraphobia: A preliminary report of effectiveness. *Behavior Therapy*, **14**, 545–556.

Holden, N. L. (1990). Is anorexia nervosa an obsessive–compulsive disorder? *British Journal of Psychiatry*, **157**, 1–5.

Holloway, W. & McNally, R. J. (1987). Effects of anxiety sensitivity on response to hyperventilation. *Journal of Abnormal Psychology*, **96**, 330–334.

Holt, P. E. & Andrews, G. (1989a). Provocation of panic: Three elements of the panic reaction in four anxiety disorders. *Behaviour Research and Therapy*, **27**, 253–261.

Holt, P. E. & Andrews, G. (1989b). Hyperventilation and anxiety in panic disorder, social phobia, GAD and normal controls. *Behaviour Research and Therapy*, **27**, 453–460.

Hoogduin, C. A. L. & Duivenvoorden, H. J. (1988). A decision model in the treatment of obsessive–compulsive neurosis. *British Journal of Psychiatry*, **152**, 516–521.

Hoogduin, C. A. L. & Hoogduin, W. A. (1984). The out-patient treatment of patients with an obsessive–compulsive disorder. *Behaviour Research and Therapy*, **22**, 455–460.

Hoon, P. W. (1979). The assessment of sexual arousal in women. In M. Hersen, R. M. Eisler & P. M. Miller (Eds), *Progress in Behavior Modification*, Vol. 7. New York: Academic Press.

Hoon, P., Wincze, J. & Hoon, E. (1977). A test of reciprocal inhibition: Are anxiety and sexual arousal in women mutually inhibitory? *Journal of Abnormal Psychology*, **86**, 65–74.

Hope, D. A. & Heimberg, R. G. (1988). Public and private self-consciousness and social anxiety. *Journal of Personality Assessment*, **52**, 629–639.

Hope, D. A., Gansler, A. D. & Heimberg, R. G. (1989). Attentional focus and causal attributions in social phobia: Implications from social psychology. *Clinical Psychology Review*, **9**, 49–60.

Hope, D. A., Rapee, R. M., Heimberg, R. G. & Dombeck, M. J. (1990). Representations of the self in social phobia: Vulnerability to social threat. *Cognitive Therapy and Research*, **14**, 177–189.

Hornsveld, R. J., Kraaimaat, F. W. & van Dam-Baggen, R. M. J. (1979). Anxiety/discomfort and handwashing in obsessive–compulsive and psychiatric control patients. *Behaviour Research and Therapy*, **17**, 223–228.

Hout van den, M. A. (1988). The explanation of experimental panic. In S. Rachman & J. D. Maser (Eds), *Panic. Psychological Perspectives*. Hillsdale, NJ: Erlbaum.

Hout van den, M. A. & Griez, E. (1984). Panic symptoms after inhalation of carbon dioxide. *British Journal of Psychiatry*, **144**, 503–507.

Hout van den, M. A., van der Molen, M. A., Griez, E. & Lousberg, H. (1987). Specificity of interoceptive fears to panic disorders. *Journal of Psychopathology and Behavioral Assessment*, **9**, 99–106.

Hout van den, M., Emmelkamp, P. M. G., Kraaykamp, H. & Griez, E. (1988). Behavioral treatment of obsessive–compulsives: Inpatients vs outpatient. *Behaviour Research and Therapy*, **26**, 331–332.

Hout van den, M. A., de Jong, P., Zandbergen, J. & Merkelbach, H. (1990). Waning of panic sensations during prolonged hyperventilation. *Behaviour Research and Therapy*, **28**, 445–448.

Hudson, B. (1974). The families of agoraphobics treated by behaviour therapy. *British Journal of Social Work*, **4**, 51–59.

Hugdahl, K. (1981). The three-systems model of fear and emotion—a critical examination. *Behaviour Research and Therapy*, **19**, 75–85.

Hutchings, D., Denney, D., Basgall, J. & Houston, B. (1980). Anxiety management and applied relaxation in reducing general anxiety. *Behaviour Research and Therapy*, **18**, 181–190.

Hyler, S. E., Riedler, R. O., Williams, J., Spitzer, R. L., Lyons, M. & Hendler, J. (1989). A comparison of self-report and clinical diagnosis of DSM-III personality disorder in 552 patients. *Comprehensive Psychiatry*, **30**, 170–178.

Ingram, R. E. & Kendall, P. C. (1986). Cognitive clinical psychology: Implications of an information processing perspective. In R. E. Ingram (Ed.), *Information Processing Approaches to Clinical Psychology*. Orlando, FL: Academic Press.

Ingram, R. E. & Kendall, P. C. (1987). The cognitive side of anxiety. *Cognitive Therapy and Research*, **5**, 523–536.

Insel, T. R. & Akiskal, H. S. (1986). Obsessive–compulsive disorder with psychotic features: A phenomenologic analysis. *American Journal of Psychiatry*, **143**, 1527–1533.

Insel, T. R., Zahn, T. & Murphy, D. L. (1985). In A. H. Tuma & J. Maser (Eds), *Anxiety and the Anxiety Disorders*. Hillsdale, NJ: Erlbaum.

Izard, C. E. (1971). *The Face of Emotion*. New York: Appleton-Century-Crofts.

Izard, C. E. (1972). Anxiety: A variable combination of interacting fundamental emotions. In C. D. Spielberger (Ed.), *Anxiety. Current Trends in Theory and Research*, Vol. 1. New York: Academic Press.

Izard, C. E. (1977). *Human Emotions*. New York: Plenum.

Izard, C. E. (1990). Facial expressions and the regulation of emotions. *Journal of Personality and Social Psychology*, **58**, 487–498.

Jacobson, N. S., Wilson, L. & Tupper, C. (1988). A clinical significance of treatment gains resulting from exposure-based interventions for agoraphobia: A reanalysis of outcome data. *Behavior Therapy*, **19**, 539–554.

Jakes, I. (1989a). Salkovskis on obsessional–compulsive neurosis: A critique. *Behaviour Research and Therapy*, **27**, 673–675.

Jakes, I. (1989b). Salkovskis on obsessional–compulsive neurosis: A rejoinder. *Behaviour Research and Therapy*, **27**, 683–684.

James, W. (1884). What is an emotion? *Mind*, **9**, 188–205. (Reprinted in M. Arnold (Ed.), *The Nature of Emotion*. Harmondsworth: Penguin, 1968.)

Janis, I. L. (1951). *Air War and Emotional Distress*. New York: McGraw-Hill.

Janis, I. L. (1958). *Psychological Stress: Psychoanalytic and Behavioral Studies of Surgical Patients*. New York: Wiley.

Jannoun, L., Oppenheimer, C. & Gelder, M. (1982). A self-help treatment manual for anxiety state patients. *Behavior Therapy*, **13**, 103–111.

Jannoun, L., Munby, M., Catalan, J. & Gelder, M. (1980). A home-based treatment program for agoraphobia: Replication and controlled evaluation. *Behavior Therapy*, **11**, 294–305.

Jansson, L. & Öst, L-G. (1982). Behavioral treatment for agoraphobia: An evaluative review. *Clinical Psychology Review*, **2**, 311–336.

Jansson, L., Jerremalm, A. & Öst, L-G. (1986). Follow-up of agoraphobia patients treated with exposure *in vivo* or applied relaxation. *British Journal of Psychiatry*, **149**, 486–490.

Jansson, L., Öst, L-G. & Jerremalm, A. (1987). Prognostic factors in the behavioral treatment of agoraphobia. *Behavioural Psychotherapy*, **15**, 31–44.

Jenike, M. A. (1986). Predictors of treatment failure. In M. A. Jenike, L. Baer & W. E. Minichiello (Eds), *Obsessive–Compulsive Disorders: Theory and Management*. Littleton, MA: PSG.

Jenike, M. A., Baer, L., Minichiello, W. E., Schwartz, C. E. & Carey, R. J. Jr. (1986). Concomitant obsessive–compulsive disorder in schizotypal personality disorder. *American Journal of Psychiatry*, **143**, 530–532.

Jenkins, C. D. (1976). Recent evidence supporting psychologic and social risk factors for coronary disease. *New England Journal of Medicine*, **294**, 1033–1038.

Jenkins, C. D. (1983). Psychosocial and behavioral factors. In N. M. Kaplan & J. Stamler (Eds), *Prevention of Coronary Heart Disease: Practical Management of the Risk Factors*. Philadelphia, PA: Saunders.

Jenkins, C. D. (1988). Epidemiology of cardiovascular diseases. *Journal of Consulting and Clinical Psychology*, **56**, 324–332.

Jerremalm, A., Jansson, L. & Öst, L-G. (1986a). Cognitive and physiological reactivity and the effects of different behavioural methods in the treatment of social phobia. *Behaviour Research and Therapy*, **24**, 171–180.

Jerremalm, A., Jansson, L. & Öst, L-G. (1986b). Individual response patterns and the effects of different behavioural methods in the treatment of dental phobia. *Behaviour Research and Therapy*, **24**, 587–596.

Joffe, R. T., Swinson, R. P. & Regan, J. J. (1988). Personality features of obsessive–compulsive disorder. *American Journal of Psychiatry*, **145**, 1127–1129.

Johansson, J. & Öst, L-G. (1982). Perception of autonomic reactions and actual heart rate in phobic patients. *Journal of Behavioral Assessment*, **4**, 133–143.

Johnson, J. E. (1984). Psychological interventions and coping with surgery. In A. Baum, S. E. Taylor & J. E. Singer (Eds), *Handbook of Health Psychology*, Vol. IV: *Social Psychological Aspects of Health*. Hillsdale, NJ: Erlbaum.

Johnson, J. E. & Leventhal, H. (1974). Effects of accurate expectations and behavioral instructions on reactions during a noxious medical examination. *Journal of Personality and Social Psychology*, **29**, 710–718.

Johnson, J. E., Lauver, D. R. & Nail, L. M. (1989). Process of coping with radiation therapy. *Journal of Consulting and Clinical Psychology*, **57**, 358–364.

Johnson, J. E., Leventhal, H. & Dabbs, J. (1971). Contribution of emotional and instrumental responses in adaption to surgery. *Journal of Personality and Social Psychology*, **20**, 55–64.

Johnson, J. E., Morrissey, J. F. & Leventhal, H. (1973). Psychological preparation for an endoscopic examination. *Gastrointestinal Endoscopy*, **19**, 180–182.

Johnson, J. E., Fuller, S. S., Endress, M. P. & Rice, V. H. (1978a). Altering patients' responses to surgery: An extension and replication. *Research in Nursing and Health*, **1**, 111–121.

Johnson, J. E., Rice, V. H., Fuller, S. S. & Endress, M. P. (1978b). Sensory information, instruction in a coping strategy and recovery from surgery. *Research in Nursing and Health*, **1**, 4–17.

Johnston, D. W. (1985). Psychological interventions with cardiovascular disease. *Journal of Psychosomatic Research*, **29**, 447–456.

Johnston, M., Johnston, D. W., Wiles, H., Burns, L. E. & Thorpe, G. L. (1984). Cumulative scales for the measurement of agoraphobia. *British Journal of Clinical Psychology*, **23**, 133–144.

Jones, R. G. (1969). A factored measure of Ellis' irrational belief system, with personality and adjustment correlates (doctoral dissertation, Texas Technical College, 1968). *Dissertation Abstracts International*, **29**, 4379B–4380B. (University Microfilms No. 69–6443).

Jones, W. H. & Russell, D. (1982). The social reticence scale: An objective measure of shyness. *Journal of Personality Assessment*, **46**, 629–631.

Kaloupek, D. G. & Stoupakis, T. (1985). Coping with a stressful medical procedure: Further investigation with volunteer blood donors. *Journal of Behavioral Medicine*, **8**, 131–148.

Kaloupek, D., Scott, J. & Khatami, V. (1985). Assessment of coping strategies associated with syncope in blood donors. *Journal of Psychosomatic Research*, **29**, 207–214.

Kaloupek, D. G., White, H. & Wong, M. (1984). Multiple assessment of coping strategies used by volunteer blood donors: Implications for preparatory training. *Journal of Behavioral Medicine*, **7**, 35–60.

Kanter, N. J. & Goldfried, M. R. (1979). Relative effectiveness of rational restructuring and self-control desensitization in the reduction of interpersonal anxiety. *Behavior Therapy*, **10**, 472–490.

Kaplan, H. S. (1974). *The New Sex Therapy*. New York: Brunner Mazel.

Kaplan, H. S. (1979). *Disorders of Sexual Desire*. New York: Brunner Mazel.

Kaplan, H. S. (1981). *The New Sex Therapy*. New York: Brunner Mazel.

Kaplan, H. S. (1983). *The Evaluation of Sexual Disorders*. New York: Brunner Mazel.

Kaplan, H. S. (1988). Anxiety and sexual dysfunction. *Journal of Clinical Psychiatry*, **49** (Suppl. 10), 21–25.

Kaplan, R. M., Atkins, C. J. & Lenhard, L. (1982). Coping with stressful sigmoidoscopy: Evaluation of cognitive and relaxation procedures. *Journal of Behavioral Medicine*, **5**, 67–82.

Kaptein, A. A. (1982). Psychological correlates of length of hospitalization and rehospitalization in patients with acute severe asthma. *Social Science and Medicine*, **16**, 725–729.

Kaptein, A. A. & van Rooijen, E. (1990). Behavioural medicine—some introductory remarks. In A. A. Kaptein, H. M. van der Ploeg, B. Garssen, P. J. G. Scheurs & R. Beunderman (Eds), *Behavioural Medicine: Psychological Treatment of Somatic Disorders*. Chichester: Wiley.

Karacan, I. (1982). Nocturnal penile tumescence as a biological marker in assessing erectile dysfunction. *Psychosomatics*, **23**, 349–360.

Karno, M., Hough, R. L., Burman, M. A., Escobar, J. I., Timbers, D. M., Santana, F. & Boyd, J. H. (1987). Lifetime prevalence of specific psychiatric disorders among Mexican Americans and non-Hispanic whites. *Archives of General Psychiatry*, **44**, 695–701.

Karno, M., Golding, J. M., Sorenson, S. B. & Burnam, M. A. (1988). The epidemiology of obsessive compulsive disorder in five U.S. communities. *Archives of General Psychiatry*, **45**, 1094–1099.

Kellner, R. (1983). The prognosis of treated hypochondriasis. A clinical study. *Acta Psychiatrica Scandinavica*, **67**, 69–79.

Kellner, R. (1985). Functional somatic symptoms and hypochondriasis. *Archives of General Psychiatry*, **42**, 821–833.

Kellner, R. (1986). *Somatization and Hypochondriasis*. New York: Praeger.

Kellner, R. (1990). Somatization: The most costly comorbidity? In J. D. Maser & C. R. Cloninger (Eds), *Comorbidity of Mood and Anxiety Disorders*. Washington, DC: American Psychiatric Press.

Kellner, R., Slocumb, J. C., Wiggins, R. J., Abbott, P., Romanik, R. & Winslow, W. W. (1986). The relationship of hypochondriacal fears and beliefs to anxiety and depression. *Psychiatric Medicine*, **4**, 15–24.

Kellner, R., Abbott, P., Winslow, W. W. & Pathak, D. (1987). Fears, beliefs and attitudes in DSM-III hypochondriasis. *Journal of Nervous and Mental Disease*, **175**, 20–25.

Kenardy, J., Evans, L. & Oei, T. P. S. (1988a). The importance of cognitions on panic attacks. *Behavior Therapy*, **19**, 471–483.

Kenardy, J., Oei, T. P. S. & Evans, L. (1990). Hyperventilation and panic attacks. *Australian and New Zealand Journal of Psychiatry*, **24**, 261–267.

Kenardy, J., Oei, T. P. S., Ryan, P. & Evans, L. (1988b). Attribution of panic attacks. *Journal of Anxiety Disorders*, **2**, 243–251.

Kendall, P. C. (1983). Methodology and cognitive–behavioural assessment. *Behavioural Psychotherapy*, **11**, 285–301.

Kendall, P. C. & Hollon, S. D. (1981). Assessing self-referent speech: Methods in the measurement of self-statements. In P. C. Kendall & S. D. Hollon (Eds), *Assessment Strategies for Cognitive–Behavioral Interventions*. New York: Academic Press.

Kendall, P. C. & Ingram, R. E. (1987). The future for cognitive assessment of anxiety: Let's get specific. In L. Michelson & L. M. Ascher (Eds), *Anxiety and Stress Disorders: Cognitive Behavioral Assessment and Treatment*. New York: Guildford Press.

Kendall, P. C., Williams, L., Pechacek, T. F., Graham, L. E., Sisslak, C. & Herzoff, N. (1979). Cognitive–behavioral and patient education interventions in cardiac catheterization procedures: The Palo Alto Medical Psychology Project. *Journal of Consulting and Clinical Psychology*, **47**, 49–58.

Kendler, K. S., Heath, A. C., Martin, A. G. & Eaves, L. J. (1987). Symptoms of anxiety and symptoms of depression: Same genes, different environments. *Archives of General Psychiatry*, **44**, 451–457.

Kenny, T. F., Mowbray, R. M. & Lalani, S. (1978). Faradic disruption and obsessive ideation in the treatment of obsessive neurosis: A controlled study. *Behavior Therapy*, **9**, 209–221.

Kenyon, F. E. (1965). Hypochondriasis: A survey of some historical, clinical and social aspects. *British Journal of Psychiatry*, **119**, 305–307.

Kilmann, P. R. (1978). The treatment of primary and secondary orgasmic dysfunction: A methodological review of the literature since 1970. *Journal of Sex and Marital Therapy*, **4**, 155–175.

Kilmann, P. R. & Auerbach, R. (1979). Treatments of premature ejaculation and psychogenic importance: A critical review of the literature. *Archives of Sexual Behavior*, **8**, 81–100.

Kinsey, A. C., Pomeroy, W. B. & Martin, C. E. (1948). *Sexual Behavior in the Human Male*. Philadelphia, PA: Saunders.

Kinsey, A. C., Pomeroy, W. B., Martin, C. W. & Gebhard, P. H. (1953). *Sexual Behavior in the Human Female*. Philadelphia, PA: Saunders.

Kinsman, R. A., Dirks, J. F. & Jones, N. F. (1982). Psychomaintenance of chronic physical illness: Clinical assessment of personality styles affecting medical management. In T. Millon, C. Green & R. Meagher (Eds), *Handbook of Clinical Health Psychology*. New York: Plenum.

Kinsman, R. A., Dahlem, N. W., Spector, S. L. & Staudenmayer, H. (1977). Observations on subjective symptomatology, coping behavior, and medical decisions in asthma. *Psychosomatic Medicine*, **39**, 102–119.

Kinsman, R. A., Dirks, J. F., Jones, N. F. & Dahlem, N. W. (1980). Anxiety reduction in asthma: Four catches to general application. *Psychosomatic Medicine*, **42**, 397–405.

Kirsch, I. (1985a). Self-efficacy and expectancy: Old wine with new labels. *Journal of Personality and Social Psychology*, **49**, 824–830.

Kirsch, I. (1985b). Response expectancy as a determinant of experience and behavior. *American Psychologist*, **40**, 1189–1202.

Klass, E. T., DiNardo, P. A. & Barlow, D. H. (1989). DSM-III-R personality diagnoses in anxiety disorder patients. *Comprehensive Psychiatry*, **30**, 251–258.

Klein, D. F. (1964). Delineation of two drug-responsive anxiety syndromes. *Psychopharmacologia*, **5**, 397–408.

Klein, D. F. (1980). Anxiety reconceptualized. *Comprehensive Psychiatry*, **21**, 411–427.

Klein, D. F. (1981). Anxiety reconceptualized. In D. F. Klein & J. Rabkin (Eds), *Anxiety: New Research and Changing Concepts*. New York: Raven Press.

Klein, D. F. (1988). In reply. *Archives of General Psychiatry*, **45**, 387–388.

Klein, D. F. & Gorman, J. M. (1987). A model of panic and agoraphobic development. *Acta Psychiatrica Scandinavica*, **76**, 87–95.

Klein, D. F., Ross, D. C. & Cohen, P. (1987). Panic and avoidance in agoraphobia: Application of path analysis to treatment studies. *Archives of General Psychiatry*, **44**, 377–385.

Klein, D. F., Zitrin, C. M. & Woerner, M. G. (1977). Imipramine and phobia. *Psychopharmacology Bulletin*, **13**, 24–27.

Kleiner, L. & Marshall, W. L. (1985). Relationship difficulties and agoraphobia. *Clinical Psychology Review*, **5**, 581–595.

Kleiner, L. & Marshall, W. L. (1987). The role of interpersonal problems in the development of agoraphobia with panic attacks. *Journal of Anxiety Disorders*, **1**, 313–323.

Kleiner, L., Marshall, W. L. & Spevack, M. (1987). Training in problem-solving and exposure treatment for agoraphobics with panic attacks. *Journal of Anxiety Disorders*, **1**, 219–238.

Kleinginna, P. R. & Kleinginna, A. M. (1981). A categorised list of emotion definitions with suggestions for a consensual definition. *Motivation and Emotion*, **5**, 348–379.

Kleinknecht, R. A. (1982). The origins and remission of fear in a group of tarantula enthusiasts. *Behaviour Research and Therapy*, **20**, 437–443.

Kleinknecht, R. A. (1987). Vasovagal syncope and blood/injury fear. *Behaviour Research and Therapy*, **25**, 175–178.

Kleinknecht, R. A. (1988). Specificity and psychosocial correlates of blood/injury fear and fainting. *Behaviour Research and Therapy*, **26**, 303–309.

Kleinknecht, R. A. & Bernstein, D. (1978). Assessment of dental fear. *Behavior Therapy*, **9**, 626–634.

Kleinknecht, R. A. & Lenz, J. (1989). Blood/injury fear, fainting and avoidance of medically-related situations: A family correspondence study. *Behaviour Research and Therapy*, **27**, 537–547.

Kleinknecht, R. A. & Thorndike, R. M. (1990). The mutilation questionnaire as a predictor of blood/injury fear and fainting. *Behaviour Research and Therapy*, **28**, 429–437.

Kleinknecht, R. A., Klepac, R. & Alexander, L. (1973). Origins and characteristics of fear of dentistry. *Journal of the American Dental Association*, **86**, 842–848.

Kleinknecht, R. A., McGlynn, F. D., Thorndike, R. M. & Harkavy, J. (1984). Factor analysis of the dental fear survey with cross-validation. *Journal of the American Dental Association*, **106**, 59–61.

Kleinknecht, R. A., Lenz, J., Ford, G. & DeBerard, S. (1990). Types and correlates of blood/injury-related vasovagal syncope. *Behaviour Research and Therapy*, **28**, 289–295.

Klepac, R. K. (1975). Successful treatment of avoidance of dental work by desensitization or increasing pain tolerance. *Journal of Behavior Therapy and Experimental Psychiatry*, **6**, 307–310.

Klerman, G. L. (1986). Current trends in clinical research on panic attacks, agoraphobia, and related anxiety disorders. *Journal of Clinical Psychiatry*, **47**, 37–39.

Klingman, A., Melamed, B. G., Cuthbert, M. I. & Hermecz, D. A. (1984). Effects of participant modeling on information acquisition and skills utilization. *Journal of Consulting and Clinical Psychology*, **52**, 414–422.

Klorman, R., Weerts, T. C., Hastings, J. E., Melamed, B. G. & Lang, P. J. (1974). Psychometric description of specific-fear questionnaires. *Behavior Therapy*, **5**, 401–409.

Klorman, R., Hilpert, P. L., Michael, R., LaGana, C. & Sveen, O. B. (1980). Effects of coping and mastery modeling on experienced and inexperienced pedodontic patients' disruptiveness. *Behavior Therapy*, **11**, 156–168.

Klosko, J. S., Barlow, D. H., Tassinari, R. & Cerny, J. A. (1990). A comparison of alprazolam and behavior therapy in treatment of panic disorder. *Journal of Consulting and Clinical Psychology*, **58**, 77–84.

Kockott, G., Dittman, F. & Nusselt, L. (1975). Systematic desensitization of erectile impotence: A controlled study. *Archives of Sexual Behavior*, **4**, 493–499.

Kockott, G., Feil, W., Revenstorf, D., Aldenhoff, J. & Besinger, U. (1980). Symptomatology and psychological aspects of male sexual inadequacy: Results of an experimental study. *Archives of Sexual Behavior*, **9**, 457–475.

Korff von, M. R., Eaton, W. W. & Keyl, P. M. (1985). The epidemiology of panic attacks and panic disorder. *American Journal of Epidemiology*, **122**, 970–981.

Kozak, M. J., Foa, E. B. & McCarthy, P. R. (1988). Obsessive–compulsive disorder. In C. G. Last & M. Hersen (Eds), *Handbook of Anxiety Disorders*. New York: Pergamon Press.

Kozak, M. J., Foa, E. B. & Steketee, G. (1988). Process and outcome of exposure treatment with obsessive–compulsives: Psychophysiological indicators of emotional processing. *Behavior Therapy*, **19**, 157–169.

Kringlen, E. (1965). Obsessional neurotics: A long-term follow-up. *British Journal of Psychiatry*, **111**, 709–722.

Kringlen, E. (1970). Natural history of obsessional neurosis. *Seminars in Psychiatry*, **2**, 403–419.

Kushner, M. G. & Beitman, B. D. (1990). Panic attacks without fear: An overview. *Behaviour Research and Therapy*, **28**, 469–479.

Laird, J. D. (1984). The role of facial response in the experience of emotion: A reply to Tourangeau and Ellsworth, and others. *Journal of Personality and Social Psychology*, **47**, 909–917.

Lane, T. W. & Borkovec, T. D. (1984). The influence of therapeutic expectancy/ demand on self-efficacy ratings. *Cognitive Therapy and Research*, **8**, 95–106.

Lang, P. J. (1968). Fear reduction and fear behavior: Problems in treating a construct. In J. M. Schlien (Ed.), *Research in Psychotherapy*, Vol. 3. Washington DC: American Psychological Association.

Lang, P. J. (1970). Stimulus control, response control, and the desensitization of fear. In D. J. Levis (Ed.), *Learning Approaches to Therapeutic Behaviour Change*. Chicago, IL: Aldine.

Lang, P. J. (1971). The application of psychophysiological methods to the study of psychotherapy and behavior modification. In A. E. Bergin & S. L. Garfield (Eds), *Handbook of Psychotherapy and Behavior Change*. New York: Wiley.

Lang, P. J. (1985). The cognitive psychophysiology of emotion: Fear and anxiety. In A. H. Tuma & J. D. Maser (Eds), *Anxiety and the Anxiety Disorders*. Hillsdale, NJ: Erlbaum.

Lang, P. J., Rice, D. G. & Sternbach, R. A. (1972). The psychophysiology of emotion. In N. S. Greenfield & R. A. Sternbach (Eds), *Handbook of Psychophysiology*. New York: Holt, Rinehart & Winston.

Lange, C. G. (1885). *The Emotions* (English translation 1922). Baltimore, MD: Williams & Wilkins.

Lange, J. D., Wincze, J. P., Zwick, W., Feldman, S. & Hughes, K. (1981). Effects of demand for performance, self-monitoring of arousal, and increased sympathetic nervous system activity on male erectile response. *Archives of Sexual Behavior*, **10**, 443–464.

Langeluddecke, P. M. (1985). Psychological aspects of irritable bowel syndrome. *Australian and New Zealand Journal of Psychiatry*, **19**, 218–226.

Langeluddecke, P., Goulston, K. & Tennant, C. (1990). Psychological factors in dyspepsia of unknown cause: A comparison with peptic ulcer disease. *Journal of Psychosomatic Research*, **34**, 215–222.

Langer, E. J., Janis, I. E. & Wolfer, J. A. (1975). Reduction of psychological stress in surgical patients. *Journal of Experimental Social Psychology*, **11**, 155–165.

Langosch, W. (1984). Behavioural interventions in cardiac rehabilitation. In A. Steptoe & A. Mathews (Eds), *Health Care and Human Behaviour*. London: Academic Press.

Langosch, W., Steer, P., Brodner, G., Kallinke, D., Kulick, B. & Heim, P. (1982). Behavior therapy with coronary heart disease patients: Results of a comparative study. *Journal of Psychosomatic Research*, **26**, 475–484.

Lapouse, R. & Monk, M. A. (1959). Fears and worries in a representative sample of children. *American Journal of Orthopsychiatry*, **29**, 803–818.

Last, C. G. & Strauss, C. C. (1989). Obsessive–compulsive disorder in childhood. *Journal of Anxiety Disorders*, **3**, 295–302.

Last, C. G., Strauss, C. C. & Francis, G. (1987). Comorbidity among childhood anxiety disorders. *Journal of Nervous and Mental Disease*, **175**, 726–730.

Latimer, P. R. (1981). Irritable bowel syndrome: A behavioural model. *Behavioural Research and Therapy*, **19**, 475–483.

Latimer, P. R., Sarna, S. K., Campbell, D., Latimer, M. R., Waterfall, W. E. & Daniel, E. E. (1981). Colonic motor activity and myoelectrical activity: A comparative study of normal patients, psychoneurotic patients and patients with irritable bowel syndrome (IBS). *Gastroenterology*, **80**, 893–901.

Laughran, T. P. & Kass, D. (1975). Desensitization of sexual dysfunction: the present status. In A. Gurman & D. Rice (Eds), *Couples in Conflict*, New York: Aronson.

Lautch, H. (1971). Dental phobia. *British Journal of Psychiatry*, **119**, 151–158.

Lazarus, R. S. (1966). *Psychological Stress and the Coping Process*. New York: McGraw-Hill.

Lazarus, R. S. (1968). Emotions and adaptation: Conceptual and empirical relations. In W. J. Arnold (Ed.), *Nebraska Symposium on Motivation*. Lincoln, NE: University of Nebraska Press.

Lazarus, R. S. (1982). Thoughts on the relation between emotion and cognition. *American Psychologist*, **37**, 1019–1024.

Lazarus, R. S. (1984). On the primacy of cognition. *American Psychologist*, **39**, 124–129.

Lazarus, R. S. (1991). Cognition and motivation in emotion. *American Psychologist*, **46**, 352–367.

Lazarus, R. S. & Folkman, S. (1984). *Stress, Appraisal, and Coping*, New York: Springer-Verlag.

Lazarus, R. S. & Smith, C. A. (1988). Knowledge and appraisal in the cognition–emotion relationship. *Cognition and Emotion*, **2**, 281–300.

Lazarus, R. S., Kanner, A. D. & Folkman, S. (1980). Emotions: A cognitive phenomenological analysis. In R. Plutchik & H. Kellerman (Eds), *Emotion: Theory, Research and Experience*, Vol. 1. New York: Academic Press.

Leary, M. R. (1982). Social anxiety. In L. Weeler (Ed.), *Review of Personality and Social Psychology*, Vol. 3. Beverly Hills, CA: Sage.

Leary, M. R. (1983a). *Understanding Social Anxiety*. Beverly Hills, CA: Sage.

Leary, M. R. (1983b). Social anxiousness: The construct and its measurement. *Journal of Personality Assessment*, **47**, 66–75.

Leary, M. R. & Schlenker, B. R. (1981). The social psychology of shyness: A self-presentational model. In J. T. Tedeschi (Ed.), *Impression Management Theory and Social Psychological Research*. New York: Academic Press.

LeBoeuf, A. & Lodge, J. (1980). A comparison of frontalis EMG feedback training and progressive relaxation in the treatment of chronic anxiety. *British Journal of Psychiatry*, **137**, 279–284.

Leger, L. A. (1978). Spurious and actual improvement in the treatment of pre-occupying thoughts by thought stopping. *British Journal of Social and Clinical Psychology*, **17**, 373–377.

Leigh, J. M., Walker, J. & Janaganathan, P. (1977). Effect of preoperative anaesthetic visit on anxiety. *British Medical Journal*, **2**, 987–989.

Lelliott, P. & Marks, I. (1988). The cause and treatment of agoraphobia. *Archives of General Psychiatry*, **45**, 388–389.

Lelliott, P., Marks, I., McNamee, G. & Tobena, A. (1989). Onset of panic disorder with agoraphobia: Toward an integrated model. *Archives of General Psychiatry*, **46**, 100–104.

Lent, R. W., Russell, R. K. & Zamostny, K. P. (1981). Comparison of cue-controlled desensitization, rational restructuring, and a credible placebo in the treatment of speech anxiety. *Journal of Consulting and Clinical Psychology*, **49**, 608–610.

Lesser, I. M. & Rubin, R. T. (1986). Diagnostic considerations in panic disorders. *Journal of Clinical Psychiatry*, **47**, Suppl., 4–10.

Leventhal, H. (1979). A perceptual-motor processing model of emotion. In P. Pliner, K. Blankenstein & I. M. Spigel (Eds), *Perception of Emotion in Self and Others*. New York: Plenum.

Leventhal, H. (1980). Toward a comprehensive theory of emotion. In L. Berkowitz (Ed.), *Advances in Experimental Social Psychology*, Vol. 13. New York: Academic Press.

Leventhal, H. (1984). A perceptual-motor theory of emotion. In L. Berkowtiz (Ed.), *Advances in Experimental Social Psychology*, Vol. 17. New York: Academic Press.

Leventhal, H. & Johnson, J. E. (1983). Laboratory and field experimentation: Development of a theory of self-regulation. In P. J. Woodridge, M. H. Schmitt, J. K. Skipper & R. C. Leonard (Eds), *Behavioural Science and Nursing Theory*. St Louis: C. V. Mosby.

Leventhal, H. & Mosbach, P. (1983). A perceptual-motor theory of emotion. In J. T. Cacioppo & R. E. Petty (Eds), *Social Psychophysiology: A Sourcebook*. New York: Guildford Press.

Leventhal, H. & Scherer, K. R. (1987). The relationship of emotion to cognition: A functional approach to a semantic controversy. *Cognition and Emotion*, **1**, 3–28.

Leventhal, H. & Tomarken, A. J. (1986). Emotion: Today's problems. *Annual Review of Psychology*, **37**, 565–610.

Ley, R. (1985a). Agoraphobia, the panic attack, and the hyperventilation syndrome. *Behaviour Research and Therapy*, **23**, 79–81.

Ley, R. (1985b). Blood, breath and fears: A hyperventilation theory of panic attacks and agoraphobia. *Clinical Psychology Review*, **5**, 271–285.

Ley, R. (1987a). Panic disorder and agoraphobia: Fear of fear or fear of the symptoms produced by hyperventilation. *Journal of Behavior Therapy and Experimental Psychiatry*, **18**, 305–316.

Ley, R. (1987b). Panic disorder: A hyperventilation interpretation. In L. Michelson & L. M. Ascher (Eds), *Anxiety and Stress Disorders. Cognitive Behavioral Assessment and Treatment*. New York: Guildford Press.

Ley, R. A. (1988a). Hyperventilation and lactate infusion in the production of panic attacks. *Clinical Psychology Review*, **8**, 1–18.

Ley, R. (1988b). Panic attacks during relaxation and relaxation induced anxiety: A hyperventilation interpretation. *Journal of Behavior Therapy and Experimental Psychiatry*, **19**, 253–259.

Ley, R. (1988c). Panic attacks during sleep: A hyperventilation–probability model. *Journal of Behavior Therapy and Experimental Psychiatry*, **19**, 181–192.

Ley, R. (1989). Dyspneic-fear and catastrophic cognitions in hyperventilatory panic attacks. *Behaviour Research and Therapy*, **27**, 549–554.

Liberman, R. P., King, L. W., de Risi, W. J. & McCann, M. (1975). *Personal Effectiveness*. Champaign, IL: Research Press.

Liebowitz, M. R. & Klein, D. F. (1979). Assessment and treatment of phobic anxiety. *Journal of Clinical Psychiatry*, **40**, 486–492.

Liebowitz, M. R., Gorman, J. M., Fyer, A. J. & Klein, D. F. (1985). Social phobia: Review of a neglected anxiety disorder. *Archives of General Psychiatry*, **42**, 729–736.

Lindsay, S. J. E. (1983). The fear of dental treatment: A critical and theoretical analysis. In S. Rachman (Ed.), *Contributions to Medical Psychology*, Vol. 3. Oxford: Pergamon Press.

Lindsay, W. R., Gamsu, C. V., McLaughlin, E., Hood, E. M. & Espie, C. A. (1987). A controlled trial of treatments for generalized anxiety. *British Journal of Clinical Psychology*, **26**, 3–15.

Lipowski, Z. J. (1976). Psychosomatic medicine: An overview. In O. Hill (Ed.), *Modern Trends in Psychosomatic Medicine*, Vol. 3. London: Butterworths.

Lipowski, Z. J. (1977). Psychosomatic medicine in the seventies: An overview. *American Journal of Psychiatry*, **134**, 223–244.

Lloyd, G. G. & Deakin, H. G. (1975). Phobias complicating treatment of uterine carcinoma. *British Medical Journal*, **5**, 440.

Lobitz, W. & LoPiccolo, J. (1972). New methods in the behavioral treatment of sexual dysfunction. *Journal of Behavior Therapy and Experimental Psychiatry*, **3**, 265–271.

LoPicollo, J. & LoPicollo, L. (1979). *Handbook of Sex Therapy*. New York: Plenum Press.

LoPiccolo, J. L. & Stock, W. E. (1985). Treatment of sexual dysfunction. *Journal of Consulting and Clinical Psychology*, **54**, 158–167.

Lowe, J. & Carroll, D. (1985). The effects of spinal injury on the intensity of emotional experience. *British Journal of Clinical Psychology*, **24**, 135–136.

Lowe, M. R. & Cautela, J. R. (1978). A self-report measure of social skill. *Behavior Therapy*, **9**, 535–544.

Lucock, M. P. & Salkovskis, P. M. (1988). Cognitive factors in social anxiety and its treatment. *Behaviour Research and Therapy*, **26**, 297–302.

Ludwick-Rosenthal, R. & Neufeld, R. W. J. (1988). Stress management during noxious medical procedures: An evaluative review of outcome studies. *Psychological Bulletin*, **104**, 326–342.

Lum, L. C. (1976). The syndrome of habitual chronic hyperventilation. In O. W. Hill (Ed.), *Modern Trends in Psychosomatic Medicine*, Vol. 3. London: Butterworths.

Lyketsos, G., Arapakis, G., Psaras, M., Photiou, I. & Blackburn, I. M. (1982). Psychological characteristics of hypertensive and ulcer patients. *Journal of Psychosomatic Research*, **26**, 255–262.

Lynch, P., Bakal, D. A., Whitelaw, W. & Fung, T. (1991). Chest muscle activity and panic anxiety: A preliminary investigation. *Psychosomatic Medicine*, **53**, 80–89.

MacAlpine, I. (1957). Syphilophobia. *British Journal of Venereal Disease*, **33**, 92–99.

Macaulay, J. L. & Kleinknecht, R. A. (1989). Panic and panic attacks in adolescents. *Journal of Anxiety Disorders*, **3**, 221–241.

MacDonald, M. R. & Kuiper, N. A. (1983). Cognitive–behavioral preparation for surgery. *Clinical Psychology Review*, **3**, 27–39.

MacLeod, C., Mathews, A. & Tata, P. (1986). Attentional bias in emotional disorders. *Journal of Abnormal Psychology*, **95**, 15–20.

Maddux, J. E., Norton, L. W. & Leary, M. R. (1988). Cognitive components of social anxiety: An investigation of the integration of self-presentation theory and self-efficacy theory. *Journal of Social and Clinical Psychology*, **6**, 180–190.

Mahoney, M. J. (1974). *Cognition and Behavior Modification*. Cambridge, MA: Ballinger.

Maller, R. G. & Reiss, S. (1987). A behavioral validation of the anxiety sensitivity index. *Journal of Anxiety Disorders*, **1**, 265–272.

Mannuzza, S., Fyer, A. B., Liebowitz, M. R. & Klein, D. F. (1990). Delineating the boundaries of social phobia: Its relationship to panic disorder and agoraphobia. *Journal of Anxiety Disorders*, **4**, 41–59.

Manstead, A. S. R. (1988). The role of facial movement in emotion. In H. L. Wagner (Ed.), *Social Psychophysiology: Theory and Clinical Applications*. Chichester: Wiley.

Manstead, A. S. R. & Wagner, H. L. (1981). Arousal, cognition and emotion: An appraisal of two-factor theory. *Current Psychological Review*, **1**, 35–54.

Marchandise, B., Bourassa, M. G., Chaitman, B. R. & Lesperance, J. (1978). Angiographic evaluation of the natural history of normal coronary atherosclerosis. *American Journal of Cardiology*, **41**, 216–220.

Marchione, K. E., Michelson, L., Greenwald, M. & Dancu, C. (1987). Cognitive–behavioral treatments of agoraphobia. *Behaviour Research and Therapy*, **25**, 319–328.

Margraf, J. (1991). Ambulatory psychophysiological monitoring of panic attacks. *Journal of Psychophysiology* (in press).

Margraf, J. & Ehlers, A. (1988). Panic attacks in nonclinical subjects. In I. Hand & H.-U. Wittchen (Eds), *Panic and Phobias. 2. Treatments and Variables Affecting Course and Outcome*. Berlin: Springer-Verlag.

Margraf, J. & Ehlers, A. (1989). Etiological models of panic—medical and biological aspects. In Baker, R. (Ed.), *Panic Disorder: Theory Research and Therapy*. Chichester: Wiley.

Margraf, J., Ehlers, A. & Roth, W. T. (1986a). Sodium lactate infusion and panic attacks: A review and critique. *Psychosomatic Medicine*, **48**, 23–51.

Margraf, J., Ehlers, A. & Roth, W. T. (1986b). Panic attacks: Theoretical models and empirical evidence. In I. Hand & H.-U. Wittchen (Eds), *Panic and Phobias*. Berlin: Springer-Verlag.

Margraf, J., Taylor, C. B., Ehlers, A., Roth, W. T. & Agras, W. S. (1987). Panic attacks in the natural environment. *Journal of Nervous and Mental Disease*, **175**, 558–565.

Marks, I. M. (1969). *Fears and Phobias*. London: Heinemann.

Marks, I. M. (1970). The classification of phobic disorders. *British Journal of Psychiatry*, **116**, 377–386.

Marks, I. M. (1971). Phobic disorders four years after treatment: A prospective follow-up. *British Journal of Psychiatry*, **118**, 683–688.

Marks, I. M. (1972). Flooding (implosion) and related treatments. In W. S. Agras (Ed.), *Behavior Modification*. Boston, MA: Little, Brown.

Marks, I. M. (1973). The reduction of fear: Towards a unifying theory. *Journal of the Canadian Psychiatric Association*, **18**, 9–12.

Marks, I. M. (1978). Exposure treatments. In S. Agras (Ed.), *Behavior Modification*, 2nd edn. Boston, MA: Little, Brown.

Marks, I. M. (1985). Behavioral treatment of social phobia. *Psychopharmacology Bulletin*, **21**, 615–618.

Marks, I. M. (1987a). Comment on S. Lloyd Williams' 'On anxiety and phobia'. *Journal of Anxiety Disorders*, **1**, 181–196.

Marks, I. M. (1987b). *Fears, Phobia, and Rituals*. Oxford: Oxford University Press.

Marks, I. M. (1988). Blood–injury phobia: A review. *American Journal of Psychiatry*, **145**, 1207–1213.

Marks, I. M. & Mathews, A. M. (1979). Brief standard self-rating for phobic patients. *Behaviour Research and Therapy*, **17**, 263–267.

Marks, I. M., Boulougouris, J. & Marset, P. (1971). Flooding v desensitization for phobic patients: A crossover study. *British Journal of Psychiatry*, **119**, 353–375.

Marks, I. M., Hodgson, R. & Rachman, S. (1975). Treatment of obsessive–compulsive neurosis by *in vivo* exposure: A 2-year follow-up and issues in treatment. *British Journal of Psychiatry*, **127**, 349–364.

Marks, I. M., Stern, R. S., Mawson, D., Cobb, J. & MacDonald, R. (1980). Clomipramine and exposure for obsessive–compulsive rituals. *British Journal of Psychiatry*, **136**, 1–25.

Marshall, G. D. & Zimbardo, P. G. (1979). Affective consequences of inadequately explained physiological arousal. *Journal of Personality and Social Psychology*, **37**, 970–988.

Martelli, M. F., Auerbach, S. M., Alexander, J. & Mercuri, L. (1987). Stress management in the health care setting: Matching interventions with patient coping styles. *Journal of Consulting and Clinical Psychology*, **55**, 201–207.

Martin, M., Williams, E. M. & Clark, D. M. (1991). Does anxiety lead to selective processing of threat-related information? *Behaviour Research and Therapy*, **29**, 147–160.

Marzillier, J. S., Lambert, C. & Kellett, J. (1976). A controlled evaluation of systematic desensitization and social skills training for socially inadequate psychiatric patients. *Behaviour Research and Therapy*, **14**, 225–238.

Maslach, C. (1979). Negative emotional biasing of unexplained arousal. *Journal of Personality and Social Psychology*, **37**, 953–969.

Masters, W. H. & Johnson, V. E. (1970). *Human Sexual Inadequacy*. Boston, MA: Little, Brown.

Matarazzo, J. D. (1982). Behavioral health's challenge to academic, scientific, and professional psychology. *American Psychologist*, **37**, 1–14.

Mathews, A. (1988a). Anxiety and the processing of threatening information. In V. Hamilton, G. Bower & N. Frijda (Eds), *Cognitive Perspectives on Emotion and Motivation*. Dordrecht, The Netherlands: Kluwer.

Mathews, A. (1988b). Cognitive factors in the treatment of anxiety states. In I. Hand & H.-U. Wittchen (Eds), *Panic and Phobias. 2. Treatment and Variables Affecting Course and Outcome*. Berlin: Springer-Verlag.

Mathews, A. (1990). Why worry? The cognitive function of anxiety. *Behaviour Research and Therapy*, **28**, 455–468.

Mathews, A. & Eysenck, M. W. (1987). Clinical anxiety and cognition. In H. J. Eysenck & I. Martin (Eds), *Theoretical Foundations of Behavior Therapy*. New York: Plenum.

Mathews, A. & MacLeod, C. (1985). Selective processing of threat cues in anxiety states. *Behaviour Research and Therapy*, **23**, 563–569.

Mathews, A. & MacLeod, C. (1986). Discrimination of threat cues without awareness in anxiety states. *Journal of Abnormal Psychology*, **95**, 131–138.

Mathews, A. & MacLeod, C. (1987). An information processing approach to anxiety. *Journal of Cognitive Psychotherapy: An International Quarterly*, **1**, 105–115.

Mathews, A. & Ridgeway, V. (1981). Personality and surgical recovery: A review. *British Journal of Clinical Psychology*, **20**, 243–260.

Mathews, A. & Ridgeway, V. (1984). Psychological preparation for surgery. In A. Steptoe & A. Mathews (Eds), *Health Care and Human Behaviour*. London: Academic Press.

Mathews, A. M. Gelder, M. G. & Johnston, D. W. (1981). *Agoraphobia: Nature and Treatment*. New York: Guildford Press.

Mathews, A., Richards, A. & Eysenck, M. (1989b). Interpretation of homophones related to threat in anxiety states. *Journal of Abnormal Psychology*, **98**, 31–34.

Mathews, A., Bancroft, J., Whitehead, A., Hackmann, A., Julier, D., Bancroft, J.,

Gath, D. & Shaw, P. (1976a). The behavioural treatment of sexual inadequacy: A comparative study. *Behaviour Research and Therapy*, **14**, 427–436.

Mathews, A. M., Johnston, D. W., Lancashire, M., Munby, M., Shaw, P. N. & Gelder, M. G. (1976b). Imaginal flooding and exposure to real phobic situations: Treatment outcome with agoraphobic patients. *British Journal of Psychiatry*, **129**, 362–371.

Mathews, A. M., Teasdale, J., Munby, M., Johnston, D. & Shaw, P. (1977). A home-based treatment program for agoraphobia. *Behavior Therapy*, **8**, 915–924.

Mathews, A. M., Mogg, K., May, J. & Eysenck, M. (1989a). Implicit and explicit memory bias in anxiety. *Journal of Abnormal Psychology*, **98**, 236–240.

Mathews, A., May, J., Mogg, K. & Eysenck, M. (1990). Attentional bias in anxiety: Selective search or defective filtering? *Journal of Abnormal Psychology*, **99**, 166–173.

Matsumoto, D. (1987). The role of facial response in the experience of emotion: More methodological problems and a meta-analysis. *Journal of Personality and Social Psychology*, **52**, 769–774.

Matthews, K. A. & Haynes, S. G. (1986). Type A behavior pattern and coronary disease risk: Update and critical evaluation. *American Journal of Epidemiology*, **123**, 923–960.

Mattick, R. P. & Peters, L. (1988). Treatment of severe social phobia: Effects of guided exposure with and without cognitive restructuring. *Journal of Consulting and Clinical Psychology*, **56**, 251–260.

Mattick, R. P., Peters, L. & Clarke, J. C. (1989). Exposure and cognitive restructuring for social phobia: A controlled study. *Behavior Therapy*, **20**, 3–23.

Mattick, R. P., Andrews, G., Hadzi-Pavlovic, D. & Christensen, H. (1990). Treatment of panic and agoraphobia: An integrative review. *Journal of Nervous and Mental Disease*, **178**, 567–756.

Mavissakalian, M. (1985). Male and female agoraphobia: Are they different? *Behaviour Research and Therapy*, **4**, 469–471.

Mavissakalian, M. (1986). The fear questionnaire: A validity study. *Behaviour Research and Therapy*, **24**, 83–85.

Mavissakalian, M. (1987). Trimodal assessment in agoraphobia research: Further observations on heart rate and synchrony/desynchrony. *Journal of Psychopathology and Behavioral Assessment*, **9**, 89–98.

Mavissakalian, M. (1988). The relationship between panic, phobic and anticipatory anxiety in agoraphobia. *Behaviour Research and Therapy*, **26**, 235–240.

Mavissakalian, M. & Barlow, D. H. (1981). *Phobia: Psychological and Pharmacological Treatment*. New York: Guildford Press.

Mavissakalian, M. & Michelson, L. (1982). Patterns of psychophysiological change in the treatment of agoraphobia. *Behaviour Research and Therapy*, **20**, 347–356.

Mavissakalian, M. & Michelson, L. (1983). Self-directed *in vivo* exposure practice in behavioral and pharmacological treatments of agoraphobia. *Behavior Therapy*, **14**, 506–519.

Mavissakalian, M. & Michelson, L. (1986). Agoraphobia: Relative and combined effectiveness of therapist-assisted *in vivo* exposure and imipramine. *Journal of Clinical Psychiatry*, **47**, 117–122.

Mavissakalian, M., Hamann, M. S. & Jones, B. (1990). Correlates of DSM-III personality disorders in obsessive–compulsive disorder. *Comprehensive Psychiatry*, **31**, 481–489.

Mavissakalian, M., Michelson, L., Greenwald, D., Kornblith, S. & Greenwald, M. (1983). Cognitive–behavioral treatments of agoraphobia: Short- and long-term efficacy of paradoxical intention vs. self-statement training. *Behaviour Research and Therapy*, **21**, 75–86.

Mayou, R. A. (1983). A controlled trial of early rehabilitation after myocardial infarction. *Journal of Cardiac Rehabilitation*, **3**, 397–402.

McCann, B. S., Woolfolk, R. L. & Lehrer, P. M. (1987). Specificity of response to treatment: A study of interpersonal anxiety. *Behaviour Research and Therapy*, **25**, 129–136.

McCarthy, B. W. (1972). Short term implosive therapy: Case study. *Psychological Reports*, **30**, 589–590.

McConaghy, N. (1988). Sexual dysfunction and deviation. In A. S. Bellack & M. Hersen (Eds), *Behavioral Assessment*, 3rd edn. New York: Pergamon Press.

McCrae, R. R., Bartone, P. T. & Costa, P. T. Jr (1976). Age, anxiety, and self-reported health. *Aging and Human Development*, **7**, 49–58.

McEwan, K. L. & Devins, G. M. (1983). Is increased arousal in social anxiety noticed by others? *Journal of Abnormal Psychology*, **92**, 417–421.

McFall, M. E. & Wollersheim, J. P. (1979). Obsessive–compulsive neurosis: A cognitive behavioral formulation and approach to treatment. *Cognitive Therapy and Research*, **3**, 333–348.

McFall, R. (1982). A review and reformulation of the concept of social skills. *Behavioral Assessment*, **4**, 1–33.

McGovern, K. B., Stewart, R. C. & LoPiccolo, J. (1975). Secondary orgasmic dysfunction. I. Analysis and strategies for treatment. *Archives of Sexual Behavior*, **4**, 265–275.

McIntosh, J. H., Nasiry, R. W., Frydman, M., Waller, S. L. & Piper, D. W. (1983). The personality pattern of patients with chronic peptic ulcer. A case-control study. *Scandinavian Journal of Gastroenterology*, **18**, 945–950.

McKeon, J., McGuffin, P. & Robinson, P. (1984). Obsessive–compulsive neurosis following head injury: A report of four cases. *British Journal of Psychiatry*, **144**, 190–192.

McKeon, J., Roa, B. & Mann, A. (1984). Life events and personality traits in obsessive–compulsive neurosis. *British Journal of Psychiatry*, **144**, 185–189.

McKinley, J. C. & Hathaway, S. R. (1940). A Multiphase Personality Schedule (Minnesota): II. A differential study of hypochondriasis. *Journal of Psychology*, **10**, 255–268.

McNally, R. J. (1987). Preparedness and phobias: A review. *Psychological Bulletin*, **101**, 283–303.

McNally, R. J. (1990). Psychological approaches to panic disorder: A review. *Psychological Bulletin*, **108**, 403–419.

McNally, R. J. & Lorenz, M. (1987). Anxiety sensitivity in agoraphobics. *Journal of Behavior Therapy and Experimental Psychiatry*, **18**, 3–11.

McNally, R. J. & Steketee, G. S. (1985). The etiology and maintenance of severe animal phobias. *Behaviour Research and Therapy*, **23**, 431–435.

McNally, R. J., Foa, E. B. & Donnell, C. D. (1989). Memory bias for anxiety information in patients with anxiety disorder. *Cognition and Emotion*, **3**, 27–44.

McNally, R. J., Riemann, B. C. & Kim, E. (1990). Selective processing of threat cues in panic disorder. *Behaviour Research and Therapy*, **28**, 407–412.

McNally, R. J., Kaspi, S. P., Reimann, B. C. & Zeitlin, S. B. (1990). Selective processing of threat cues in post-traumatic stress disorder. *Journal of Abnormal Psychology*, **89**, 403–419.

McPherson, F. M., Brougham, L. & McLaren, S. (1980). Maintenance of improvement in agoraphobic patients treated by behavioural methods—four-year follow-up. *Behaviour Research and Therapy*, **18**, 150–152.

Medalie, J. H. & Goldbourt, U. (1976). Angina pectoris among 10 000 men. *American Journal of Medicine*, **60**, 910–921.

Meichenbaum, D. (1977). *Cognitive–behavior Modification*. New York: Plenum.

Meichenbaum, D. & Cameron, R. (1983). Stress inoculation training: Toward a general paradigm for training coping skills. In D. Meichenbaum & M. E. Jeremko (Eds), *Stress Reduction and Prevention*. New York: Plenum Press.

Meichenbaum, D. H., Gilmore, J. B. & Fedoravicius, A. (1971). Group insight versus group desensitization in treating speech anxiety. *Journal of Consulting and Clinical Psychology*, **36**, 410–421.

Meier, S., McCarthy, P. R. & Schmeck, R. R. (1984). Validity of self-efficacy as a predictor of writing performance. *Cognitive Therapy and Research*, **8**, 107–120.

Melamed, B. G. (1979). Behavioral approaches to fear in dental settings. In M. Hersen, R. Eisler & P. Miller (Eds), *Progress in Behavior Modification*, Vol. 7. New York: Academic Press.

Melamed, B. G. & Siegel, L. J. (1975). Reduction of anxiety in children facing surgery by modeling. *Journal of Consulting and Clinical Psychology*, **43**, 511–521.

Melamed, B. G., Dearborn, M. & Hermecz, D. A. (1983). Necessary considerations for surgery preparation: Age and previous experience. *Psychosomatic Medicine*, **45**, 517–525.

Melamed, B. G., Siegel, L. J. & Ridley-Johnson, R. (1988). Coping in children facing medical stress. In T. M. Field, P. M. McCabe & N. Schneiderman (Eds), *Stress and Coping Across Development*. Hillsdale, NJ: Erlbaum.

Melamed, B. G., Hawes, R. R., Heiby, E. & Glick, J. (1975). Use of filmed modeling to reduce uncooperative behavior of children during dental treatment. *Journal of Dental Research*, **54**, 797–801.

Melamed, B. G., Yurcheson, R., Fleece, L., Hutcherson, S. & Hawes, R. (1978). Effects of film modeling on the reduction of anxiety-related behaviors in individuals varying in levels of previous experience in the stress situation. *Journal of Consulting and Clinical Psychology*, **46**, 1357–1367.

Mellman, T. A. & Uhde, T. W. (1989). Electroencephalographic sleep in panic disorder. *Archives of General Psychiatry*, **46**, 178–184.

Mendel, J. & Klein, D. (1969). Anxiety attacks and subsequent agoraphobia. *Comprehensive Psychiatry*, **10**, 190–195.

Mendeloff, A. I. (1975). The epidemiology of idiopathic inflammatory bowel disease. In J. B. Kirsner & R. G. Shorter (Eds), *Inflammatory Bowel Disease*. Philadelphia, PA: Lea & Febiger.

Merckelbach, H., van Hout, W., van den Hout, M. & Mersch, P. (1989a). Psychophysiological and subjective reactions of social phobics and normals to facial stimuli. *Behaviour Research and Therapy*, **27**, 289–294.

Merckelbach, H., de Ruiter, C., van den Hout, M. A. & Hoekstra, R. (1989b). Conditioning experiences and phobias. *Behaviour Research and Therapy*, **27**, 657–662.

Merluzzi, T. V. & Biever, J. (1987). Role-playing procedures for the behavioral assessment of social skill: A validity study. *Behavioral Assessment*, **9**, 361–377.

Merluzzi, T. V., Burgio, K. L. & Glass, C. R. (1984). Cognition and psychopathology: An analysis of social introversion and self-statements. *Journal of Consulting and Clinical Psychology*, **52**, 1102–1103.

Mersch, P. P. A., Emmelkamp, P. M. G., Bogels, S. M. & van der Sleen, J. (1989). Social phobia: Individual response patterns and the effects of behavioral and cognitive interventions. *Behaviour Research and Therapy*, **27**, 421–434.

Metzger, R. L., Miller, M. L., Cohen, M., Sofka, M. & Borkovec, T. D. (1990). Worry changes decision making: The effect of negative thoughts on cognitive processing. *Journal of Clinical Psychology*, **46**, 78–88.

Meyer, T. J., Miller, M. L., Metzger, R. L. & Borkovec, T. D. (1990). Development and validation of the Penn State Worry questionnaire. *Behaviour Research and Therapy*, **28**, 487–495.

Meyer, V. (1966). Modification of expectations in cases with obsessional rituals. *Behaviour Research and Therapy*, **4**, 273–280.

Meyer, V. & Levy, R. (1973). Modification of behavior in obsessive–compulsive disorders. In H. E. Adams & P. Unikel (Eds), *Issues and Trends in Behavior Therapy*. Springfield, IL: Charles C. Thomas.

Michelson, L. (1984). The role of individual differences, response profiles and treatment consonance in anxiety disorders. *Journal of Behavioral Assessment*, **6**, 349–368.

Michelson, L. (1986). Treatment consonance and response profiles in agoraphobia: The role of individual differences in cognitive, behavioural and physiological treatments. *Behaviour Research and Therapy*, **24**, 263–275.

Michelson, L. (1987). Cognitive–behavioral assessment and treatment of agoraphobia. In L. Michelson, & L. M. Ascher (Eds), *Anxiety and Stress Disorders. Cognitive–Behavioral Assessment and Treatment*. New York: Guildford Press.

Michelson, L. K. & Marchione, K. (1991). Behavioral, cognitive and pharmacological treatments of panic disorder with agoraphobia: Critique and synthesis. *Journal of Consulting and Clinical Psychology*, **59**, 100–114.

Michelson, L. & Mavissakalian, M. (1983). Temporal stability of self-report measures in agoraphobia research. *Behaviour Research and Therapy*, **21**, 695–698.

Michelson, L. & Mavissakalian, M. (1985). Psychophysiological outcome of behavioral and pharmacological treatments of agoraphobia. *Journal of Consulting and Clinical Psychology*, **53**, 229–236.

Michelson, L., Mavissakalian, M. & Marchione, K. (1985). Cognitive and behavioral treatments of agoraphobia: Clinical, behavioral and psychophysiological outcome. *Journal of Consulting and Clinical Psychology*, **53**, 913–925.

Michelson, L., Mavissakalian, M. & Marchione, K. (1988). Cognitive, behavioral, and physiological treatments of agoraphobia: A comparative outcome investigation. *Behavior Therapy*, **19**, 97–120.

Michelson, L., Mavissakalian, M., Marchione, K., Dancu, D. & Greenwald, M. (1986). The role of self-directed *in vivo* exposure practice in cognitive, behavioral and psychophysiological treatments of agoraphobia. *Behavior Therapy*, **17**, 91–108.

Michelson, L., Marchione, K., Greenwald, M., Glanz, L., Testa, S. & Marchione, N. (1990a). Panic disorder: Cognitive–behavioral treatment. *Behaviour Research and Therapy*, **28**, 141–151.

Michelson, L., Mavissakalian, M., Marchione, K., Ulrich, R. F., Marchione, N. & Testa, S. (1990b). Psychophysiological outcome of cognitive, behavioral and psychophysiologically based treatments of agoraphobia. *Behaviour Research and Therapy*, **28**, 127–139.

Milgram, N. W., Krames, L. & Alloway, T. M. (1977). *Food Aversion Learning*. New York: Plenum.

Milgrom, P., Fiset, L., Melnick, S. & Weinstein, P. (1988). The prevalence and practice management consequences of dental fear in a major U.S. city. *Journal of the American Dental Association*, **116**, 641–647.

Miller, D., Acton, T. M. G. & Hedge, B. (1988). The worried well: Their identification and management. *Journal of the Royal College of Physicians of London*, **22**, 158–165.

Miller, D., Green, J., Farmer, R. & Carroll, G. (1985). A 'pseudo-AIDS' syndrome following from a fear of AIDS. *British Journal of Psychiatry*, **146**, 550.

Miller, M. P., Murphy, P. J. & Miller, T. P. (1978). Comparison of electromyographic feedback and progressive relaxation training in treating circumscribed anxiety stress reactions. *Journal of Consulting and Clinical Psychology*, **46**, 1291–1298.

Miller, N. E. (1951). Learnable drives and rewards. In S. S. Stevens (Ed.), *Handbook of Experimental Psychology*. New York: Wiley.

Miller, S. M. & Mangan, C. E. (1983). Interaction effects of information and coping style in adapting to gynecologic stress: Should the doctor tell all? *Journal of Personality and Social Psychology*, **45**, 223–236.

Mills, H. L., Agras, W. S., Barlow, D. H. & Mills, J. R. (1973). Compulsive rituals treated by response prevention. *Archives of General Psychiatry*, **28**, 524–527.

Milner, A. D., Beech, H. R. & Walker, V. J. (1971). Decision processes and obsessional behaviour. *British Journal of Social and Clinical Psychology*, **10**, 88–89.

Milton, F. & Hafner, J. (1979). The outcome of behavior therapy for agoraphobia in relation to marital adjustment. *Archives of General Psychiatry*, **36**, 807–811.

Mineka, S. (1987). A primate model of phobic fears. In H. J. Eysenck & I. Martin (Eds), *Theoretical Foundations of Behavior Therapy*. New York: Plenum.

Mineka, S., Davidson, M., Cook, M. & Keir, R. (1984). Observational conditioning of snake fear in rhesus monkeys. *Journal of Abnormal Psychology*, **93**, 355–372.

Minichiello, W. E., Baer, L. & Jenike, M. A. (1987). Schizotypal personality disorder: A poor prognostic indicator for behavior therapy in the treatment of obsessive–compulsive disorders. *Journal of Anxiety Disorders*, **1**, 273–276.

Minichiello, W. E., Baer, L., Jenike, M. A. & Holland, A. (1990). Age of onset of major subtypes of obsessive–compulsive disorders. *Journal of Anxiety Disorders*, **4**, 147–150.

Minski, L. & Desai, M. M. (1955). Aspects of personality in peptic ulcer patients. *British Journal of Medical Psychology*, **28**, 113–134.

Mischel, W. (1973). Toward a cognitive social learning reconceptualisation of personality. *Psychological Review*, **80**, 252–283.

Mitchell, C. M. & Drossmann, D. A. (1987). The irritable bowel syndrome: Understanding and treating a biopsychosocial illness disorder. *Annals of Behavioral Medicine*, **9**, 13–18.

Mitchell, K. R. (1978). Self-management of spastic colitis. *Journal of Behavior Therapy and Experimental Psychiatry*, **9**, 269–273.

Modigliani, A. (1968). Embarrassment and embarrassibility. *Sociometry*, **31**, 313–326.

Mogg, K. & Marden, B. (1990). Processing of emotional information in anxious subjects. *British Journal of Clinical Psychology*, **29**, 227–229.

Mogg, K. & Mathews, A. (1990). Is there a self-referent mood-congruent recall bias in anxiety? *Behaviour Research and Therapy*, **28**, 91–92.

Mogg, K., Mathews, A. & Weinman, J. (1987). Memory bias in clinical anxiety. *Journal of Abnormal Psychology*, **96**, 94–98.

Mogg, K., Mathews, A. & Weinman, J. (1989). Selective processing of threat cues in anxiety states: A replication. *Behaviour Research and Therapy*, **27**, 317–323.

Mohr, D. C. & Beutler, L. E. (1990). Erectile dysfunction: A review of diagnostic and treatment procedures. *Clinical Psychology Review*, **10**, 123–150.

Molen van der, G. M., van den Hout, M. A. & Halfens, R. (1988). Agoraphobia and locus of control. *Journal of Psychopathology and Behavioral Assessment*, **10**, 269–275.

Molen van der, G. M., van den Hout, M. A., Vroemen, J., Lousberg, H. & Griez, E. (1986). Cognitive determinants of lactate-induced anxiety. *Behaviour Research and Therapy*, **24**, 677–680.

Monteiro, W., Marks, I. M. & Ramm, E. (1985). Marital adjustment and treatment outcome in agoraphobia. *British Journal of Psychiatry*, **146**, 383–390.

Moore, N. (1965). Behavior therapy in bronchial asthma: A controlled study. *Journal of Psychosomatic Research*, **9**, 257–276.

Morokoff, P. J. & Heiman, J. R. (1980). Effects of erotic stimuli on sexually functional and dysfunctional women: Multiple measures before and after therapy. *Behaviour Research and Therapy*, **18**, 127–137.

Morris, C. (1991). Non-ulcer dyspepsia. *Journal of Psychosomatic Research*, **35**, 129–140.

Mowrer, O. H. (1939). A stimulus–response analysis of anxiety and its role as a reinforcing agent. *Psychological Review*, **46**, 553–565.

Mowrer, O. H. (1960). *Learning Theory and Behavior*. New York: Wiley.

Mowrer, O. H. & Lamoreaux, R. R. (1946). Fear as an intervening variable in avoidance conditioning. *Journal of Comparative Psychology*, **39**, 29–50.

Mukerji, V., Beitman, B. D., Alpert, M. A., Hewitt, J. E. & Basha, I. M. (1987). Panic attack symptoms in patients with chest pain and angiographically normal coronary arteries. *Journal of Anxiety Disorders*, **1**, 41–46.

Mumford, E., Schlesinger, H. J. & Glass, G. V. (1982). The effects of psychological intervention on recovery from surgery and heart attacks: An analysis of the literature. *American Journal of Public Health*, **72**, 141–151.

Munby, J. & Johnston, D. W. (1980). Agoraphobia: The long-term follow-up of behavioural treatment. *British Journal of Psychiatry*, **137**, 418–427.

Munjack, D. J., Kanno, P. H. & Oziel, L. J. (1978). Ejaculatory disorders: Some psychometric data. *Psychological Reports*, **43**, 783–787.

Munro, A. (1980). Monosymptomatic hypochondriacal psychosis (MHP): New aspects of an old syndrome. *Journal of Psychiatric Treatment and Evaluation*, **2**, 79–86.

Murray, E. J. & Foote, F. (1979). The origins of fear of snakes. *Behaviour Research and Therapy*, **17**, 489–493.

Murray, R. M., Cooper, J. E. & Smith, A. (1979). The Leyton Obsessional Inventory: An analysis of the responses of 73 obsessional patients. *Psychological Medicine*, **9**, 305–311.

Myers, J. K., Weissman, M. M., Tischler, C. E., Holzer, C. E., III, Orvaschel, H., Anthony, J. C., Boyd, J. H., Burke, J. D., Jr., Kramer, M. & Stoltzman, R. (1984). Six-month prevalence of psychiatric disorders in three communities. *Archives of General Psychiatry*, **41**, 959–967.

Nagle, R., Gangola, R. & Picton-Robinson, I. (1971). Factors influencing return to work after myocardial infarction. *The Lancet*, **ii**, 454–456.

Naismith, L. D., Robinson, J. F., Shaw, G. B. & MacIntyre, M. M. (1979). Psychological rehabilitation after myocardial infarction. *British Medical Journal*, **67**, 439–442.

Neff, D. F. & Blanchard, E. B. (1987). A multi-component treatment for irritable bowel syndrome. *Behavior Therapy*, **18**, 72–83.

Nemetz, G. H., Craig, K. D. & Reith, G. (1978). Treatment of female sexual dysfunction through symbolic modeling. *Journal of Consulting and Clinical Psychology*, **46**, 62–73.

Newton, A., Kindness, K. & McFadyen, M. (1983). Patients and social skills groups: Do they lack social skills? *Behavioural Psychotherapy*, **11**, 116–126.

Ney, T. & Gale, A. (1988). A critique of laboratory studies of emotion with particular reference to psychophysiological aspects. In H. L. Wagner (Ed.), *Social Psychophysiology and Emotion*. Chichester: Wiley.

Norton, G. R. & Jehu, D. (1984). The role of anxiety in sexual dysfunctions: A review. *Archives of Sexual Behavior*, **2**, 165–183.

Norton, G. R., Cox, B. J. & Malan, J. (1990). Nonclinical panickers: A critical review. Manuscript submitted.

Norton, G. R., Dorward, J. & Cox, B. J. (1986). Factors associated with panic attacks in nonclinical subjects. *Behavior Therapy*, **17**, 239–252.

Norton, G. R., Harrison, B., Hauch, J. & Rhodes, L. (1985). Characteristics of people with infrequent panic attacks. *Journal of Abnormal Psychology*, **94**, 216–221.

Norton, G. R., Cairns, S. L., Wozney, K. A. & Malan, J. (1988a). Panic attacks and psychopathology in nonclinical panickers. *Journal of Anxiety Disorders*, **2**, 319–331.

Norton, G. R., Schaefer, E., Cox, B. J., Doward, J. & Wozney, K. (1988b). Selective memory effects in nonclinical panickers. *Journal of Anxiety Disorders*, **2**, 169–177.

Noyes, R., Anderson, D. J., Clancy, J., Crowe, R. R., Slymen, D. J., Ghoneim, M. M. & Heinricks, J. V. (1984). Diazepam and propranolol in panic disorder and agoraphobia. *Archives of General Psychiatry*, **41**, 287–292.

Noyes, R., Reich, J., Clancy, J. & O'Gorman, T. W. (1986). Reduction in hypochondriasis with treatment of panic disorder. *British Journal of Psychiatry*, **149**, 631–635.

Nunn, J. D., Stevenson, R. J. & Whalan, G. (1984). Selective memory effects in agoraphobic patients. *British Journal of Clinical Psychology*, **23**, 195–201.

O'Banion, K. & Arkowitz, H. (1977). Social anxiety and selective memory for affective information about the self. *Social Behavior and Personality*, **5**, 321–328.

Obler, M. (1973). Systematic desensitization in sexual disorders. *Journal of Behavior Therapy and Experimental Psychiatry*, **4**, 93–101.

O'Brien, G. T. & Barlow, D. H. (1984). Agoraphobia. In S. M. Turner (Ed.), *Behavioral Theory and Treatment of Anxiety*. New York: Plenum Press.

Ockene, I. S., Shay, M. J., Alpert, J. S., Weiner, B. H. & Dalen, J. E. (1980). Unexplained chest pain in patients with normal coronary arteriograms. *New England Journal of Medicine*, **303**, 1249–1252.

Odom, J. V., Nelson, R. O. & Wien, K. S. (1978). The differential effectiveness of five treatment procedures on three response systems in a snake phobia analogue study. *Behavior Therapy*, **9**, 936–942.

Oei, T. P. S., Wanstall, K. & Evans, L. (1990). Sex differences in panic disorder with agoraphobia. *Journal of Anxiety Disorder*, **4**, 317–324.

Ohman, A. (1979). Fear relevance, autonomic conditioning, and phobias: A laboratory model. In P. O. Sjoden, S. Bates & W. S. Dockens III (Eds), *Trends in Behavior Therapy*. New York: Academic Press.

Ohman, A. (1986). Face the beast and fear the face: Animal and social fears as prototypes for evolutionary analyses of emotion. *Psychophysiology*, **23**, 123–145.

Ohman, A. & Dimburg, U. (1984). An evolutionary perspective on human social behavior. In W. M. Waid (Ed.), *Sociophysiology*. New York: Springer-Verlag.

Ohman, A., Dimburg, U. & Öst, L-G. (1985) Animal and social phobias: Biological constraints on learned fear responses. In S. Reiss & R. R. Bootzin (Eds), *Theoretical Issues in Behavior Therapy*. New York: Academic Press.

Oldenberg, B., Perkins, R. J. & Andrews, G. (1985). Controlled trial of psychological intervention in myocardial infarction. *Journal of Consulting and Clinical Psychology*, **53**, 852–859.

O'Neill, G. W. (1985). Is worry a valuable concept? *Behaviour Research and Therapy*, **23**, 479–480.

Öst, L-G. (1985). Ways of acquiring phobias and outcome of behavioural treatments. *Behaviour Research and Therapy*, **23**, 683–689.

Öst, L-G. (1987) Age of onset in different phobias. *Journal of Abnormal Psychology*, **96**, 223–229.

Öst, L-G. (1988). Applied relaxation vs progressive relaxation in the treatment of panic disorder. *Behaviour Research and Therapy*, **26**, 13–22.

Öst, L-G. (1990). The agoraphobia scale: An evaluation of its reliability and validity. *Behaviour Research and Therapy*, **28**, 323–329.

Öst, L-G. & Hugdahl, K. (1981). Acquisition of phobias and anxiety response patterns in clinical patients. *Behaviour Research and Therapy*, **19**, 439–447.

Öst, L-G. & Hugdahl, K. (1983). Acquisition of agoraphobia, mode of onset and anxiety response patterns. *Behaviour Research and Therapy*, **21**, 623–631.

Öst, L-G. & Hugdahl, K. (1985). Acquisition of blood and dental phobia and anxiety response patterns in clinical patients. *Behaviour Research and Therapy*, **23**, 27–34.

Öst, L-G., Jerremalm, A. & Jansson, L. (1984a). Individual response patterns and the effects of different behavioral methods in the treatment of agoraphobia. *Behaviour Research and Therapy*, **22**, 697–707.

Öst, L-G., Jerremalm, A. & Johansson, J. (1981). Individual response patterns and the effects of different behavioral methods in the treatment of social phobia. *Behaviour Research and Therapy*, **19**, 1–16.

Öst, L-G., Johansson, J. & Jerremalm, A. (1982). Individual response patterns and the effects of different behavioral methods in the treatment of claustrophobia. *Behaviour Research and Therapy*, **20**, 445–460.

Öst, L-G., Sterner, U. & Lindahl, I-L. (1984c) Physiological response in blood phobics. *Behaviour Research and Therapy*, **22**, 109–117.

Öst, L-G., Lindahl, I-L., Sterner, U. & Jerremalm, A. (1984b). Exposure *in vivo* vs applied relaxation in the treatment of blood phobia. *Behaviour Research and Therapy*, **22**, 205–216.

Ottaviani, R. & Beck, A. T. (1987). Cognitive aspects of panic. *Journal of Anxiety Disorders*, **1**, 15–28.

Palace, E. M. & Gorzalka, B. B. (1990). The enhancing effects of anxiety on arousal in sexually dysfunctional and functional women. *Journal of Abnormal Psychology*, **99**, 403–411.

Palmer, R. L., Stonehill, E., Crisp, A. H., Waller, S. L., & Misiewicz, J. J. (1974). Psychological characteristics of patients with irritable bowel syndrome. *Postgraduate Medical Journal*, **50**, 416–419.

Parker, G. (1979). Reported parental characteristics of agoraphobics and social phobics. *British Journal of Psychiatry*, **135**, 555–560.

Parkinson, L. & Rachman, S. (1981). Intrusive thoughts: The effects of an uncontrived stress. *Advances in Behaviour Research and Therapy*, **3**, 111–118.

Pauli, P., Marquardt, C., Hartl, L., Nutzinger, D. O., Hozl, R. & Strain, F. (1991). Anxiety induced by cardiac perceptions in patients with panic attacks: A field study. *Behaviour Research and Therapy*, **29**, 137–145.

Pennebaker, J. W. (1982). *The Psychology of Physical Symptoms*. New York: Springer-Verlag.

Perkins, C. C. Jr (1955). The stimulus conditions which follow learned responses. *Psychological Review*, **62**, 341–348.

Perkins, C. C. Jr (1968). An analysis of the concept of reinforcement. *Psychological Review*, **75**, 155–172.

Persons, J. B. & Foa, E. B. (1984). Processing of fearful and neutral information by obsessive–compulsives. *Behaviour Research and Therapy*, **22**, 259–265.

Persson, G. & Nordlund, C. L. (1985). Agoraphobics and social phobics: Differences in background factors, syndrome profile and therapeutic response. *Acta Psychiatrica Scandinavica*, **7**, 148–159.

Peterson, L. (1989). Coping by children undergoing stressful medical procedures: Some conceptual, methodological, and therapeutic issues. *Journal of Consulting and Clinical Psychology*, **57**, 380–387.

Peterson, L. & Shigetomi, C. (1981). One-year follow-up of elective surgery child patients receiving preoperative preparation. *Journal of Pediatric Psychology*, **7**, 43–48.

Peterson, L., Schultheis, K., Ridley-Johnson, R., Miller, D. J. & Tracy, K. (1984). Comparison of three modeling procedures on the presurgical and postsurgical reactions of children. *Behavior Therapy*, **15**, 197–203.

Peterson, R. A. & Heilbronner, R. L. (1987). The anxiety sensitivity index: Construct validity and factor analytic structure. *Journal of Anxiety Disorders*, **1**, 117–121.

Philip, A. E., Cay, E. L., Vetter, N. J. & Stuckey, N. A. (1979). Personal traits and the physical, psychiatric and social state of patients one year after a myocardial infarction. *International Journal of Rehabilitation Research*, **2**, 479–487.

Philpott, R. (1975). Recent advances in the behavioural measurement of obsessional illness: Difficulties common to these and other instruments. *Scottish Medical Journal*, **20**, 33–40.

Pickett, C. & Clum, G. A. (1982). Comparative treatment strategies and their interaction with locus of control in the reduction of surgical pain and anxiety. *Journal of Consulting and Clinical Psychology*, **50**, 439–441.

Pickles, A. & van den Broek, M. (1988). Failure to replicate evidence for phobic schemata in agoraphobic patients. *British Journal of Clinical Psychology*, **27**, 271–272.

Pilkonis, P. A. & Zimbardo, P. G. (1979). The personal and social dynamics of shyness. In C. E. Izard (Ed.), *Emotions in Personality and Psychopathology*. New York: Plenum Press.

Pilowsky, I. (1967). Dimensions of hypochondriasis. *British Journal of Psychiatry*, **113**, 88–93.

Pilowsky, I. (1970). Primary and secondary hypochondriasis. *Acta Psychiatrica Scandinavica*, **46**, 273–285.

Pinto, R. P. & Hollandsworth J. G. (1989). Using videotape modeling to prepare children psychologically for surgery: Influence of parents and costs versus benefits of providing preparation services. *Health Psychology*, **8**, 79–95.

Plutchik, R. (1980). *Emotion: A Psychoevolutionary Synthesis*. New York: Harper & Row.

Plutchik, R. (1984). Emotions: A general psychoevolutionary theory. In K. R. Scherer & P. Ekman (Eds), *Approaches to Emotion*. Hillsdale, NJ: Erlbaum.

Plutchik, R. (1985). On emotion: The chicken-and-egg problem revisited. *Motivation and Emotion*, **9**, 197–200.

Pollard, C. A. & Henderson, J. G. (1988). Four types of social phobia in a community sample. *Journal of Nervous and Mental Disease*, **176**, 440–445.

Pollard, C. A., Pollard, H. J. & Corn, K. J. (1989). Panic onset and major life events in the lives of agoraphobics: A test of contiguity. *Journal of Abnormal Psychology*, **98**, 318–321.

Power, K. G., Jerrom, D. W. A., Simpson, R. J., Mitchell, M. J. & Swanson, V. (1989). A controlled comparison of cognitive–behaviour therapy, diazepam and placebo in the management of generalized anxiety. *Behavioural Psychotherapy*, **17**, 1–14.

Pruzinsky, T. & Borkovec, T. D. (1990). Cognitive and personality characteristics of worriers. *Behaviour Research and Therapy*, **28**, 507–512.

Przybyla, D. P. J. & Byrne, D. (1984). The mediating role of cognitive processes in self-reported sexual arousal. *Journal of Research in Personality*, **18**, 54–63.

Rabavilas, A. D., Boulougouris, J. C. & Stefanis, C. (1977). Duration of flooding sessions in the treatment of obsessive–compulsive patients. *Behaviour Research and Therapy*, **14**, 349–355.

Rachman, S. (1976a). The passing of the two-stage theory of fear and avoidance: Fresh possibilities. *Behaviour Research and Therapy*, **14**, 125–131.

Rachman, S. (1976b). The modification of obsessions: A new formulation. *Behaviour Research and Therapy*, **14**, 437–443.

Rachman, S. (1977). The conditioning theory of fear acquisition: A critical examination. *Behaviour Research and Therapy*, **15**, 375–387.

Rachman, S. (1978). *Fear and Courage*. San Francisco, CA: Freeman.

Rachman, S. (1979). The return of fear. *Behaviour Research and Therapy*, **17**, 164–167.

Rachman, S. (1980). Emotional processing. *Behaviour Research and Therapy*, **18**, 51–60.

Rachman, S. (1981). The primacy of affect: Some theoretical implications. *Behaviour Research and Therapy*, **19**, 279–290.

Rachman, S. (1983a). The modification of agoraphobic avoidance behaviour? Some fresh possibilities. *Behaviour Research and Therapy*, **21**, 567–574.

Rachman, S. (1983b). Obstacles to the successful treatment of obsessions. In E. B Foa & P. M. G. Emmelkamp (Eds), *Failures in Behavior Therapy*. New York: Wiley.

Rachman, S. (1984a). A reassessment of the 'primacy of affect'. *Cognitive Therapy and Research*, **8**, 279–290.

Rachman, S. (1984b). Anxiety disorders: Some emerging theories. *Journal of Behavioral Assessment*, **6**, 281–299.

Rachman, S. (1984c). Agoraphobia: A safety-signal perspective. *Behaviour Research and Therapy*, **22**, 59–70.

Rachman, S. (1984d). The experimental analysis of agoraphobia. *Behaviour Research and Therapy*, **22**, 631–640.

Rachman, S. (1985). An overview of clinical and research issues in obsessional–compulsive disorders. In M. Mavissakalian, S. M. Turner & L. Michelson (Eds), *Obsessive–Compulsive Disorder*. New York: Plenum Press.

Rachman, S. (1990). *Fear and Courage*, 2nd edn. New York: W. H. Freeman.

Rachman, S. (1991). Neo-conditioning and the classical theory of fear acquisition. *Clinical Psychology Review*, **11**, 155–173.

Rachman, S. & Hodgson, R. I. (1974). Synchrony and desynchrony in fear and avoidance. *Behaviour Research and Therapy*, **12**, 311–318.

Rachman, S. & Hodgson, R. (1980). *Obsessions and Compulsions*. Englewood Cliffs, NJ: Prentice-Hall.

Rachman, S. & Levitt, K. (1985). Panics and their consequences. *Behaviour Research and Therapy*, **23**, 585–600.

Rachman, S. & Maser, J. D. (Eds) (1988). *Panic. Psychological Perspectives*. Hillsdale, NJ: Erlbaum.

Rachman, S. & de Silva, P. (1978). Abnormal and normal obsessions. *Behaviour Research and Therapy*, 16, 233–248.

Rachman, S., Levitt, K. & Lopatka, C. (1987). Panic: The links between cognitions and bodily symptoms—1. *Behaviour Research and Therapy*, 25, 411–423.

Rachman, S., Levitt, K. & Lopatka, C. (1988a). Experimental analysis of panic—III. Claustrophobic subjects. *Behaviour Research and Therapy*, 26, 41–52.

Rachman, S., Lopatka, C. & Levitt, K. (1988b). Experimental analysis of panic—II. Panic patients. *Behaviour Research and Therapy*, 26, 33–40.

Rachman, S., Cobb, J., Grey, S., McDonald, B., Mawson, D., Sartory, G. & Stern, R. (1979). The behavioural treatment of obsessional-compulsive disorders with and without clomipramine. *Behaviour Research and Therapy*, 17, 462–478.

Rachman, S., Craske, M., Tallman, K. & Solyom, C. (1986). Does escape behavior strengthen agoraphobic avoidance? A replication. *Behavior Therapy*, 17, 366–384.

Raguram, R. & Bhude, A. (1985). Patterns of phobic neurosis: A retrospective study. *British Journal of Psychiatry*, 147, 557–560.

Ramsey, G. (1943). The sexual development of boys. *American Journal of Psychology*, 56, 217.

Rapee, R. M. (1985a). Distinctions between panic disorder and generalized anxiety disorder. *Australian and New Zealand Journal of Psychiatry*, 19, 227–232.

Rapee, R. M. (1985b). A case of panic disorder treated with breathing retraining. *Journal of Behavior Therapy and Experimental Psychiatry*, 16, 63–65.

Rapee, R. M. (1986). Differential response to hyperventilation in panic disorder and generalized anxiety disorder. *Journal of Abnormal Psychology*, 95, 24–28.

Rapee, R. M. (1987). The psychological treatment of panic attacks: Theoretical conceptualization and review of evidence. *Clinical Psychology Review*, 7, 427–438.

Rapee, R. M. & Barlow, D. H. (1989). Psychological treatment of unexpected panic attacks: Cognitive/behavioural component. In Baker, R. (Ed.), *Panic Disorder: Theory, Research and Therapy*. Chichester: Wiley.

Rapee, R. M. & Murrell, E. (1988). Predictors of agoraphobic avoidance. *Journal of Anxiety Disorders*, 2, 203–217.

Rapee, R M., Ancis, J. R. & Barlow, D. H. (1988a). Emotional reactions to physiological sensations: panic disorder patients and non-clinical Ss. *Behaviour Research and Therapy*, 26, 265–269.

Rapee, R. M., Craske, M. G. & Barlow, D. H. (1990). Subject-described features of panic attacks using self-monitoring. *Journal of Anxiety Disorders*, 4, 171–181.

Rapee, R. M., Litwin, E. M. & Barlow, D. H. (1990). Life events in panic disorder: A comparison study. *American Journal of Psychiatry*, 147, 640–644.

Rapee, R. M., Mattick, R. & Murrell, E. (1986). Cognitive mediation in the affective component of spontaneous panic attacks. *Journal of Behavior Therapy and Experimental Psychiatry*, 17, 245–253.

Rapee, R. M., Sanderson, W. C. & Barlow, D. H. (1988b). Social phobia features across DSM-III-R anxiety disorders. *Journal of Psychopathology and Behavioral Assessment*, 10, 287–299.

Rapoport, J. L. (1986). Annotation childhood obsessive compulsive disorder. *Journal of Child Psychology and Psychiatry*, 27, 289–295.

Rapoport, J. L. (Ed.) (1989). *Obsessive–Compulsive Disorder in Children and Adolescence*. New York: American Psychiatric Press.

Rappaport, N. B., McAnulty, D. P., Waggoner, C. D. & Brantley, C. J. (1987). Cluster analysis of Minnesota Multiphasic Personality Inventory (MMPI) profiles in a chronic headache population. *Journal of Behavioral Medicine*, 10, 49–60.

Raskin, M., Bali, L. R. & Peeke, H. V. (1980). Muscle biofeedback and transcendental meditation; a controlled evaluation of efficiency in the treatment of chronic anxiety. *Archives of General Psychiatry*, **37**, 93–97.

Raskin, M., Johnson, G. & Rondestvedt, J. W. (1973). Chronic anxiety treated by feedback induced muscle relaxation. *Archives of General Psychiatry*, **28**, 263–267.

Rasmussen, S. A. & Eisen, J. L. (1988). Clinical and epidemiologic findings of significance to neuropharmacological trials in OCD. *Psychopharmacological Bulletin*, **24**, 466–467.

Rasmussen, S. A. & Tsuang, M. T. (1984). The epidemiology of obsessive compulsive disorder. *Journal of Clinical Psychiatry*, **45**, 450–457.

Rasmussen, S. A. & Tsuang, M. T. (1986). Clinical characteristics and family history in DSM-III obsessive–compulsive disorder. *American Journal of Psychiatry*, **43**, 317–322.

Rasmussen, S. A. & Tsuang, M. T. (1987). Obsessive–compulsive disorder and borderline personality disorder. *American Journal of Psychiatry*, **144**, 121–122.

Ray, C. (1979). Examination stress and performance on a color word interference test. *Perceptual and Motor Skills*, **49**, 400–402.

Razin, A. M. (1982). Psychological intervention in coronary artery disease: A review. *Psychosomatic Medicine*, **44**, 363–387.

Reading, A. E. (1979). The short term effects of psychological preparation for surgery. *Social Science and Medicine*, **13**, 641–654.

Reed, G. (1969a). Under-inclusion—a characteristic of obsessional personality disorder: 1. *British Journal of Psychiatry*, **115**, 781–785.

Reed, G. (1969b). Under-inclusion—a characteristic of obsessional personality disorder: 2. *British Journal of Psychiatry*, **115**, 787–790.

Reed, G. (1977a). Obsessional disorder and remembering. *British Journal of Psychiatry*, **130**, 177–183.

Reed, G. (1977b). Obsessional cognition: Performance on two numerical tasks. *British Journal of Psychiatry*, **130**, 184–185.

Reed, G. F. (1983). Obsessional–compulsive disorder: A cognitive/structural approach. *Canadian Psychology*, **24**, 169–180.

Reed, G. F. (1985). *Obsessional Experience and Compulsive Behavior: A Cognitive–Structure Approach*. New York: Academic Press.

Regier, D. A., Burke, J. D. & Burke, K. C. (1990). Comorbidity of affective and anxiety disorders in the NIMH epidemiologic catchment area program. In J. D. Maser & C. R. Cloninger (Eds), *Comorbidity of Mood and Anxiety Disorders*. Washington, DC: American Psychiatric Press.

Regier, D. A., Boyd, J. H., Burke, J. D., Rae, D. S., Myers, J. K., Kramer, M., Robins, L. N., George, L. K., Karno, M. & Locke, B. Z. (1988). One-month prevalence of mental disorders in the United States. *Archives of General Psychiatry*, **45**, 977–986.

Rehm, L. P. & Marston, A. R. (1968). Reduction of social anxiety through modification of self-reinforcement. *Journal of Consulting and Clinical Psychology*, **32**, 565–574.

Reisenzein, R. (1983). The Schachter theory of emotion: Two decades later. *Psychological Bulletin*, **94**, 239–264.

Reiss, S. (1980). Pavlovian conditioning and human fear: An expectancy model. *Behavior Therapy*, **11**, 380–396.

Reiss, S. (1987). Theoretical perspectives on the fear of anxiety. *Clinical Psychology Review*, **7**, 585–596.

Reiss, S. (1991). Expectancy model of fear, anxiety and panic. *Clinical Psychology Review*, **11**, 141–153.

Reiss, S. & McNally, R. J. (1985). Expectancy model of fear. In S. Reiss & R. R. Bootzin (Eds), *Theoretical Issues in Behavior Therapy*. New York: Academic Press.

Reiss, S., Peterson, R. A., Gursky, D. M. & McNally, R. J. (1986). Anxiety sensitivity, anxiety frequency, and the prediction of fearfulness. *Behaviour Research and Therapy*, **24**, 1–8.

Renneberg, B., Goldstein, A. J., Phillips, D. & Chambless, D. L. (1991). Intensive behavioral group treatment of avoidant personality disorder and social sensitivity: A pilot study. *Behavior Therapy*, **21**, 363–377.

Renshaw, D. C. (1988). Profile of 2376 patients treated at Loyola Sex Clinic between 1972 and 1987. *Sexual and Marital Therapy*, **3**, 111–117.

Rescorla, R. A. (1988). Pavlovian conditioning: It's not what you think it is. *American Psychologist*, **43**, 151–160.

Rescorla, R. A. & Wagner, A. R. (1972). A theory of Pavlovian conditioning: Variations in the effectiveness of reinforcement and nonreinforcement. In A. H. Black & W. F. Prokasky (Eds), *Classical Conditioning. II. Current Research and Theory*. New York: Appleton-Century-Crofts.

Reynolds, B. (1977). Psychological treatment methods and outcome results for erectile dysfunctions. *Psychological Bulletin*, **84**, 1218–1238.

Rice, K. M. & Blanchard, E. B. (1982). Biofeedback in the treatment of anxiety disorders. *Clinical Psychology Review*, **2**, 557–577.

Richards, A. & Millwood, B. (1989). Colour-identification of differentially valenced words in anxiety. *Cognition and Emotion*, **3**, 171–176.

Richter, J. E., Obrecht, W. F., Bradley, L. A., Young, L. D. & Anderson, K. O. (1986). Psychological comparison of patients with nutcracker oesophagus and irritable bowel syndrome. *Digestive Disease Science*, **31**, 131–138.

Richter, R. & Dahme, B. (1982). Bronchial asthma in adults; there is little evidence for the effectiveness of behavioral therapy and relaxation. *Journal of Psychosomatic Research*, **26**, 533–540.

Rickels, K., Schweitzer, E. & Lucki, I. (1987). Benzodiazepine side effects. In R. E. Hales & A. T. Frances (Eds), *Psychiatry Update: APA Annual Review*. Washington, DC: American Psychiatric Association.

Ridgeway, V. & Mathews, A. (1982). Psychological preparation for surgery: A comparison of methods. *British Journal of Clinical Psychology*, **21**, 271–280.

Rimm, D. C., Janda, L. H., Lancaster, D. W., Nahl, M. & Dittmar, K. (1977). An exploratory investigation of the origin and maintenance of phobias. *Behaviour Research and Therapy*, **15**, 231–238.

Riskind, J. H., Beck, A. T., Brown, G. B. & Steer, R. A. (1987). Taking the measure of anxiety and depression: Validity of reconstructed Hamilton Scales. *Journal of Nervous and Mental Disease*, **175**, 474–479.

Robertson, J., Wendiggensen, P. & Kaplan, I. (1983). Towards a comprehensive treatment for obsessional thoughts. *Behaviour Research and Therapy*, **21**, 347–356.

Robins, L. N., Helzer, J. E., Weissman, M. M., Orvaschel, H., Guenberg, E., Burke, J. D. & Regier, D. A. (1984). Lifetime prevalence of specific psychiatric disorders in three sites. *Archives of General Psychiatry*, **41**, 949–958.

Rogers, M. & Reich, P. (1986). Psychological intervention with surgical patients: Evolution of outcome. *Advances in Psychosomatic Medicine*, **15**, 23–50.

Roper, G. & Rachman, S. (1976). Obsessional–compulsive checking: Experimental replication and development. *Behaviour Research and Therapy*, **14**, 25–32.

Roper, G., Rachman, S. & Hodgson, R. (1973). An experiment on obsessional checking. *Behaviour Research and Therapy*, **11**, 271–277.

Roper, G., Rachman, S. & Marks, I. M. (1975). Passive and participant modelling in exposure treatment of obsessive–compulsive neurotics. *Behaviour Research and Therapy*, **13**, 271–279.

Rosen, J. C., Grubman, J. A., Bevins, T. & Frymoyer, J. W. (1987). Musculoskeletal status and disability of MMPI profile subgroups among patients with low back pain. *Health Psychology*, **6**, 581–598.

Rosen, R. C. & Beck, J. G. (1988). *Patterns of Sexual Arousal; Psychophysiological Processes and Clinical Applications*. New York: Guildford Press.

Rosenberg, H. & Upper, D. (1983). Problems with stimulus/response equivalence and reactivity in the assessment and treatment of obsessive–compulsive neurosis. *Behaviour Research and Therapy*, **21**, 177–180.

Roy-Byrne, P. P., Mellman, T. A. & Uhde, T W. (1988). Biological findings in panic disorder: Neuroendocrine and sleep related abnormalities. *Journal of Anxiety Disorders*, **2**, 17–29.

Rubin, R. D. & Merbaum, M. (1971). Self-imposed punishment versus desensitization. In R. D. Rubin, H. Fensterheim, A. A. Lazarus & C. M. Franks (Eds), *Advances in Behavior Therapy*. New York: Academic Press.

Ruff, G. A. & St Lawrence, J. S. (1985). Premature ejaculation: Past research progress, future directions. *Clinical Psychology Review*, 5, 627–639.

Ryan, W. A., Kelly, M. G. & Fielding, J. F. (1983). Personality and the irritable bowel syndrome. *Irish Medical Journal*, **76**, 140–141.

Ryle, A. & Hamilton, M. (1962). Neurosis in 50 married couples. *Journal of Mental Science*, **108**, 265.

Ryle, J. A. (1948). Nosophobia. *Journal of Mental Science*, **94**, 1–17.

Saile, H., Burgmeier, R. & Schmidt, L. R. (1988). A meta-analysis of studies on psychological preparation of children facing medical procedures. *Psychology and Health*, **2**, 107–132.

Salge, R. A., Beck, J. G. & Logan, A. C. (1988). A community survey of panic. *Journal of Anxiety Disorders*, **2**, 157–167.

Salkovskis, P. M. (1983). Treatment of an obsessional patient using habituation to audiotaped ruminations. *British Journal of Clinical Psychology*, **22**, 311–313.

Salkovskis, P. M. (1985). Obsessive–compulsive problems: A cognitive behavioural analysis. *Behaviour Research and Therapy*, **25**, 571–583.

Salkovskis, P. M. (1988a). Phenomenology, assessment and the cognitive model of panic. In S. J. Rachman & J. Maser (Eds), *Panic; Psychological Perspectives*. Hillsdale, NJ: Erlbaum.

Salkovskis, P. M. (1988b). Intrusive thoughts and obsessional disorders. In D. Glasgow & N. Eisenberg (Eds), *Current Issues in Clinical Psychology*. London: Gower.

Salkovskis, P. M. (1989a). Obsessions and compulsions. In J. Scott, J. M. G. Williams & A. T. Beck (Eds), *Cognitive Therapy: A Clinical Casebook*. London: Croom-Helm.

Salkovskis, P. M. (1989b). Cognitive–behavioural factors and the persistence of intrusive thoughts in obsessional problems. *Behaviour Research and Therapy*, **27**, 677–682.

Salkovskis, P. M. (1989c). Obsessive and intrusive thoughts: Clinical and non-clinical aspects. In P. M. G. Emmelkamp, W. T. A. M. Everaerd, F. Kraaimaat, & M. J. M. van Son (Eds), *Fresh Perspectives on Anxiety Disorders*. Amsterdam: Swets & Zeitlinger.

Salkovskis, P. M. (1989d). Somatic disorders. In K. Hawton, P. M. , J. W. Kirk, & D. M. Clark (Eds), *Cognitive Behaviour Therapy for Psych. blems: A Practical Guide.* Oxford: Oxford University Press.

Salkovskis, P. M. & Clark, D. M. (1986). Cognitive and physiological processe, the maintenance and treatment of panic attacks. In I. Hand & H.-U. Wittchen (Eds), *Panic and Phobias. Empirical Evidence of Theoretical Models and Long-term Effects of Behavioral Treatments.* Berlin: Springer-Verlag.

Salkovskis, P. M. & Clark, D. M. (1990). Affective responses to hyperventilation: A test of the cognitive model of panic. *Behaviour Research and Therapy*, **28**, 51–61.

Salkovskis, P. M. & Harrison, J. (1984). Abnormal and normal obsessions: A replication. *Behaviour Research and Therapy*, **22**, 549–552.

Salkovskis, P. M. & Warwick, H. M. C. (1985). Cognitive therapy of obsessive–compulsive disorder—treating treatment failures. *Behavioural Psychotherapy*, **13**, 243–255.

Salkovskis, P. M. & Warwick, H. M. C. (1986). Morbid preoccupations, health anxiety and reassurance: A cognitive behavioural approach to hypochondriasis. *Behaviour Research and Therapy*, **24**, 597–602.

Salkovskis, P. M. & Warwick, H. M. C. (1988). Cognitive therapy of obsessive–compulsive disorder. In C. Perris, I. M. Blackburn & H. Perris (Eds), *The Theory and Practice of Cognitive Therapy.* Heidelberg: Springer-Verlag.

Salkovskis, P. M. & Westbrook, D. (1989). Behaviour therapy and obsessional ruminations: Can failures be turned into success? *Behaviour Research and Therapy*, **27**, 149–160.

Salkovskis, P. M., Clark, D. M. & Hackman, A. (1991). Treatment of panic attacks using cognitive therapy without exposure or breathing retraining. *Behaviour Research and Therapy*, **29**, 161–166.

Salkovskis, P. M., Jones, D. R. O. & Clark, D. M. (1986a). Respiratory control in the treatment of panic attacks: Replication and extension with concurrent measurement of behaviour and pCO_2. *British Journal of Psychiatry*, **148**, 526–532.

Salkovskis, P. M., Warwick, H. M. C., Clark, D. M. & Wessels, D. J. (1986b). A demonstration of acute hyperventilation during naturally occurring panic attacks. *Behaviour Research and Therapy*, **24**, 91–94.

Sammons, M. T. & Karoly, P. (1987). Psychosocial variables in irritable bowel syndrome: A review and proposal. *Clinical Psychology Review*, **7**, 187–204.

Sanavio E. (1988). Obsessions and compulsions: The Padua inventory. *Behaviour Research and Therapy*, **26**, 169–177.

Sanavio, E. & Vidotto, G. (1985). The components of the Maudsley Obsessional–Compulsive Questionnaire. *Behaviour Research and Therapy*, **23**, 659–662.

Sandberg, B. & Bilding, A. (1976). Duodenal ulcer in army trainees during basic military training. *Journal of Psychosomatic Research*, **20**, 61–74.

Sanderson, W. C. & Barlow, D. H. (1991). A description of patients with DSM-III-Revised generalized anxiety disorder. *Journal of Nervous and Mental Disease* (in press).

Sanderson, W. C., Rapee, R. M. & Barlow, D. H. (1989). The influence of an illusion of control on panic attacks induced via the inhalation of 5.5% carbon dioxide-enriched air. *Archives of General Psychiatry*, **46**, 157–162.

Sanderson, W. C., DiNardo, P. A., Rapee, R. M. & Barlow, D. H. (1990). Syndrome co-morbidity in patients diagnosed with a DSM-III-Revised anxiety disorder. *Journal of Abnormal Psychology*, **99**, 308–312.

Sandin, B. & Chorot, P. (1989). The incubation theory of fear/anxiety: experimental investigation in a human laboratory model of Pavlovian conditioning. *Behaviour Research and Therapy*, **27**, 9–18.

Sarrel, D. M. & Masters, W. H. (1982). Sexual molestation of men by women. *Archives of Sexual Behavior*, **11**, 117–131.

Sartory, G. & Master, D. (1984). Contingent negative variation in obsessional–compulsive patients. *Biological Psychology*, **18**, 253–267.

Schachter, S. & Singer, J. (1962). Cognitive, social and physiological determinants of emotional state. *Psychological Review*, **69**, 379–399.

Scherer, K. R. (1982). Emotion as a process: Function, origin and regulation. *Social Science Information*, **21**, 555–570.

Scherer, K. R. (1984). Emotion as a multicomponent process. A model and some cross-cultural data. In P. Shaver (Ed.), *Review of Personality and Social Psychology*, Vol. 5. *Emotions, Relationships and Health*. Beverly Hills, London & New Delhi: Sage.

Schlenker, B. R. & Leary, M. R. (1982). Social anxiety and self-presentation: A conceptualisation and model. *Psychological Bulletin*, **92**, 641–669.

Schneier, F. R., Fyer, A. J., Martin, L. Y., Ross, D., Mannuzza, S., Liebowitz, M. R., Gorman, J. M. & Klein, D. F. (1991). A comparison of phobic subtypes within panic disorder. *Journal of Anxiety Disorders*, **5**, 66–75.

Schultheis, W., Peterson, L. & Selby, V. (1987). Preparation for stressful medical procedures and person × treatment interactions. *Clinical Psychology Review*, **7**, 329–352.

Schwartz, G. E. & Weiss, S. M. (1978). Yale conference on behavioral medicine: A proposed definition and statement of goals. *Journal of Behavioral Medicine*, **1**, 3–12.

Schwartz, G. E., Davidson, R. J. & Goleman, D. J. (1978). Patterning of cognitive and somatic processes in self-regulation of anxiety: Effects of meditation versus exercise. *Psychosomatic Medicine*, **40**, 321–328.

Schwartz, R. M. & Garamoni, G. L. (1986). A structural model of positive and negative states of mind: Asymmetry in the internal dialogue. In P. C. Kendall (Ed.), *Advances in Cognitive–Behavioral Research and Therapy*, Vol. 5. New York: Academic Press.

Schwartz, R. M. & Garamoni, G. L. (1989). Cognitive balance and psychopathology: Evaluation of an information processing model of positive and negative states of mind. *Clinical Psychology Review*, **9**, 271–294.

Schwartz, R. M. & Michelson, L. (1987). States of mind model: Cognitive balance in the treatment of agoraphobia. *Journal of Consulting and Clinical Psychology*, **55**, 557–565.

Schwarz, S. P. & Blanchard, E. B. (1990). Inflammatory bowel disease: A review of the psychological assessment and treatment literature. *Annals of Behavioral Medicine*, **12**, 95–105.

Schwarz, S. P. & Blanchard, E. B. (1991). Evaluation of a psychological treatment for inflammatory bowel disease. *Behaviour Research and Therapy*, **29**, 167–177.

Schwarz, S. P., Taylor, A. E., Scharff, L. & Blanchard, E. B. (1990). Behaviorally treated irritable bowel syndrome patients: A four-year follow-up. *Behaviour Research and Therapy*, **28**, 331–335.

Seligman, M. E. P. (1970). On the generality of the laws of learning. *Psychological Review*, **77**, 406–418.

Seligman, M. E. P. (1971). Phobias and preparedness. *Behavior Therapy*, **2**, 307–320.

Seligman, M. E. P. & Hager, J. (Eds) (1972). *Biological Boundaries of Learning*. New York: Appleton-Century-Crofts.

Seligman, M. E. P. & Johnston, J. C. (1973). A cognitive theory of avoidance learning. In F. J. McGuigan & D. B. Lumsden (Eds), *Contemporary Approaches to Conditioning and Learning*. Washington, DC: Winston & Sons.

Seligman, M. E. P., Maier, S. F. & Solomon, R. L. (1971). Unpredictable and uncontrollable aversive events. In F. R. Brush (Ed.), *Aversive Conditioning and Learning*. New York: Academic Press.

Seyrek, S. K., Corah, N. L. & Pace, L. F. (1984). Comparison of three distraction techniques in reducing stress in dental patients. *Journal of the American Dental Association*, **108**, 327–329.

Shabsin, H. S. & Whitehead, W. E. (1988). Psychophysiological disorders of the gastrointestinal tract. In W. Linden (Ed.), *Biological Barriers in Behavioral Medicine*. New York: Plenum.

Shahar, A. & Merbaum, M. (1981). The interaction between subject characteristics and self control procedures in the treatment of interpersonal anxiety. *Cognitive Therapy and Research*, **5**, 221–224.

Shaw, P. M. (1979). A comparison of three behaviour therapies in the treatment of social phobia. *British Journal of Psychiatry*, **134**, 620–623.

Shear, M. K., Kligfield, P., Harshfield, G., Devereux, R. B., Polan, J. J., Man, J. J., Pickering, M. K. & Frances, A. J. (1987). Cardiac rate and rhythm in panic patients. *American Journal of Psychiatry*, **144**, 633–637.

Shear, M. K., Ball, G. G., Josephson, St. G. & Gitlin, B. (1988). Cognitive–behavioral treatment of panic. In I. Hand & H.-U. Wittchen (Eds), *Panic and Phobias. 2. Treatment and Variables Affecting Course and Outcome*. Berlin, Springer-Verlag.

Sheehan, D. V. (1986). Tricyclic antidepressants in the treatment of panic and anxiety disorders. *Psychosomatics*, **27**, 10–16.

Sheehan, D. V., Ballenger, J. & Jacobsen, G. (1980). Treatment of endogenous anxiety with phobic, hysterical and hypochondriacal symptoms. *Archives of General Psychiatry*, **37**, 51–59.

Sheehan, D. V., Sheehan, K. E. & Minichiello, W. E. (1981). Age of onset of phobic disorders: a reevaluation. *Comprehensive Psychiatry*, **22**, 544–553.

Sheffield, B. F. & Carney, M. W. P. (1976). Chron's disease: A psychosomatic illness? *British Journal of Psychiatry*, **128**, 446–450.

Sher, K. J., Frost, R. O. & Otto, R. (1983). Cognitive deficits in compulsive checkers: An exploratory study. *Behaviour Research and Therapy*, **20**, 357–363.

Sher, K. J., Mann, B. & Frost, R. O. (1984). Cognitive dysfunction in compulsive checkers: Further explorations. *Behaviour Research and Therapy*, **22**, 493–502.

Sher, K. J., Frost, R. O., Kushner, M., Crews, T. M. & Alexander, J. B. (1989). Memory deficits in compulsive checkers: Replication and extension in a clinical sample. *Behaviour Research and Therapy*, **27**, 66–69.

Shields, J. (1962) *Monozygotic Twins Brought up Apart and Brought up Together*. London: Oxford University Press.

Shields, J. (1973). Heredity and psychological abnormality. In H. J. Eysenck (Ed.), *Handbook of Abnormal Psychology*, 2nd edn. London: Pitman.

Shiloh, M., Paz, G. F. & Homannai, Z. T. (1984). The use of pheoxybenzamine treatment in premature ejaculation. *Fertility and Sterility*, **42**, 659–661.

Shipley, R. H., Butt, J. H. & Horwitz, B. (1979). Preparation to reexperience a stressful medical examination: Effect of repetitious videotape exposure and coping style. *Journal of Consulting and Clinical Psychology*, **47**, 485–492.

Shipley, R. H., Butt, J. H., Horwitz, B. & Farbry, J. E. (1978). Preparation for a stressful medical procedure: Effect of amount of stimulus preexposure and coping style. *Journal of Consulting and Clinical Psychology*, **46**, 499–507.

Shull, G. R. & Sprenkle, D. H. (1980). Retarded ejaculation: Reconceptualization and implications for treatment. *Journal of Sex and Marital Therapy*, **6**, 234–246.

Shusterman, L. R. (1973). The treatment of impotence by behavior modification techniques. A review. *Journal of Sex Research*, **9**, 226–240.

Siegel, L. J. & Peterson, L. (1980). Stress reduction in young dental patients through coping skills and sensory information. *Journal of Consulting and Clinical Psychology*, **48**, 785–787.

Sime, A. M. (1976). Relationship of preoperative fear, type of coping and information received about surgery to recovery from surgery. *Journal of Personality and Social Psychology*, **34**, 716–724.

Simon, A. & Ward, L. O. (1982). Sex-related patterns of worry in secondary school pupils. *British Journal of Clinical Psychology*, **21**, 63–64.

Simpson, M. E. (1980). Societal support and education. In I. W. Kutask & L. B. Schlesinger (Eds), *Handbook on Stress and Anxiety*. San Francisco, CA: Jossey-Bass.

Sinnott, A., Jones, R. B., Scott-Fordham, A. & Woodward, R. (1981). Augmentation of *in vivo* exposure treatment for agoraphobia by the formation of neighbourhood self-help groups. *Behaviour Research and Therapy*, **19**, 339–347.

Sirota, A. D. & Mahoney, M. J. (1974). Relaxation on cue: The self-regulation of asthma. *Journal of Behavior Therapy and Experimental Psychiatry*, **5**, 65–66.

Slater, E. & Shields, J. (1969). Genetical aspects of anxiety. *British Journal of Psychiatry*, **3**, 62–71.

Smedslund, J. (1978). Bandura's theory of self-efficacy: A set of common sense theorems. *Scandinavian Journal of Psychology*, **19**, 1–14.

Smith, R. C., Greenbaum, D. A., Vancouver, J. B., Henry, R. L., Reinhart, M. A., Greenbaum, R. B., Dean, H. A. & Mayle, J. E. (1990). Psychosocial factors are associated with health care seeking rather than diagnosis in irritable bowel syndrome. *Gastroenterology*, **98**, 293–301.

Smith, T. W., Follick, M. J. & Korr, K. S. (1984). Anger, neuroticism, Type A behavior and the experience of angina. *British Journal of Medical Psychology*, **57**, 249–252.

Smith, T. W., Ingram, R. E. & Brehm, S. S. (1983). Social anxiety, anxious self-preoccupation, and recall of self-relevant information. *Journal of Personality and Social Psychology*, **44**, 1276–1283.

Snaith, R. P., Bridges, C. W. K. & Hamilton, M. (1976). The Leeds scales for the self-assessment of anxiety and depression. *British Journal of Psychiatry*, **128**, 156–165.

Snowdon, J. (1980). A comparison of written and post hoc forms of the Leyton obsessional inventory. *Psychological Medicine*, **10**, 165–170.

Sokol, L., Beck, A. T., Greenberg, R. L., Wright, F. D. & Berchick, R. J. (1989). Cognitive therapy of panic disorder. A nonpharmacological alternative. *Journal of Nervous and Mental Disease*, **177**, 711–716.

Solyom, L. & Kingstone, E. (1973). An obsessive neurosis following morning glory seed ingestion treated by aversion relief. *Journal of Behavior Therapy and Experimental Psychiatry*, **4**, 293–295.

Solyom, L., Ledwidge, B. & Solyom, C. (1986). Delineating social phobia. *British Journal of Psychiatry*, **149**, 464–470.

Solyom, L., Silberfeld, M. & Solyom, C. (1976). Maternal overprotection in the etiology of agoraphobia. *Canadian Psychiatric Association Journal*, **21**, 109–113.

Solyom, L., Zamanyadek, D., Ledwick, B. & Kenny, F. (1971). Aversion relief treatment of obsessional neurosis. In R. Rubin (Ed.), *Advances in Behavior Therapy*. London: Academic Press.

Solyom, L., Beck, P., Solyom, C. & Hugel, R. (1974). Some etiological factors in phobic neurosis. *Canadian Psychiatric Association Journal*, **19**, 69–78.

Sotile, W. M. & Kilmann, P. R. (1978). Effects of group systematic desensitization on female orgasmic dysfunction. *Archives of Sexual Behavior*, **7**, 477–492.

Southworth, S. & Kirsch, I. (1988). The role of expectancy in exposure-generated fear reduction in agoraphobia. *Behaviour Research and Therapy*, **26**, 113–120.

Spector, I. P. & Carey, M. P. (1990). Incidence and prevalence of the sexual dysfunctions: A critical review of the empirical literature. *Archives of Sexual Behavior*, **19**, 389–408.

Spence, S. H. (1985). Group versus individual treatment of primary and secondary orgasmic dysfunction. *Behaviour Research and Therapy*, **23**, 539–548.

Spetch, M. L., Wilkie, D. M. & Pinel, J. P. J. (1981). Backward conditioning: A re-evaluation of the empirical evidence. *Psychological Bulletin*, **89**, 163–175.

Spielberger, C. D. (1966). The effects of anxiety on complex learning and academic achievement. In C. D. Spielberger (Ed.), *Anxiety and Behaviour*. London: Academic Press.

Spielberger, C. D. (1972). Anxiety as an emotional state. In C. D. Spielberger (Ed.), *Anxiety: Current Trends in Theory and Research*, Vol. 1. New York: Academic Press.

Spielberger, C. D., Gorsuch, R. L. & Lushene, R. E. (1970). *Manual for the State–Trait Anxiety Inventory*. Palo Alto, CA: Consulting Psychologists Press.

Spielberger, C. D., Pollans, C. H. & Worden, T. V. (1984). Anxiety disorders. In S. M. Turner & M. Hersen (Eds), *Adult Psychopathology and Diagnosis*. New York: Wiley.

Staats, A. W. & Eifert, G. H. (1990). The paradigmatic behaviorism theory of emotions: Basis for unification. *Clinical Psychology Review*, **10**, 539–566.

Stanley, M. A., Turner, S. M. & Borden, J. W. (1990). Schizotypal features in obsessive–compulsive disorder. *Comprehensive Psychiatry*, **31**, 511–518.

Steketee, G. (1988). Intra- and interpersonal characteristics predictive of long-term outcome following behavioral treatment of obsessive–compulsive disorders. In I. Hand & H.-U. Wittchen (Eds), *Panic and Phobias. 2. Treatment and Variables Affecting Course and Outcome*. Berlin: Springer-Verlag.

Steketee, G. (1990). Personality traits and disorders in obsessive–compulsives. *Journal of Anxiety Disorders*, **4**, 1–14.

Steketee, G. & Tynes, L. L. (1991). Behavioral treatment of obsessive–compulsive disorder. In M. T. Pato & J. Zohar (Eds), *Clinical Psychiatry with Obsessive–Compulsive Disorders*. American Psychiatric Press (in press).

Steketee, G., Foa, E. B. & Grayson, J. B. (1982). Recent advances in the behavioral treatment of obsessive–compulsives. *Archives of General Psychiatry*, **39**, 1365–1371.

Steketee, G., Grayson, J. B. & Foa, E. B. (1985). Obsessive–compulsive disorder: Differences between washers and checkers. *Behaviour Research and Therapy*, **23**, 197–201.

Steketee, G., Grayson, J. B. & Foa, E. B. (1987). A comparison of characteristics of obsessive–compulsive disorder and other anxiety disorders. *Journal of Anxiety Disorders*, **1**, 325–335.

Steptoe, A. (1985). Psychological aspects of bronchial asthma. In S. Rachman (Ed.), *Contributions to Medical Psychology*, Vol. 3. Oxford: Pergamon Press.

Steptoe, A. & Wardle, J. (1988). Emotional fainting and the psychophysiologic response to blood and injury: Autonomic mechanisms and coping strategies. *Psychosomatic Medicine*, **50**, 402–417.

Stern, M. J. & Cleary, P. (1981). National heart disease and exercise project. Psychosocial changes observed during a low-level exercise program. *Archives of Internal Medicine*, **141**, 1463–1467.

Stern, R. S. (1978). Obsessive thoughts: The problems of therapy. *British Journal of Psychiatry*, **133**, 233–239.

Stern, R. S. & Cobb, J. P. (1978). Phenomenology of obsessive–compulsive neurosis. *British Journal of Psychiatry*, **132**, 233–239.

Stern, R. S. & Marks, I. M. (1973). Brief and prolonged flooding: A comparison of agoraphobic patients. *Archives of General Psychiatry*, **28**, 270–276.

Sternberger, L. G. & Burns, G. L. (1990a). Maudsley Obsessional–Compulsive Inventory: Obsessions and compulsions in a nonclinical sample. *Behaviour Research and Therapy*, **28**, 337–340.

Sternberger, L. G. & Burns, G. L. (1990b). Compulsive Activity Checklist and the Maudsley Obsessional–Compulsive Inventory: Psychometric properties of two measures of obsessive–compulsive disorder. *Behavior Therapy*, **21**, 117–127.

Sternberger, L. G. & Burns, G. L. (1990c). Obsessions and compulsions: Psychometric properties of the Padua Inventory with an American college population. *Behaviour Research and Therapy*, **28**, 341–345.

Stone, S. V. & Costa, P. T. Jr (1990). Disease-prone personality or distress-prone personality? The role of neuroticism in coronary heart disease. In H. S. Friedman (Ed.), *Personality and Disease*. New York: Wiley.

Stone, S. V. & Costa, P. T. Jr (1990). Disease-prone personality or distress-prone personality? The role of neuroticism in coronary heart disease. In H. S. Friedman (Ed.), *Personality and Disease*. New York: Wiley.

Strassberg, D. S., Mahoney, J. M., Schaugaard, M. & Hale, V. F. (1990). The role of anxiety in premature ejaculation: A psychophysiological model. *Archives of Sexual Behavior*, **19**, 251–257.

Stravynski, A. & Greenberg, D. (1989). Behavioural psychotherapy for social phobia and dysfunction. *International Review of Psychiatry*, **1**, 207–218.

Stravynski, A., Elie, R. & Franche, R. L. (1989). Perception of early parenting by patients diagnosed avoidant personality disorder: A test of the separation hypothesis. *Acta Psychiatrica Scandinavica*, **90**, 415–420.

Stravynski, A., Grey, S. & Elie, R. (1987). Outline of the therapeutic process in social skills training with socially dysfunctional patients. *Journal of Consulting and Clinical Psychology*, **55**, 224–228.

Stravynski, A., Marks, I. & Yule, W. (1982). Social skills problems in neurotic outpatients: Social skills training with and without cognitive modification. *Archives of General Psychiatry*, **39**, 1378–1385.

Stravynski, A., Lesage, A., Marcouiller, M. & Elie, R. (1989). A test of the therapeutic mechanism in social skills training with avoidant personality disorder. *Journal of Nervous and Mental Diseases*, **177**, 739–744.

Street, L. L., Craske, M. & Barlow, D. H. (1989). Sensations, cognitions and the perception of cues associated with expected and unexpected panic attacks. *Behaviour Research and Therapy*, **27**, 189–198.

Strongman, K. T. (1987). *The Psychology of Emotion*, 3rd edn. Chichester: Wiley.

Stroop, J. R. (1935). Studies of interference in serial verbal reactions. *Journal of Experimental Psychology*, **18**, 643–662.

Sturgiss, E. T. & Scott, R. (1984). Simple phobias. In S. M. Turner (Ed.), *Behavioral Theories and Treatment of Anxiety*. New York: Plenum Press.

Suinn, R. (1976). Anxiety management training to control general anxiety. In J. Krumboltz & C. Thoresen (Eds), *Counseling Methods*. New York: Holt, Rinehart & Winston.

Suinn, R. (1984). Generalized anxiety disorder. In S. Turner (Ed.), *Behavioral Theories and Treatment of Anxiety*. New York: Plenum Press.

Suinn, R. & Richardson, F. (1971). Anxiety management training: A nonspecific behavior therapy program for anxiety control. *Behavior Therapy*, **2**, 498–510.

Suls, J. & Fletcher, B. (1985). The relative efficacy of avoidant and nonavoidant coping strategies: A meta-analysis. *Health Psychology*, **4**, 249–288.

Suls, J. & Wan, C. K. (1989). Effects of sensory and procedural information on coping with stressful medical procedures and pain: A meta-analysis. *Journal of Consulting and Clinical Psychology*, **57**, 372–379.

Sutton-Simon, K. & Goldfried, M. R. (1979). Faulty thinking patterns in two types of anxiety. *Cognitive Therapy and Research*, **3**, 193–203.

Svedlund, J., Sjodin, I., Ottosson, J. O. & Dotevall, G. (1983). Controlled study of psychotherapy of irritable bowel syndrome. *The Lancet*, **ii**, 589–591.

Swedo, S. E., Rapoport, J. L., Leonard, H., Lenane, M. & Cheslow, D. (1989). Obsessive–compulsive disorder in children and adolescence. *Archives of General Psychiatry*, **46**, 335–341.

Talley, N. J. & Piper, D. W. (1986). Comparison of the clinical features and illness behavior of patients presenting with dyspepsia of unknown cause (essential dyspepsia) and organic disease. *Australian Journal of Medicine*, **16**, 352–359.

Talley, N. J., Phillips, S. F., Bruce, B., Twomey, C. K., Zinsmeister, A. R. & Melton, L. J. III (1990). Relation among personality and symptoms in nonulcer dyspepsia and the irritable bowel syndrome. *Gastroenterology*, **99**, 327–333.

Tallis, F., Eysenck, M. & Mathews, A. (1991). Elevated avoidance requirements and worry. *Personality and Individual Differences*, **12**, 21–27.

Tarrier, N. & Main, C. J. (1986). Applied relaxation training for generalised anxiety and panic attacks: The efficacy of a learnt coping strategy on subjective reports. *British Journal of Psychiatry*, **149**, 330–336.

Tarter, R. E., Switala, J., Garra, J., Edwards, K. L. & van Thiel, T. J. (1987). Inflammatory bowel disease: Psychiatric status of patients before and after disease onset. *International Journal of Psychiatry in Medicine*, **17**, 173–181.

Tasto, D. L. (1977). Self-report schedules and inventories. In A. R. Ciminero, K. S. Calhoun & H. E. Adams (Eds), *Handbook of Behavioral Assessment*. New York: Wiley.

Taylor, C. B., Telch, M. J. & Haavik, D. (1983). Ambulatory heart rate changes during panic attacks. *Journal of Psychiatric Research*, **17**, 261–266.

Taylor, C. B., Houston-Miller, N., Ahn, D. K., Haskell, W. & DeBusk, R. F. (1986a). The effects of exercise training programs on psychosocial improvement in uncomplicated postmyocardial infarction patients. *Journal of Psychosomatic Research*, **30**, 581–587.

Taylor, C. B., Sheikh, J., Agras, W. S., Roth, W. T., Margraf, J., Ehlers, A., Maddock, R. J. & Gossard, D. (1986b). Ambulatory heart rate changes in patients with panic attacks. *American Journal of Psychiatry*, **143**, 478–482.

Taylor, S. E. & Clarke, L. F. (1986). Does information improve adjustment to noxious medical procedures? In M. J. Saks & L. Saxe (Eds), *Advances in Applied Social Behavior*. Hillsdale, NJ: Erlbaum.

Tearnan, B. H., Telch, M. J. & Keefe, P. (1984). Etiology and onset of agoraphobia: A critical review. *Comprehensive Psychiatry*, **25**, 51–62.

Teasdale, J. (1974). Learning models of obsessive–compulsive disorder. In H. R. Beech (Ed.), *Obsessional States*. London: Methuen.

Teasdale, J. (1988). Cognitive models and treatments of panic: A critical evaluation. In S. Rachman & J. D. Maser (Eds), *Panic. Psychological Perspectives*. Hillsdale, NJ: Erlbaum.

Telch, M. J., Lucas, J. A. & Nelson, P. (1989b). Nonclinical panic in college students: An investigation of prevalence and symptomatology. *Journal of Abnormal Psychology*, **98**, 300–306.

Telch, M. J., Tearnan, B. H. & Taylor, C. B. (1983). Antidepressant medication in the treatment of agoraphobia: A critical review. *Behaviour Research and Therapy*, **21**, 505–517.

Telch, M. J., Agras, S., Taylor, B., Roth, W. T. & Gallen, C. (1985). Combined pharmacological and behavioral treatment for agoraphobia. *Behaviour Research and Therapy*, **23**, 325–335.

Telch, M. J., Brouilard, M., Telch, C. F., Agras, S. & Taylor, B. (1989a). Role of cognitive appraisal in panic-related avoidance. *Behaviour Research and Therapy*, **27**, 373–383.

Theorell, T. (1983). Psychosocial intervention as part of rehabilitation after a myocardial infarction. *International Rehabilitation Medicine*, **5**, 185–188.

Thompson, D. R. & Meddis, R. (1990). A prospective evaluation of in-hospital counselling for first time myocardial infarction men. *Journal of Psychosomatic Research*, **34**, 237–248.

Thompson, D. R., Webster, R. A., Cordle, C. J. & Sutton, T. W. (1987). Specific sources and patterns of anxiety in male patients with first time myocardial infarction. *British Journal of Medical Psychology*, **60**, 343–348.

Thorndike, E. L. (1935). *The Psychology of Wants, Interests and Attitudes*. New York: Appleton-Century-Crofts.

Thorpe, G. & Burns, L. (1983). *The Agoraphobia Syndrome*. Chichester: Wiley.

Thyer, B. (1985). Audiotaped exposure therapy in a case of obsessional neurosis. *Journal of Behavior Therapy and Experimental Psychiatry*, **16**, 271–273.

Thyer, B. A. (1987). *Treating Anxiety Disorders*. Newbury Park, CA: Sage.

Thyer, B. A. & Himle, J. (1985). Temporal relationship between panic attack onset and phobic avoidance in agoraphobia. *Behaviour Research and Therapy*, **23**, 607–608.

Thyer, B. A., Himle, J. & Curtis, G. C. (1985a). Blood–injury–illness phobia: A review. *Journal of Clinical Psychology*, **41**, 451–459.

Thyer, B. A., Nesse, R. M., Cameron, O. G. & Curtis, G. C. (1985b). Agoraphobia: A test of the separation anxiety hypothesis. *Behaviour Research and Therapy*, **23**, 75–78.

Thyer, B. A., Parrish, R. T., Curtis, G. C., Nesse, R. M. & Cameron, O. (1985c). Age of onset of DSM-III anxiety disorders. *Comprehensive Psychiatry*, **26**, 113–122.

Tolman, E. C. (1932). *Purposive Behavior in Animals and Men*. New York: Appleton-Century-Crofts.

Tomkins, S. S. (1962). *Affect, Imagery, Consciousness*, 2 vols. Springer-Verlag: New York.

Tomkins, S. S. (1980). Affect as amplification: Some modifications of theory. In R. Plutchik & H. Kellerman (Eds), *Emotion: Theory, Research and Experience*, Vol. 1: *Theories of Emotion*. New York: Academic Press.

Torgersen, S. (1983). Genetic factors in anxiety disorders. *Archives of General Psychiatry*, **40**, 1085–1089.

Torgersen, S. (1986). Childhood and family characteristics in panic and generalized anxiety disorders. *American Journal of Psychiatry*, **143**, 630–632.

Townsend, R. E., House, J. F. & Addario, D. (1975). A comparison of biofeedback-mediated relaxation and group therapy in the treatment of chronic anxiety. *American Journal of Psychiatry*, **132**, 598–601.

Trelawny-Ross, C. & Russell, O. (1987). Social and psychological responses to myocardial infarction: Multiple determinants of outcome at six months. *Journal of Psychosomatic Research*, **31**, 125–130.

Trower, P. (1981). Social skills disorder: Mechanisms of failure. In R. Gilmore & S. Duck (Eds), *Personal Relationships in Disorder*. London: Academic Press.

Trower, P. (1984). A radical critique and reformulation: From organism to agent. In P. Trower (Ed.), *Radical Approaches to Social Skills Training*. London: Croom-Helm.

Trower, P. & Gilbert, P. (1989). New theoretical conceptions of social anxiety and social phobia. *Clinical Psychology Review*, **9**, 19–35.

Trower, P. & Turland, D. (1984). Social phobia. In S. M. Turner (Ed.), *Behavioral Theories and Treatment of Anxiety*. New York: Plenum.

Trower, P., Bryant, B. & Argyle, M. (1978a). *Social Skills and Mental Health*. London: Methuen.

Trower, P., Yardly, K., Bryant, B. & Shaw, P. (1978b). The treatment of social failure: A comparison of anxiety-reduction and skills-acquisition procedures on two social problems. *Behavior Modification*, **2**, 41–60.

Trull, T. J., Nietzel, M. T. & Main, A. (1988). The use of meta-analysis to assess the clinical significance of behavior therapy for agoraphobia. *Behavior Therapy*, **19**, 527–538.

Turner, S. M. & Beidel, D. C. (1985). Empirically derived subtypes of social anxiety. *Behavior Therapy*, **16**, 384–392.

Turner, S. M. & Beidel, D. C. (1988a). Some further comments on the measurement of social phobia. *Behaviour Research and Therapy*, **26**, 411–413.

Turner, S. M. & Beidel, D. C. (1988b). *Treating Obsessive–Compulsive Disorder*. New York: Pergamon Press.

Turner, S. M. & Beidel, D. C. (1989). Social phobia: Clinical syndrome, diagnosis, and comorbidity. *Clinical Psychology Review*, **9**, 3–18.

Turner, S. M. & Michelson, L. (1984). Obsessive–compulsive disorders. In S. M. Turner (Ed.), *Behavioral Theories and Treatment of Anxiety*. New York: Plenum Press.

Turner, S. M., Beidel, D. C. & Larkin, K. T. (1986a). Situational determinants of social anxiety in clinic and nonclinic samples: Physiological and cognitive correlates. *Journal of Consulting and Clinical Psychology*, **54**, 523–527.

Turner, S. M., Beidel, D. C. & Townsley, R. M. (1990). Social phobia: Relationship to shyness. *Behaviour Research and Therapy*, **28**, 497–505.

Turner, S. M., McCann, M. & Beidel, D. C. (1987). Validity of the social avoidance and distress and fear of negative evaluation scales. *Behaviour Research and Therapy*, **25**, 113–115.

Turner, S. M., Hersen, M., Bellack, A. S. & Wells, K. C. (1979). Behavioral treatment of obsessive–compulsive neurosis. *Behaviour Research and Therapy*, **17**, 95–106.

Turner, S. M., McCann, S. M., Beidel, D. C. & Mezzich, J. E. (1986b). DSM-III classification of the anxiety disorders: A psychometric study. *Journal of Abnormal Psychology*, **95**, 168–172.

Turner, S. M., Beidel, D. C., Dancu, C. V. & Keys, D. J. (1986c). Psychopathology of social phobia and comparison to avoidant personality disorder. *Journal of Abnormal Psychology*, **95**, 389–394.

Turner, S. M., Beidel, D. C., Dancu, C. V. & Stanley, M. A. (1989a). An empirically derived inventory to measure social fears and anxiety: The social phobia and anxiety inventory. *Psychological Assessment: A Journal of Consulting and Clinical Psychology*, 1, 35–40.

Turner, S. M., Stanley, M. A., Beidel, D. C. & Bond, L. (1989b). The social phobia and anxiety inventory: Construct validity. *Journal of Psychopathology and Behavioral Assessment*, 11, 221–234.

Turner, S. M., Beidel, D. C., Borden, J. W. & Jacob, R. G. (1991). Social phobia: Axis I and II correlates. *Journal of Abnormal Psychology*, 100, 102–106.

Twentyman, C. T. & McFall, R. M. (1975). Behavioral training of social skills in shy males. *Journal of Consulting and Clinical Psychology*, 43, 384–395.

Tyrer, P. (1976). *The Role of Bodily Feelings in Anxiety*. London: Oxford University Press.

Tyrer, P., Casey, P. & Gall, J. (1983). Relationship between neurosis and personality disorder. *British Journal of Psychiatry*, 142, 404–408.

Tyrer, P., Lee, I. & Alexander, J. (1980). Awareness of cardiac function in anxious, phobic and hypochondriacal patients. *Psychological Medicine*, 10, 171–174.

Tyrer, P. J., Rutherford, D. & Huggett, T. (1981). Benzodiazepine withdrawal symptoms and propariolol. *Lancet*, i, 520.

Uhde, T. W., Roy-Byrne, P. P., Gillin, J. C., Mendelson, W. B., Boulenger, J.-P., Vittone, B. J. & Post, R. M. (1984). The sleep of patients with panic disorder: A preliminary report. *Psychiatry Research*, 12, 251–259.

Uhde, T. W., Roy-Byrne, P. P., Vittone, B., Siever, L. & Post, R. M. (1985). Phenomenology and neurobiology of panic disorder. In A. H. Tuma & J. D. Maser (Eds), *Anxiety and the Anxiety Disorders*. Hillsdale, NJ: Erlbaum.

Venn, J. R. & Short, J. G. (1973). Vicarious classical conditioning of emotional responses in nursery school children. *Journal of Personality and Social Psychology*, 28, 249–255.

Vermilyea, J. A., Boice, R. & Barlow, D. H. (1984). Rachman and Hodgson (1974) a decade later: How do synchronous response systems relate to the treatment of agoraphobia? *Behaviour Research and Therapy*, 22, 615–621.

Vernon, D. T. W. & Bigelow, D. W. (1974). Effect of information about a potentially stressful situation on responses to stress impact. *Journal of Personality and Social Psychology*, 29, 50–59.

Vingerhoets, A. J. J. M. (1985). The role of the parasympathetic division of the autonomic nervous system in stress and the emotions. *International Journal of Psychosomatics*, 32, 28–32.

Vingerhoets, A. J. J. M. & Schomaker, L. R. B. (1989). Emotional fainting: Its physiological and psychological aspects. In C. D. Spielberger, I. G. Sarason & J. Strelau (Eds), *Stress and Anxiety*, Vol. 12. New York: Hemisphere.

Volans, P. J. (1976). Styles of decision-making and probability appraisal in selected obsessional and phobic patients. *British Journal of Social and Clinical Psychology*, 15, 303–317.

Von Korff, M., Shapiro, S., Burke, J. D., Teitelbaum, M., Skinner, E. A., German, P., Turner, R. W., Klein, L. & Burns, B. (1987). Anxiety and depression in a primary care clinic. *Archives of General Psychiatry*, 44, 152–156.

Wallace, L. (1984). Psychological preparation as a method of reducing the stress of surgery. *Journal of Human Stress*, 10, 62–79.

Wardle, J. (1982). Fear of dentistry. *British Journal of Medical Psychology*, 55, 119–126.

Wardle, J. & Jarvis, M. (1981). The paradoxical fear response to blood, injury and illness—a treatment report. *Behavioural Psychotherapy*, **9**, 13–24.

Wardle, J., Ahmad, T. & Hayward, P. (1990). Anxiety sensitivity in agoraphobia. *Journal of Anxiety Disorders*, **4**, 325–333.

Warwick, H. M. C. (1989). A cognitive–behavioural approach to hypochondriasis and health anxiety. *Journal of Psychosomatic Research*, **33**, 705–711.

Warwick, H. M. C. & Marks, I. M. (1988). Behavioural treatment of illness phobia. *British Journal of Psychiatry*, **152**, 239–241.

Warwick, H. M. C. & Salkovskis, P. M. (1989). Cognitive therapy of hypochondriasis. In J. Scott, J. M. G. Williams & A. T. Beck (Eds), *Cognitive Therapy in Clinical Practice*. London: Croom-Helm.

Warwick, H. M. C. & Salkovskis, P. M. (1990). Hypochondriasis. *Behaviour Research and Therapy*, **28**, 105–117.

Watson, D. & Friend, R. (1969). Measurement of social–evaluative anxiety. *Journal of Consulting and Clinical Psychology*, **33**, 448–451.

Watson, J. B. & Morgan, J. J. B. (1917). Emotional reactions and psychological experimentation. *American Journal of Psychology*, **28**, 163–174.

Watson, J. B. & Rayner, R. (1920). Conditioned emotional reactions. *Journal of Experimental Psychology*, **3**, 1–14.

Watts, F. N. (1983). Affective cognitive: Sequel to Zajonc and Rachman. *Behaviour Research and Therapy*, **21**, 89–90.

Watts, F. N. (1988). Agoraphobia: The changing face of treatment. In F. N. Watts (Ed.), *New Developments in Clinical Psychology*, Vol. II. Chichester: Wiley/BPS.

Watts, F. N. (1989). Attentional strategies and agoraphobic anxiety. *Behavioural Psychotherapy*, **17**, 15–26.

Watts, F. N., McKenna, F. P., Sharrock, R. & Trezise, L. (1986). Colour naming of phobia-related words. *British Journal of Psychology*, **77**, 97–108.

Weiss, E. & English, O. S. (1957). *Psychosomatic Medicine*. Philadelphia, PA: Saunders.

Weissman, M. M. (1985). The epidemiology of anxiety disorders: Rates, risks and familial patterns. In A. H. Tuma & J. D. Maser (Eds), *Anxiety and the Anxiety Disorders*. Hillsdale, NJ: Erlbaum.

Weissman, M. M., Leaf, P. J., Blazer, D. G., Boyd, J. D. & Florio, L. F. (1986). The relationship between panic disorder and agoraphobia: An epidemiologic perspective. *Psychopharmacology Bulletin*, **22**, 787–791.

Welch, G. W., Hillman, L. C. & Pomare, E. W. (1985). Psychoneurotic symptomatology in the irritable bowel syndrome: A study of reporters and non-reporters. *British Medical Journal*, **291**, 1382–1384.

Wells, J. K., Howard, G. S., Nowlin, W. F. & Vargas, M. J. (1986). Presurgical anxiety and postsurgical pain and adjustment: Effects of a stress inoculation procedure. *Journal of Consulting and Clinical Psychology*, **54**, 831–835.

Welner, A., Reich, T., Robin, G., Fishman, R. & van Doren, T. (1976). Obsessive–compulsive neurosis: Record, follow-up and family studies, 1. Inpatient record study. *Comprehensive Psychiatry*, **17**, 527–539.

Westphal, C. (1871). Die Agoraphobie: Eine neuropathische Erscheinung. *Archiv für Psychiatrie und Nervenkrankheiten*, **3**, 138–161.

White, W. B. & Baker, L. H. (1987). Ambulatory blood pressure monitoring in patients with panic disorder. *Archives of Internal Medicine*, **147**, 1973–1975.

Whitehead, W. E. (1985). Psychotherapy and biofeedback in the treatment of irritable bowel syndrome. In N. W. Read (Ed.), *Irritable Bowel Syndrome*. London: Grune & Stratton.

Whitehead, W. E. & Schuster, M. M. (1985). *Gastrointestinal Disorders. Behavioral and Physiological Basis for Treatment*. London: Academic Press.

Whitehead, W. E., Engel, B. T. & Schuster, M. M. (1980). Irritable bowel syndrome: Physiological and psychological differences between diarrhoea-predominant and constipation-predominant patients. *Digestive Diseases and Sciences*, **25**, 404–413.

Whitehead, W. E., Bosmajian, L., Zonderman, A. B., Costa, P. T. & Schuster, M. M. (1988). Symptoms of psychological distress associated with irritable bowel syndrome. *Gastroenterology*, **95**, 709–714.

Wicklund, R. A. (1975). Objective self-awareness. In L. Berkowitz (Ed.), *Advances in Experimental Social Psychology*, Vol. 8. New York: Academic Press.

Wiklund, I., Sanne, H., Vedine, A. & Wilhelmsen, C. (1985). Coping with myocardial infarction: A model with clinical applications, a literature review. *International Rehabilitation Medicine*, **7**, 167–175.

Williams, J. M. G., Watts, F. N., MacLeod, C. & Mathews, A. (1988). *Cognitive Psychology and Emotional Disorders*. Chichester: Wiley.

Williams, S. L. (1985). On the nature and measurement of agoraphobia. In M. Hersen, P. Miller & R. Eisler (Eds), *Progress in Behavior Modification*. New York: Academic Press.

Williams, S. L. (1987). On anxiety and phobia. *Journal of Anxiety Disorders*, **1**, 161–180.

Williams, S. L. (1991). Guided mastery treatment of agoraphobia: Beyond stimulus exposure. In M. Hersen, R. M. Eisler & P. M. Miller (Eds), *Progress in Behavior Modification*. Orlando: Academic Press.

Williams, S. L. & Rappoport, A. (1983). Cognitive treatment in the natural environment for agoraphobics. *Behavior Therapy*, **14**, 299–313.

Williams, S. L. & Watson, N. (1985). Perceived danger and perceived self-efficacy as cognitive determinants for acrophobic behavior. *Behavior Therapy*, **14**, 299–313.

Williams, S. L. & Zane, G. (1989). Guided mastery and stimulus exposure treatments for severe performance anxiety in agoraphobics. *Behaviour Research and Therapy*, **27**, 237–245.

Williams, S. L., Dooseman, G. & Kleifield, E. (1984). Comparative effectiveness of guided mastery and exposure treatments for intractable phobias. *Journal of Consulting and Clinical Psychology*, **52**, 505–518.

Williams, S. L., Kinney, P. J. & Falbo, J. (1989). Generalization of therapeutic changes in agoraphobia: The role of perceived self-efficacy. *Journal of Consulting and Clinical Psychology*, **57**, 436–442.

Williams, S. L., Turner, S. M. & Peer, D. F. (1985). Guided mastery and performance desensitization treatments for severe acrophobia. *Journal of Consulting and Clinical Psychology*, **53**, 237–247.

Wilson, G. T. (1984). Fear reduction methods and the treatment of anxiety disorders. In G. T. Wilson, C. M. Franks, K. D. Brownell & P. C. Kendall (Eds), *Annual Review of Behavior Therapy: Theory and Practice*, Vol. 9. New York: Guildford Press.

Wilson, J. F. (1981). Behavioral preparation for surgery. Benefit or harm? *Journal of Behavioral Medicine*, **4**, 79–102.

Wilson, J. F., Moore, R. W., Randolph, S. & Hanson, B. J. (1982). Behavioral preparation of patients for gastrointestinal endoscopy: Information, relaxation, and coping style. *Journal of Human Stress*, **8**, 13–23.

Wilson-Barnett, J. (1984). Interventions to alleviate patients' stress: A review. *Journal of Psychosomatic Research*, **28**, 63–72.

Winton, W. M. (1986). The role of facial response in self-reports of emotion: A critique of Laird. *Journal of Personality and Social Psychology*, **50**, 808–812.

Wisocki, P. A. (1988). Worry as a phenomenon relevant to the elderly. *Behavior Therapy*, **19**, 369–379.

Wittchen, H.-U. (1986). Epidemiology of panic attacks and panic disorders. In I. Hand & H.-U. Wittchen (Eds), *Panic and Phobias. Empirical Evidence of Theoretical Models and Long-term Effects of Behavioral Treatments*. Berlin: Springer-Verlag.

Wlazlo, Z., Schroeder-Hartwig, K., Hand, I., Kaiser, G. & Munchau, N. (1990). Exposure *in vivo* vs social skills training for social phobia: Long-term outcome and differential effects. *Behaviour Research and Therapy*, **28**, 181–193.

Wolchik, S. A., Beggs, V., Wincze, J. P., Sakheim, D. K., Barlow, D. H. & Mavissakalian, M. (1980). The effects of emotional arousal on subsequent sexual arousal in men. *Journal of Abnormal Psychology*, **89**, 595–598.

Wolpe, J. (1958). *Psychotherapy by Reciprocal Inhibition*. Stanford, CA: Stanford University Press.

Wolpe, J. (1973). *The Practice of Behavior Therapy*, 2nd edn. New York: Pergamon Press.

Wolpe, J. (1978a). Self-efficacy theory and psychotherapeutic change: A square peg for a round hole. *Advances in Behaviour Research and Therapy*, **1**, 231–236.

Wolpe, J. (1978b). Comments on 'A test of reciprocal inhibition' by Hoon, Wincze, and Hoon. *Journal of Abnormal Psychology*, **87**, 452–454.

Wolpe, J. & Lang, P. (1964). A fear schedule for use in behaviour therapy. *Behaviour Research and Therapy*, **2**, 27–30.

Wolpe, J. & Rachman, S. (1960). Psychoanalytic 'evidence': A critique based on Freud's case of little Hans. *Journal of Nervous and Mental Disease*, **131**, 135–148.

Wolpe, J. & Rowan, V. C. (1988). Panic disorder: A product of classical conditioning. *Behaviour Research and Therapy*, **26**, 441–450.

Woodruff, R. & Pitts, F. N. (1964). Monozygotic twins with obsessional neurosis. *American Journal of Psychiatry*, **120**, 1075–1080.

Woods, S. W., Charney, D. S., Loke, J., Goodman, W. K., Redmond, D. E. & Heninger, G. R. (1986). Carbon dioxide sensitivity in panic anxiety. *Archives of General Psychiatry*, **43**, 900–909.

Woodward, R. & Jones, R. B. (1980). Cognitive restructuring treatment: A controlled trial with anxious patients. *Behaviour Research and Therapy*, **18**, 401–407.

York, D., Borkovec, T. D., Vasey, M. & Stern, R. (1987). Effects of worry and somatic anxiety induction on thoughts, emotion and physiological activity. *Behaviour Research and Therapy*, **25**, 523–526.

Yorkston, N. J., McHugh, R. B., Brady, R., Serber, M. & Sergeant, H. G. S. (1974). Verbal desensitization in bronchial asthma. *Journal of Psychosomatic Research*, **18**, 371–376.

Young, D. T., Kotte, T. E., McCall, M. M. & Blume, D. (1982). A prospective controlled study of inhospital myocardial infarction rehabilitation. *Journal of Cardiac Rehabilitation*, **2**, 32–40.

Yule, W. & Fernando, P. (1980). Blood phobia—beware. *Behaviour Research and Therapy*, **18**, 587–590.

Zachary, R. A., Friedlander, S., Huang, L. N., Silverstein, S. & Leggott, P. (1985). Effects of stress-relevant and -irrelevant filmed modeling on children's responses to dental treatment. *Journal of Pediatric Psychology*, **10**, 383–401.

Zafiropoulou, M. & McPherson, F. M. (1986). 'Preparedness' and the severity of outcome of clinical phobias. *Behaviour Research and Therapy*, **24**, 221–222.

Zajonc, R. B. (1980). Feeling and thinking: Preferences need no inferences. *American Psychologist*, **35**, 151–175.

Zajonc, R. B. (1984). On the primacy of affect. *American Psychologist*, **39**, 117–123.

Zimbardo, P. G. (1977). *Shyness*. Reading, MA: Addison-Wesley.

Zitrin, C. M., Klein, D. F., Woerner, M. G. & Ross, D. C. (1983). Treatment of phobias: 1. Comparison of imipramine hydrochloride and placebo. *Archives of General Psychiatry*, **40**, 125–138.

Zucker, D., Taylor, C. B., Brouillard, M., Ehlers, A., Margraf, J., Telch, M., Roth, W. T. & Agras, W. S. (1989). Cognitive aspects of panic attacks. Content, cause and relationship to laboratory stressors. *British Journal of Psychiatry*, **155**, 86–91.

Zung, W. W. K. (1971). A rating instrument for anxiety disorders. *Psychosomatics*, **12**, 371–379.

Index

Agoraphobia 1, 6, 22, 29, 32, 36, 40, 43, 47, 49, 59, 62–63, 67, 76, 80, 86–87, 101, 103, 109–140, 235, 242
  age of onset 48, 111, 137
  assessment of 121–126
  definition of 109–110
  and early family environment 48, 112–113
  and the marital context 113–116, 138
  prevalence of 110, 137
  theories of 117–126
Agoraphobia Scale (AS) 122
Agoraphobic Cognitions Questionnaire (ACQ) 98–99, 121–122
Ambulatory monitoring of physiological reactions 90–91, 97–98, 142–143
Animal phobia 22–23, 34, 47
  see also Dog phobia
Anorexia nervosa 163
Anxiety management training 69–70, 153–154, 158, 266
Anxiety sensitivity 32, 43, 79, 89, 112, 120
Anxiety Sensitivity Index (ISI) 79
Applied relaxation 71, 104, 127, 136, 251
Asthma 253–259, 276
Attentional bias 36–42, 57–58, 92–93, 149–150, 158
Attentional focus 196–200
Audience anxiety 46, 50, 58, 75
Automatic thoughts 73, 170–171
Avoidant personality disorder 47–51, 64, 68, 75, 164

Backward conditioning 27
Beck Anxiety Inventory 151
Behaviour therapy 2, 156, 221
Behavioural avoidance test 123–124
Behavioural inhibition system (BIS) 18, 29–31, 148
Benzodiazepines 83, 99, 101
Biofeedback 94, 152–154, 250
Blood/injury fears 231–232, 242–245, 248–249, 251–252
Blushing 49, 59, 82, 110
Bodily sensations,
  misinterpretation of 86, 236–237
  perception of 58–59, 74, 79, 81–82, 84–93, 96, 110, 117
  see also Interoceptive cues; Interoceptive conditioning
Body Sensation Questionnaire (BSQ) 82, 98–99, 121–122
Breathing retraining 87, 101–108
Bulimia 163

Cannon's theory 8–9
Cardiovascular disease 254
Childhood separation anxiety 113
Classical conditioning 20–28, 42, 51
Claustrophobia 6
Cognitions
  as determinants of emotional state 11–15
  and anxiety 35–44, 53–57, 87
Cognitive appraisal 207–210
Cognitive–arousal theories 8
Cognitive avoidance 147, 181

Cognitive–behaviour therapy 73
    99–102, 154, 156, 207, 228, 240
    see also Cognitive therapy
Cognitive deficit 167–168
Cognitive expectancy theory 31–32
Cognitive restructuring 72–73, 101,
    103–104, 108, 114, 134, 154
Cognitive–Somatic Anxiety
    Questionnaire 98, 144, 151
Cognitive therapy 67, 69–75,
    103–107, 134–136, 154–158,
    183–184, 210, 223–226
Compulsive Activity Checklist (CAC)
    173–174
Compulsive behaviours 159, 162, 169
Compulsive personality
    see Obsessive–compulsive
    personality disorder
Concordance
    see Discordance
Coping 272
    emotion-focused 209–210, 219
    problem-focused 209–210, 219
Coping preparation 217–218
Coping skills 249–251
Coping styles 215–216, 218–220,
    222–223, 228
Coronary heart disease 268–276
    see also Hypertension; Myocardial
    infarction
Crohn's disease
    see Inflammatory bowel disease
    (IBD)

Darwinian evolutionary theories 9–10
Dating anxiety 46, 66
Dental Anxiety Scale (DAS) 246–247,
    250
Dental Fear Survey (DFS) 246–248
Dental phobia/dental fears 6, 23, 67,
    217–219, 221–222, 231, 242–243,
    249–251
Dependent personally disorder 163
Depression 163–166, 183–185, 188,
    235, 240, 256, 261–262, 267,
    270–271
Desynchrony 4, 125–126, 196
Discordance 4, 89, 125
Disease phobia
    see Illness phobia

Dispositional anxiety
    see Personality
Dog phobia 2, 23, 26
Duodenal ulcers
    see Stomach ulcers
Dyspepsia of unknown origin (DUO)
    260

Equipotentiality 23
Embarrassibility Scale 61
Embarrassment 16, 46, 50, 54, 62
Emotion 2, 6–16
Emotional drive theory 207–209
Emotional processing 147
Erectile disorder
    see Erectile dysfunction
Erectile dysfunction 188, 190–191,
    193, 197, 201–202, 204–205
Exposure based treatment 34, 63–65,
    68–70, 72–73, 75, 101–103,
    105–108, 126–136, 155, 176–185,
    240–242, 248, 252
    improvement rates for 131–132, 182
    procedural variations in 128–130,
        176–182
    self-directed 123, 135
    and spouse involvement 115–116,
        132–133, 179–180

Facial feedback 10–11
Fainting 243–246, 251
Fear of fear 32, 59, 89, 109, 117–120,
    138
Fear of Negative Evaluation Scale
    (FNE) 61–62, 70, 141
Fear Questionnaire (FQ) 61, 121–122,
    246–247
Fear Survey Schedule (FSS) 61, 121,
    154, 246–247

Gastrointestinal disease 219, 254,
    259–268, 276
    see also Inflammatory bowel disease
        (IBD); Irritable bowel syndrome
        (IBS); Stomach ulcers
Gender differences 48, 110–111, 140,
    143, 161, 245
Generalised anxiety
    see Generalised Anxiety Disorder

Generalised Anxiety Disorder (GAD)
2, 37, 39–40, 43, 47–48, 62,
79–81, 86–87, 139–158
assessment of 150–152
definition of 139–140, 157
prevalence of 130–131, 157
theories of 148–150
treatment of 153–157

Hamilton Anxiety Scale (HAS) 152
Head injury 163
Health anxiety 230–231, 237, 240–241
see also Hypochondriasis; Illness
phobia
Health psychology 253
Height phobia 34, 48
Histrionic personality disorder 164
Hypertension 253, 268–269
Hyperventilation 84–89, 91, 94–96,
102–103, 108, 144
Hypoactive sexual desire disorder
188, 190
Hypochondriasis 230–242, 261, 265,
269
assessment of 238–239
definition of 232–233
prevalence of 234
theories of 236–237
treatment of 240–241

Illness Attitude Scale (IAS) 238–239
Illness phobia 230–236, 238–241
categories of 329
definition of 231–232
prevalence of 233–234
theories of 236–237
treatment of 240–241
Illness-related anxiety 257, 270–272,
276
Incubation 26–27, 42
Individual differences
see Personality
Inflammtory bowel disease (IBD) 153,
259–260
Information processing 92, 167–168
see also Attentional bias
Information provision 207–217,
223–225, 228, 249–250, 272, 275
Information-seeking theory 210

Inhibited female orgasm 189, 192,
201, 203–205
Inhibited male orgasm 189, 192, 202
Interaction Anxiousness Scale 61
Interoceptive conditioning 84, 96–97,
108
Interoceptive cues 94, 95, 107
Irrational beliefs 56, 59, 63, 70, 72,
167, 184
Irritable bowel syndrome (IBS)
230–231, 261–265

James–Lange theory 7–8

Leyton Obsessional Inventory (LOI)
172–173
life events 77–78, 116–117, 162, 254,
269
Locus of control 65, 215–216

Marital adjustment 113–116
Maudsley Obsessionive–Compulsive
Inventory (MOCI) 163, 167–168,
172–174
Medication
see Benzodiazepine; Pharmacological
treatment
Memory bias 40, 56–57, 92–93, 150,
163, 167–168
Mobility Inventory (MI) 121–122
Modelling 24, 29, 34, 66, 203, 207,
220–223, 226–227, 248–250
MMPI Hypochondriasis Scale 238
Multicomponent process models of
emotion 10–12, 43, 57–59, 88,
157
Mutilation Questionnaire (MQ)
246–247
Myocardial infarction 268, 270–276
rehabilitation subsequent to 272–276

Neurosis 1, 19
Neuroticism 17, 227–228, 235, 254,
257, 261, 265, 269

Observational learning 24, 220

Obsessive–compulsive
   see Obsessive–compulsive disorder
Obsessional thoughts 160, 163, 169,
   178, 181–182, 184
Obsessive–compulsive disorder 1, 26,
   31, 37, 43, 63, 80, 139, 140,
   159–185, 235, 237, 240
   age of onset 162
   assessment of 171–176
   definition of 159–160
   prevalence of 161–162
   theories of 169–171
   treatment of 176–184
Obsessive–compulsive personality
   disorder 164, 167–168
Overvalued ideation 183, 185

Padua Inventory (PI) 173–174
Panic 1, 4, 23, 35, 39–40, 43, 47, 59,
   62, 76–108, 109–110, 117–119,
   137, 139–140, 236–237, 267, 269
   and association with agoraphobic
      avoidance 76, 109–110,
      118–120
   cued–uncued 82, 94
   definition of 76
   expected–unexpected 82, 107
   induction of 83–84, 87
   nocturnal 93–96, 108
   non-clinical 78–79, 107
   non-fearful 89
   prevalence of 77–78
   related to general anxiety 79–81,
      91, 93, 142–145, 157
   relaxation-induced 94–95
   theories of 83–99
   treatment of 99–107
Panic Attack Questionnaire (PAQ) 98
Panic Attack Symptom Questionnaire
   99
Paradoxical intention 134–137
Penn State Worry Questionnaire
   (PSWQ) 151
Performance demand 186, 191, 195
Personality 2, 16–18, 111–112, 138,
   214–217, 227, 256–257, 261–263,
   265–267, 269–270, 276
   see also Anxiety sensitivity; Coping
      styles; Locus of control;
      Neuroticism; Trait anxiety

Pharmacological treatment 80,
   101–102, 107–108, 155–156, 183,
   240
Post traumatic stress disorder 1–2, 39
Premature ejaculation 189–193,
   201–203
Preparation for surgery 207–229
   techniques of 210–226, 228
   theories of 208–210
   with children 220–222, 228
Preparatory-response theory 210
Preparedness 25–26, 29
Primacy of affect 5, 13–14
Psychoanalytic 19–20, 200, 240, 253
Psychosexual dysfunction 1, 43,
   186–206
   assessment of 190–191
   and attentional focus 196–200
   definition of 186, 188–189
   prevalence of 189–190, 205
   treatment of 200–205
Psychosomatic medicine 253–254
Psychosomatic Rating Scale 98
Public speaking phobia 47

Rational Emotive Therapy (RET) 65,
   67, 69, 72, 134, 184, 201
Reciprocal inhibition 191, 194
Relaxation 67, 70, 101, 104–106,
   135–137, 153, 158, 178–179, 186,
   191, 201, 208, 210, 212, 216–220,
   223–226, 228, 248–250, 257–259,
   264, 268, 273, 276
   see also Applied relaxation
Response prevention 177–178, 185
Retarded ejaculation
   see Inhibited male orgasm
Ruminations
   see Obsessional thoughts

Schizophrenia 163–164
Schizotypal personality disorder
   164–165
Safety-signal theory 210
Safety signals 117, 120–121, 138
Selective memory
   see Memory bias
Selective processing
   see Attentional bias
Self-awareness 58

Self-consciousness 58, 74
Self-efficacy 33–35, 42, 118, 130, 220
Self-evaluation 54, 72
Self instructional training (SIT) 65,
    69, 71, 134, 183, 251
Self-monitoring 97, 104, 123, 151,
    174
Self-statements 54–55, 63, 104, 105,
    214, 224
Sensate focus 198, 201
Sex therapy 201–202, 204, 206
Shame 50, 90
Shyness 45–46, 49–50, 58, 75
Shyness Scale 61
Simulated Social Interaction Test 60
Social anxiety
    see Social phobia
Social Avoidance and Distress Scale
    (SADS) 56, 61–62, 70, 141
Social Interaction Self Statement Test
    (SISST) 55–56, 59, 62–63, 71
Social Performance Survey Schedule
    61
Social Phobia 2, 6, 36, 39, 43, 45–75,
    80–81, 87, 103, 108, 139–141, 161
    age of onset 48
    assessment of 59–63
    definition of 45–46
    and parental rearing 48
    prevalence of 45–46, 74
    relationship to other anxiety
        disorders 47–49
    relationship to avoidant personality
        disorder 49–51
    theories of 51–59, 74
    treatment of 63–74
Social Phobia and Anxiety Inventory
    62
Social Reticence Scale 61
Social Situations Questionnaire 61

Social skills 50, 59, 72, 74, 75
    deficit model 51–53
    training 63, 66–69, 73, 75
Somatoform disorders 232–234
Spectatoring 201
Stage fright 46
Standardised walks 123–124
State anxiety 38, 70, 214, 227, 250,
    261
State Trait Anxiety Inventory (STAI)
    144, 151
States of Mind (SOM) model 55,
    130–131
Stomach ulcers 253, 265–266, 259
Synchrony
    see Desynchrony
Systematic desensitisation 63–64, 70,
    126, 176–177, 186, 191, 201–206,
    248, 250, 257–258, 276–277

Thought stopping 178
Three-systems analysis of anxiety
    3–6, 25
Trait anxiety 17–18, 38–39, 43, 70,
    227–228, 261, 265, 269
Two factor theory 28–29, 169

Ulcerative colitis
    see Inflammatory bowel disease

Worry 4, 39, 87, 138–139, 144–148,
    150–151, 157–158, 208, 211, 235,
    262

Yale-Brown Obsessive–Compulsive
    Scale, 171–172